VBScript Sourcebook

Mary Jane Mara

WILEY COMPUTER PUBLISHING

John Wiley & Sons, Inc.
New York • Chichester • Weinheim • Brisbane • Singapore • Toronto

Publisher: Robert Ipsen
Editor: Carol Long
Assistant Editor: Pam Sobotka
Managing Editor: Brian Snapp
Electronic Products/Associate Editor: Mike Green
Text Design & Composition: Benchmark Productions, Boston, MA

Designations used by companies to distinguish their products are often claimed as trademarks. In all instances where John Wiley & Sons, Inc., is aware of a claim, the product names appear in initial capital or ALL CAPITAL LETTERS. Readers, however, should contact the appropriate companies for more complete information regarding trademarks and registration.

This book is printed on acid-free paper.

This publication is designed to provide accurate and authoritative information in regard to the subject matter covered. It is sold with the understanding that the publisher is not engaged in rendering legal, accounting, or other professional services. If legal advice or other expert assistance is required, the services of a competent professional person should be sought.

The content of this book is based on Preview 2 of Internet Explorer 4.0. There may have been changes made to the product since this release. Therefore, screen shots and examples may not be identical to the final product.

For current information about Microsoft Internet Information Server 4.0, you should visit http://www.microsoft.com/

Library of Congress Cataloging-in-Publication Data:

Mara. Mary Jane, 1948-
        VBScript sourcebook / Mary Jane Mara.
                    p.   cm.
        Includes index.
        ISBN 0-471-19106-X (alk. paper)
        1. VBScript (Computer program language) 2. Internet programming.
        3. HTML (Document markup language)   I. Title.
        QA76.73.V27M37   1997
        005.2'762--dc21   97-17967
                                                                  CIP

Printed in the United States of America.
10 9 8 7 6 5 4 3 2 1

Contents

Acknowledgments   xiii

Introduction   xiv

Part One Introducing VBScript   **1**

Chapter 1 Welcome to the Family   3
ActiveX Scripting Engines   4
The Power of Scripting   5
    HTML versus Extension Scripting Languages   5
    Using VBScript and JavaScript   7
    Using VBScript in Other HTML Tags   9
Getting Started   12
    Hardware and Software Requirements   13
    Your First Script   15
Frequently Asked Questions   19
    What Is the Relationship of VBScript to Java?   19
    What Is VBScript's Relationship to the Visual Basic Family?   20
    Can I Use VBScript on the Server Side of My Site?   20
    Is VBScript Secure?   21
    What Are Cookies?   21
    What Are the Restrictions for Using VBScript in My Own Applications?   21
What's Next?   22

Chapter 2 The HTML Document Object Model   23
Object-Based and Event-Driven Languages   24
    HTML Objects   24
    HTML Events   24
    Enter VBScript and JavaScript   25
    First Steps   25
The VBScript Object Hierarchy   27
Object Properties and Methods   32
    Properties Are Sources of Information   32
    Methods Are PreProgrammed Sets of Actions   38
    Functions Are Methods without Objects   41
Understanding and Using Arrays   43
    The Length Property   44
    The Index Position   44
Passing and Evaluating Data   47
    Working with Variables   48
    Scoping Your Variables   51
    How Expressions Are Constructed and Evaluated   54
    Naming Your Variables   56
What's Next?   57

Contents

Chapter 3 The Basics of VBScript   59

VBScript Rules of Syntax   59
  VBScript Is Not Case-Sensitive   60
  Use of Parentheses   61
  Lines, Spaces, Tabs, and Quotes   63
  Commenting Your Code   65
  Built-In Statements   66
Writing Your Own Procedures   67
  Subroutines   67
  Functions   69
  Calling Your Procedures   70
Using Control Structures   72
  Decision Control Structures   73
  Looping Control Structures   77
  Combining and Exiting Control Structures   81
What's Next?   82

Part Two The VBScript Language   83

Chapter 4 VBScript Objects   85

Documentary Sources   85
The VBScript Objects   86
  All Array   87
  Anchor Object   87
  Applets Array   88
  Body Object   88
  Button Object   89
  Checkbox Object   91
  Document Object   93
  Elements Array   97
  Embeds Array   100
  Event Object   101
  Err Object   101
  Form Object   102
  Frame Object   105
  Hidden Object   107
  History Object   109
  Image Object   110
  Link Object   111
  Location Object   114
  Navigator Object   116
  <OBJECT> Tag   117
  Options Array   118
  Password Object   119
  Plugins Array   121
  Radio Object   121
  Reset Object   124
  Script Object   126
  Select Object   127

Selection Object   131
Submit Object   131
Text Object   134
Textarea Object   136
TextRange Object   139
Visual Object   140
Window Object   141
What's Next?   145

Chapter 5 Object Properties   **147**
The Built-In Properties of VBScript Objects   147
Action Property   149
ALinkColor Property   149
AppCodeName Property   150
AppName Property   151
AppVersion Property   151
Checked Property   152
Cookie Property   152
DefaultChecked Property   155
DefaultValue Property   156
Encoding Property   156
FgColor Property   156
Hash Property   157
Host Property   157
Hostname Property   158
Href Property   158
LastModified Property   158
Length Property   159
LinkColor Property   160
Method Property   160
Name Property   162
Opener Property   163
Parent Property   163
Pathname Property   163
Port Property   164
Protocol Property   164
Referrer Property   164
Search Property   165
SelectedIndex Property   165
Self Property   166
Status Property   166
Target Property   166
Title Property   167
Top Property   167
userAgent Property   167
Value Property   168
VLinkColor Property   169
What's Next?   170

Chapter 6 Object Methods   171

The Built-In Methods of VBScript Objects	171
Use of Parentheses with Methods	172
Add Method	173
Alert Method	173
Back Method	174
Blur Method	175
Clear Method	176
ClearTimeout Method	179
Click Method	182
Close Method	182
Collapse Method	183
CommonParentElement Method	184
Confirm Method	184
Contains Method	185
CreateElement Method	186
CreateRange Method	186
CreateTextRange Method	187
Duplicate Method	187
ElementFromPoint Method	187
Empty Method	187
ExecuteCommand Method	188
Expand Method	188
Focus Method	188
Forward Method	190
GetMember Method	190
Go Method	190
InRange Method	191
IsEqual Method	191
Item Method	191
Move Method	192
MoveEnd Method	192
MoveStart Method	192
Move Method	193
Navigate Method	193
Open Method	193
ParentElement Method	198
PasteHTMLMethod	198
Prompt Method	199
QueryCommandEnabled Method	202
QueryCommandIndeterm Method	202
QueryCommandState Method	203
QueryCommandSupported Method	203
QueryCommandText Method	203
RangeFromElement Method	203
Reload Method	204
Remove Method	204

RemoveMember Method   204
Replace Method   204
Reset Method   205
Scroll Method   205
ScrollIntoView Method   205
Select Method   205
SetMember Method   207
SetTimeout Method   207
ShowModalDialog Method   210
Start Method   210
StartPainting Method   210
Stop Method   211
StopPainting Method   211
Submit Method   211
Tags Method   212
Write Method   213
WriteLn Method   218
ZOrder Method   220
What's Next?   221

Chapter 7 Event Handlers   **223**
New Way to Process Events   224
The VBScript Event Handlers   225
onAbort Handler   226
onAfterUpdate Handler   226
onBeforeUpdate Handler   227
onBlur Handler   227
onBounce Handler   229
onChange Handler   230
onClick Handler   231
onDblClick Handler   233
onError Handler   235
onFinish Handler   235
onFocus Handler   235
onHelp Handler   236
onKeyDown Handler   237
onKeyPress Handler   238
onKeyUp Handler   238
onLoad Handler   238
onMouseDown Handler   239
onMouseMove Handler   240
onMouseOut Handler   241
onMouseOver Handler   241
onMouseUp Handler   243
onReadyStateChange Handler   244
onReset Handler   244
onSelect Handler   244
onStart Handler   244

onSubmit Handler   245
onUnload Handler   245
What's Next?   248

Chapter 8 Functions and Constants   **249**
The VBScript Functions and Constants   250
Use of Parentheses with Functions   250
Abs Function   251
Array Function   251
Asc Function   252
Atn Function   252
CBool Function   253
CByte Function   253
CCur Function   254
CDate Function   254
CDbl Function   255
Chr Function   255
CInt Function   256
CLng Function   257
Color Constants   258
Cos Function   259
CSng Function   259
CStr Function   259
Date and Time Functions   260
Exp Function   265
Filter Function   265
Fix Function   267
FormatCurrency Function   267
FormatDateTime Function   268
FormatNumber Function   268
FormatPercent Function   269
Hex Function   270
Int Function   270
InputBox Function   271
InStr Function   272
InStrRev Function   274
IsArray Function   276
IsDate Function   276
IsEmpty Function   277
IsNull Function   277
IsNumeric Function   278
IsObject Function   279
Join Function   279
LBound Function   281
LCase Function   281
Left Function   282
Len Function   282
Log Function   282

LTrim Function	283
MsgBox Function	283
Mid Function	287
Oct Function	287
Replace Function	288
Right Function	289
Rnd Function	289
Round Function	290
RTrim Function	291
ScriptEngine Function	292
ScriptEngineBuildVersion Function	292
ScriptEngineMajor|MinorVersion Function	292
Sgn Function	292
Sin Function	293
Space Function	293
Split Function	294
Sqr Function	295
StrComp Function	296
String Function	296
strReverse Function	296
Tan Function	297
TypeName Function	297
UBound Function	298
UCase Function	299
VarType Function	300
What's Next?	301

Chapter 9 Statements — **303**

Controlling Program Flow	303
Call Statement	304
Const Statement	305
Dim Statement	307
Do Until Statement	310
Do While Statement	311
Erase Statement	312
Exit Do Statement	313
Exit For Statement	314
Exit Function Statement	314
Exit Sub Statement	315
For Statement	316
For Each Statement	318
Function Statement	319
If Statement	321
On Error Resume Next Statement	324
Randomize Statement	324
Redim Statement	324
Rem Statement	325
Select Case Statement	326

Set Statement	327
Sub Statement	328
What's Next?	331

Chapter 10 Operators and Keywords — 333

The VBScript Operators and Keywords	333
Addition Operator	334
And Operator	334
Concatenation Operator	335
Division Operators	336
Does Not Equal Operator	336
Empty Keyword	337
Equals Operator	337
Equivalence Operator	338
Exponent Operator	339
False Keyword	339
Greater Than Operator	339
Implication Operator	340
Is Operator	341
Less Than Operator	341
Modulus Operator	342
Multiplication Operator	342
Negation Operator	343
Not Operator	343
Nothing Keyword	344
Null Keyword	344
Or Operators	345
Preserve Keyword	346
True Keyword	347
Operator Precedence	347
What's Next?	349

Part Three VBScript in the Real World — 351

Chapter 11 Scripting the Behavior of Built-In Objects — 353

Overview of the Easy Reader Page	353
The Easy Reader Scripts	356
Segment 1: Opening Prompts	357
Segment 2: Dynamic Page Generation	359
Segment 3: The Animal Sounds Game	362
Segment 4: The Color Game	364
Segment 5: The Button Game	368
Putting the Easy Reader Page Together	370
The Full Script	371
What's Next?	375

Chapter 12 Writing Your Own Procedures — 377

Overview of the Membership Application Page	378
The Membership Application Scripts	382

Segment 1: Validating the Name Fields   382
Segment 2: Validating the Date Field   386
Segment 3: Validating the E-mail Address   388
Segment 4: Validating the Phone Fields   390
Segment 5: Checking Required Fields   400
Putting the Membership Application Page Together   405
The Full Script   406
What's Next?   415
Correction to the Phone Script   416

Chapter 13 Creating Your Own Arrays   **417**
Overview of the Shopping List Page   418
The Shopping List Scripts   422
Segment 1: Setting Up the Shopping List Array   424
Segment 2: Creating the User's Shopping List and Calculating the Order Total   428
Segment 3: Displaying the Selected Catalog Items   440
Segment 4: Submitting the Order Form   443
Putting the Shopping List Page Together   445
The Full Script   445
What's Next?   453

Chapter 14 Troubleshooting Your Scripts   **455**
Browser Support Problems   456
Quality Assurance Testing   456
Unit Testing   457
Integration Testing   458
System Testing   459
Five Steps to Effective Testing   460
Solving Anomalous Behavior Problems   462
Who's Responsible for the Problem?   462
Where Is the Script Failing?   467
Why Is the Script Failing?   469
Error Handling   478
Bypassing Errors in a Script   478
Handling Errors in a Script   480
What's Next?   488

Part Four Advanced VBScript   **489**

Chapter 15 The Joys of Dynamic HTML   **491**
Chapter Structure   492
Overview of the Puzzle Page   494
The Puzzle Page Scripts   495
Segment 1: Error Handling   496
Segment 2: Drag 'n' Drop   497
Segment 3: Scramble Operation   502
Segment 4: Viewing Original Picture   503
Putting the Puzzle Page Together   505
The Full Script   505

What's Next?   510

Chapter 16 Working with Bound Data Across Frames   **511**
Data-Binding   511
Scripting Across Frames   513
Overview of the Client Address Book   514
The Client Address Book Scripts   515
  Segment 1 of controls.htm: Alpha Buttons   522
  Segment 2 of controls.htm: Table/Record View   524
  Segment 1 of addresses.htm: Data-Binding   526
  Segment 2 of addresses.htm: Browsing   527
  Segment 1 of tables.htm: Data Binding   531
  Segment 2 of tables.htm: Column Sorting   533
Putting the "Addresses" Frameset Together   534
  The FRAMESET Script   534
  The CONTROLS FRAME Script   535
  The MIDDLE Frame Script   538
  The VIEWER Frame Scripts   538
What's Next?   545

Chapter 17 Working with External Objects   **547**
Overview of the Recipe Page   548
The Recipe Page Scripts   549
  Segment 1 of banner.htm: Horizontal Marquee   552
  Segment 2 of banner.htm: Mouse Down   552
  Segment 3 of banner.htm: Mouse Up   556
  Segment 1 of viewerx.htm: Vertical Marquee   559
  Segment 2 of viewerx.htm: The Button   560
Putting the "Recipe" Frameset Together   560
  The FRAMESET Script   561
  The BANNER Frame Script   561
  The VIEWERX Frame Script   566
  The VIEWERY Frame Script   567
  The TITLE Marquee Script   568
  The INGREDIENTS Marquee Script   569
  The INSTRUCTIONS Marquee Script   569
More to Come   570

Appendix A What's on the Web Site   **571**

Appendix B Color Chart   **573**
Popular Hexadecimal Equivalents   573
  Basic Colors   573
  Other Colors   573

Appendix C Most Commonly Used ASCII Codes   **575**

Index   **577**

Acknowledgments

Many thanks to . . .

My husband, Jerry Daniels, whose consistently excellent technical advice sees me through many a dark moment.

My children, Rose and Joe Daniels, whose patience and understanding make it possible for me to immerse myself in complex projects.

My agent, Margot Maley of Waterside Productions, for putting the project together.

My friends Dewey Gaedcke and Marianne Linde at Complete Data Solutions in Austin, Texas, for generously allowing the use of their equipment, network, and other strategic resources.

The folks at Wiley who helped transform my thoughts into a coherent, well-designed book, including Pam Sobotka, Carol Long, Brian Snapp, and Hans Gilde.

Dedication

To my late parents, Andy and Billie Mara, for their love and encouragement.

Introduction

In the early months of 1990, something extraordinary happened. A cooperating pair of server and multimedia presentation technologies edged its way quietly onto a little-known, sparsely traveled thoroughfare known as the Internet. For almost four years, this soon-to-become-major turning point in the information revolution went virtually unnoticed. Finally, word of the landmark Hypertext Transfer Protocol (HTTP) and its presentation partner, Hypertext Markup Language (HTML), began trickling slowly across the Net. Then came "Mosaic," a graphical, user-friendly browser application that allowed even novice computer users to navigate the Net's subnet of HTTP servers with ease. When the close of 1993 brought with it versions of Mosaic for all major computing platforms, it was the watershed event the world had long been unconsciously awaiting. Suddenly, the Internet and its World Wide Web of HTTP servers weren't just for breakfast anymore.

Thanks almost entirely to the accessible and seductive display of information on the World Wide Web—and the rapidly evolving technologies for viewing that information—the Internet is now in a growth spurt second only to the one that occurred when a Big Bang ignited the universe. Never has anything in the annals of human history possessed the Web's potential to turn the world's disparate populations into one big global family. Fueling this happy belief are predictions by International Data Corporation (IDC) that traffic on the Web will skyrocket to 163 million users, conducting 100 billion dollars' worth of commerce by the dawn of the third millennium, just a few years hence.

This relentless march of progress (and traffic) on the World Wide Web is both a blessing and a curse for hardworking webmasters everywhere. As the Web's audience grows, so does its appetite for meaningful user services accompanied by more profound sensual experiences, powered by increasingly complex artificial intelligence engines. For many, the World Wide Web is the living counterpart of an electronic world long portrayed by Hollywood as far more advanced than the most progressive sites of the current day. Those who have worked with computers since command line was king are understandably thrilled by the rapid evolution of the Web's multimedia and interactive capabilities. Yet, with visions of *Blade Runner*, *Johnny Mnemonic*, and *Disclosure* dancing in their heads, it's no wonder that the newly computer literate are a little disappointed in the light-of-day reality of the heavily hyped Web.

About This Book

The *VBScript Sourcebook* is for webmasters eager to turn disappointment into wonder, and Hollywood's dream into human reality, by adding one of the most strategic of the emerging web page extension languages to their growing arsenal of web-weaving tools. As part of the popular Wiley Sourcebook Series, the *VBScript Sourcebook* is designed to be your definitive guide to Microsoft's new web page scripting extension language, fully supported on both the client and the server side by Microsoft's Internet Explorer browser and Internet Information Server (IIS) suite.

Is This Sourcebook for Me?

This book is for webmasters and HTML authors with all levels of programming expertise who wish to enhance their internal and external web sites with this powerful yet friendly extension language. Although a working knowledge of HTML is required, no other programming experience is necessary. So, if you're an experienced HTML user, this book is for you if you want to do any or all of the following:

- Be in the forefront of web development.

- Take advantage of the mounting supply of available applets, plug-ins, and ActiveX controls to enrich your HTML pages with state-of-the-art sound, video, animation, and database interaction.

- Provide sophisticated local (page-based) services to visitors, including self-validating forms, automatic order processing, user-adapted surveys, dynamically generated (created on-the-fly) pages, and interactive games.

- Harness the power of dynamic HTML and the fully exposed document object model.

- Become a Visual Basic programmer.

A Word to Macintosh and UNIX Users

At the time of publication, Internet Explorer 3.01 had just been made available for the 68K and PowerMac systems, finally allowing Mac-based IE users to interpret pages containing JavaScript. No support for VBScript was included in this version, however, and—surprisingly enough—none forecast. The UNIX versions of IE lag even further behind. For all its huffing and puffing about open standards and be-all and end-all Internet access, Microsoft's visible commitment to cross-platform support is sadly lacking. If Microsoft doesn't correct this myopic, Windows-centric behavior, it may prove to be the Achilles heel that trips up the software giant's bid for Internet supremacy.

Meanwhile, Microsoft claims that it does indeed intend to support the full gamut of ActiveX technologies (including VBScript) on the Macintosh, and that third parties are working to provide similar support to UNIX users. If that support is actually made available by the time this book hits the stands, then the *VBScript Sourcebook* is certainly a good tutorial resource for Mac or UNIX users interested in mastering VBScript.

To find out whether VBScript is supported in the latest version of IE for Macintosh, first check the Microsoft site at www.microsoft.com to be sure that you have the most up-to-date version. Then, browse that site to find out what's new in the current version. If you can't find any information on whether or not this version supports VBScript, place this simple script into the <HEAD> portion of any HTML document:

```
<HEAD>
<SCRIPT LANGUAGE="VBScript">


alert("Hello.")


</SCRIPT>
</HEAD>
```

If an alert containing the word "Hello" is presented as soon as you load the page into your IE browser, then your version of this browser *is* VBScript-enabled. If not, then it isn't yet ready to interpret VBScript. Be sure that both "Scripting" and "ActiveX Controls" are enabled in the "Web Content" section of your IE Preferences (found on the Edit menu) before you try this test. When these items are properly enabled, your Mac IE (assuming you have version 3.01 or higher) will properly interpret the preceding script, if the specified language is changed to "JavaScript."

```
<HEAD>
<SCRIPT LANGUAGE="JavaScript">

alert("Hello.")

</SCRIPT>
</HEAD>
```

Even if your current Mac version of IE supports VBScript, if it is not version 4 or higher, it probably doesn't support all of the new language elements introduced in version 3 of the VBScript engine (in order to support DHTML). However, none of the scripting examples in Part III of the book use the DHTML extension elements and should therefore all be interpretable by your version of the browser. Part IV's examples, however, may *not* be sensible to your IE browser since the scripts in this section rely heavily on DHTML elements.

There is no current information from Microsoft on what kind of IE support is, or will be, available to UNIX users. If you are a UNIX user, however, it is supposed that, if you have a UNIX version of IE, you could try the example scripts to see if your version is JavaScript and/or VBScript-enabled.

What's in This Sourcebook?

Like all books in Wiley's critically acclaimed Sourcebook Series, the *VBScript Sourcebook* presents its subject methodically, starting with the most basic VBScript information and ending with advanced scripting procedures and examples.

- Chapters 1 through 3 explain the basics necessary to understanding and using VBScript in your web pages.

- Chapters 4 through 10 comprise a complete reference to the VBScript language, including all the new objects, properties, methods, events, and other extensions provided for in the new DHTML object model.

- Chapters 11 through 14 provide beginner-to-intermediate tutorials that show you how to put VBScript to use in the real Web world.

- Chapters 15 through 18 cover advanced programming techniques that show you how to build pages that integrate the full power of ActiveX, DHTML, and VBScript into serious web applications.

Those with previous programming experience may prefer to skip the early chapters and move right to the advanced material. To help you decide what's best for you, here are suggested starting points based on prior experience:

If you are...	Begin with...
New to HTML	An HTML book
Familiar with HTML but new to VBScript and programming	Chapter 1
New to VBScript but have some programming experience (other than HTML)	Chapter 2
New to VBScript but have some object-based programming experience (e.g., JavaScript)	Chapter 3
New to VBScript but have Visual Basic programming experience	Chapter 3
Somewhat familiar with VBScript and object-based programming	Chapter 4
Familiar with VBScript and object-based programming	Chapter 11
Very familiar with VBScript and object-based programming	Chapter 15

> **NOTE** Even if you're a very experienced JavaScript user, if you're not familiar with Visual Basic programming and/or the new DHTML model you should peruse Chapters 2 and 3 to acquaint yourself with important differences between JavaScript and VBScript. You'll find significant deviations in things like datatype support, implementation of subroutines that are not functions, and variations in syntax.

Sourcebook Conventions

In additional to the basic chapter text, throughout this book you'll find occasional notes, tips, sidebars, and lots of example scripts, as well as frequent references to files on the companion Web Site or to resources on the World Wide Web.

> **NOTES, TIPS, & WARNINGS** Special notes, helpful hints, warnings, and any other additional information deemed noteworthy are brought to your attention using this format.

> ## Sidebars
> Supporting information not critical to the current discussion but nevertheless valuable to your knowledge of VBScript is presented in this sidebar format.

Example Script Format

VBScript and HTML examples are displayed in a special font to clearly distinguish actual code from explanatory text. The scripting font is also monospaced to make it easier to see which indented (or nested) lines of VBScript belong together (you'll discover the importance of this in Chapter 3). Coding conventions (standards used in writing the script examples) are also discussed in Chapter 3.

Here's how a script example looks:

```
<SCRIPT LANGUAGE="VBScript">
<!--

Function HelloFunction

        alert("Hello.")

End Function


-->
</SCRIPT>
```

> **WWW** URLs to helpful Web resources are included in these sections.

What's on the Web Site?

The Companion Web site contains scripts and ancillary files for viewing all of the Web applications discussed in Parts III and IV of this book. Each set of files appears within the folder that corresponds to its chapter. For instance, all of the files for running the "Puzzle Page" application are found in the Chapter 15 folder.

Details on how to copy the files to your hard drive, and which file to open within IE4 so you can begin viewing and using the application (or Web pages), are provided at the beginning of each chapter, following the "Web site" heading.

NOTE This book was written in "Internet time," which means that versions can change quickly. For up-to-the-minute updates, please visit the companion Web site at www.wiley.com/compbooks/mara

---

Part One
Introducing VBScript

The first section of the *VBScript Sourcebook* is dedicated to getting you up and scripting quickly, regardless of whether you're a beginning programmer, or simply new to VBScript. Part I's three chapters methodically explore the underlying framework that supports Web-based scripting languages, from the object-based programming concepts that form the foundation, to the actual mechanics of adding extension scripts to HTML pages.

Chapter 1 is a general introduction to Web scripting languages that compares and contrasts VBScript and Netscape's JavaScript, provides step-by-step instructions for composing VBScripts within HTML documents, and answers frequently asked VBScript questions. Chapter 2 takes an in-depth look at the Document Object Model that drives object-based, event-driven languages—with a special emphasis on the impact of Dynamic HTML. Chapter 3 completes your introduction to VBScript with a detailed review of the elements of the VBScript language, and its critical rules of syntax.

Welcome to
the Family

As the latest and friendliest addition to Microsoft's Visual Basic family of languages, Visual Basic, Scripting Edition is set to play a pivotal role in Microsoft's efforts to establish ActiveX as the premier architecture for developing Internet and intranet applications. ActiveX is a framework (or set of rules) for using virtually any standard development language to build software components that can talk to each other. As a proper subset of the ActiveX-based Visual Basic language, the easy-to-learn, simple-to-write VBScript is poised to do a fair share of that talking.

In fact, in its debut assignment, VBScript is challenging Netscape's JavaScript as the de facto scripting language for enhancing the play and display of Web pages. While Netscape furiously debugged early, quirky versions of Navigator's JavaScript interpreter, Microsoft used the time to re-architect Internet Explorer to talk to ActiveX controls. Once this feat was accomplished, the MS team simply built an ActiveX scripting engine to house VBScript, and voilà—the ActiveX-friendly components (Internet Explorer and the VBScript engine) were ready to converse.

The combination of Visual Basic inheritance and ActiveX architecture allowed VBScript to burst onto the Web scene in a state roughly par to the more established JavaScript (which is to say that they both suffer from approximately the same proportion of bugs, even though JavaScript is supposedly more mature). This isn't really that surprising when you consider that Netscape's JavaScript sprang from Sun Microsystems' newly minted Java language, while VBScript inherited not only the look and feel but the power, stability, and support of a more time-tested ancestor.

ActiveX Scripting Engines

An ActiveX scripting engine is a specific type of ActiveX control that contains all the information necessary for any ActiveX-aware application to understand the engine's resident scripting language. For instance, when Netscape finally gets around to releasing a version of Navigator with native ActiveX (perhaps by the time you read this), that browser's ability to talk to ActiveX controls will automatically allow it to also talk to any ActiveX scripting engine, including the VBScript engine.

ActiveX scripting engines are built upon a Document Object Model (DOM) that evolved from the Scripting Object Model first used by Netscape to define JavaScript. This object model is discussed in detail in Chapter 2 but suffice it to say that the focus of any scripting language supported by this model is on dictating the action the application should take when a user interacts in a specific way with an object. The specific ways in which users interact with objects are called *events*. Scripting languages with this kind of object/event focus are called *object-based* and *event-driven*.

A good example is the submission of an HTML form when a user clicks the form's **Submit** button. The user's click is the *event*, the **Submit** button is the *object*, and the resulting action is the submission of the form. See? Even our old friend HTML is object-based and event-driven!

Languages built upon this object paradigm have long been thought to produce more efficient, stable, and (perhaps most important for rapid application development) *reusable* code. Fully object-oriented languages like C++ (or the legendary SmallTalk) are based on a stricter, more powerful object model than languages which are merely object-based. Object-oriented programming (OOP) allows developers to build custom object classes, define inheritance paths, and generally create their own little universes. If you don't know what any of this means, don't worry about it. You don't need to understand the ins and outs of object-oriented programming to master an object-based scripting language. And less powerful though it may be, the world of object-based languages is nevertheless potent enough to set your Web pages on fire—and much friendlier to fledgling programmers than OOP. (See Chapter 2 for a full review of the Document Object Model.)

Microsoft's decision to follow an object model for Web scripting languages so closely akin to the JavaScript model makes it easier for webmasters to learn multiple languages. However, it also made it simpler for Microsoft to enable Internet Explorer to speak JavaScript (or JScript, as Microsoft prefers to call it). The company's developers only had to define the rules of the JavaScript language, syntax, and execution model within the framework of a scripting engine already designed and constructed to support JavaScript's object model. Not a bad day's work. (Okay, it probably took more than a day.)

The Power of Scripting

Perhaps you find the recent industry attention to Web page scripting languages confusing, considering the fact that you've been "scripting" your Web pages with HTML since day one. As this book progresses you will, in fact, discover a great deal of similarity between the construction of HTML and the syntax of languages like VBScript and JavaScript. There are, however, significant differences in power and scope.

HTML versus Extension Scripting Languages

The biggest difference between a simple though capable markup language like HTML and a true scripting language like VBScript is the latitude the latter gives you to tell the browser how to respond to events occurring within the page, such as the loading of the page into the browser, the selection of a radio button, or the clicking of a hypertext link.

To return to our previous example of a user clicking the "Submit" button on a form in a Web page: Using only HTML you do indeed have the power to modify the way the form is submitted but only via its allowed arguments. For instance, you can specify in the <FORM> tag's ACTION argument that it be sent to a given e-mail address instead of being submitted directly to the server. This ability to control the form submission process is wonderful but limited to what the current version of HTML allows.

With the additional help of an extension language like VBScript, however, you could direct the browser to check required fields on the form and, if any are empty, prompt the user to fill them before submitting the form. You could add further instructions to determine if the Phone field (for example) contains a valid telephone number, using a validation routine that could be written to support international numbers as well as local phone formats. Moreover, you could script a confirmation page to be generated on-the-fly when the user submits the form, recapping the information provided in the form by the user and thanking the user for the submission.

Of course, the HTML language specification is under constant revision and, if current proposals pass in committee, may soon be empowered to perform limited field-level forms validation on its own. The keyword, however, is "limited," since the simplicity of HTML syntax confines it to the most standard expressions of any operation it addresses. The more complex syntax of an extension scripting language allows it to not only respond in myriad if-then-else ways to a single action on a page, but to track a user's actions; collect and review form input; discern information about the user's environment like browser-in-use, type of display, and operating system; and then compile all of this feedback into a customized response to the current user.

One of the most exciting attributes of a language like VBScript is its ability to orchestrate complex interactions between multiple third-party applets. While, again,

---

What about Dynamic HTML?

Doesn't Dynamic HTML increase the power and scope of the HTML language and thereby reduce (or even obviate) the need for external scripting?

The word "dynamic" is somewhat misleading when applied to recent enhancements to both Internet Explorer's and Navigator's support of HTML. DHTML *does not*—as you might reasonably suppose—refer to new ways of writing HTML to allow the automatic updating of pages on the client side without constant recourse to the server, or without the need for external scripting. DHTML refers, rather, to an intensified relationship between HTML and languages like VBScript, JavaScript, and Java.

With the advent of the Internet Explorer 4.0 version of DHTML, the entire HTML document is now entirely "exposed" to these external programming languages. Newcomers to these languages may find such a concept confusing prior to digesting Chapters 2 and 3. But readers of these chapters, as well as past Java and JavaScript coders, will understand quite well that the previously limited access to HTML "objects" has now been expanded to allow your scripting language and/or your applets and controls to access any object created by HTML, such as, say, the individual elements of a table that were previously unavailable for external interaction.

Chapter 2 provides more details but the short explanation is that DHTML-enabled browsers now support a more expanded object model (more objects) with an attendant expansion of properties, methods, and events. Moreover, the entire superstructure for intercepting events has been redesigned and reconstructed to support "event bubbling," allowing objects at the top of the Object Hierarchy (presented in Chapter 2) to choreograph events for lower-level objects. The net result (pun intended) is an astonishing increase in power and scope all right—not for HTML but for external Web languages like VBScript. Looks like you picked the right time to roll up your sleeves and learn it.

HTML provides tags for embedding and displaying plug-ins, applets, and controls on a page, getting those objects to talk meaningfully to each other is a job for a language like VBScript. Using VBScript, for instance, Microsoft's Agent Control (whose demo version flies a little talking "Genie" character around a page) could be scripted to know which movie a user is viewing in the popular Macromedia Shockwave plug-in, and then be further scripted to narrate additional information about that movie while it's playing.

Using VBScript and JavaScript

VBScript is, of course, best known as a Web page extension language identical in overall function to Netscape's JavaScript. Both are "high-level" computer languages closer in syntax to human languages than to the strict zeros and ones of low-level machine code. The downside is, the closer a computer language is to a spoken language, the slower its code runs. But, what VBScript and JavaScript lack in speed is made up for a thousand-fold in ease of learning and implementation.

Both VBScript and JavaScript may be used to add local programming operations to HTML pages. This means that you can "program" your Web pages to perform services for your users right inside the page instead of reconnecting to the server to execute a cgi application (a server helper application conforming to the "Common Gateway Interface").

Pages can be scripted to respond in unlimited ways to a variety of user actions. You've already discovered that if a user clicks a form's "Submit" button, a script in that page can verify that all the form's fields have been filled. If all fields *are* filled, your script can allow the submission. If one or more fields are empty, your script can direct the user to fill in these fields and submit the form again. Page-based services like these save your visitor connection and transfer time while significantly reducing the load on your poor server.

As a past webmaster, you'll be pleased to discover that both JavaScript and VBScript are typed right alongside (and sometimes *inside*) the familiar HTML tags used to create Web pages. In the first instance, to distinguish extension scripting from vanilla HTML you simply place your lines of VBScript or JavaScript between the HTML <SCRIPT></SCRIPT> tags, identifying the scripting language you're using via this tag's LANGUAGE argument.

```
<SCRIPT LANGUAGE="VBScript">

[VBScript Statements]

</SCRIPT>
```

The <SCRIPT> tag takes up to four arguments but only its LANGUAGE argument is required. The other three optional arguments are:

- **SRC=**: The answer to this argument is the URL of an external file containing additional scripts. The browser uses this URL to load a specified file along with the master page, so scripts in the page can also call upon (run) scripts in the external file. At the present time, only JavaScript uses external files so this argument isn't yet used with VBScript (although it may be by the time you read this).

```
<SCRIPT LANGUAGE="JavaScript" SRC="extScriptFile.js">

[JavaScript Statements]

</SCRIPT>
```

- **FOR=**: The answer to this argument is the name of an object (such as *Button1*). This argument is not recognized by Navigator 3.0 although Navigator 4.0 allows it.

- **EVENT=**: The answer to this argument is the name of an *event handler*, a scripting element empowered to handle a specified user or browser event (such as *Click*). This argument is not recognized by Navigator 3.0 but Navigator 4.0 allows it.

The FOR and EVENT arguments allow you to link an object and an event to the enclosed script. If *Click* is the event and *Button1* is the specified object, the enclosed script is executed whenever the user clicks a button called "Button1."

```
<SCRIPT LANGUAGE="VBScript" FOR="Button1" EVENT="onClick()">

[VBScript Statements]

</SCRIPT>
```

You'll learn more about these arguments in subsequent tutorials. For the purpose of getting started there are only two more things you need to know about creating and using scripts inside the <SCRIPT> tags:

1. Unless you have complete control over the browser your visitors use (which may be the case, if you're running an intranet), or you simply don't care to accommodate non-VBScript-aware browsers, you should place HTML comment tags around the VBScript statements in the <SCRIPT> tag to hide this code from unaware browsers. Otherwise, failing to recognize <SCRIPT> as a valid tag, down-level browsers will simply display the raw text of the tag and its contained statements on the page.

```
<SCRIPT LANGUAGE="VBScript>
<!--

[script statements]

-->
</SCRIPT>
```

2. You may place <SCRIPT> tags virtually anywhere in an HTML document but, unless there's good reason to do otherwise, it's often best to locate your VBScripts inside a single <SCRIPT> tag in the <HEAD> portion of your HTML document. This is especially true of scripts that are called upon to execute from multiple "objects" in the document, for example, all of the hyperlinks on a page. Since all browsers routinely load the <HEAD> portion of a document first, you won't need to worry whether a precipitous user event (we've all clicked a link while the page is still loading) will cause the browser to try to execute a script that isn't yet loaded.

```
<HEAD>
<SCRIPT LANGUAGE="VBScript>
<!--

[script statements]

-->
</SCRIPT>
</HEAD>
```

Using VBScript in Other HTML Tags

Veteran JavaScripters are familiar with another method of embedding scripts into HTML, which allows you to place scripts inside any HTML tag. Prior to the introduction of IE4's DHTML (and full exposure of the HTML document model), tag-level scripts could only be placed inside tags that created an interactive object on the page. In the past, this didn't include, for example, the <HR> tag which placed a horizontal line on the page but didn't previously detect any user action.

Today, thanks to DHTML and IE4's universal ability to detect user events, *virtually all tags now accept tag-level scripts*. This is with the obvious exception of tags that do not produce a visible element, such as the <HTML> tag itself, the <HEAD> and <META> tags, the <NOBR> and <NOFRAMES> tags, and subsidiary tags like <OPTION> and <PARAM> whose parent tags receive events for them.

Scripts placed into HTML tags (other than the <SCRIPT> tag) become the answer to a new argument for that tag, and that new argument is the event that is going to

Inline Scripts

There are times when a script won't work unless it's placed within the <BODY> of its HTML document. For instance, a script that adds additional HTML to the current document as the page is loaded *must* appear at the exact point where that HTML string is to be displayed on the resulting page. Such a requirement necessitates placement of the enclosing <SCRIPT> tag within the document's <BODY> tags.

Scripts appearing within the document <BODY> are called "inline" scripts, just like pictures referenced within <IMG> tags in the <BODY> are called inline images. Inline scripts are executed (run) during page load—as soon as the browser arrives at the section in the HTML document where the script resides. This is the same rule that the browser applies to an inline image, which is displayed on the page in the same place as its tag appears in the parent HTML document.

While it's difficult to quantify all of the circumstances when it may be advantageous or even necessary to place a <SCRIPT> tag in the <BODY> of a document, you'll actually get the basic idea very rapidly from simply reviewing the tutorial in Chapter 11, when you're ready for that level of instruction. Its scripts are strewn throughout an HTML page, and you'll find the chapter text disclosing the reasons for each script's placement more enlightening than a theoretical discourse on the same material.

handle the script. The term used to describe a script's handling event is known generically and appropriately, in both VBScript and JavaScript, as an *event handler*. An event handler is simply the name of the event, preceded by the word "on."

Here's an example. If you want a script to execute when the page is loaded, you might place it inside that page's <BODY> tag—using the *load* event handler as an argument within that tag, and your script as its answer:

```
<BODY onLoad="[script statements]">
```

Basically, placing this script inside the <BODY> tag tells the browser to execute that script "on" the loading of the page. The next script argument/answer setup tells the browser to execute the script "on" the clicking of its resident button:

```
<INPUT TYPE="button" onClick="[script statements]">
```

In JavaScript, longer or more universal routines are usually placed between <SCRIPT> tags in the <HEAD> portion of a document, then executed by an event handler inside the target object. In the following example, when the user clicks the button object named "Button1," a script called "myFunction()" is executed:

```
<HTML>
<HEAD>
<SCRIPT LANGUAGE="JavaScript">

function myFunction()   {

    [script statements that execute when Button 1 is clicked];

}

</SCRIPT>
</HEAD>
<BODY>
<FORM>

<INPUT TYPE="button" NAME="Button1" onClick="myFunction()">

</FORM>
</BODY>
</HTML>
```

While VBScript allows you to follow the same procedure, you also have other alternatives. For instance, you can place a *subroutine* (list of related actions) in the <HEAD> of your document that already knows it must run when the page is loaded or when a certain button is clicked.

```
<HTML>
<HEAD>
<SCRIPT LANGUAGE="VBScript">

sub Button1_onClick

    [script statements that execute when Button 1 is clicked]

End sub

</SCRIPT>
</HEAD>
<BODY>
<FORM>
```

```
<INPUT TYPE="button" NAME="Button1">

</FORM>
</BODY>
</HTML>
```

Alternatively, you can use the previously described EVENT and FOR arguments in the enclosing <SCRIPT> tag to designate the object and event that will execute the enclosed script.

```
<HTML>
<HEAD>

<SCRIPT LANGUAGE="VBScript" EVENT="onClick()" FOR="Button1">

    [script statements that execute when Button 1 is clicked]

</SCRIPT>

</SCRIPT>
</HEAD>
<BODY>
<FORM>

<INPUT TYPE="button" NAME="Button1" onClick="myFunction()">

</FORM>
</BODY>
</HTML>
```

In succeeding chapters, you'll gradually learn the best way to write your scripts. Once you know more about VBScript's syntax (its written construction—or grammar, if you will), it'll become almost second nature to know where things go and how to best set up a page-worth or a frameset-worth of scripts. Even in this short discussion, you've bitten off a major piece of what you need to know to begin scripting.

Getting Started

When you *are* ready to begin scripting, where do you start? Will you need to get a copy of the VBScript engine? Not if you've already installed Internet Explorer 3.0 or higher. The VBScript engine is actually nothing more than a .dll file that is automatically placed into your Windows/System Directory when you install Internet Explorer.

The latest version of the VBScript engine is always bundled with the latest version of Internet Explorer. Each time you retrieve a newer version of the browser, the "Vbscript.dll" file is also updated (if changes have been made to the VBScript engine). Although this saves you the trouble of keeping track of updates to the engine, you'll still need to know what changes, additions, and corrections have been made to the language by visiting the VBScript home page whenever new versions of Internet Explorer appear.

> **W W W** VBScript home page:
>
> www.microsoft.com/vbscript/

To begin scripting, all you need to do is open any HTML (or simple text) editor and begin typing. When you're ready to test your script, you'll need to have the latest version of Internet Explorer installed on your system. To test the script, you simply load the page into the browser using File > Open—just as you would to test a vanilla HTML page.

> **W A R N I N G** When you first install Internet Explorer, choose View > Options > Security and make sure that the "Run ActiveX scripts" checkbox is selected. If it isn't, your browser won't even try to interpret VBScripts or JavaScripts in yours or anyone else's pages. You should also enable "ActiveX controls and plug-ins" and "Java programs" if you want to play around with these objects in your own pages or view them in pages authored by others.

Hardware and Software Requirements

Internet Explorer and your favorite HTML editor are all you really need to add VBScript to your Web pages. Hardware and system requirements for the latest version of Internet Explorer for your operating system are posted on the Internet Explorer Download Pages.

W W W Internet Explorer Download Pages:

www.microsoft.com/ie/download/

However, you may want to take advantage of some of the helpful supporting software and documentation available on the Microsoft Web site for free use or trail:

- The ActiveX Control Pad with the HTML Layout Control automates some of your basic scripting tasks and provides excellent script setup support for embedding applets and controls into your pages.

- If you want your pages to work with both Internet Explorer and Netscape Navigator, you'll need to install the ScriptActive plug-in (a demo version is available at www.ncompuss.com) that allows Navigator to use ActiveX controls and the VBScript engine.

- The Microsoft Script Debugger is a helpful aid to debugging your scripts and, if there's one thing you can count on in this life it's the fact that your scripts (along with everyone else's) will have bugs. At the time of publication, however, the debugger was not ready for IE4.

The Trials and Tribulations of Supporting Navigator, Too

Currently, producing VBScripted pages comprehensible to the Navigator browser is a thankless task, due to limitations in Navigator's support of ActiveX (and therefore, VBScript). If Navigator continues to withhold support of ActiveX your only recourse at this time is the ScriptActive plug-in from NCompass. However, since ScriptActive is a third-party production, there are two distinct drawbacks:

1. ScriptActive's support of VBScript necessarily lags behind Microsoft's evolving VBScript spec. At press time, for instance, ScriptActive didn't support VBScript 3.0, rendering all of the DHTML-dependent code examples in this book insensible to this plug-in.

2. ScriptActive is a commercial product that must be installed on the machines of Navigator-prone visitors to your site. Current pricing is

$21.50 for a single user license and $115.00 for 10 user licenses. Call (604) 606-0950 for information on licenses for redistribution.

To truly pursue the creation of cross-browser pages, you'll need to assess the current state of Navigator and the ScriptActive plug-in to determine the latitude and limitations you'll face in implementing VBScript; and you'll certainly need to test your pages in all the versions of Navigator that you intend to support.

What about Mac Visitors to Your Site? You should also consider visitors to your site who are running Mac versions of Internet Explorer or Navigator. Currently, there is no ScriptActive plug-in available for the Mac, however, assuming Microsoft has fulfilled its promise to provide cross-platform support for ActiveX and IE, there should soon be (if there isn't now) a VBScript-enabled IE for the Mac. If so, you'll need to know the version of the VBScript engine supported on the Mac. History clearly shows that Microsoft is not above allowing the Mac's IE to lag well behind the Windows versions.

Until cross-platform and cross-browser support of VBScript matures, you may find it best to create a separate branch of pages for your non-Windows visitors using browsers other than Internet Explorer.

W W W Pick up the latest ScriptActive information at the NCompass site:

www.ncompasslabs.com/scriptactive/

Your First Script

Nothing brings a new technical subject into sharper focus more quickly than a simple example. As a tip of the hat to early programming environments, it's traditional to produce a "Hello, World!" message with your first piece of working code. Accordingly, the VBScript in the following example creates a new HTML document that says "Hello, World!" as soon as the user presses the **Click Me** button on the original page.

The original page displays a single button for the user to click (see Figure 1.1). When the user clicks that button, the browser becomes aware of a *Click* event generated by the button object whose name is "myButton." As the only object on the page, it certainly wouldn't take a rocket scientist to figure out the source of the click. However, this is a simple example; a real page is likely to have multiple objects in it, and possibly multiple buttons. So, an easy method for identifying the source object is necessary.

```
<HTML>
<HEAD>
<TITLE>Hello World Page</TITLE>

<SCRIPT LANGUAGE="VBScript">
<!--

sub myButton_onClick

        document.open
        document.write("<CENTER><B>Hello, World!</B></CENTER>")
        document.close

End sub

-->
    </SCRIPT>

    </HEAD>

    <BODY>

    <FORM>

    <CENTER>
    <INPUT TYPE="button" NAME="myButton" VALUE="Click Me!">
    </CENTER>

    </FORM>

    </BODY>

    </HTML>
```

Since the VBScript subroutine in the <HEAD> of the document references both *myButton* and the *onClick* handler, the subroutine's three action statements are run only if the button is clicked (Figure 1.2).

Figure 1.1 Here's an illustration of the original page.

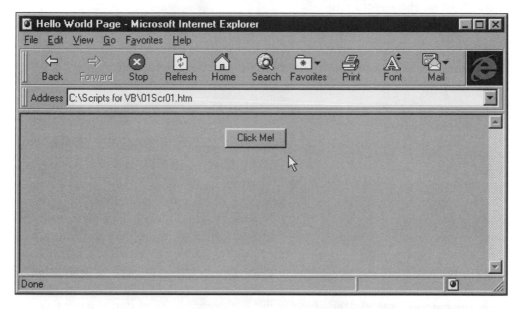

Figure 1.2 Here's an illustration of the new page that is displayed when the user presses the "Click Me" button shown in Figure 1.1.

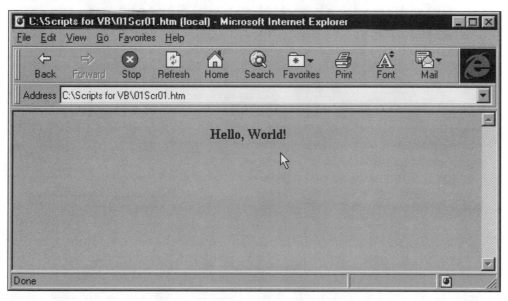

The "Sub myButton_onClick" script contains three lines of code, asking the browser to do three specific things:

1. **document.open**: Asks the browser to (basically) create a new document.

2. **document.write()**: Asks the browser to use the HTML script that appears between the parentheses (to the right of *write*) as the basis of the new document.

3. **document.close**: Asks the browser to close the document (or text) stream, and present the page.

When the browser completes these three tasks, a page displaying the "Hello, World!" message, centered and bolded, is displayed in the browser, in place of the original page containing the "Click Me" button.

An important item to note in this example script is the "object.action" construction used to present the script's three commands to the browser. This procedure of tying words together with a dot (.) is standard syntax for more than just Internet domain names. It is used by both VBScript and JavaScript to attach sets of predefined actions to their objects—telling the browser, in effect, to execute those actions upon the target object.

In the current example, the object is the *document* (or page) that is getting created. The predefined actionsets (more properly called *methods*) are *open*, *write*, and

A Few Words about the Sub Statement

JavaScript users may be perplexed at this point by the use of the "substatement" to house subroutines (ordered lines of code describing one or more actions to the browser). This is because, in JavaScript, all subroutines are housed in functions.

You can also write functions in VBScript but, in this language, only lists of actions that result in a returned value are placed into a function statement. Action lists that do not return a value are ordinarily placed into a substatement. If you're used to JavaScript, this may seem like an academic distinction at first, but it's actually a very logical, orderly (and traditional) way to write code. Reserving the function statement for routines that return a value makes it very easy to glance through a script and immediately know which blocks of code return values. As you'll learn in subsequent chapters, any coding convention that makes it easier to read and understand the code is well worth applying.

close. Whenever VBScript supports a prescribed list of actions for an object, that actionset is assigned a specific word (such as *write*). The word becomes the name of one of the object's methods, and that name, alone, can henceforth be used to describe the entire actionset to the browser. More on objects, methods, and other scripting elements in Chapter 2.

Frequently Asked Questions

The *most* frequently asked questions about VBScript have already been answered in either the Introduction or earlier in this chapter. If you've read through this material you certainly already know enough to move on to the next chapter. But, if you're a dyed-in-the-wool computer type (a.k.a. *real nerd*), then you may be interested in some of the less-pressing, but still impressive details of VBScript's short but eventful life.

What Is the Relationship of VBScript to Java?

Java is Sun Microsystems' million-dollar baby—but that wasn't always the case. The fact is, Java failed in its original mission to provide a development language that could be used across a multitude of hardware devices (handheld computers, cellular phones, garage-door openers—you name it). Thanks to some quick thinking on the part of one of Sun's resident whiz kids, however, Java changed horses in midstream and became the perfect answer to the Net's need for a platform-independent programming language.

Derived from the object-oriented C++, Java is a full-fledged OOP environment. Its code may be written once, then compiled separately for every operating system that boasts a Java Virtual Machine (all major ones do)—allowing the same code to run on a variety of computer platforms. Java*Script*, as noted earlier, is a scripting language *based on Java*. It was written by the folks at Netscape (who bought the rights to do so from Sun) and not by the original developers of the Java language.

VBScript has no direct relationship to Java but many people erroneously believe that VBScript is to ActiveX what JavaScript is to Java. This is clearly not the case, since Java is a language that JavaScript is based upon while ActiveX is only a framework for creating componentry software (ActiveX controls) and not a language at all. The language that VBScript is based upon is Visual Basic. Strangely enough, you can use either Java or Visual Basic (or C++, or any other viable computer language) within the ActiveX framework to create ActiveX controls. VBScript can then, in turn, interact with the created control. If that control was created using the Java language, then VBScript can talk to that Java component. But that's really nothing new since VBScript can also talk to Java applets, which, to date, are *only* written in Java.

What Is VBScript's Relationship to the Visual Basic Family?

You could say that Visual Basic Scripting Edition (to use its formal name) is the grandchild of the Visual Basic Development Environment, and the child of Visual Basic for Applications (VBA)—a language first used to customize Microsoft Excel, then extended to other members of the Microsoft Office suite. Thus, if you know Visual Basic or VBA (or both), you'll find VBScript very familiar indeed. VBScript is, in fact, 100 percent compatible with all members of the Visual Basic family, which means you can actually cut and paste whole code segments from one to the other with very little need for modification.

VBScript is a lightweight, interpreted version of Visual Basic for Applications. The term "lightweight" means that VBScript is simpler and less powerful than its predecessors; but, this simplified structure makes it less difficult to learn. It also speeds up the time it takes to translate VBScript into machine code (zeros and ones), which is the only way you can really talk to a computer. Any speed gain in this area is important to VBScript, since each line of code produced by interpreted languages must be translated into machine code *every time that line of code is run*. This means that, when the user clicks a button on a Web page which executes a VBScript or a JavaScript, that script must be interpreted (translated into zeros and ones) *before* its instructions can be understood (much less executed) by the computer. If the user clicks the button to execute the script again, it must reinterpreted before script is executed.

Precompiled languages like Java and Visual Basic, on the other hand, are permanently turned into machine language when compiled. Applications running on compiled code never have to wait for an interpretation prior to the execution of its commands. Sitting in a middle ground are languages that are *runtime* compiled. This kind of code is only interpreted the first time it is run in each session. The resulting machine language translation remains in memory for the duration of that session. Look for future versions of Internet Explorer and other high-powered browsers to incorporate runtime compiling into their featuresets.

Can I Use VBScript on the Server Side of My Site?

Yes. If your server is running Windows NT 4.0 or higher you can set up and use Microsoft's Internet Information Server (IIS) 3.0. Then, in addition to writing .htm files to be interpreted by the browser, you'll be writing .asp files (Active Server Pages) that are interpreted by the server, which creates Web pages from these scripts on-the-fly.

VBScript for the server is virtually identical to VBScript for the browser, with the addition of a few new server-based objects (such as the server itself). After you've gotten a complete handle on writing client-side VBScript, copy the necessary files for installing IIS onto your NT machine and consult Microsoft's accompanying documentation to try your hand at server-side VBScript.

Is VBScript Secure?

Security means many things to many people on the Internet. However, since one of VBScript's major purposes is for use in scripting Web pages, Microsoft has created it as a "safe subset" of the Visual Basic language. This means that VBScript does not include any file I/O commands, or have any direct access to the operating system that sits on the client's machine—with exception of the placement and retrieval of cookies.

What Are Cookies?

Cookies are little tidbits of information that can be deposited on a client's machine in the browser's cookie file and retrieved later—but only by a page presented by the server that placed the cookie there. Cookies are usually used to track things like how often a user has visited a site, the last time the user visited the site, page choices made by the user on previous visits...fairly harmless stuff. Nevertheless, cookies are still quite controversial since (under certain circumstances) they can be inserted on the user's machine without the user's knowledge or permission.

The many limits, restrictions, and user concerns surrounding cookies are discussed in detail in Chapter 4, in the section on the VBScript "cookie" object.

What Are the Restrictions for Using VBScript in My Own Applications?

If you're a registered Microsoft Developer you can license and use the VBScript engine for free. Microsoft provides binary implementations of VBScript for the 32-bit Windows API, the 16-bit Windows API, and the Macintosh as part of the ActiveX SDK, available for both Windows and Macintosh from the Microsoft site.

W W W   ActiveX home page:

www.microsoft.com/intdev/sdk/

What's Next?

By now you should have a decent handle on how VBScript fits into the ActiveX scheme of things, and a basic understanding of how to incorporate scripts into your HTML documents. The next chapter changes focus from these relatively mechanical considerations to the broader programming concepts inherent in the Document Object Model that forms the foundation of object-based scripting. This model is presented in Chapter 2, along with the Object Hierarchy that proceeds from it and supports the working concepts critical to mastering an object-based scripting language.

2

The HTML Document
Object Model

As an ActiveX Scripting Engine, VBScript inherits an architecture for scripting languages first defined by Netscape and exemplified by Netscape's JavaScript for the Web. Thanks to Microsoft's support of this emerging object-based language model, it is first in line to become the standard for all scripting languages used by Web browsers (or other likely software components) to provide a means to customize, extend, and integrate the behavior of cooperating applications.

It's good news for users when competing companies like Microsoft and Netscape join forces to adopt and promote standards like the object model for scripting languages. Basing VBScript (and all other ActiveX Scripting Engine languages) upon the same architectural model as JavaScript makes it easier for webmasters to be multilingual and therefore better equipped to flexibly extend their Web sites. Unfortunately, from this initial common ground, the two companies are now veering off in significantly different directions with their separate implementations of DHTML. Don't they know or care that keeping up with advances in the various Web-enabling technologies is hard enough without companies reinventing the wheel with every new tool and toy?

DHTML differences aside, if you're already well-versed in either Microsoft's or Netscape's version of JavaScript, you can be up and running in VBScript in a very short time, because (for the most part) even the DHTML-enabled version of VBScript supports the same basic objects and fundamental events as JavaScript. Since you already understand the nature and use of objects, properties, methods, events, et al., all you need is a rapid review of VBScript's syntactical variations (Chapter 3) and a solid reference to all of its language elements, including the DHTML extensions (Chapters 4–10) to begin weaving this sister scripting language into your Web pages.

On the other hand, if VBScript is the first Web scripting language you've chosen to learn, once you've mastered it, you'll have a leg up on the learning curve when and if you move on to JavaScript. After absorbing the slightly more complex VBScript environment—with its larger vocabulary and provision for a wider variety of datatypes, and the like—you'll find it very easy indeed to master JavaScript. The first step toward learning both languages is a clear understanding of the underlying model for object-based, event-driven scripting languages.

Object-Based and Event-Driven Languages

Chapter 1 observed that the focus of any language supported by an object model is on ". . . dictating the action the application should take when a user interacts in a specific way with an object. The specific ways in which users interact with objects are called *events*. Scripting languages with this kind of object/event focus are called *object-based* and *event-driven*." These programming buzzwords may feel foreign at first glance, but the fact of the matter is, you are already deeply familiar with an object-based, event-driven scripting language called HTML.

HTML Objects

Many of the tags that you place into your HTML documents result in the display of objects on a Web page. The <HTML> tag itself represents the top-level object at your disposal: the *document* that houses your HTML script. The <BODY> tag represents the displayed area of that document, where any <ANCHOR>, <IMG>, or <INPUT> tags you place between those <BODY> tags are displayed as *links*, *images*, and *form elements*, respectively. And these are only some of the HTML objects that you can script to appear in your Web pages. Many others exist or are on the drawing board for the ever-evolving HTML specification.

HTML Events

Regardless of which HTML objects you choose to include in your Web page scripts, you realize, of course, that none are either created or displayed merely because you type their tags into a text file. Such display can only occur in the *event* that the page is loaded into a Web-enabled browser application. Another way of stating this would be to say that the HTML document and its internal objects are displayed whenever a load [page] event is executed in relation to that document.

Once the page is loaded and displayed, the browsing user may cause other events to occur in relation to visible objects on the page. The links created by <ANCHOR> tags may be clicked—causing a *click* event to execute for that link—which, in turn, executes an *unload* event for the exiting page and a *load* event for the incoming page. On the new page, the user might type information into a series of text fields on a form, then click a Submit button. This last action generates a *click* event for the Submit button, which then also generates *submit* event for the form. The *firing* of the submit event signals the browser to execute its internal form submission routine, based on your answers to the METHOD and ACTION arguments in the <FORM> tag.

Enter VBScript and JavaScript

When you augment your HTML scripts with VBScript or JavaScript, you increase your ability to manipulate HTML-created objects and their associated events by at least an order of magnitude. In some instances, you become empowered to create objects without recourse to HTML. Moreover, VBScript and JavaScript cover a much broader territory of browser-generated objects and events—made broader still by the advent of dynamic HTML, giving you access to additional interface items and allowing you more control over the browser's response to executed events (see Figure 2.1).

First Steps

Since both JavaScript and VBScript are *object-centric,* after getting a grip on how and where VBScript is written into an HTML document (covered in Chapter 1), the next order of business is to become familiar with the terms used to name all of the objects that may be created or otherwise manipulated by the language (just as you likely learned, and endeavor to keep abreast of, all the possible tags that may be used to create or manipulate objects via HTML). Once you become familiar with its built-in objects, it's a good idea to study all of the recognized events in VBScript's (or any programming language's) interpreted environment (in this case, the browser),which may be used to dictate the circumstances and order in which your code is executed.

When you've completed Chapters 1–3 (Part I) of the *VBScript Sourcebook,* you'll know how, where, and in what format to write your code. This is basically all you need to know to start VBScripting your Web pages. To inject meaningful content into your scripts, however, it's a good idea to take the time to peruse the exhaustive VBScript vocabulary provided in Part II, which offers descriptions and scripting examples for all of the VBScript Objects, Object Properties, Object Methods, Supported Events, Built-in Functions, Constants, Statements, Operators, and Keywords. But before you embark on such an up-close and personal inspection of the language, step back and take a wide-angle look at the VBScript Hierarchy of Objects that forms the foundation of the HTML Document Object Model.

Working with Events

Using events to control the execution of code is the cornerstone technique for *event-driven* programming. In order to use this technique to its fullest, you must know which events are perceptible to—and therefore interceptable by—your scripts. In the VBScript/browser environment your scripts can (for instance) perceive and intercept a user's click over any button. The following script results in a notification alert if the user clicks its containing button:

```
<INPUT TYPE="button" onClick="alert('You just clicked my button.')">
```

But you cannot perceive, or intercept, the movement of the mouse over the spot in a document where a <NOBR> tag has been placed. Not only does this tag produce no visible evidence of its existence, but it cannot detect any event even if the mouse pointer happens to stumble across its virtual place in the document. The following script would *never* execute:

```
<NOBR onMouseMove="alert('You just moved the mouse pointer over me.')">
```

In addition to studying a language's allowable events, it is also important to note which events are attached to which objects. The <NOBR> example uses an HTML element that not only doesn't support the *mouseMove* event, but isn't even a recognized object in either VBScript or JavaScript.

On the other side of that coin, just because an object is recognized by your scripting language, it doesn't mean that all events are applicable to that object. While DHTML has certainly broadened the playing field, validating more events for many more objects (text fields, for example, now accept the *click* event), the application of events is still far from universal.

The aforementioned *click* event, for example, is now applicable to the *document* object. The *blur* event, however, (fired when a previously targeted object loses the cursor's focus) is not applicable to the document object. Clicking from one empty area on a page to another empty area (areas with no other valid objects), for instance, would never result in the execution of an onBlur script attached to the document object. For the blur event to be processed, it must occur in relation to an object in the document that is capable of firing a message regarding that event—such as a text field on the page—to notify the browser that the object has just lost the document focus.

Figure 2.1 In an object-based, event-driven scripting language like VBScript: (a) the user interacts with a created object; (b) an event message is fired that tells the browser the name of the affected object and the executing event; and, (c) scripts attached to that object/event sequence are executed.

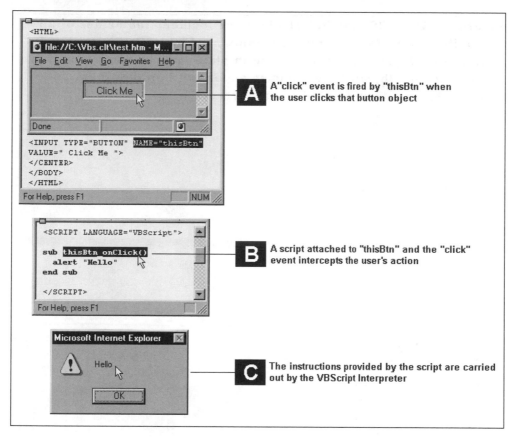

The VBScript Object Hierarchy

All object-centric coding environments (whether object-based or fully object-oriented) define an Object Hierarchy. This hierarchy describes the *scope* of each object and its place in the developmental pecking order for the given programming environment. Communication between objects flows in a single direction, from top to bottom. Objects that sit above other objects in the hierarchy thus enjoy the broadest scope, or influence, over the objects shown in Figure 2.2

While memorizing all the available VBScript objects is almost a no-brainer (there aren't that many), a more subtle task is understanding and appreciating the scope of each object. Such awareness is essential to realizing what you can and cannot do in

Figure 2.2 The VBScript Object Hierarchy includes the names of all of the built-in objects that may be manipulated by VBScript or JavaScript. Object names appearing in plain text may be used, as is, to refer to the object. Object names appearing in italics must be referred to by a user-created pseudonym.

```
window
        event
    history
    location
    navigator
    visual
    document
        all
        anchors
        applets
        body
        embeds
        frames
        images
        links
        plugins
        scripts
        selection
        forms
            elements
            button
            checkbox
            hidden
            image
            radio
            reset
            text
            textarea
            submit
            password
            <object>
            select
                options
```

your scripts; and knowing VBScript's capabilities and limitations is critical to producing a well-designed Web application.

For instance, a script in a parent window can tell a child window what to do, but the child window cannot tell the parent window what to do. (Makes sense, doesn't it?) This is an important piece of knowledge to have if you intend to script events between windows. It is also valuable to know that variable information contained only in a script inside <FORM> tags is not available to scripts in the <BODY> or <HEAD> (which are part of the document object). This is because the form object is a child of the document object, and *communication only flows down*, not up, the hierarchy (just as it does in a dysfunctional corporation).

The Object Hierarchy for languages adhering to the HTML Document Object Model (DOM) is, more or less, the same for each spin-off language (otherwise, a language could hardly be said to fit the standard model). Thus, if you know the JavaScript Object Hierarchy, you also know the VBScript Object Hierarchy.

> **T I P** If you're not yet familiar with the addition of objects, methods, properties, and events precipitated by DHTML for either language, then you'll need to closely review the language reference chapters in Part II to augment your working knowledge of this *new age* VBScript—or check out the Netscape site to bring your JavaScript education up to date.

The top object in both hierarchies (both before and after the addition of DHTML) is the *window* that displays a Web page. In either language, you can use this object to create your own browser windows—dictating width and height and window dressing (such as toolbars, resize boxes, or horizontal and vertical scrolls). You can force the display of a new document in the current window, indicate the document that a newly created window will display, or change the document display in one or more of the frames in a current frameset.

All other objects in the hierarchy are contained within a browser window and, thus, sit below the *window* object, on the second tier of the hierarchy:

- The *event* object provides the name of the currently firing event.

- The *history* object provides the list of the current session's visited pages.

- The *location* object provides the address of the currently displayed page or frameset.

- The *navigator* object provides information about the browser in use.

- The *visual* object provides information about the current visitor's monitor.

- The *document* object represents all of the other objects contained in the parent HTML document.

> **NOTE** There are two additional JavaScript objects whose operations are provided for in VBScript by built-in functions. In JavaScript, these items are known as the Date and Math objects. Because these items are not objects in both languages, they are not included in the official hierarchy. All of the items in the Object Hierarchy shown in this chapter are available in both languages, using the same naming conventions (except for the visual object, which is called screen in JavaScript).

Almost all of the objects appearing in the hierarchy may be referenced by either its generic name (shown in Figure 2.2), or by a pseudonym assigned to the object via VBScript or the NAME argument inside the object's HTML tag. Objects that may be referenced by a generic name are shown in plain text in the figure, while objects referenced only by pseudonym (a given name) appear in italics. The following button object, for instance, cannot be referred to as "button" in a script because there may potentially be more than one button in the current page or frameset. You can, however, refer to it as "myButton," if you give it that name.

```
<INPUT TYPE="button" NAME="myButton">
```

On the other hand, since the window is the top object you don't need to type the word "window" in a script when referring to the current window. When you leave out the window name, the current window is automatically assumed. If you want to access a window that is *not* current, however, you'll need to refer to that window by a name that you previously gave it, or by another valid window identifier like "parent," "self," or "top." (See Chapter 4's section on the Window Object for more details.)

While all objects in the hierarchy are subsidiary to the window object, a few of these other objects also have subsidiary objects of their own. In such cases, the subsidiary object is considered a child of the object directly above it, and a grandchild or great-grandchild (or, in one instance, great-great-grandchild) of the window object. The *document* object, for instance, is parent to the following objects, which sit below the document, on the third tier of the hierarchy:

- The *links* object represents an array or collection of hypertext links on the page created by the <A HREF> tag.

- The *anchors* object represents an array or collection of the named targets on the page created by the <A NAME> tag.

- All *applets*, *plugins*, and *embeds* (that are not inside <FORM> tags) represent all of the embedded objects in the page created by the <OBJECT>, <EMBED>, or <APPLET> tags.

Why Isn't Navigator the Top Object?

Since the browser application has a much broader, affective scope on the client's machine than a mere window within that browser, you may be wondering why the *navigator* object isn't top gun in the Object Hierarchy.

Basically, because both JavaScript and VBScript are *safe* languages that limit your ability to manipulate the user's machine to what can be displayed in the browser window (with the exception of saving and retrieving cookies, or little packets of information, on the client machine).

Both VBScript and JavaScript have been constrained in this way to ensure a comfort zone for browsing users who might otherwise shy away from travelling to unknown Web sites for fear of how scripts on those sites might manipulate their machines and personal data. (Some are already nervous about the cookies that may be set.) Thus, all you can *do* with the *navigator* object is discover attributes of its identity, such as its application name or version number. This severely restricted ability to interact with the navigator object is why it sits below the much more powerful *window* object.

- The *frames* object represents an array or collection of all frames associated with the current frameset document.
- The *body* object defines the beginning and end of the document.
- The *selection* object represents any currently selected text on the page.
- The *all* object represents an array or collection of all subsidiary document objects (i.e., all of the objects that sit anywhere below the document in the Object Hierarchy).
- The *scripts* object represents an array or collection of all scripts in the page enclosed by <SCRIPT> tags. (This doesn't include scripts attached to other HTML tags.)
- The *forms* object represents an array or collection of all forms in the page created by the <FORM> tag.

The *forms* object is the parent of any element contained between its <FORM> tag, including embedded applets or controls—and an array of all the form's elements called the *elements* array (discussed later in this chapter).

One of the members of the form's elements array is the *select* object, which is parent to all of its contained *options*. Select objects are created whenever a <SELECT> tag appears in a form, and its subsidiary collection of options are the sum of all <OPTION> tags placed between the <SELECT> tags to create the items in the resulting scrollable list or pop-up menu.

Object Properties and Methods

Once again, you are already familiar with the properties and methods associated with objects through your experience with HTML. Whenever you answer the NAME argument for a button you are setting a property for that *button* object. Whenever you answer the ROWS and COLS arguments for a <TEXTAREA> tag you are setting properties for that *textarea* object. Whenever you answer the ACTION argument for a <FORM> tag you are indicating which method the browser will use to submit the form object.

Properties Are Sources of Information

Properties are handy little guys to have around because they house information about the characteristics of an associated object that either affect that object's onscreen appearance, or are used internally by scripts to identify and manipulate that object—or both. The number of ROWS and COLS dictated for a textarea object affect the displayed size of the resulting text field. The NAME of a button is

Embedded Objects

When objects like ActiveX controls or Java applets are embedded in a Web page via the HTML <OBJECT>, <APPLET>, or <EMBED> tags, these items also become objects in the current hierarchy. Although you cannot use the tags themselves in a script, like other objects whose names are italicized in Figure 2.2, you can refer to embedded objects using the answer to that object's NAME argument. In other words, an applet whose NAME="myApplet" may be referenced in a script as simply "myApplet."

The place of an embedded object in the hierarchy is determined by the location of its tag within the scripted page. If the tag occurs outside of any <FORM> tags, it is considered a third-tier object (see Figure 2.2). If it occurs inside <FORM> tags, it is considered a *child* of that form object and relegated to the fourth tier below the form object (where all form *elements* sit).

As a member of the third tier of the hierarchy, the embedded object becomes a member of its associated array (applets, plugins, or embeds). As a child of the form object, however, it also becomes a member of the general elements array.

not shown on screen but it may be used in a script to identify that button and, thereby, manipulate it. The VALUE placed into a text field via its tag appears as data in that field when the page is displayed, but it may also be used by an internal script to determine whether to execute a conditional statement that basically declares: if *this* is in the field, do one thing—if *that* is in the field, do another thing.

Suppose that you've answered a text field's VALUE argument with the string: "Please type your name into this field." If the user clicks or tabs out of that field (thereby firing the blur event for that field), you can check to see if that string is still sitting in the field. If so, you know that the user hasn't typed anything into it, and you can ask the user to please fill in the field before submitting the form. The following script checks the *value* property of a field whose NAME="username," and presents an alert if the user has failed to revise the original contents of the field:

```
onBlur="if username.value = 'Please type your name into this field.' then

    alert('Please fill in the Name field before submitting this form.')

end if"
```

As a rule, all of the arguments used to set the properties of HTML tags are also available as properties in VBScript (or JavaScript), and almost always have the same name. To discover the current property setting for a given object, you simply type the object's name—preceded by the name(s) of its parent(s)—in a decimal-delimited list that ends with the name of the property whose data you seek to discover or manipulate:

```
window.document.myForm.myTextField.value
```

> **TIP** Although the window is the patriarch of all VBScript objects, as previously noted, you only need to use it when referring to objects associated with a window or frame that is not attached to the current script. When you omit the window reference, the current (script's) window is automatically assumed. When you use the generic name of the window (as in the preceding example), the current window is also assumed. Thus, the reference to a text field's value property may be (and most often is) written as:
>
> ```
> document.myForm.myTextField.value
> ```

As far as the VBScript interpreter (or browser) is concerned, the decimal-delimited name of an object and property is synonymous with the actual information contained in that property. In the current example, document.formName.myTextField.value means the exact same thing to the interpreter as the contents that appear in the referenced field. With this in mind, you could, for instance, write a script that presents a personalized welcome as soon as the user exits the name field after changing its contents (hopefully resulting in a message that includes the user's *real* name) (see Figure 2.3).

```
<FORM NAME="myForm">

<b>Name</b>:

<INPUT TYPE="text" NAME="myTextField"

onChange="alert('Welcome to my page, ' & document.myForm.myTextField.value
& '.')">

</FORM>
```

Figure 2.3 Thanks to the value property of the text field object, this alert message can be scripted to include the contents of the Name field.

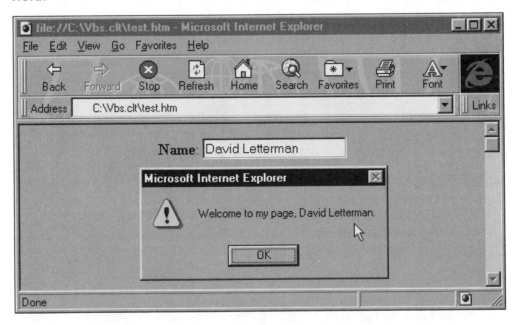

> **TIP** In VBScript, when the script referencing a form element appears *inside* the parent form's tags, you may omit both the document *and* the form object, and refer to the element simply by pseudonym:
>
> ```
> myTextField.value
> ```

Reading and Writing Object Properties

Some properties do more than simply reveal their current values. They allow you to set those values from within your scripts. These properties are called "read-write," while properties that only allow you to get values are called "read-only."

All of the navigator object's properties are read-only, and it's easy to understand why. Its *appName* property, for instance, returns the name of the current browser. You can discover this name and use it, say, as the basis of an if-then-else condition that determines which page to display next in the current window (using, by the way, the read-write *href* property of the location object):

```
if navigator.appName = "Microsoft Internet Explorer" then

    location.href = "explorer.htm"

else

    location.href = "nonexplorer.htm"

end if
```

While the appName property allows you to discover the name of the current browser, and react in an unlimited number of ways to this piece of intelligence—for obvious reasons, you cannot (and should not be able to) change the name of that browser.

On the other hand, using various scripting techniques, there are many properties whose values may be changed in midstream without harmful (and usually with helpful) results. A familiar example of a read-write property is the value property of a text field, used in a previous example. In addition to allowing you to discover the current contents of the field, this property also lets you change the contents of that field. This ability is illustrated by the following simple script. When the user types numbers into text1 and text2—then tabs or clicks into text3 (making text3 the current focus of the document, which fires the focus event for that field)—the onFocus script inside text3's tag executes, placing the sum of the first two fields into text3 (see Figure 2.4).

Figure 2.4 The sum of the first two fields appears in the third field when field 3 receives the focus event.

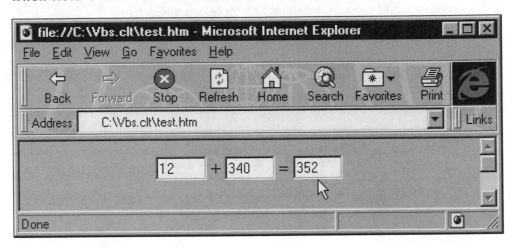

```
<FORM NAME="myForm">

<INPUT TYPE="text" NAME="text1" SIZE-5 VALUE=0>

<b>+</b>

<INPUT TYPE="text" NAME="text2" SIZE=5 VALUE=0>

<b>=</b>

<INPUT TYPE="text" NAME="text3" SIZE=5 VALUE=0

onFocus="text3.value=text1.value+text2.value">

</FORM>
```

Shared Properties

Many properties belong to multiple objects. The value property used in several examples is not only attached to text objects but to several form elements as well, including buttons, checkboxes, radios, and the submit and reset objects. Not all properties belong to all objects, however. Buttons, checkboxes, radios, text objects, document objects, and window objects all have *name* properties, but only the first four share the value property. Document and window objects do not accept this property.

Shared properties don't always behave the same with every object, either. While the value property of a text field holds the contents of that field, the value property of a button holds its displayed name, and the value property of a checkbox holds the answer to its VALUE argument—which is not displayed but used to identify the checkbox in the string generated during the form submission process.

The more you know about an object's attached properties and property behaviors, the more control you have over the appearance of objects in your miniature Web universe. You can also use the information provided about objects by their properties to further control the flow of activity within your pages. You can set up an event-driven script to pass data via object properties, and use that data to drive further scripting processes. While the initial script must be kicked off by an event, once the event is fired, the remaining script can be *data-driven*. (More on this concept in the discussion on variables later in this chapter.)

> **TIP** In addition to sharing properties, almost all of the objects in the DOM Object Hierarchy are also properties of their parents (a frighteningly feudal thought). Only the window object, which is parentless for our purposes, exists as a relatively "pure object." This fact serves to reinforce the idea that objects belonging to other objects must often be addressed using a very formal string that includes the parent, grandparent, and so forth. But it also means that objects that sit below other objects in the hierarchy may contain data about the parent object. The navigator object, for instance, doubles as a *property* of the window object that holds information regarding the browser that is running that window. This information can only be revealed, however, through the use of both the navigator object and one of *its own* associated properties, such as appName or appVersion.

Additional, detailed information on the built-in properties associated with each VBScript object may be found in Chapter 4, and the properties themselves are covered in detail in Chapter 5. Because there are so many properties, and because many reiterate over multiple objects (are attached to more than one object) with subtly changing behaviors, it is much harder to memorize all of the properties and their object-based behaviors than it is to memorize the objects. Do the best you can to absorb the property material in the reference section so you'll at least have a general notion of the scope of available properties and behaviors while you script. As long as you have this underlying notion you can always refer back to the reference section in this book or to Microsoft's online documentation to refresh your memory of a property's particulars.

> **W W W** You can find the VBScript Language Reference in English at this address:
>
> www.microsoft.com/vbscript/us/vbslang/vbstoc.htm
>
> Other languages' versions may be found at this root URL:
>
> www.microsoft.com/vbscript/

Methods Are PreProgrammed Sets of Actions

Like properties, methods are also attached to certain objects. However, while properties *in*form on their associated objects, methods *per*form on those objects.

Built-in object methods are usually set up to perform simple-to-complex series of tasks that the language's users might otherwise be unable to perform for themselves (given the limits of the language at hand). These series of tasks, or actionsets, are preprogrammed by the language's original authors to perform, in one fell swoop, what those authors suppose to be commonly desired application functions.

The window object has a method called open, which represents a commonly desired function in GUI applications. As you probably guessed, this method is used to open new windows in the user's browser. It became a built-in method of the window object because the authors of both VBScript and JavaScript considered the ability to script the display of multiple windows in a graphical application like a Web browser to be an environmental necessity.

Rather than expand either scripting language's glossary to allow you to laboriously script the creation of new windows yourself (which would actually involve programming at a lower level than any simple scripting language really ever allows), the VBScript and JavaScript authors wrote a block of code to do the grunt work for you. This code block is attached as a method to the window object and is called upon to do its job whenever the window's open method is invoked by script. Your use of one word, the name of the method, is all that the interpreter needs to execute that entire block of code.

Like properties, methods are attached to their objects by a single decimal. Although methods must usually be explicitly attached to an object, in the case of the window object, the current window is implied when you present the method by itself. The following lines of script are identical to the interpreter.

```
window.open()
open()
```

Shared Methods

As with properties, methods can also reiterate over multiple objects. The open method, to continue with it as an example, is also attached to the document object.

> **NOTE** When you invoke the *window.open()* method you are, in effect, creating a new instance of the window object—a process known in object-oriented programming circles as *instantiation*.

But, like reiterated properties, this method behaves quite differently when hooked to the document object. In this association, it opens what is referred to as a "text stream" in the current document. This text (or document) stream may then be used in conjunction with the *document.write()* method to dynamically generate new HTML for the current page or for a new page.

> **WARNING** An opened text stream must be closed by the *document.close()* method when you're done writing to it or the browser will freeze. (For more information on the document object's open, write, and close methods, see Chapter 6.)

Although the open method can be presented alone if you intend to create a new window from the current window, it must be explicitly attached to the document object, using the familiar decimal delimiter. Otherwise, the interpreter assumes that you are calling the method for the window (and not the document) object.

```
document.open()
```

> **NOTE** There are times in VBScript when ending parentheses are not necessary; and there are times when they *cannot* be used. However, ending parentheses are always required with JavaScript methods, and are sometimes required with VBScript. Parentheses are used to show example methods throughout this chapter, because that is the common syntax. You'll find a fuller discussion of the VBScript variations to this rule in the next chapter on VBScript syntax.

Methods with Arguments

As you know, many HTML tags allow arguments to be placed within the tag. Sometimes these arguments are optional and sometimes they are required—but at all times they provide a welcome means for fine-tuning the display of the associated tag. HTML arguments and their answers are placed between the angle brackets that enclose the element's opening tag—or, in the case of empty tags that stand alone, within the element's only tag.

```
<TAGNAME ARG1="answer1" ARG2="answer2">
```

In a similar way, the answers to method arguments are placed between the method's opening and closing parentheses, in a comma-delimited list. Unlike HTML arguments, however, an argument label is usually not included:

```
object.method(answer1,answer2)
```

If you are answering an argument by passing a container that houses the actual answer (such as the name of a text field whose contents are the argument's answer), you my pass the answer to the method in an unquoted string:

```
object.method(myTextField.value)
```

However, if you are passing an actual text string meant to answer the argument (such as text that you want to display in a field), then you are required to enclose the answer in quotes:

```
object.method("hello, world!")
```

When you are providing answers to multiple arguments, commas must be placed between them, with enclosing quotes considered part of its enclosed answer:

```
object.method("hello",myTextField.value,"goodbye")
```

TIP Don't be concerned if you feel a little lost within some of the code-writing details in this chapter. This information is expanded upon in the next chapter on syntax. So keep a relaxed mind as you read through this text, and your understanding will start to "snowball" as you peruse the basics of VBScript construction in Chapter 3.

Using Argument Labels

There are times when a method takes a multipart answer to a single argument. When this happens, argument labels become required in the method parentheses. An example is the window.open() method, which allows four arguments:

1. The URL of the document that should be loaded into the new window.

2. The name of the target window.

3. The parts of the new window.

4. The size of the new window.

The third and fourth arguments are both sub-argument groups that take a multi-part answer. The part group's sub-arguments include toolbar, location, directories, status, menubar, and scrollbars; resizable Answers to this argument are passed using these standard argument labels, with the entire argument group enclosed in one set of quotes.

The following example script opens a vanilla window without any optional parts. To simplify the example, the optional *size* argument group is omitted. Note how the string that contains answers to the toolbar, location, directories, and status sub-arguments are answered following the equals sign (just like arguments in HTML tags); and that the entire argument group is enclosed by a single set of quotation marks.

```
window.open("this.html","newWind","toolbar=no,location=no,directories=no,
status=no")
```

Functions Are Methods without Objects

Both VBScript and JavaScript provide a core set of built-in functions that behave much the same as methods. Like methods, functions are stored procedures that may be run simply by invoking the function's name in a script. However, while invoked methods often result in visible changes to the environment (say, the creation of a new window or document), functions usually return some kind of value that is then acted upon internally by a script:

```
abs(number)   ' returns the absolute value of the passed number
```

As you can see by the syntax used in the abs() example, functions are not attached to any object and may therefore be used anywhere, any time, without connection to any object and without requiring the presence of any object except the window and document objects. These two objects must exist for a function to run because the document object houses the script that contains the function call; and the window object displays that document. You don't even need to explicitly attach the function to an event. If you type it all by itself between <SCRIPT> tags that appear in the <HEAD> or <BODY> of the page (not inside an <INPUT> tag), it automatically executes when the page is loaded.

TIP Any line of script appearing all by itself between <SCRIPT> tags in the <HEAD> or <BODY> of the page is implicitly attached to the load event.

There are exceptions to these fine distinctions between methods and functions. For instance, like many methods, the msgBox() function results in a visible change by returning a dialog box displaying a message string. This is reminiscent of the window object's alert() method, which also returns a dialog box displaying a message string. Also, like functions, the alert() method (along with all window methods) can be invoked for the current window without actually referring to that window in the script. As a result, window methods often appear to be syntactically identical to functions in a script:

```
alert(stri ng)
' a window method that returns a dialog box displaying the passed string

msgBox(string,parts,title)
' a built-in function that returns a dialog box displaying the passed string,
' with prescribed buttons and dialog box title
```

The rules for passing answers to functions that take arguments are the same as the rules for passing answers to methods that take arguments:

When to Include and When to Omit Arguments

Naturally, you must answer all arguments that are required by the method or function (and this information is provided for each method or function in the appropriate reference sections in Part II). You can skip all optional arguments, provided none of those arguments occur in the argument string *before* an argument you wish to answer.

Suppose a function takes two optional arguments. You don't care about the first argument but you want to provide a special answer to the second argument. Under the circumstances, you must provide some kind of answer to the first argument before you type an answer to the second one. Otherwise, the interpreter will take your answer to the second argument as an answer to the *first* argument—because it appears in that argument's *place*. The interpreter usually has a default answer to optional arguments that are omitted when you call a function or method, and you can use this answer (if you know it) as a placeholder before providing a non-default answer to a later argument.

Here's an example: The split() function stakes one required argument, the string to be split. Following that it takes three optional arguments including the *delimiter* to use in splitting the string, the *count* or number of substrings to return, and the *compare* type to use in evaluating the string.

If you wanted to split a 5-word sentence into two pieces containing words 1 and 2 of the sentence (respectively), you must answer the first argument with the 5-word sentence, and the third argument with the number 2. Answering the second argument may seem unnecessary since the target delimiter is the space between each word, and that's the default answer to the delimiter argument. However, if you only pass the sentence string, followed by the number 2, the interpreter will think you want to use "2" as the delimiter. Finding no 2s in the string, it'll return empty-handed. To avoid this error you must pass it the default delimiter " as a placeholder answer to the second argument.

As you read through the reference material on methods and functions in Part II, you'll find that each item's reference shows its arguments in the order in which the interpreter is expecting them, indicates whether an argument is required or not, and provides information on default answers to optional arguments (if available). With only a few exceptions, optional arguments usually follow required arguments. In the few instances where the VBScript developers have goofed and put an optional argument before a required argument, you'll have to provide at least a placeholder answer to the optional argument at all times—since the required argument that follows it, by definition, must always be answered.

Knowing an object's methods and method behaviors is as important as knowing the scope of its properties, because so much may be accomplished with a single word when you invoke a method. Ditto with built-in functions. In addition to the methods and functions reference material provided in Part II of this book, you can keep abreast of the latest information regarding these important language elements by frequently reviewing Microsoft's online documentation.

W W W VBScript Language Reference:

www.microsoft.com/vbscript/us/vbslang/vbstoc.htm

Understanding and Using Arrays

Some of the objects in the Object Hierarchy double as "array objects." An array object is an index of all like-objects in the current environment. Documentation for version 3.0 (and higher) of the VBScript engine now calls these array objects "object collections." It's a fancier phrase but the meaning remains the same as when the lowly term "array" was used. You can correctly refer to these language elements using either term, and both are used throughout this book—although array is used more often.

Through the grace of arrays, you can write one line of script to get or set a property, or invoke a method for all of the objects currently belonging to the array (or collection), rather than dealing with the objects one at a time.

The Length Property

The first thing you need to know about any array is how many of the prescribed objects are currently contained in that array. You can immediately determine this number by using a special property that VBScript and JavaScript attach to all array objects, the *length* property:

```
arrayName.length
' represents the number of objects that currently exist for the named array
```

One of the array objects in the hierarchy is frames. Via the length property, you can discover the number of frames in the current frameset. Since you probably created the frameset yourself, you may wonder at the value of discovering what you already know. But, do you really know? Will you always know? Will this number always remain the same while your scripted page is running? If you are working from a script in a parent window, can you assume that the user still has the originally designated frameset on display in a previously created window?

You'll be surprised how handy it is to be able to retrieve the length of an array any time you please. It's one of the easiest (and most elegant) ways to set up a *repeat loop* to execute the same procedure for every item in a given array. If you scripted the loop to run for the exact number of items you originally created for that array, you'd be engaging in a programming practice known as hard coding—which is neither flexible nor farsighted, considering how often pages are redesigned and revised.

Scripts that rely on hard-coded values must be rewritten whenever objects are added to or subtracted from the referenced array. Sometimes this can't be helped. But in the current example, a much better approach is to set up the loop to run for the *length* of the current array. This is called "soft-coding" and it is greatly preferred, since it allows you to make changes to the number of objects in the referenced array without rewriting your code—always a plus!

The Index Position

Another extremely useful attribute of an array object is its built-in index of every item in its array. This index allows you to reference an object without using (or even knowing) its name. You may remember that italicized objects in the hierarchy in Figure 2.2 must be referred to by a pseudonym, and not the generic name shown in the figure. The fact is, these objects may also be referenced by position in the index of any array to which the object belongs. An object in an array receives it index position according to when it is created in the current document:

- The first <FRAME> tag listed below the opening <FRAMESET> tag in an HTML document receives the first index position in the *frames* array. The next

<FRAME> tag receives the second position, and any <FRAME> tags below that receive the subsequent positions.

- The first position in the *forms* array references the first set of <FORM> tags in the HTML document. If another set of <FORM> tags appears below the first <FORM> tags in that same document, that form receives the second index position, and so on.

To refer to a member of an array (or object collection) by index position, you type the name of the array followed by the target object's numbered position in the index. The first item in the array is always numbered zero (not 1), and may be referenced by that position using the following syntax:

```
arrayName(0) for VBScript - OR -  arrayName[0] for JavaScript
```

> **N O T E** Parentheses enclose index position information in VBScript, although brackets are used in JavaScript.

All Built-In Arrays Are Zero-Based

The first position in every built-in VBScript (and JavaScript) array is not numbered 1; it is numbered 0. This is a long-standing tradition in programming languages, and many believe that only never-see-the-sun engineering-types could have imposed it upon us. Why the imposition continues in these supposedly friendlier 4GL languages remains an open question.

A zero-based numbering system not only takes a little adjustment in thinking but it also creates a few minor problems. When you get the length of an array, for instance, the length property begins its count at 1 (not 0). This means that if the frames array contained three items, it would have a length of 3 but array positions of 0, 1, and 2. Therefore, to reference the last item in this array using the length property, you must subtract 1 from the retrieved length to arrive at a digit that represents the last item's true array position:

```
frames(0)
frames(1)
frames(2)       ' the last index position in the frames array

frames(frames.length)     ' the same as frames(3), which doesn't exist
frames(frames.length-1)    ' the same as frames(2)
```

It's difficult for the novice to fully comprehend the value of array position information, but after a little scripting experience you're certain to be singing its praises. A good example of its power occurs in relation to the *elements* array.

Each form object has its own elements array, which indexes all of the elements in that form. It doesn't matter whether these elements are buttons, text fields, select objects, or a combo of these or any other possible form elements. Regardless of type, all of these items automatically become objects in the elements array when their parent form is created by the <FORM> tag. Like all other arrays, the elements array assigns positions according to order of creation, *not element type*. As tags for the various elements in a form appear within its <FORM> tags, so do they appear in the resulting elements array.

It's good coding practice to name each form element that you create so that you can call it by that name in your scripts. This is another form of flexible coding, since you can move the element anywhere in the form and not have to rewrite your script if that script refers to the element by pseudonym.

There are times, however, when it is much more efficient to use a form elements array position rather than its given name. What if you wanted to know which of 10 radio choices the user has selected? You could implement the following "if" script 10 times to determine the currently selected button in a radio button group:

```
if theForm.radio1.checked =  true then

    theSelectedRadio = theForm.radio1.value

else if theForm.radio2.checked = true then

    theSelectedRadio = theForm.radio2.value

else if theForm.radio3.checked = true then...
```

Or you could use elements array position information to write a much shorter script to perform the same service:

```
for i = 0 to 9

    if theForm.elements(i).checked =  true then

        theSelectedRadio = theForm.elements(i).value
        exit for

    end if

next
```

You may not be familiar with all of the VBScript language elements used in this script but you can see that it runs through elements 0 through 9 in the referenced form (all 10 radios) until it reaches the checked item, whose value is then placed into a variable container for safekeeping. (Variables are coming up next.) Script number two is clearly a more elegant and easy solution to this kind of problem—and therein lies the power of array position information.

Passing and Evaluating Data

Toward the end of the section on properties, the idea of driving scripts with data received the briefest mention, but it is of the utmost importance. In both of the scripting languages under discussion here, data is second in importance only to events—and only because initial scripting actions cannot execute until an event is fired to trigger that execution. But once the event has triggered the script, its job is done, while the work of data has only just begun.

You already know that data concerning the status of objects may be passed via an object's properties, but what you may not know is that there are other ways to retrieve data, and other types of data to retrieve. And the more the merrier, since it is the passage and evaluation of data that determines the execution path of an event-triggered script. Of course, the event-firing actions that the user takes on the page certainly determines the order in which scripts are executed; just as the actions not taken determine which scripts shall remain silent during the current session. You want to be aware of this reality when you script your pages. However, having accepted the fact that you cannot control the user's actions, you must then turn your focus to what you *can* control.

Once the user has taken the initial action needed to trigger a script, control shifts to you and your script. In all but the simplest HelloWorld-like scripts, nine times out of ten, the execution of your scripts will require data retrieved from the environment:

- What has the user typed into the Name field?

- How many points has the user accrued in the current game?

- What is the URL of the page the user exited in order to load this page?

The answers to these and a thousand yet-to-be-posed questions will determine which internal scripting path your current user will travel. For the most part, you'll be retrieving information from object properties, a procedure that's already been thoroughly discussed. You may also, however, need the information that a function can provide (what is the current date and time, relative to the user's system?), a notion that's also been fully discussed.

An important avenue for retrieving and storing data that has not yet been fully investigated, however, is a language element known as a *variable*—so-called because the information it contains can vary throughout the session (just like text in an editable field might be revised over and over again).

Working with Variables

A variable is a data container that you create for yourself as a temporary resting place for data that you wish to track. Creating variables is as easy as naming and registering a pet—you just need to figure out what to call it and then provide its name to the proper authorities. (Actually, it's easier than registering a pet.) In JavaScript, you notify the interpreter of the instantiation of a variable by declaring its name following the *var* statement (for variable). In VBScript, you declare your variables using the *dim* statement (for dimension):

```
dim myVariable
```

You can assign data to a variable as soon as you create it, or you can leave it uninitialized. In loosely typed languages like JavaScript and VBScript, uninitialized variables are not yet typecast (assigned to a datatype)—which is not quite the same as being empty. (More on variable datatyping in a moment.)

You assign data to a variable by using an *assignment operator,* which is the equals sign in both VBScript and JavaScript:

```
dim myVariable
myVariable = "hello"
var myVariable = "hello"
```

> **WARNING** Although JavaScript lets you declare and populate a variable in a single line of code, VBScript requires you to perform these operations on separate lines, as shown in the previous example.

Once you put data into the variable, it inherits that data's *datatype*. Simply put, if you put a number into the variable, it becomes a number variable; if you put a quoted string into it, it becomes a string variable. As previously mentioned, these two scripting languages are loosely typed, which means that you do not have to typecast (assign a datatype to) a variable as soon as you create it—and your created variable doesn't have to remain a strict type throughout its lifetime (the duration of its script).

In stricter coding environments like C++ and Java, a variable *has* to have a declared type and, once it does, it can *never* be used to house a different type of data. If you try to pass string data to a number variable, you'll get an ugly error. In both JavaScript and VBScript, however, your variable can start life as a number variable and switch to a string variable in mid-stream. This schizophrenic behavior has its drawbacks (addressed to some degree in Chapter 14 on debugging) but, by and large, it makes scripting easier. Through loose datatyping you can (for instance) add a string of numbers together, place them into a variable, and then use that variable and its original number information to create a string of text containing that number:

```
dim myVariable = 2+2+3
myVariable = "The answer is " & myVariable
alert(myVariable)
```

In the preceding script, myVariable begins its short life as a number variable containing the value "7," derived from an expression that adds 2, 2, and 3. The variable container itself is then concatenated to a text string, and the whole thing is placed back into myVariable—which becomes a string container in the process. The myVariable string container is then passed to the alert() method, which displays the string as its message (shown in Figure 2.5). You could *never* do something like that in C++.

> **TIP** Did you notice that you only need to use the *dim* statement the first time you type the variable. After that, its name can stand alone. In theory, if you have not declared a script to be "option explicit," you can create variables without using the dim statement at all. In practice, however, this omission is an open invitation to disaster (discussed further in Chapter 14).

Figure 2.5 The final contents of myVariable appear in the alert dialog box.

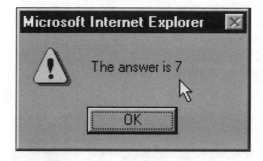

Datatype Handling in VBScript

Like JavaScript, when you declare a variable in VBScript it inherits the only real datatype that actually exists in these loosely typed languages. Microsoft calls it a "variant." This datatype behaves in a fairly flexible way, automatically treating the variable as a number if numbers are placed into it; as a string, if a text string is placed into it; or a date, if a recognizable date string is placed into it.

In VBScript, you can further refine this variant "super-type" by converting the variable's data to one of the allowable subtypes shown in Table 2.1.

Table 2.1 VBScript Data Subtypes

Subtype	Description
Empty	An uninitialized variant, whose value is 0 for numeric variables or a zero-length string ("") for string variables
Null	A variant that intentionally contains no data
Boolean	A variant that contains either true or false
Byte	A variant that contains an integer from 0 to 255
Integer	A variant that contains an integer from –32,768 to 32,767
Currency	A variant that contains a floating-point integer from –922,337,203,685,477.5808 to 922,337,203,685,477.5808
Long	A variant that contains an integer from –2,147,483,648 to 2,147,483,648
Single	A variant that contains a single-precision, floating-point number in the range –3.402823E38 to –1.401298E-45 for negative values; 1.401298E-45 to 3.402823E38 for positive values
Double	A variant that contains a double-precision, floating-point number in the range –1.79769313486232E308 to –4.94065645841247E-324 for negative values; 4.94065645841247E-324 to 1.79769313486232E308 for positive values
Date/Time	A variant that contains a number representing a date between January 1, 100 and December 31, 9999
String	A variant that contains a variable-length string (which may be up to 2 billion characters)

Table 2.1 *Continued.*

Subtype	Description
Object	A variant that contains an object created by the set statement (see Chapter 9)
Error	A variant that contains an error number

For most scripting purposes, the variant supertype and its automatic handling of numbers, strings, and dates, will suffice. If you need to convert a variable to one of the other subtypes, however, the necessary conversion functions are described in Chapter 8.

TIP You may have noticed that numbers (i.e., integers), strings, and dates are included as subtypes, even though the variant supertype already allows for them. This is in case a variable is converted to a subtype and you wish to convert it back to one of these general types.

Creating Array Variables

So far in this discussion, the focus has been on scalar (or single-value) variables. In the previous section, however, you learned how arrays can be used to manipulate multiple values across a collection of objects. You'll find instructions for creating your own arrays (or object collections) using the dim statement in Chapter 9, as well as information on how to create a "dynamic" array in the section on the *redim* statement in that same chapter. In Chapter 13, you'll find examples of both woven into working scripts.

Scoping Your Variables

Where you declare a variable in a script determines the scope of that variable, just as an object's position in the DOM hierarchy determines its scope.

Global Variables Receive the Broadest Scope

If you want the information in some of your variables to be available to every line of script in the current page, you must declare them in a place that is *outside the control structures used in those scripts.* Microsoft calls these "script-level variables." A good practice is to declare script-level variables in the <HEAD> section of the page, right below the opening <SCRIPT> tag. The declarations should sit outside of any user-created procedure, or conditional or repeat control structure, that may also be contained between the same <SCRIPT> tags.

In the following example, three global variables are declared and then initialized with data. The information in these variables is not only available to the shown sub (thisRoutine()), but to any other script that references these globals in the current page.

```
<HEAD>
<SCRIPT LANGUAGE="VBScript">

dim myVariable1,myVariable2,myVariable3

myVariable1 = document.forms(0).elements.length
myVariable2 = false
myVariable3 = "hello"

sub thisRoutine()

    if myVariable2 = true then

        for i = 0 to myVariable1-1

            document.forms(0).elements(i).value - myVariable3

        next

    end if

end sub

</SCRIPT>
```

> **N O T E** As the preceding example shows, you can declare multiple variables using the same dim statement by presenting the names of the variables in a comma-delimited string:
>
> ```
> dim myVariable1,myVariable2,myVariable3
> ```

The Scope of Local Variables Is Relative

If you want the information in a variable to remain within the confines of a certain section of script, you should declare it at the place in the script where the variable is used. Microsoft calls these "procedure-level variables," although, if you place the variable inside a control structure within a procedure (such as, an if statement or repeat loop), it will only be available for the duration of that statement or loop. It will not be available to the entire procedure. If the variable is only needed within the control structure, then this is the proper place for it. Be careful, however, not to embed a variable any further than you need to within a section of script, or it may be unavailable to statements outside of that section that need to use it.

The following script would place "undefined" into the alert dialog box, because that is what is contained in myVariable when the alert method receives it. How can that be when the if conditional certainly puts either "true" or "false" into the variable? Because the variable is declared within the "if" statement nested inside the sub statement, making it local to the if statement alone. The alert method—though also contained within the sub statement—is called *outside* of the if conditional, beyond the scope of the myVariable declaration. The interpreter therefore correctly treats it as an uninitialized variable.

```
sub myProc()

    document.forms(0).elements(0).value = "type here"

    if document.forms(0).elements(0).value = "type here" then

        dim myVariable

myVariable = false

    else

        myVariable = true

    end if

    alert(myVariable)

end sub
```

To correct this problem, the scope of myVariable must be broadened to include the entire sub procedure, not just the if conditional:

```
sub myProc()

    dim myVariable

    document.forms(0).elements(0).value = "type here"
```

```
if document.forms(0).elements(0).value = "type here" then

    myVariable = false

else

    myVariable = true

end if

alert(myVariable)

end sub
```

How Expressions Are Constructed and Evaluated

Even in the short course of the book so far, you've seen examples of data derived from the interpreter's evaluation of compound expressions. These expressions are created by marrying two or more sources of data with operators suited to the task. Here are two recent examples that do just that:

```
myVariable = 2+2+3 ' uses the add operator (+) to add numbers

myVariable = "The answer is " & myVariable

' uses the VBScript concatenation operator (&) to piece together a string
```

Chapter 10 presents detailed information on all of the available VBScript operators—and that information isn't repeated here. However, in addition to checking out that chapter to discover what operators are available to perform which operations, you also need to be aware of a few rules regarding the construction and evaluation of expressions.

The Importance of Operator Precedence

Since there's no way to know ahead of time all the expressions you might need to create, the most important thing to learn is which operators do what, and which operations take precedence over other operations. Here's an example of the importance of operator precedence. The multiplication operator (*) takes precedence over the addition operator (+). This is a very important piece of information to have if you want to add 2 and 2 together, then multiply the result by 3. If you write your expression in the following order, it'll evaluate to 8, because the second 2 is multiplied by 3 *first*, and then the first two is added to the result:

```
2+2*3 = 8
```

You can override the rules of precedence through the judicious use of parentheses. The following parenthetical expression is evaluated first, *then* the result is multiplied by three, producing the desired result of 12:

```
(2+2)*3 = 12
```

Although parentheses can re-order operator precedence by forcing the evaluation of parenthetical expressions first, in left-to-right order, operator precedence rules continue to apply within the parentheses themselves:

```
(2+2*3)/2 = 4
(2+2)*3/2 = 6
```

You'll find a chart showing Operator Precedence at the end of Chapter 10.

Supplying Values to an Expression

The values used to create an expression can be supplied by any valid data container, including an object property, a variable, an array object, a function, a method, or the actual data itself. The following examples are all valid methods for constructing expressions in VBScript. (Some of the operators and other language elements are not used in JavaScript, so these expressions don't serve as universal examples.)

```
dim expireDate

expireDate = dateAdd("m",1,theCurDate)

' adds 30 days to the current date, previously placed into theCurDate variable
' using the dateAdd() function (discussed in Chapter 8)

-------------------------------------------------------------------
if confirm("Do you want to place an order?") = true then

' executes the if condition if the user clicks OK in the confirmation dialog
' box, an action which returns the VBScript constant "true" to the if statement

-------------------------------------------------------------------
dim num1,num2,num3

num1 = 12          ' puts 12 into num1

num2 = num1*3      ' multiplies 12 by 3, and puts 36 into num2

num3 = (num1+num2)*num1
' adds 12 to 36, multiplies the result by 3, and puts 144 into num3
```

> **TIP** If you use an operator between inapproriate types of data (such as the arithmetic add operator between two strings), VBScript, in some instances, modifies the operation accordingly. If, for instance, you do use the plus sign between two strings, instead of the string concatenator operator (&), the interpreter goes ahead and concatenates the string for you. This is one area in which loose datatyping saves the day.

Naming Your Variables

When you're creating complex scripts for several interactive Web pages, the way you name your variables can help or hinder your progress more than you might imagine. Savvy programmers try to use names that serve to identify the kind of data they expect to find in that variable. Chapter 3 includes some suggested scripting conventions. You may decide to adopt some or all of these conventions along with the following suggestions for naming all your created elements—be they variables, subs, functions, arguments (for subs or functions), objects, or arrays.

Whether you adopt a logical naming convention for your variables is neither here nor there to VBScript or JavaScript. Neither care what you call a variable as long as you don't give it the same name as a built-in element in the scripting environment. All of these words are reserved by the interpreter. You cannot, for instance, name a variable that houses information about the current document "document," because that name is reserved for the document object.

You can, however, call it something like "curDoc"—which may be better than "document" for your purposes because it's shorter (less typing). An even better name, however, would describe the type of data the variable is meant to hold concerning the current document. If you intend to house the document title in this variable, you might try the following name:

```
dim docTitle
```

```
docTitle = document.title
```

If docTitle is a global variable, you might want to identify it as such by putting a "g_" in front of it. Others suggest that local variables also be identified but that isn't really necessary. Since there are only two types of variables, those not preceded by "g_" are obviously local.

```
dim g_docTitle = document.title
```

It can also be helpful to use words in your variable that help to identify the type of data it is meant to track. For instance, you might use the word "date" somewhere in the name of any variable meant to house a date; or place the word "is" in front of any Boolean (true or false) variable, indicating that it either "is" true, or "is" false. Such strategies result in scripts that read more like your native tongue, making it easier to understand scripts at a glance, and keep track of what you're doing as you code. (If English isn't your native language, by all means, use your language's equivalents.)

```
isRegUser
' is true if user's name is in the registered user list, is false if not
```

> **TIP** Sometimes new programmers (after the fashion of hard-core hackers) consider it a matter of pride to produce code that cannot be easily understood by others. You'll be sorry if you follow this practice, because even a few hours away from your code can turn it so "cold" you can't remember what in blazes you were trying to do with it. If you're working with others who need to understand your code, too, you'll be setting up everyone (including yourself) for certain failure. Really smart coders realize that the more the code reads like a human—rather than a machine, language—the easier it is to decode as the days and the inevitable revisions wear on.

Naming Restrictions

The following restrictions apply to all the names that you create within your scripts, including variable names, procedures names, argument names, constant names, et al:

- A name must be unique within the scope of its declaration.
- A name cannot match any of the words reserved by the scripting language in use.
- A name must begin with an alphabetic character.
- A name must not exceed 255 characters.
- A name cannot contain an embedded decimal.

What's Next?

Although it's possible to continue describing the basic principles of the HTML Document Object Model and object-based, event-driven programming in general terms, the time has come to focus on the particular ways that these principles and ideas are implemented in VBScript.

The major concepts have all been covered—and you should now have a pretty good grasp on how objects and their properties and methods interact, how events kick off the process, where functions fit into the picture, how data can be used to control a script's execution—and a general notion of how variables, expressions, and operators aid the process. In the next chapter, you'll learn exactly how all of these elements may be pieced together to create viable scripts that conform to the VBScript rules of syntax.

The Basics of
VBScript

The general rules of syntax and procedures for actually writing VBScript code are relatively simple and straight-forward, if you don't try to swallow it all in one gulp. These rules and procedures are presented in this chapter in their simplest states to get you up and scripting quickly. You won't be shown every possible script format because that's not the way most people learn. You'll get a solid grounding in basic script construction, and you'll build upon this knowledge through discussions and examples in subsequent chapters. In particular, fine points in the scripting of control structures (introduced in this chapter) are dealt with in detail in Chapter 9, and visited and revisited in the variety of scripting examples presented throughout the book.

VBScript Rules of Syntax

The rules of syntax of a language provide information about how the various language elements and programming control structures (explained momentarily) must be written so that the interpreter (or compiler) can recognize your intentions and properly implement them. Virtually all of the information in this chapter revolves around how to type VBScript—character by character—

into whatever text editor you wish to use. Before digging into this task, however, here are a few basic rules you should understand before you start scripting.

VBScript Is Not Case-Sensitive

Unlike JavaScript—which *is* case-sensitive—all of the VBScript language elements may be typed in upper, lower, or mixed case; however you please. In this particular regard, VBScript can be said to be more "forgiving" than JavaScript, meaning it won't return an error if you mix cases in your variable or object names or forget the upper-lowercase sequence of a method or function:

```
thisVariable and thisvariable
' these two words are one variable to VBScript, and two variables to JavaScript


setTimeout() and SetTimeout()
' both are correct formats of this method in VBScript; the second format returns
' an error in JavaScript
```

The case-insensitivity of VBScript is helpful in two ways:

1. **It reduces the risk of typographical errors that produce bugs in the code.** This is a great thing, since each character in every script must be hand-typed into the Web page, even if you use an HTML editor. With the exception of a *little* help from the ActiveX Control Pad reviewed in Chapter 16, none of the major HTML editors currently offer support for extension scripting languages.

2. **It provides yet another means of making code readable.** You can use case to distinguish language elements. Some scripters, for instance, opt to capitalize all of VBScript's built-in statements, making it easy to quickly determine if all opening and closing portions of the statement are properly presented; as well as to get a quick overview of what's happening inside a complex script. This could be overkill in small scripts. But long, intricate scripts are more comprehensible and less overwhelming when they offer such reassuring visual cues.

```
DIM g_myVariable

SUB myProc()

    IF [condition] THEN

        [statement]
        [statement]
        [statement]
        [statement]
```

```
    ELSE

        [statement]

    END IF

        [statement]
        [statement]

END SUB
```

There is one minor drawback to the case insensitivity of VBScript. It reduces the number of characters that you can use to produce unique names. Whereas in JavaScript, you could use the same name for two different variables by merely changing case, VBScript would view same-name variables with the same scope (discussed later in this chapter) as the same variable regardless of case variations:

```
TOTAL and total

' in JavaScript "TOTAL" could house a grand total, and "total" could house a
' subtotal; in VBScript, these two words would represent the same variable
```

Use of Parentheses

In Chapter 2, you learned to write methods, functions, and subs with enclosing parentheses whether or not the method, function, or sub takes arguments. The appearance of these parentheses is required in all instances in JavaScript. In VBScript, however, this is not so. It is not only unnecessary to use parentheses to enclose the answers to method, function, and sub arguments in every instance; there are times when scripts won't run if parentheses are present. To confuse the issue even further, there are other times when scripts won't run if enclosing parentheses are *absent*.

While the current Microsoft VBScript documentation doesn't clearly provide all the details regarding the use of parentheses, the following general rules appear to be true in test scripts run with the current version of the browser.

Enclosing parentheses are acceptable—and may even be required—in the following instances:

1. When a method, function, or sub is included in a line of script-level code (lines of script that stand alone, outside of any sub or function statement):

```
<SCRIPT LANGUAGE="VBScript">

document.write("Hello, World.")

</SCRIPT>
```

2. When a method, function, or sub is included within a conditional or repeat loop control structure (discussed later in this chapter):

```
<SCRIPT LANGUAGE="VBScript">

sub thisProc()

    if document.forms(0).fld1.value <> "" then

document.write(document.forms(0).fld1.value)

    end if

end sub

</SCRIPT>
```

3. When a method, function, or sub is included in the opening line of a conditional or repeat loop control structure (parentheses are required):

```
<SCRIPT LANGUAGE="VBScript">

sub thisProc()

    if confirm("Do you want to place an order?") = true then

navigate("order.htm")

    end if

end sub

</SCRIPT>
```

4. When a method, function, or sub is included in a variable assignment statement:

```
DIM myVariable
myVariable = round(1.5768)
```

Enclosing parentheses may be omitted—and this omission may even be required—in the following instances:

5. When a method, function, or sub is included within a sub or function statement, but not inside a conditional or repeat loop control structure:

```
<SCRIPT LANGUAGE="VBScript">

sub thisProc()
```

```
document.write "Hello, World."

end sub

</SCRIPT>
```

6. When a method, function, or sub is part of a script that answers an HTML tag argument, as long as it is in a line by itself and not contained within a conditional or repeat loop control structure:

```
<INPUT TYPE="button" onClick="myFunction '12','hello'">
```

> **N O T E** When you use the call statement (discussed in "Calling Your Procedures") to invoke a sub or function that you've written, you *must* include the procedure's enclosing parentheses:
>
> ```
> <INPUT TYPE="button" onClick="CALL myFunction('12','hello')">
> ```

As noted, these rules have been derived not just through published VBScript documentation but from usage with the current version of the Internet Explorer browser. If you find that you are receiving errors in your own (or in these) scripts—even when following what appears to be the proper syntax for the current scripting situation—it may be that your version of Internet Explorer has been updated with new rules. By all means, lose or use the parentheses as the interpreter dictates.

Lines, Spaces, Tabs, and Quotes

Neither JavaScript nor VBScript processes excess lines, spaces, or tabs in your code. The following script appears exactly the same to the interpreter in both its collapsed and expanded formats. However, which do you prefer to read?

Collapsed Format

```
dim g_myVariable
sub myProc()
if g_myVariable = true then
document.forms(0).field.value = "Yes"
dim curDate
curDate = date
else
document.forms(0).field.value = "No"
end if
alert("This procedure is done.")
end sub
```

Expanded Format

```
DIM g_myVariable

SUB myProc()

    IF g_myVariable = true THEN

        document.forms(0).field.value = "Yes"
        DIM curDate
curDate = date

    ELSE

        document.forms(0).field.value = "No"

    END IF

    alert("This procedure is done.")

END SUB
```

> **TIP** You can take advantage of a more effective method of collapsing your typed code by using colons to delimit short commands and place them on a single line. You could use this strategy, for instance, to populate several variables in only one line of code. Although the spaces in this example are, once again, superfluous—they do help make the line of script more readable.
>
> ```
> var1 = 1 : var2 = 2 : var3 = 3 : var4 = 4 : var5 = 5
> ```

Scripters generally take full advantage of the line-space-tab blindness of the interpreter to make code readable. Most adhere to an unspoken rule that indents any section of code that is subordinate to another section. Any lines of script that appear inside a substatement might be indented four spaces (or one tab) past the substatement itself. If that line of code begins another control structure (such as an if conditional), the lines of code within that structure are indented four more spaces (or one more tab). This is called "nesting" statements, and it makes scripts very readable.

```
DIM g_myVariable

SUB myProc()

    alert("This procedure is running.")
```

```
    IF g_myVariable = true THEN

        document.forms(0).field.value = "Yes"
        DIM curDate
curDate = date

    END IF

END SUB
```

Quotes are a different story, and are not only recognized but required by the interpreter whenever literal (exact text string) values are passed. If you try to put an unquoted string into a container, the interpreter will tell you that your value is not defined:

```
alert("hello")    ' displays "hello" in the alert dialog box
alert(hello)      ' displays "undefined" in the alert dialog box
```

Nested quotes are allowed if double quotes are used on the outside, and single quotes within:

```
<INPUT TYPE="button" onClick="alert('hello')">
```

Commenting Your Code

VBScript also ignores any text that appears on a line to the right of the REM (for remarks) statement. You can use this built-in statement to provide explanatory comments with your code. These comments can help you and others understand what a block of code is supposed to be doing.

It is not necessary to fully explain everything the code is doing. To do so would probably result in more comments than actual code. Since there is a limit to the number of characters that you can have in one scripted page, and since the longer the script is the slower the page loads, you want to keep your comments brief and to the point:

```
function isZip(zipFld) REM checks if contents of Zip field are valid
```

An alternative to the REM statement is the apostrophe ('), which also causes the VBScript interpreter to ignore everything on the line to its right:

```
function isZip(zipFld) ' checks if contents of Zip field are valid
```

You can use either, depending on which makes it easier for you to read and review your code. The apostrophe is used in this book to save character space, but you might prefer to use the REM statement in all caps to really emphasize where remarks occur. Whichever comment prefix you choose must appear at the beginning of every line of comment. The following script and associated remarks would return an error.

```
function isZip(zipFld) REM checks to see if the contents of Zip field, passed in
                       REM answer to the zipFld argument, represent a valid zip
```

To avoid errors, remarks that take up multiple lines should be written like this:

```
function isZip(zipFld)    REM checks to see if the contents of Zip field,
                          REM passed in answer to the zipFld argument,
                          REM represent a valid zip
```

Or this:

```
function isZip(zipFld)    ' checks to see if the contents of Zip field,
                          ' passed in answer to the zipFld argument,
                          ' represent a valid zip
```

Built-In Statements

You may have noted that term "statement" seems to pop up every where. Built-in statements are the language elements used to make scripts and their purpose and order of execution comprehensible to the interpreter. Just as HTML imposes a document structure that allows the browser to coherently present the page, VBScript requires the use of the proper statement set to tell the interpreter where a user-created procedure or function begins and ends; to notify the interpreter that a variable is being declared; or to tell the interpreter how a conditional script or repeat loop should be executed.

The specific language and placement rules required to accomplish these tasks actually vary quite a bit between VBScript and JavaScript. VBScript provides statements that allow users to create two kinds of procedures (subroutines and functions), while JavaScript currently allows only functions. VBScript provides if-then-else and select-case statements for if conditions, while JavaScript provides if-else (the "then" is implied) and switch-case statements. Moreover, the statements used to formulate conditionals, repeat loops, and to perform other operations differ, here and there, between the languages.

If you are a past-JavaScripter, in the scripting examples thus far presented you may have noted the absence of curly brackets and semi-colons, the presence of end statements, the different look of the VBScript if-then-else control structure, and differences in the way a counting repeat loop is written. The differences are not huge, and you'll learn them swiftly; but this early evidence should convince you of the value of reviewing these structures in this chapter, and their implementation details presented in Chapter 9, before making any assumptions about how VBScript is written based on previous experience writing JavaScript.

> **TIP** Novices may find it confusing that the term "statement" is also used to describe the lines of code written between the official VBScript statements. You could say that official statements are provided by the language; while unique statements are created by the user in much the same way that the language offers, for instance, built-in functions—but also allows users to create their own.

Writing Your Own Procedures

There are two VBScript statement sets that allow you to create stored procedures— or blocks of code that you may be called upon to execute from other scripts: *sub* and *function*.

Subroutines

From its prevalent use in previous examples, you may already be familiar by osmosis with the subroutine statement set which begins with the *sub* statement and ends with the *end sub* statement.

```
sub myProc()

    [statements]


end sub
```

You can name your procedure anything you want (the example uses the name "myProc()"), as long as you avoid the naming restrictions listed in Chapter 2, and include ending parentheses *regardless of whether the sub takes arguments*.

As you may recall from Chapter 1, the sub statement doubles as a method for binding a script to an object and event. When doing so, a special naming convention is enforced, beginning with the name of the object (which *must* be a pseudonym and not an array position like "document.thisForm.elements(1)"), followed by an underscore, followed by the name of the target event handler, and ending with an empty parenthesis.

```
sub     thisButton_onClick()

    [statements]


end sub
```

When and How to Create Arguments

You should already be quite at home with the concept of arguments and answers from your previous HTML experience with tags that take both required and optional arguments. You can pass information to your own procedures and functions using a similar argument/answer mechanism. How do you know when to create arguments for your procedures and functions; and how do you create them if needed?

There are many ways to pass data back and forth in VBScript, but one of the slickest ways to get data to a sub or function you've created is to pass it as the answer to one of its own arguments. Of course, you can only pass information to your procedure if it exists *before* the procedure is run. Keep in mind that any data that is going to be created by the procedure's execution won't be available until the script is run.

Here's an example of when to create an argument. If a field is set up to call a procedure that requires information about the state of that field at the time of the call, you've got a good reason for adding an argument to that procedure.

The following onBlur script is executed when the user tabs or clicks out of a field named "fld1." The script's only job is to call a sub named "myProc()," which takes one argument called "fieldValue." Accordingly, when the field's internal onBlur handler calls myProc(), it also passes the value property of that field as an answer to myProc's fieldValue argument. If the field is empty, an alert informs the user that the field is required and must be filled.

```
<INPUT TYPE="field" NAME="fld1" onBlur="myProc(fld1.value)">

sub myProc(fieldValue)

    if fieldValue = "" then

        alert("You must fill in this required field.")

    end if

end sub
```

You can optionally halt the execution of a sub in mid-stream using the exit *sub* statement. For complete details on the sub statement, see Chapter 9.

Functions

The second method for creating a stored procedure has also been mentioned already. It is provided by the *function* statement set, which may be used to construct blocks of code whose execution result in a returned value.

> **TIP** The value returned by your created functions is always a variant, just like the values contained in your created variables. For information on variant datatypes, see Chapter 2.

The format of user-created functions follows almost the exact same structure as that of the sub statement, beginning with the *function* statement, in this case, and ending with the *end function* statement. In order for the function to return a value, however, you must include a line of script that looks very much as if you were assigning a value to a variable with the same name as the function, sans parentheses. The line bolded in the following example shows the syntax used to assign the value derived by other operations in the function, and which you presumably wish to return to the calling script.

```
function didSelect(selOpt,selVal)

    if selOpt <> 0 then

        didSelect = "You selected " & selVal

    else

        didSelect = "Please select something from the list."

    end if

end function
```

```
<SELECT NAME="list"
onChange="alert(didSelect(list.options.selectedIndex,list.options(list.options
.selectedIndex).value))">
```

In the example just shown, a function named didSelect() is called whenever an option is selected from a select object named list. The function, however, is not the first operation called by the select object. First, it calls the alert method. From within the alert method, didSelect() is called to show you that it's possible to nest functions within other functions or methods. didSelect's two arguments are answered by providing the options array position of the currently selected option, and the value assigned to that option.

> **TIP**   Note that the value of the selected option is derived, in part, by using the same object property used to derive the number of the selected option. This is because the number of the selected option is the same as its position in the options array. Since that number can't be known until the user makes a selection, the list.options.selected statement provides the options array position information needed by both the first and the second arguments:
>
> ```
> didSelect(list.options.selected,list.options(list.options.selected).value
> ```

If the selected option is not 0 in the array, the alert presents the first message with the words "You selected" followed by the value of the selected option. If the array position is 0 (which, by the way, is displayed as "nothing selected" in our imaginary list), the second message results, asking the user to select something.

Calling Your Procedures

The functions and subroutines that you write are called upon to execute their internal statements in the same way that you call upon built-in functions and methods to execute their stored procedures. All you need to do is name the function or sub in a related script.

Related script is any script whose scope includes the script containing your function or sub. Scripts that exist within the same HTML document can call any sub or function that appears in the <HEAD> portion of your document, or anywhere in the <BODY> *except* within <FORM> tags. The preferred way is to place a universal procedure into the <HEAD> of your document.

```
<HEAD>

<SCRIPT LANGUAGE="VBScript>

sub mySub()

    alert("Hello, World.")

end sub

</SCRIPT>
```

```
</HEAD>

<BODY onLoad="mySub()">
```

If a procedure is only apropos to one or more of the elements in a form, then you can certainly place that procedure within that form's tags without problems. If so, this is a very expedient place to put a script tied to elements on that form—allowing you to use the short form of the elements' names (as noted in Chapter 2).

```
<FORM>

<SCRIPT LANGUAGE="VBScript>

sub field1_onBlur()

    field1.value = "Hello, World."

end sub

</SCRIPT>

<INPUT TYPE="text" NAME="field1">

</FORM>
```

> **WARNING** If the browser in use might be Netscape Navigator (or any of a number of other popular browsers, like the one used by members of America Online), there may be sequential problems with processing scripts within a form's tags. The previous example, for instance, would generate an error in Navigator during page load. This is because Navigator would read through the sub script first, and try to locate an element named "field1"" before it has been created—resulting in a no-such-object error. All things considered, the original recommendation made in Chapter 1 stands: Unless you have a good reason to place a script in the document <BODY>, it's usually best to place it within the <SCRIPT> tag into the <HEAD> of the document.

Your own original procedures can be called from anywhere inside other procedures you've created. In the following example, a user-created function named myFunction() is called from a sub named mySub().

```
sub mySub()

    if myFunction() = true then

        [statements]

    end if

end sub
```

Your procedures can also be called using lines of code that stand alone within the <SCRIPT> tag, and are automatically attached to the onLoad event (and, therefore, executed as soon as the page is loaded):

```
<SCRIPT LANGUAGE="VBScript">

if myFunction() = true then

        [statements]

end if

</SCRIPT>
```

Your procedures may also be called from within the onEventHandler scripts that may be placed inside any HTML tag:

```
<INPUT TYPE="button" onClick="if myFunction() = true then

    [statements]

end if">
```

There is also an optional *call* statement that can be used to call your subs and functions but it is not required. See Chapter 9 for details on its use.

```
<INPUT TYPE="button" onClick="call mySub()>
```

Using Control Structures

Thus far, we've discussed how to control the execution of scripts by attaching them to designated objects and events, as well as how to use data to drive the process further. Once the script has been triggered by a fired event, however, you can't drive the process with data alone. You need to know how to use your language's inherent control structures to steer the process this way or that way—based on the evaluation of that data.

A control structure dictates the way a particular block of code is written in order to lead the interpreter through a decision-making process—or to instruct the interpreter to repeat certain operations under certain conditions.

Decision Control Structures

When you want to write a script that executes one group of statements if condition A exists, and another group of statements if condition B exists, you need to use what is known as a conditional format. Conditional formats let your code make decisions based on what the current user has or has not done, to date, on your page. If the user hasn't filled in certain fields, or has checked a particular checkbox, or has populated one of the frames in your frameset with one document instead of another, and so forth, you can write a script that behaves differently according to these variable conditions.

If-Then-Else Conditions

The most flexible conditional format available in VBScript is the if-then-else conditional statement set. It allows you to provide multiple *decision* branches for multiple conditions. It begins with the keyword "if," followed by an expression that describes the condition which must be met *if its attached statements are to be executed*. You can write a simple if statement that only executes if the condition is met, or you can write a compound statement that executes one set of statements if the condition *is* met, and a second set of statements if the condition is *not* met, by adding an *else* clause:

```
if [expression] then

    [statement set A]

else

    [statement set B]

end if
```

Added flexibility is afforded to the if conditional format by the inclusion of an *elseif* clause that allows you to create decision branches for multiple conditions:

```
if [expression A] then

    [statement set A]
```

```
elseif [expression B] then

    [statement set B]

elseif [expression C] then

    [statement set C]

elseif [expression D] then

    [statement set D]

end if
```

You can combine the elseif and else clauses if, say, you have two separate statement branches to run if one of two conditions is met, and a third set to run if neither of the first two conditions is met. In other words, you use the elseif clause whenever you need to allow for a new condition, but you use the else clause when you wish to provide a statement branch for *everything else*. This is because the elseif clause requires an expression describing its required condition, while the else clause takes no expression and is just like saying: "in all other instances, do this."

```
if [expression A] then

    [statement set A]

elseif [expression B] then

    [statement set B]

else

    [statement set C]

end if
```

Here's an example of a script that checks to see whether the user's browser is Internet Explorer, Netscape Navigator, or some other browser application. If the browser is Internet Explorer, the user is taken to a starting page optimized for that browser. If the browser is Netscape Navigator, the user is taken to a page optimized for Navigator. In all other instances, the user is taken to a page that is simplified for all standard browsers.

```
sub theBrowser()

    if navigator.appName = "Microsoft Internet Explorer" then

        navigate("ie.htm")

    elseif navigator.appName = "Netscape Navigator" then

        navigate("nav.htm")

    else

        navigator("other.htm")

    end if

    end sub
```

Case Statements

The most efficient conditional format available in VBScript is the *select case* statement set. It is a shorthand method that lets you designate multiple decision branches as long as you are only testing for one condition in every case (thus, the term "case"). It begins with the keywords "select case," followed by the expression that evaluates the data you wish to test for several cases. Within the select case control structure, you nest the individual case statements that indicate all the possible values that might result from the initial test. Nested within each internal case statement are the statements you wish to execute in the event that the given case is true.

Confused? An example will clarify everything. Let's say you have a select object on a page with three options. The value of each option is a method of payment that the user may choose when ordering items on the page. Depending on the form of payment chosen, you'll need different pieces of additional data from the user so you set up this script to take the user to an appropriate follow-up page once a method of payment is selected.

```
select case document.forms(0).selectPay.options.selectedIndex

    case 0

        navigate("check.htm")

    case 1
```

```
        navigate("credit.htm")

    case 3

        navigate("po.htm")

end select
```

> **TIP** You may have noted that both the "if-then-else" and "select case"
> examples execute one of three possible branches, depending on the eval-
> uation of a single condition. In the first example, every branch depends
> upon the results of a single test, which checks to see which browser is in
> use. In the second example, every branch also depends on the results of a
> single test, which checks to see what item the user has chosen from a list.
> Could you use the select case statement in place of the if statement in the
> previous example? Yes, if you use the "case else" keywords in place of
> the final "else" clause (shown next). If your if statement was testing for
> more than one condition, however, you couldn't use the select-case for-
> mat. For instance, if one branch of an if statement needs to execute if a
> certain field is not empty, and another needs to execute if the field is
> empty *and* a particular radio button choice has been made.
>
> ```
> sub theBrowser()
>
>     select case navigator.appName
>
>       case "Microsoft Internet Explorer" then
>
>             navigate("ie.htm")
>
>       case "Netscape Navigator" then
>
>             navigate("nav.htm")
>
>                   case else
>
>             navigator("other.htm")
>
> end select
>
> end sub
> ```

Looping Control Structures

There are many times when you'll want to perform the same basic action or set of actions more than once. You may need to check the contents of several fields on a form before allowing its submission, or review each character in a string input by the user to make sure that all the characters are numbers, or create a flashy visual effect by repeatedly executing a line of code that changes the background color of the page—or any number of other tasks that require a repeat performance, or that must be performed in relation to multiple objects.

The process of scripting the interpreter to reiterate actions is called looping, and the control structures that support looping are commonly called repeat loops. VBScript provides two basic types of repeat loop control structures.

Counting Repeat Loops

VBScript provides the "for" and "next" statement set, which allows you to set up a counter that repeats the loop for the designated number of times. Each time the loop is run, 1 is added to the count which is kept by a "counting variable" (which is "i" in the example shown). When the count reaches the designated number, the loop stops running.

```
for i = 1 to 10

    [statements]


next
```

This control structure, in effect, says: "for as long as the counting variable i equals any number from 1 to 10, keep executing the enclosed statements." The first time the loop is run, i = 1. When the "next" keyword is encountered, the i variable is automatically incremented by 1. When the interpreter loops around to the "for" statement again, the i variable is incremented to 2 . . . and so it goes, until i = 11 and the loop stops executing. It stops executing when i reaches 11 because, at that point, the condition for executing the loop's internal statements is no longer met.

Another way to write a counting "for" loop includes the "step" keyword. When this keyword is absent, the interpreter assumes that you want to increment the counting variable by 1 with each occurrence of the "next" statement. If you want to perform the enclosed operation only when i equals an even number from 1 to 10, you should explicitly use the step keyword, indicating that 2 is to be added to i whenever the "next" statement is encountered:

```
for i = 2 to 10 step 2

    [statements]

next
```

As with all other situations in VBScript, you don't have to use an actual number (or even know the number) that defines the range of the loop. Many counting loops depend, for instance, upon the length of an array for their upward-limit number (as shown by example in the previous chapter).

The fact is, however, that any number required by the counting loop can be defined by any element in the current environment that evaluates to a number, including user inputs on the current page. Execution of the following script would cause the background of the page to flash from red, to white, to blue for the number of times represented by the user's age (as input into an Age field on the page's first form).

```
for i = 1 to document.forms(0).ageField.value

    document.bgColor = "red"
    document.bgColor - "white"
    document.bgColor = "blue"

next
```

> **TIP** You can also use a special form of the "for" statement to execute a set of statements for every element in a given array, or for every object in a collection. This loop format uses the "for each" statement, and causes its enclosed statements to execute for each member of the group passed to the statement. The following example shows how you might use the "for each" control structure to perform a repeated set of actions for every item in the elements array of a form that contains this script. (Note the use of the elements array name in both the beginning and ending lines of the control structure.)
>
> ```
> for each item in elements
>
>     [statements]
>
> next elements
> ```

Do Loops

VBScript also provides the "do" and "loop" statement set, which allows you to repeat a loop under specific circumstances. The "do while" form of the do loop statement lets you script a loop to be repeated as long as a certain condition exists.

do while The following "do" statement uses the "while" keyword to repeat the loop as long as a variable named "theStatus" equals "true." When the "addTo25()" subroutine is run, "true" is placed into a variable called "theStatus," and a zero is placed into a field named "fld1." When the "do while" statement is executed for the first time, 1 is added to the zero in fld1, changing the value of that field to 1 right before the browsing user's eyes (although it all happens too fast for the user to see anything but the final number; to slow it down, you'd need to include a timer like the one used in the Chapter 18 example).

When the loop is executed for the 25th time, the if condition finally evaluates to true and false is placed into theStatus, rendering the while clause no longer true, and stopping the execution of the loop. The effect of this script is to clear fld1 each time it is run, then let the field count from 1 to 25 and stop.

```
sub addToFld()

        DIM theStatus
        theStatus = true
        document.forms(0).fld1.value = 0

        do while theStatus = true

                document.forms(0).fld1.value = document.forms(0).fld1.value + 1

                if document.forms(0).fld1.value = 25 then

                    theStatus = false

                end if

        loop

end sub
```

Another form of the "do while" statement allows you to check the while clause without looping the interpreter back to the top (which may result in a slight performance gain if you've packed a lengthy script inside your loop):

```
sub addToFld()

        DIM theStatus
        theStatus = true
        document.forms(0).fld1.value = 0

    do

            document.forms(0).fld1.value = document.forms(0).fld1.value + 1

            if document.forms(0).fld1.value = 25 then

                theStatus = false

            end if

        loop while theStatus = true

end sub
```

do until You can also create a loop that executes *until* a specified condition is met. The same addTo25() example could be rewritten to use this form of a conditional repeat loop as follows:

```
sub addTo25()

        DIM theStatus
        theStatus = true
        document.forms(0).fld1.value = 0

    do until theStatus = false

            document.forms(0).fld1.value = document.forms(0).fld1.value + 1

            if document.forms(0).fld1.value = 25 then

                theStatus = false
            end if

    loop
```

```
end sub
```

As with the "do while" loop control structure, a variation of the "do until" loop lets you check the condition without looping back to the top of the structure:

```
sub addTo25()

    DIM theStatus
    theStatus = true
    document.forms(0).fld1.value = 0

    do

        document.forms(0).fld1.value = document.forms(0).fld1.value + 1

        if document.forms(0).fld1.value = 25 then

            theStatus = false

        end if

    loop until theStatus = false

end sub
```

Combining and Exiting Control Structures

There are many ways to interweave conditional and looping control structures to create complex and highly discriminating scripts whose operations vary greatly depending upon the current user's actions and inputs. In addition to mixing and matching control structures, you can also invoke a variety of exit statements to stop a script cold if and when given conditions are met.

Here's an example script that combines two control structures with an exit statement. The subordinate "if" control structure is nested within a "for" loop control structure and contains an exit statement that allows the loop to be exited. If x becomes true *before* the loop is finished executing for all of its expressed steps, the loop stops executing and the interpreter jumps to the next presented statement beyond the loop, or stops all activities if no new statements are presented.

```
for i = 2 to 10 step 2

    [statements]
```

```
    if x = true

        exit for

    end if

next
```

By making strategic use of the proper "exit" statement, the previous addTo25() procedure could be written a little more tersely to perform the exact same routine:

```
sub addTo25()

    document.forms(0).fld1.value = 0

    for 1 to 25

        document.forms(0).fld1.value = document.forms(0).fld1.value + 1

        if document.forms(0).fld1.value = 25 then

            exit for

        end if

    loop

end sub
```

See Chapter 9 for detailed information on each of VBScript's control structures, including all the available exit statements that allow you to stop a script in its tracks, and not do anything else—a very handy capability when you want to actively respond to some conditions but not others.

What's Next?

Now that you have a working knowledge of how scripts are written to control program flow, you're ready to play with VBScript on your own for a little while. A good way to do so is to familiarize yourself with all the VBScript language elements at your disposal by perusing Part II, and experimenting with script ideas as you go along. When you've finished providing yourself with this broad VBScript foundation, you'll be more than prepared for the tutorials in Part III.

Part Two
The VBScript Language

Part II of the *VBScript Sourcebook* provides definitions for most of the basic VBScript terms available for use in your scripts. It is based on version 3.0 of the VBScript scripting engine (Vbscript.dll) provided with Internet Explorer 4.0. This upgrade of Internet Explorer includes DHTML, the wide-open HTML Document Object Model that exposes every tag (*excepting* the <PARAM> tag, and *including* the <SCRIPT> tag) to the VBScript engine. All tags are now objects or members of object collections (a.k.a. *arrays*). The arguments associated with those tags are (for the most part) all exposed as properties or methods to the VBScript and JavaScript engines within the IE4 browser.

Programming languages are always shifting and changing. It is, therefore, not the goal of this book to provide a microscopic analysis of every term in the VBScript lexicon. Rather, the purpose of Part II is to give you a broad overview of its available language elements, with an eye to mastering the general methods for incorporating these terms into your scripts.

A second task of this portion of the book is to expose you to the scope of the VBScript language, so you'll have a working understanding of what it can and cannot do. Toward these twin ends, many terms are presented in detail, while terms implemented similarly to those exhaustively discussed are covered more briefly.

Each definition in Part II begins with the proper spelling of the referenced term. Although VBScript is *not case-sensitive*, terms *must* be spelled correctly for the interpreter to recognize and apply them appropriately. Each definition also includes example syntax, short example scripts (as needed), and explanations and tips regarding the term's use. Terms are divided into groups according to their role in the VBScript development environment:

- VBScript's built-in Objects are described in Chapter 4.
- The built-in Properties of VBScript's Objects are described in Chapter 5.
- The built-in Methods of VBScript's Objects are described in Chapter 6.
- VBScript's built-in Functions are described in Chapter 7.
- VBScript's available Event Handlers are described in Chapter 8.
- VBScript's controlling Statements are described in Chapter 9.
- VBScript's Arithmetic, Concatenation, and Logical Operators are described in Chapter 10.

Chapter

4

VBScript Objects

This chapter includes all of VBScript's built-in objects, while Chapters 6, 7, 8, 9, and 10 cover all of the known methods, events, functions, and other VBScript particulars. Only Chapter 5, "Object Properties," has been abridged, due to the large number of HTML arguments that have become VBScript properties (over 200 and counting). Since all HTML arguments that have been translated into VBScript arguments behave similarly, and are invoked in the same way, a representative sampling of these properties (many with detailed explanations and examples) is provided in the next chapter, along with the Web site address of Microsoft's more complete properties posting.

Documentary Sources

Descriptions of the behavior of individual language elements are based on information provided by Microsoft, enhanced wherever possible by the author's working knowledge of the language. Many existing problems with language elements are not reported here because—thanks to the rapidity of software revision on the Web—you may well be working with a version of the supporting software that fixes earlier problems. Problems *are* occasionally addressed in these chapters, however; especially if it appears that Microsoft's documentation and the actual behavior of the language element are in conflict.

If you find terms that do not behave essentially as described in this section—and the descriptions fail to mention any anomalies—consult

Microsoft's online VBScript documentation to see if the behavior of that item has changed since this book was published. Be advised, however, that—at the time of publication—Microsoft's VBScript documentation was found to contain numerous typographical errors, and some surprising syntax mistakes, apparently resulting from excessive cutting and pasting. (Some of these errors may be repeated here, if detected.) So, review documented changes carefully and, if it still seems as if a term does not behave as specified, report the problem as a bug to Microsoft.

W W W   For the latest information on VBScript, see:

www.microsoft.com/vbscript/

Report VBScript bugs to support at:

microsoft.com

Chapter 2's explanation of the Document Object Model included a discussion of the VBScript Object Hierarchy. This hierarchy, as you may recall, refers to the relative order of VBScript Objects, starting with the top-level Object (window) and ending with the lowest-level Object (the options array). This chapter takes an in-depth look at each Object in this hierarchy, and explains how to create scripts using these objects.

The VBScript Objects

For easy reference, VBScript's built-in Objects are presented here in alphabetical order; not according to the Object Hierarchy discussed in Chapter 2. In addition to the explanation and examples presented for each Object, each definition also includes a list of the Object's Properties, Methods, attached Events, and brief descriptions of each.

N O T E   JavaScript users won't find listings in this chapter for a Date or Math Object, although VBScript does in fact support all of the Date and Math operations currently supported by JavaScript. Math operations, however, are implemented via separate functions, like abs() (which is used to obtain the absolute value of a number) instead of Math.abs() (which performs the same service in JavaScript). Dates are similarly created in both languages using the term Date(). In JavaScript, however, this language element is referred to as the Date constructor or the Date Object. In VBScript, it is considered a built-in function. For more information on Date and Math operations, see Chapter 8.

All Array

Term: all

Example Syntax: document.all(10).tagName
```
            ' returns the string inside the tag portion of the eleventh
            ' tagged element in the parent HTML document
```

All is a third-tier object in the hierarchy, below the document object. The all object refers to all of the objects in the VBScript Object Hierarchy that sit below the document object and have been generated by an HTML tag. When an element's position in the all array is used to reference that element, the all array inherits all of the properties, methods, and events belonging to that element.

Anchor Object

Term: anchors

Example Syntax: document.anchors(0)   ' first anchor in current page
```
              document.anchors(0).name   ' name of the referenced anchor
```

Anchor is one of the third-tier objects in the VBScript Object Hierarchy. It is the child of the document object, and the grandchild of the window object. An instance of the anchor object is created for every <ANCHOR> tag in the current document that includes a NAME argument. In other words, the VBScript anchor object is only used to refer to <ANCHOR> tags in a document that target a word or phrase within that same document. (Use the link object to reference <ANCHOR> tags that include the HREF argument.)

All of the anchor objects in a document are indexed in the anchors array. Anchors are positioned in this array in the order that their applicable <ANCHOR> tags appear in the parent document. In the following example, only the fourth and fifth <ANCHOR> tags qualify as anchor objects; and these objects are first and second in the anchors array.

```
<BODY>
<A HREF="doc1.htm">        'not a member of the anchors array
<A HREF="doc2.htm">        'not a member of the anchors array
<A HREF="doc3.htm">        'not a member of the anchors array
<A NAME="word">           'document.anchors(0)
<A NAME="phrase">         'document.anchors(1)

</BODY>
```

You can reference an anchor object via its position in the anchors array:

```
document.anchors(0) 'the first named anchor in the current document
```

Since, by definition, anchor objects include a NAME argument, you can also reference an anchor by name:

```
document.thisPhrase 'references <A NAME="thisPhrase">this phrase</A>
```

Properties

name   Gets the answer to the reference anchor's NAME argument.

length   Gets the total number of items in the anchors array.

Methods and Event Handling

Anchor objects have no built-in Methods or Event Handlers.

Applets Array

Term: `applets`

Example Syntax: `document.applets(5)`
            `' sixth embedded applet in the current document`

Applets refers to all of the objects in the VBScript Object Hierarchy that are embedded via the <APPLET> tag.

Properties

className, docHeight, docLeft, docTop, docWidth, parentElement, sourceIndex, tagName, accessKey, align, height, id, style, title, width

Methods

removeMember, scrollIntoView, contains, getMember, setMember

Event Handling

onAfterUpdate, onBeforeUpdate, onBlur, onClick, onDblClick, onFocus, onHelp, onKeyDown, onKeyPress, onKeyUp, onLoad, onMouseDown, onMouseMove, onMouseOut, onMouseOver, onMouseUp, onReadyStateChange

Body Object

Term: `body`

Example Syntax: `document.body.bgColor`
                `' returns the current background color of the page`

Body is a third-tier object in the hierarchy. It is a child object (and property) of the document object, and grandchild of the window object. There is only one instance of the body object for each document.

Properties

className, docHeight, docLeft, docTop, docWidth, parentElement, sourceIndex, tagName, align, alink, background, bgColor, bgProperties, id, leftMargin, link, scroll, style, text, title, topMargin, vLink

Methods

removeMember, scrollIntoView, contains, getMember, setMember

Event Handling

onAfterUpdate, onBeforeUpdate, onBlur, onClick, onDblClick, onFocus, onHelp, onKeydown, onKeyPress, onKeyUp, onLoad, onMouseDown, onMouseMove, onMouseOut, onMouseOver, onMouseUp, onScroll

Button Object

Term: `button`

Example Syntax:

```
document.thisForm.elements(1)
' second element in the array, which is also a button
document.thisForm.thisButton
' a button in the referenced form named "thisButton"
```

Button is one of the fourth-tier objects in the VBScript Object Hierarchy. It is the child of the form object, the grandchild of the document object, and the great-grandchild of the window object. An instance of the button object is created for every <INPUT> tag in the current document whose TYPE is "button."

All of the button objects in a document are indexed along with all other form elements in the elements array. Elements are positioned in this array in the order that their tags appear in the parent form. In this example, the first (and only) button on "thisForm" is actually the second element in the elements array:

```
<FORM NAME="thisForm">

<INPUT TYPE="password">    'document.thisForm.elements(0)
<INPUT TYPE="button">      'document.thisForm.elements(1)
<TEXTAREA ROWS=2 COLS=20> 'document.thisForm.elements(2)
<INPUT TYPE="submit">      'document.thisForm.elements(3)

</FORM>
```

Since all form elements, regardless of type, appear together in the elements array, using this array to reference your subordinate form objects is not very intuitive. You'll find it more expedient to name your buttons (and all other form objects), so you can refer to them by name in your scripts.

```
<FORM NAME="thisForm">
<INPUT TYPE="button" NAME="thisButton" VALUE="Click Me">

</FORM>
```

Giving a name to the button in the preceding example script allows you to use that name to refer to the button elsewhere:

```
document.thisForm.thisButton
parent.document.thisForm.thisButton
```

Using the last example, you can reference the button from a script in a document residing in another window (as long as that window was created by the window displaying "thisForm"). If you are referring to a button from within its own <INPUT> tag, you don't need to include any reference to the document and form objects:

```
<INPUT TYPE="button" NAME="myButton" VALUE="Hello" onClick="myButton.value =
'Good-bye'">
```

Properties

form   Gets the forms array position of the button's parent form.

name   Sets or gets the name of the button defined by the <INPUT> tag's NAME argument.

value   Sets or gets the display name of the button defined by the <INPUT> tag's VALUE argument.

Methods

click   Simulates a user-click on the referenced button.

Event Handling

The onClick event handler may be attached to button objects using the <SCRIPT> tag's EVENT and FOR arguments, or by creating a subroutine that references the object and the handling event, or by using the handler as an argument inside the object's own <INPUT> tag. When using the first two methods, you can dispense with the document and form reference, and simply use the object's name.

```
<SCRIPT LANGUAGE="VBScript" FOR="thisButton" EVENT="onClick()">

    -- OR --

sub thisButton_onClick()
```

```
   -- OR --

<INPUT TYPE="button" NAME="thisButton" VALUE="Click Me" onClick="doThis()">
```

Checkbox Object

Term: checkbox

Example Syntax:

```
document.thisForm.elements(3)
' fourth element in the array, which is also a checkbox
document.thisForm.checkbox1
' a checkbox in the referenced form named "checkbox1"
```

Checkbox is one of the fourth-tier objects in the VBScript Object Hierarchy. It is the child of the form object, the grandchild of the document object, and the great-grandchild of the window object. An instance of the checkbox object is created for every <INPUT> tag in the current document whose TYPE is "checkbox."

All of the checkbox objects in a document are indexed along with all other form elements in the elements array. Elements are positioned in this array in the order that their tags appear in the parent form. In this example, the two checkbox objects on "thisForm" are actually the third and fourth elements in the elements array:

```
<FORM NAME="thisForm">

<INPUT TYPE="password">   'document.thisForm.elements(0)
<INPUT TYPE="button">     'document.thisForm.elements(1)
<INPUT TYPE="checkbox">   'document.thisForm.elements(2)
<INPUT TYPE="checkbox">   'document.thisForm.elements(3)
<INPUT TYPE="hidden">     'document.thisForm.elements(4)

</FORM>
```

Since all form elements, regardless of type, appear together in the elements array, using this array to reference your subordinate form objects is not very intuitive. You'll find it more expedient to name your checkboxes (and all other form objects), so you can refer to them by name in your scripts. If your checkboxes comprise a group (such as a group of "Yes" checkboxes repeated for each question in a list of three questions), you may want to include a number in the name:

```
<FORM NAME="thisForm">
<ol>

<li>Do you like chocolate cake?
<INPUT TYPE="checkbox" NAME="Yes1" VALUE="Yes"> YES
```

```
<li>Do you like vanilla pudding?
<INPUT TYPE="checkbox" NAME="Yes2" VALUE="Yes"> YES

<li>Do you like liver and onions?
<INPUT TYPE="checkbox" NAME="Yes3" VALUE="Yes"> YES

</ol>

</FORM>
```

Giving incremented names to the checkboxes in the preceding example script allows you to use those names to refer to specific checkboxes in other scripts:

```
document.thisForm.Yes1
document.thisForm.Yes2
document.thisForm.Yes3
```

If you are referring to a checkbox from within its own <INPUT> tag, you don't need to include any reference to the document and form objects, as shown in the following script. (Figure 4.1 shows the script's results.)

```
<INPUT TYPE="checkbox" NAME="Yes3" VALUE="Yes"

onClick="if Yes3.checked = 1 then

    confirm ('Are you kidding?')

end if">
```

Properties

form	Gets the forms array position of the checkbox's parent form.
name	Sets or gets the name of the checkbox defined by the <INPUT> tag's NAME argument.
value	Sets or gets the display name of the checkbox defined by the <INPUT> tag's VALUE argument.
checked	Sets or gets the status of the checkbox; returns a 1 if checked, and a 0 if not checked.
defaultChecked	Sets or gets the default status of the checkbox; returns "true" if checked by default, and "false" if not checked.

Methods

click	Simulates a user-click on the referenced checkbox.

Figure 4.1 If the user checks the "Yes" box next to the "liver and onions" question, a dialog asks the user to confirm this choice.

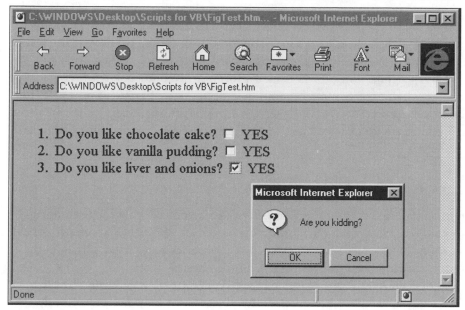

Event Handling
The onClick event handler may be attached to checkbox objects using the <SCRIPT> tag's EVENT and FOR arguments, or by creating a subroutine that references the object and the handling event, or by using the handler as an argument inside the object's own <INPUT> tag. When using the first two methods, you can dispense with the document and form reference, and simply use the button's name.

```
<SCRIPT LANGUAGE="VBScript" FOR=" thisBox" EVENT="onClick()">

    -- OR --

sub thisBox_onClick()

    -- OR --

<INPUT TYPE="checkbox" NAME="thisBox" VALUE="Click Me" onClick="doThis()">
```

Document Object
Term: document
Example Syntax:
```
document.write ("string")
'writes the string to a new document
```

Document is one of the second-tier objects in the VBScript Object Hierarchy and, as such, is also considered a property of the window object. It is the name of the object that houses the executing VBScript and all of its supporting HTML code. A document object is created whenever an HTML file is loaded into a VBScript-aware browser. A document object may contain one or more instances of three subordinate objects (link, anchor, form, and cookie) and a corresponding array for each object type (links array, anchors array, forms array, and cookie array).

Unlike the window object, you cannot use implicit syntax to refer to properties or methods of the document object. In other words, the term "document" must appear in any scriptural reference to a document's properties, methods, or subordinate objects:

```
document.location
document.open
document.formName.elementName
```

Note that even references to form objects must be preceded by the term document—unlike JavaScript, which allows syntax like forms[0].field1 to refer to a field in the current document. (Note also that JavaScript uses brackets to surround the array index position, while VBScript uses a parenthesis.)

The only exceptions to this rule of explicit syntax are objects created by the <OBJECT> tag, which may be addressed by object name only. For instance, the height and width properties of a control called "3DField" can be modified in VBScript without any direct reference to the document object, as shown here:

```
<OBJECT NAME="3DField" ... ></OBJECT>
```

This object's height and width properties may be referred to as:

```
3DField.height = 50
3DField.width = 50
```

In all other instances, the term document must be included in any statement affecting the current document:

```
modDate = document.lastModified
```

You can reference any subordinate object in a document using either the name of that object, or its position in its array. In the previous example, a form element called field1 was identified by its name, but its resident form was identified by that form's position in the current document's forms array:

```
document.forms(0).field1
```

Names are assigned to forms and their elements using the NAME argument in the object's respective tag. If both the referenced form and form element have names, you can use these names to point to that form element. For example, when the user clicks the "Who wrote the VBScript Sourcebook?" button created by the following HTML script, the string "Mary Jane Mara" is placed into the Author field (as shown in Figure 4.2).

```
<HTML>
<HEAD>

<SCRIPT LANGUAGE="VBScript" FOR="button1" EVENT="onClick()">

    document.book.author.value = "Mary Jane Mara"

</SCRIPT>

</HEAD>
<BODY>

<FORM NAME="book">

<INPUT TYPE="button" NAME="button1" VALUE="Who wrote the VBScript Sourcebook?">
<p>
<INPUT TYPE="text" NAME="author">
```

Figure 4.2 The *book* form page before clicking the button, and after clicking the button.

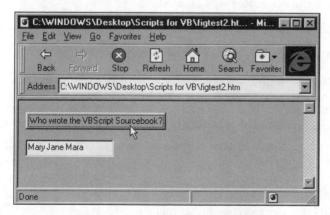

```
</FORM>

</BODY>
</HTML>
```

If a form or element has no name, you can use array positions to define both. The following object pathname refers to the second element (form control object) of the first form in the current document:

```
document.forms(0).elements(1)
```

Properties

activeElement	Gets the element that currently has the document focus.
aLinkColor	Sets or gets the color of the active links in the referenced document.
anchors	Gets the anchors array for the referenced document.
bgColor	Sets or gets the background color of the referenced document.
charset	Gets the charset of the current document.
cookie	Sets or gets the referenced document's cookie(s).
domain	Gets or sets the current domain for a pageset, for secure communication purposes.
fgColor	Sets or gets the foreground color of the referenced document.
fileSize	Size of the document in bytes.
fileCreatedDate	Gets the date the document was created.
fileModifiedDate	Gets the date the document was last modified.
fileUpdatedDate	Gets the date the document was last reloaded from the server.
forms	Gets the forms array for the referenced document.
lastModified	Returns the date that the referenced document was last modified.
linkColor	Sets or gets the color of hypertext links in the referenced document.
links	Gets the links array for the referenced document.
location	Gets the URL of the referenced document.

mimeType	Returns text/html.
referrer	Gets the URL of the document that directed the browser to the referenced document.
strReadyState	Gets the current state of a downloading file.
title	Gets the title of the referenced document.
url	An alias of the location object.
vLinkColor	Sets or gets the color of the visited links in the referenced document.

Methods

clear	Clears the referenced document from its display window.
close	Closes the document stream opened by the open method, and displays any data written to the previously opened document stream.
open	Creates a new document of a specified MIME type.
writc	Writes a specified string into the referenced document.
writeLn	Writes a specified string into the referenced document, followed by a newline character.

Event Handling

onClick, onMouseOver, onDblClick, onKeyPress, onMouseDown, onMouseMove, onMouseUp, onKeyDown, onKeyUp, onMouseOut, onReadyStateChange, onHelp, onBeforeUpdate, onAfterUpdate

Events can be attached to the document object using the sub statement. Since there is only one document object current (to the script) at any given time, it is not necessary to use a pseudonym for the document (which is a good thing, since there's no way to name the document in the HTML script).

```
sub document_onClick()
```

Elements Array

Term: `elements`
Example Syntax:
```
document.thisForm.elements(5)
' sixth element in the elements array
```

Elements refers to all of the fourth-tier objects in the VBScript Object Hierarchy—also known as form elements—and it is used to create an array of all of the subordinate objects in a referenced form. Although a form can contain a variety of subordinate objects (buttons, text fields, etc.), these objects are not assigned to separate arrays but are all lumped together in the elements array. The term elements is used as an alias for the referenced object, which can be any button, checkbox, hidden, password, radio, select, text, textarea, or <OBJECT> tag enclosed within <FORM> tags.

A form element's position in the elements array is determined by its position in the HTML document that generates it. In this example, five distinctly different form objects receive positions in the thisForm's elements array in the order in which they appear within the enclosing <FORM> tags:

```
<FORM NAME="thisForm">

<INPUT TYPE="password">    'document.thisForm.elements(0)
<INPUT TYPE="button">      'document.thisForm.elements(1)
<INPUT TYPE="text">        'document.thisForm.elements(2)
<TEXTAREA SIZE=8>          'document.thisForm.elements(3)
<INPUT TYPE="hidden">      'document.thisForm.elements(4)


</FORM>
```

Since all form elements, regardless of type, appear together in the elements array, using this array to reference your subordinate form objects is not very intuitive. An elements array position tells you nothing about the type of object you're referencing. Unless there are extenuating circumstances, you'll find it more expedient to name subordinate form objects, so you can use those names in your scripts.

Adding a NAME argument to the HTML construction used previously:

```
<INPUT TYPE="password" NAME="Pword">
```

allows you to refer to the password object as:

```
document.thisForm.Pword
```

instead of:

```
document.thisForm.elements(2)
```

If you name your elements wisely, a form object's name will also reveal its type. In this example, the use of the name "Pword" clearly identifies the element as a password object, while its position as the third item in the referenced elements array tells you only that it is the third created element within the reference form.

Assigning all subordinate form objects to a single array comes in handy when you want to reiterate the same operation over several elements in a form. Let's say you set up the following form:

```
<FORM NAME="thisForm">

Send me information on your product:
<INPUT TYPE="checkbox" NAME="button1" VALUE="Yes"><p>

Name:
<INPUT TYPE="text" NAME="Name"><p>

Street Address:
<INPUT TYPE="text" NAME="Address"><p>

City:
<INPUT TYPE="text" NAME="City">

State:
<INPUT TYPE="text" NAME="State">

Zip:
<INPUT TYPE="text" NAME="Zip"><p>

Where did you hear about us?
<TEXTAREA ROWS=12 COLS=40 NAME="Reply"><p>

<INPUT TYPE="submit">

</FORM>
```

The objects in this form are positioned in its elements array as follows:

```
<INPUT TYPE="checkbox" VALUE="Yes">        'document.thisForm.elements(0)
<INPUT TYPE="text" NAME="Name">            'document.thisForm.elements(1)
<INPUT TYPE="text" NAME="Name">            'document.thisForm.elements(2)
<INPUT TYPE="text" NAME="Name">            'document.thisForm.elements(3)
<INPUT TYPE="text" NAME="Name">            'document.thisForm.elements(4)
<INPUT TYPE="text" NAME="Name">            'document.thisForm.elements(5)
<TEXTAREA NAME="Comments">                 'document.thisForm.elements(6)
<INPUT TYPE="submit">                      'document.thisForm.elements(7)
```

As you can see, there are eight items in the elements array. When the user clicks the "Submit" button, you could check and see if any text or textarea field is empty before accepting the submission, using the array positions of your fields and a repeat loop:

```
for count = 1 to 6

    if document.thisForm.elements(count).value = "" then
```

```
        alert ("Please fill in all fields before submitting form.")

    end if

next
```

> **TIP** VBScript (like JavaScript) assigns array positions from 0. This
> example begins its count with "1" because the loop is only supposed to
> perform its operation on the second through seventh items in the array
> (which, in array-speak, are item 1 through item 6). If you knew that you
> wanted to skip the first and last elements in a form, but didn't know how
> many text items existed in the middle, you could use the length prop-
> erty of the elements array to get the total number of array items. The
> returned number, in this example, would be "8" (since the length prop-
> erty counts from "1" like normal human beings). To make up for the dif-
> ference in counting base, you must subtract 1 from the length (or 8 - 1);
> and to make sure you skip the last element (the "Submit" button), you
> must subtract 1 more (or 8 - 2):
>
> ```
> for count = 1 to document.thisForm.elements.length-2
> ```

Properties
length   Gets the total number of items in the array.

Methods and Event Handling
onAfterUpdate, onBeforeUpdate, onChange, onDblClick, onHelp, onKeyPress,
onMouseDown, onMouseUp, onMouseOut, onSelect, onBlur, onClick, onFocus,
onKeyDown, onKeyUp, onMouseMove, onMouseOver, onResize

When an ordinal position in the elements array is used to represent an element,
the elements array object inherits that element's properties, methods, and events.
With the advent of DHTML, one or more of the events listed are now available to
the objects in the elements array. For more information on which additional events
are now attached to these objects, check the Object List for each event in Chapter 7.

Embeds Array
Term: embeds
Example Syntax:
```
document.embeds(5)
' sixth embedded object in the current document
```

Embeds refers to all of the objects in the VBScript Object Hierarchy that are
embedded via the <EMBED> or <OBJECT> tag.

Properties
className, docHeight, docLeft, docTop, docWidth, parentElement, sourceIndex, tagName, accessKey, align, height, id, style, title, width

Methods
removeMember, scrollIntoView, contains, getMember, setMember

Event Handling
onAfterUpdate, onBeforeUpdate, onBlur, onClick, onDblClick, onFocus, onHelp, onKeydown, onKeyPress, onKeyUp, onLoad, onMouseDown, onMouseMove, onMouseOut, onMouseOver, onMouseUp, onReadyStateChange

Event Object

Term: event

Example Syntax:
```
window.event.srcElement
'returns the object that fired the currently event
```

Event is one of the second-tier objects in the VBScript Object Hierarchy. It is the child of (and therefore a property of) the window object, and it represents the currently active (just fired) event (if any).

The following lines of script turn an object variable called theSource into an alias for the object that fired the current event:

```
DIM theSource
SET theSource = window.event.srcElement
```

Properties
cancelBubble, returnValue, srcElement, keyCode

Err Object

Term: err

Example Syntax: `err.number 'returns number of current error, if any`

The *err* object is not included in the official Object Hierarchy, but it begins to exist as soon as you place its name in a script. Its job is to provide information when an error occurs, or to provide a means of creating and numbering your own errors (see Chapter 14). When you use the err object alone, you are inferring the use of its number property. All of the err object's properties are reset to a zero-length string whenever the "on error resume next statement" is run.

The following lines of script would present an alert if the user's actions resulted in an error number 13 (datatype mismatch). The "on error..." statement would suppress the VBScript error dialog, and the if condition (if met) would present the alternative alert. See Chapter 14 for additional information on using the err object to handle possible runtime errors in your scripts.

```
on error resume next

if err.number = 13
    alert "Please type a date into the Date field."
end if
```

Properties

number, description, source

Methods

raise, clear

Form Object

Term: forms

Example Syntax: `document.formName.submit 'submits the form`

Forms is one of the third-tier objects in the VBScript Object Hierarchy. It is the child of the document object, and the grandchild of the window object. An instance of the form object is created for every <FORM> tag occurring in the current document.

A form object may contain one or more instances of 11 subordinate objects (button, checkbox, radio, text, textarea, select, hidden, password, submit, reset, and objects created by enclosed <OBJECT> tags). The form object is assigned a single array—the elements array—which represents all types of subordinate form objects.

Form elements are positioned in the elements array in the order that they appear within their parent <FORM> tag, regardless of type. Thus, the elements appearing in the following form would be positioned in the elements array as shown:

```
<FORM NAME="thisForm">

<INPUT TYPE="button">      'document.thisForm.elements(0)
<INPUT TYPE="password">    'document.thisForm.elements(1)
<TEXTAREA ROW=2 COL=20>    'document.thisForm.elements(2)
<INPUT TYPE="submit">      'document.thisForm.elements(3)
<OBJECT ...>                'thisForm.elements(4)

</FORM>
```

References to any subordinate form element are *always* preceded by an explicit reference to the form itself. Even references to objects created by the <OBJECT> tag must contain either the name or array position of the parent form, if its enclosing tag appears between <FORM> tags.

With the exception of <OBJECT> tag elements, references to all other elements in a form must also include the term document (as shown in the previous example).

If Your Script Resides in the Form . . .

There is an exception to the explicit reference rules for form elements. If the script that references a form element is contained inside the form itself, then you don't have to refer to either the document or the parent form. You can simply use the name (or array position) of the element, all by itself. The following example form places an "OFF" button on a page. A script inside that form causes the displayed name of that button to change to "ON" when the user clicks it (see Figure 4.3). Note that the script refers to the target button as "button1," not "document.thisForm.button1."

```
<FORM NAME="thisForm">
<INPUT TYPE="button" NAME="button1" VALUE="OFF">
<SCRIPT LANGUAGE="VBScript" FOR="button1" EVENT="onClick()">

button1.value = "ON"

</SCRIPT>
</FORM>
```

Chapter 1's discussion of script placement noted that most developers favor placing <SCRIPT> tags inside the <HEAD> of a document. This procedure is still highly preferable, since the <HEAD> portion of a document is always read by *any* browser before the <BODY> portion, making it impossible for any scripted object to load and fire its script-calling event before the script itself is loaded. If you place <SCRIPT> tags throughout the <BODY> of your document, you'll have to be careful where you put them to avoid event/script misfires.

Internet Explorer loads the whole HTML page into memory before processing any user actions. But other browsers that may become VBScript-aware in the future operate differently. For instance, current versions of Navigator would not process the preceding script correctly. If the user clicked the "OFF" button the very instant it appeared on the page (and users do this!), an error would occur because Navigator would process the user event before loading the lines of code following the clicked button's <INPUT> tag.

Although placing <SCRIPT> tags outside the <HEAD> of your document is probably not a good idea, you can place scripts as answers to arguments in other tags throughout your document with relative impunity. When you refer to a form element inside its own <INPUT> tag, you can also dispense with some of VBScript's naming formalities:

```
<INPUT TYPE="button" NAME="button1" VALUE="OFF" onClick="button1.value
= 'ON'">
```

Figure 4.3 Clicking the OFF button on the page shown executes a script that changes the button's name to ON.

Properties

action   Sets or gets the URL of the application that processes the form.

elements   Places the current elements array in memory, where it may be refer-
              enced using the standard array properties.

encoding   Gets or sets the MIME type to be used in the form's encoding.

length   Used with the term "forms" to get the number of forms in the forms
              array: forms.length.

method   Sets or gets the method for formatting the form and sending it to the
              servers (currently, the only methods are GET and POST).

target   Sets or gets the name of a new window to display the results of the
              form action (e.g., a confirmation message).

Methods

submit   Submits the form.

Event Handling

You can attach the onSubmit event handler to the form object. This event handler can be used to script additional actions prior to the form's submission, or to disallow the submission entirely. The onSubmit event handler can be implemented as an argument in the <FORM> tag, or using the sub statement:

```
<FORM NAME="thisForm" onSubmit="return myFunction()"
```

```
    -OR-
```

```
sub thisForm_onSubmit()
```

You can also implement the onSubmit handler using this format:

```
document.thisForm.onSubmit = return myFunction()
```

> **WARNING** Notice the use of the keyword "return" in these imple-
> mentation strategies. You don't have to use this keyword if you just
> want to add actions to the form's submission process. However, you
> *must* use "return" if you want to *prevent the submission of the form.*
> Otherwise, as soon as your onSubmit script is done executing, the
> browser will execute its internal form submission process.

Frame Object

Term: frames

Example Syntax: frames(2) 'the third frame in the current frameset

Frames is a second-tier object in the VBScript Object Hierarchy—but for all practical purposes, it behaves just like a window (the top-level object). This is reasonable,
since a frameset is merely a way of breaking up a browser's display window into multiple windows (or window panes). Each window pane (or frame) can display its own
document; and, as a reward for this capability, each individual frame inherits all of
the window object's built-in Properties, Methods, and assigned Event Handlers.

You may reference your currently open frames in VBScript using its array position, or any of the formats used to reference a window (including, self). To access a
foreign frame (that doesn't contain the executing script), you can use the term
"top" (to refer to the topmost window in a frameset), or "parent" (to refer to the
window that created the current frame).

Your scripts can only access frames created by those scripts, or that contain your
scripted documents. To access one of your frames that is neither the top window in
a frameset nor the parent to a frame you've created, you'll need to call that frame
by name, which you can only do if you give the frame a name when you create it.
You can name a frame by providing an answer to the <FRAME> tag's NAME argument when creating a frameset:

```
<FRAMESET ROWS="25%,75%">
    <FRAME NAME="FirstFrame" SRC="First.htm">
    <FRAME NAME="SecondFrame" SRC="Second.htm">
</FRAMESET>
```

Properties

defaultStatus	Sets the default message to be displayed in the Status Bar of the frameset's window.
document	The document on display in the referenced frame.
history	Gets the history list for the referenced frame.
frames.length	Gets the number of frames in the current frameset.
location	The URL of the document in the referenced frame.
name	The name of the script's resident frame.
navigator	The current browser application.
opener	The window that opened the current frame; or, if none, the current frame.
parent	The window that created the current frame; or, if none, the current frame.
self	The current frame.
top	The topmost window in a frameset; or, if none, the current frame.
status	Sets a message to be displayed in the Status Bar of the frameset's window.

Methods

alert	Opens an Alert dialog above the frameset's window.
clearTimeout	Stops the execution of SetTimeout.
close	Closes the referenced frame.
confirm	Opens a Confirmation dialog above the frameset's window.
fireOnLoad	Sends the load event.
fireOnUnload	Sends the unload event.
navigate	Loads the document of a specified URL into the referenced frame.
open	Creates a new browser window.
prompt	Opens a User-prompt dialog above the frameset's window.
setTimeout	Sets a timer to call a function after a specified number of milli-seconds.

Event Handling

You can attach the onLoad and onUnload event handlers to frame objects via the <FRAMESET> tags. The following script contained within the <FRAMESET> tag opens the Alert dialog shown in Figure 4.4 as soon as the top frame in the frameset is loaded into the browser window:

```
<FRAMESET onLoad="alert('I am a window with two frames')">
```

Hidden Object

Term: hidden

Example Syntax:

```
document.thisForm.elements(5)
' sixth element in the array, which is also a hidden field
document.thisForm.userKey
' a hidden field in the referenced form named "userKey"
```

Hidden is one of the fourth-tier objects in the VBScript Object Hierarchy. It is the child of the form object, the grandchild of the document object, and the great-grandchild of the window object. An instance of the hidden object is created for every <INPUT> tag in the current document whose TYPE is "hidden."

All of the hidden objects in a document are indexed along with all other form elements in the elements array. Elements are positioned in this array in the order

Figure 4.4 This Alert dialog is opened above the browser's display window by the onLoad handler script in the page's <FRAMESET> tag.

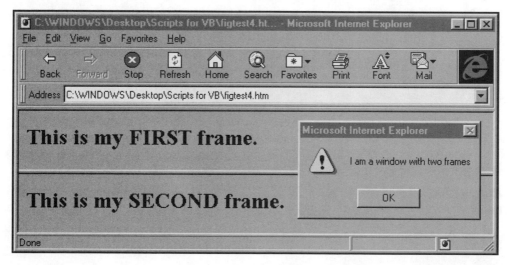

that their tags appear in the parent form. In this example, a hidden object on "thisForm" is actually the fifth element in the elements array:

```
<FORM NAME="thisForm">

<INPUT TYPE="password">   'document.thisForm.elements(0)
<INPUT TYPE="button">     'document.thisForm.elements(1)
<INPUT TYPE="radio">      'document.thisForm.elements(2)
<INPUT TYPE="radio">      'document.thisForm.elements(3)
<INPUT TYPE="hidden">     'document.thisForm.elements(4)

</FORM>
```

Since all form elements, regardless of type, appear together in the elements array, using this array to reference your subordinate form objects is not very intuitive. You'll find it more expedient to name your hidden fields (and all other form objects), so you can refer to them by name in your scripts.

```
<FORM NAME="thisForm">
<INPUT TYPE="hidden" NAME="userKey">

</FORM>
```

Naming the hidden field in the preceding example script allows you to use that name to refer to that hidden field in other scripts:

```
document.thisForm.userKey
```

If you are referring to a hidden field from within its own <INPUT> tag, you don't need to include any reference to the document and form objects:

```
<INPUT TYPE="hidden" NAME="userKey"

onBlur="if userKey.value = '' then

    alert ('Please type your password into the PASSWORD field.')

end if">
```

Properties

name   Sets or gets the name of the hidden field defined by the <INPUT> tag's NAME argument.

value   Sets or gets the contents of the hidden field.

defaultValue   Sets default contents, or gets default contents defined by the <INPUT> tag's VALUE argument.

> **TIP** Hidden objects are extremely useful for storing data during the current browser session. Even if the user leaves the hidden field's page, most browser do not clear form fields in memory until the user quits the application or clicks a reset button (which you can avoid by placing the field in a separate form object, without a reset button). When a user types a proper character string into a Password field, for instance, you can store that string in a hidden field for the duration of the session. Whenever the user navigates back to your page, you can retrieve the password from the hidden field and resubmit it to the server without asking the user to type it again. Saving the information in a variable wouldn't do the trick, since variables are emptied as soon as the resident page is unloaded.

Methods and Event Handling

Hidden objects have no built-in Methods or Event Handlers.

History Object

Term: `history`
Example Syntax:

```
history.length
'total pages in the current window's history list

indexWind.history
'history object for a window named "indexWind"
```

"History" is one of the second-tier objects in the VBScript Object Hierarchy and, as such, is also considered a property of the window object. The history object houses a list of the user's previously visited pages. Only one history object exists at any given time for the browser, and you can access it by simply using its object name:

```
history
```

You can use this list to track the pages the user has visited on your server, and even send the user back to visited pages (useful, for instance, if you created a game or test that spanned multiple pages). You can only navigate to pages in history via position in the list (since the history object has no properties that reveal URLs or page <TITLE> information).

```
<HTML>
<HEAD>

<SCRIPT LANGUAGE="VBScript" FOR="button1" EVENT="onClick()">

    history.back 2
```

```
</SCRIPT>

</HEAD>
<BODY>

<FORM>
Click this button to go back two pages:
<INPUT TYPE="button" NAME="button1" VALUE="2 Steps Back">
</FORM>

</BODY>
</HTML>
```

Properties

length	Gets the total number of pages in the history object.

Methods

back	Moves the user backward in the history list by a specified number of pages.
forward	Moves the user forward in the history list by a specified number of pages.
go	Moves the user to the page that resides at the specified position in the list.

Event Handling

The history object has no assigned Event Handlers.

Image Object

Term: images

Example Syntax:

```
document.images(0)          ' first image in current page
document.links(0).src       ' SRC URL of the first image
```

Images is one of the third-tier objects in the VBScript Object Hierarchy. It is the child of the document object, and the grandchild of the window object. An instance of the image object is created for every <IMG> tag in the current document. All of the image objects in a document are indexed in the images array. Images are positioned in this array in the order that their applicable <IMG> tags appear in the parent document.

The following example script would switch the sourced GIF image for a button created using the first <IMG> tag in a document from an Up position to a Down position.

```
if document.images(0).src = "buttonUp.gif" then

    "buttonDown.gif"  = document.images(0).src

end if
```

Properties
dataFld, dataSrc, className, docHeight, docLeft, docTop, docWidth, parentElement, sourceIndex, tagName, align, alt, border, dynSrc, height, hspace, id, isMap, loop, lowSrc, name, src, style, title, useMap, vrml, vspace, width

Methods
removeMember, scrollIntoView, contains, getMember, setMember

Event Handling
onAbort, onAfterUpdate, onBeforeUpdate, onBlur, onClick, onDblClick, onError, onFocus, onHelp, onKeydown, onKeyPress, onKeyUp, onLoad, onMouseDown, onMouseMove, onMouseOut, onMouseOver, onMouseUp, onReadyStateChange

Link Object
Term: links
Example Syntax: document.links(0)   ' first link in current page
                    document.links(0).href   ' SRC URL of the first anchor

Links is one of the third-tier objects in the VBScript Object Hierarchy. It is the child of the document object, and the grandchild of the window object. An instance of the link object is created for every <ANCHOR> tag in the current document that contains an HREF argument. (Use the anchor object to reference <ANCHOR> tags that include a NAME argument.)

All of the link objects in a document are indexed in the links array. Links are positioned in this array in the order that their applicable <ANCHOR> tags appear in the parent document:

```
<BODY>
<A HREF="doc1.htm">  'document.links(0)
<A HREF="doc2.htm">  'document.links(1)
<A HREF="doc3.htm">  'document.links(2)
<A HREF="doc4.htm">  'document.links(3)
<A NAME="phrase">     'not part of the links array

</BODY>
```

Since an <ANCHOR> tag with an HREF argument cannot be named (its NAME argument is used instead of HREF to target a text string in a current or destination page), the only way to reference a particular link in a document is via its position in the links array. The following example script causes a message to appear in the window's Status Bar when the mouse pointer is placed above the first link in the parent document, if that link's pathname is "/zebras.htm" (see Figure 4.5):

```
<HTML>
<HEAD>

<SCRIPT LANGUAGE="VBScript">

sub show_msg()

    if document.links(0).pathname = "/zebras.htm" then

        status = "Click this hypertext link for information on zebras."

    end if

end sub

</SCRIPT>

</HEAD>
<BODY>

Place the mouse pointer <A HREF="http://www.my.com/zebras.htm"
onMouseOver="show_msg("> HERE </a> and look in the Status bar.

</BODY>
</HTML>
```

Properties

hash	Sets or gets the #hash portion of the URL of the referenced link.
host	Sets or gets the hostname:port portion of the URL of the referenced link.
hostname	Sets or gets the hostname portion of the URL of the referenced link.
href	Sets or gets the complete URL of the referenced link.
length	Gets the total number of links in the referenced document.
pathname	Sets or gets the pathname portion of the URL of the referenced link.
protocol	Sets or gets the protocol portion of the URL of the referenced link.

Figure 4.5 Placing the mouse pointer over the word "here" puts a new message in the window's Status Bar.

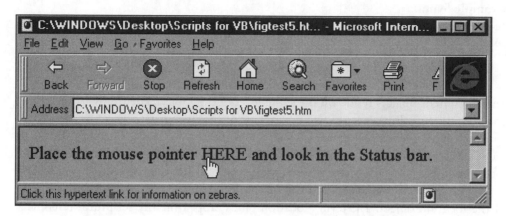

port   Sets or gets the port portion of the URL of the referenced link.

search   Sets or gets the ?search portion of the URL of the referenced link.

target   Sets or gets the name of the target window to display the URL of the referenced link.

Methods and Event Handling

Link objects have no built-in Methods, but you can attach the onClick, onMouseOver, and onMouseMove event handlers to any link object using the link's resident <ANCHOR> tag.

> **TIP** Even though link objects have no name property, the onClick, onMouseMove, and onMouseOver event handlers may still be attached to link objects using the <SCRIPT> tag's EVENT and FOR arguments, or by creating a subroutine that references the object and the handling event. Since the NAME argument in an <ANCHOR> tag is already taken (and used for creating a target for a link), instead of using the link object's name, you can use its ID, as shown in the following example:
>
> ```
> <A HREF="this.htm" ID="thisLink">
>
> <SCRIPT LANGUAGE="VBScript" FOR="thisLink" EVENT="onMouseMove()">
>
>     -- OR --
>
> sub thisLink_onClick()
> ```

Location Object

Term: `location`

Example Syntax:

```
location.href      ' the full URL of the current page
document.location  ' the full URL of the current page
```

Location is one of the second-tier objects in the VBScript Object Hierarchy and, as such, is also considered a property of the window object. Although the location and document objects reside on the same level of the Object Hierarchy—oddly enough, the location object is also a property of the document object.

The location object houses the URL of a referenced window's current HTML document. A location object is created for every HTML file displayed by the browser. The location object is assigned several properties, but no methods and no event handlers.

Unlike the window object, you cannot use implicit syntax to refer to properties of the location object. The term "location" must appear in any scriptural reference to its object properties:

```
currentPort = location.port
current#String = location.hash
```

In its role as a property of the window object, you can use the location object to change the page displayed by the referenced window. Clicking the "Show a Picture..." button created by the following script would create and bring forward a new window called newWind, and set its location object to display a picture called "texas.gif" (see Figure 4.6).

```
<HTML>
<HEAD>

<SCRIPT LANGUAGE="VBScript" FOR="button1" EVENT="onClick()">

    window.open(newWind).location = "http://www.my.com/texas.gif"

</SCRIPT>

</HEAD>
<BODY>

<FORM>
<INPUT TYPE="button" NAME="button1" VALUE="Show a Picture in a Different
Window">
</FORM>

</BODY>
</HTML>
```

Figure 4.6 Clicking the "Show a Picture..." in one window (shown in the background) brought forward a new window with the target picture in it.

Properties

hash	Sets or gets the #hash portion of the URL of the referenced window's current document.
host	Sets or gets the hostname:port portion of the URL of the referenced window's current document.
hostname	Sets or gets the hostname portion of the URL of the referenced window's current document.
href	Sets or gets the complete URL of the referenced window's current document.
pathname	Sets or gets the pathname portion of the URL of the referenced window's current document.
protocol	Sets or gets the protocol portion of the URL of the referenced window's current document.
port	Sets or gets the port portion of the URL of the referenced window's current document.
search	Sets or gets the ?search portion of the URL of the referenced window's current document.

Methods and Event Handling

The location object has no built-in Methods or Event Handlers.

Navigator Object

Term: navigator

Example Syntax: navigator.appName 'name of the current browser

Navigator is one of the second-tier objects in the VBScript Object Hierarchy and, as such, is also considered a property of the window object. The navigator object houses information about the current browser. Only one navigator object exists at any given time for the browser, and you can access it by simply using its object name:

navigator

You can use the browser object to discover, for instance, whether your current visitor is using Internet Explorer. Comment tags hide the VBScript from unaware browsers, that simply skip the lines inside the <SCRIPT> tag and load the rest of the page). Visitors browsing with Internet Explorer, however, are sent on to your "real" home page.

```
<HTML>
<HEAD>

<SCRIPT LANGUAGE="VBScript">
<!--
sub getBrowser()

    if navigator.appName = "Microsoft Internet Explorer" then

    navigate("realHome.htm")

    end if
-->
</SCRIPT>

</HEAD>
<BODY onLoad="getBrowser()">
I'm sorry…but you need Microsoft Internet Explorer to view pages on this Web
site. Please download this free browser from <A
HREF="www.microsoft.com">Microsoft</A> and return.
<p>
Thanks!
</BODY>
</HTML>
```

Properties

appCodeName   Gets the code name of the current browser.

appName   Gets the name of the current browser.

appVersion   Gets the version of the current browser.

userAgent   Gets the user agent information from the current browser.

TIP Use variations of the following script to determine the exact string returned by different properties of the Navigator object for all versions of Internet Explorer and/or Netscape Navigator that you want to script for:

```
<INPUT TYPE="button" onClick="alert (navigator.appCodeName)">
```

Methods and Event Handling

The history object has no assigned Methods or Event Handlers.

<OBJECT> Tag

Term: <OBJECT>

Example Syntax: <OBJECT CLASSID=[registered clsid] NAME="thisOb">' an object embedded in a page

```
      document.thisOb          ' an embedded object named "thisOb"
```

External Objects (e.g., ActiveX controls) that you embed in your Web pages via the <OBJECT> tag automatically become members of the Object Hierarchy. If the embedded object isn't contained within <FORM> tags, it becomes a child of the document object.

If you embed an object within <FORM> tags, that object becomes a member of the elements array, and can thereafter be referenced via its elements array position. The following embedded control named "theObject" becomes the fourth element in thisForm's elements array:

```
<FORM NAME="thisForm">
<INPUT TYPE="password">    'document.thisForm.elements(0)
<INPUT TYPE="button">      'document.thisForm.elements(1)
<INPUT TYPE="radio">       'document.thisForm.elements(2)
<OBJECT NAME="theObject"> 'document.thisForm.elements(3)
<INPUT TYPE="text">        'document.thisForm.elements(4)

</FORM>
```

The embedded object can now be referred to by name or array position:

```
thisForm.elements(3)

-OR-

thisForm.theObject
```

> **TIP** Embedded objects enjoy special status in a VBScript document. For this reason, you needn't refer to the object's parent document when calling that object, regardless of where the calling script resides:
>
> ```
> thisForm.theObject
>
> -INSTEAD OF-
>
> document.thisForm.theObject
> ```

Properties
name   Gets the name of the button defined by the <OBJECT> tag's NAME argument.

Methods and Event Handling
Since external objects are created by third-party code, supported properties, methods, and events vary from object to object. To discover this information for any object, you must read its available documentation.

Options Array
Term: options
Example Syntax: `document.forms(0).select1.options.length`
`'returns the number of options in the select object`

The *options* array object is actually a property of the select object. As such, it is the only object that presently exists on the fifth tier of the Object Hierarchy, below the fourth-tier select object. An options array is automatically created for every set of <SELECT> tags in a document. Each instance of an options array contains the total number of <OPTIONS> belonging to its associated select object.

A given option's position in this array is determined by its position within its enclosing <SELECT> tags. In this example, five options in a select object receive positions in the options array in the order in which they appear within the enclosing <SELECT> tags:

```
<SELECT NAME="choices">

<OPTION> Number 1    'document.thisForm.choices.options(0)
<OPTION> Number 2    'document.thisForm.choices.options(1)
<OPTION> Number 3    'document.thisForm.choices.options(2)
<OPTION> Number 4    'document.thisForm.choices.options(3)
<OPTION> Number 5    'document.thisForm.choices.options(4)

</SELECT>
```

Properties

defaultSelected	Gets the option that is selected by default.
index	Gets the index (position number) of a designated option.
length	Gets the total number of items in the array.
name	Gets or sets the name of the specified option.
selected	Selects the designated option.
selectedIndex	Gets the index (position number) of the selected option.
text	Gets or sets the designated option's display text.
value	Getsor sets the designated option's value.

Methods and Event Handling

Option objects have no built-in Methods or Event Handlers.

Password Object

Term: password
Example Syntax:
```
document.thisForm.elements(2)
' 3rd element in array, which is also a passsword field

document.thisForm.Pword
' a password field in the referenced form named "Pword"
```

Password is one of the fourth-tier objects in the VBScript Object Hierarchy. It is the child of the form object, the grandchild of the document object, and the great-grandchild of the window object. An instance of the password object is created for every <INPUT> tag in the current document whose TYPE is "password."

All of the password objects in a document are indexed along with all other form elements in the elements array. Elements are positioned in this array in the order that their tags appear in the parent form. In this example, the password object on "thisForm" is actually the first element in the elements array:

```
<FORM NAME="thisForm">

<INPUT TYPE="password">    'document.thisForm.elements(0)
<INPUT TYPE="button">      'document.thisForm.elements(1)
<INPUT TYPE="radio">       'document.thisForm.elements(2)
<INPUT TYPE="radio">       'document.thisForm.elements(3)
<INPUT TYPE="text">        'document.thisForm.elements(4)

</FORM>
```

Since all form elements, regardless of type, appear together in the elements array, using this array to reference your subordinate form objects is not very intuitive. You'll find it more expedient to name your password fields (and all other form objects), so you can refer to them by name in your scripts.

```
<FORM NAME="thisForm">

<INPUT TYPE="password" NAME="Pword">

</FORM>
```

Naming the password field in the example script just shown allows you to use that name to refer to that password field in other scripts:

```
document.thisForm.Pword
```

If you are referring to a password field from within its own <INPUT> tag, you don't need to include any reference to the document and form objects:

```
<INPUT TYPE="password" NAME="Pword"

onBlur="if Pword.value = '' then

    alert ('Please type your server password into this field.')

end if">
```

Properties

form	Gets the forms array position of the password field's parent form.
name	Sets or gets the name of the password field defined by the <INPUT> tag's NAME argument.
value	Sets or gets the contents of the password field.
defaultValue	Sets default contents, or gets default contents defined by the <INPUT> tag's VALUE argument.

Methods

focus   Sets the application focus to the specified password field, as if the user clicked it.

blur   Removes the application focus from the specified password field, as if the user left it.

select   Highlights the contents of the specified password field, as if the user manually selected its text.

Event Handling

Password objects have no built-in Event Handlers.

Plugins Array

Term: plugins
Example Syntax:
```
document.plugins(5)
' sixth embedded plugin in the current document
```

Plugins refers to all of the objects in the VBScript Object Hierarchy that are embedded via the <PLUGIN> tag.

Properties

className, docHeight, docLeft, docTop, docWidth, parentElement, sourceIndex, tagName, accessKey, align, height, id, style, title, width

Methods

removeMember, scrollIntoView, contains, getMember, setMember

Event Handling

onAfterUpdate, onBeforeUpdate, onBlur, onClick, onDblClick, onFocus, onHelp, onKeydown, onKeyPress, onKeyUp, onLoad, onMouseDown, onMouseMove, onMouseOut, onMouseOver, onMouseUp, onReadyStateChange

Radio Object

Term: radio
Example Syntax:
```
document.thisForm.elements(3)
' 4th element in the array, which is also a radio button
```

Radio is one of the fourth-tier objects in the VBScript Object Hierarchy. It is the child of the form object, the grandchild of the document object, and the great-grandchild of the window object. An instance of the radio object is created for every <INPUT> tag in the current document whose TYPE is "radio."

All of the radio objects in a document are indexed along with all other form elements in the elements array. Elements are positioned in this array in the order that their tags appear in the parent form. In this example, the two radio objects on "thisForm" are actually the third and fourth elements in the elements array:

```
<FORM NAME="thisForm">

<INPUT TYPE="password">  'document.thisForm.elements(0)
<INPUT TYPE="button">    'document.thisForm.elements(1)
<INPUT TYPE="radio">     'document.thisForm.elements(2)
<INPUT TYPE="radio">     'document.thisForm.elements(3)
<INPUT TYPE="hidden">    'document.thisForm.elements(4)

</FORM>
```

By definition, radio buttons come in groups of two or more, and each radio in a group is assigned the same name in order to affiliate it with its group. At any given time, only one radio in a given group may be checked—making radio buttons the ideal objects for processing mutually exclusive choices like yes/no.

Because of the HTML convention which requires you to give the *exact same name* to each radio in a group, you cannot effectively refer to a radio object by its name in your scripts. Instead, you can either place radio-specific scripts inside the <INPUT> tag of the target radio, or use the radio's elements array position to point to it. The following example creates a form with three groups of yes/no radio buttons:

```
<FORM NAME="thisForm">

<ol>

<li>Do you like chocolate cake?
<INPUT TYPE="radio" NAME="Q1" VALUE="Yes">
<INPUT TYPE="radio" NAME="Q1" VALUE="No">

<li>Do you like vanilla pudding?
<INPUT TYPE="radio" NAME="Q2" VALUE="Yes">
<INPUT TYPE="radio" NAME="Q2" VALUE="No">

<li>Do you like liver and onions?
<INPUT TYPE="radio" NAME="Q3" VALUE="Yes">
<INPUT TYPE="radio" NAME="Q3" VALUE="No">

</ol>

</FORM>
```

You would then use the following elements array positions to refer to the various radio objects in the form:

```
document.thisForm.elements(0)    'Answers Yes to Question 1
document.thisForm.elements(1)    'Answers No to Question 1
document.thisForm.elements(2)    'Answers Yes to Question 2
document.thisForm.elements(3)    'Answers No to Question 2
document.thisForm.elements(4)    'Answers Yes to Question 3
document.thisForm.elements(5)    'Answers No to Question 3
```

If you are referring to a radio from within its own <INPUT> tag, you don't need to include any reference to the document and form objects, although you still need to reference its array position:

```
<INPUT TYPE="radio" NAME="Q3" VALUE="Yes"

onClick="if elements(4).checked = 1 then

    confirm ('Are you kidding?')

end if">
```

Repeat loops may be effectively used to discover which radio in a particular group is currently checked. The following scriptlet, for instance, looks at the yes/no radios for Question 1 (in our previous example), and places a pointer to the currently checked radio into the *isChecked* variable. An isChecked2 and an isChecked3 variable could be named to house the currently selected answer to the other two questions.

```
for count = 0 to 1

    if document.thisForm.elements(count).checked then

        isChecked1 = document.thisForm.elements(count).value
        exit for

    end if

next
```

Properties

form   Gets the forms array position of the checkbox's parent form.

value   Sets or gets the display name of the radio defined by the <INPUT> tag's VALUE argument.

checked   Sets or gets the status of the radio; returns a 1 if checked and a
              0 if not checked.

defaultChecked   Sets or gets the default status of the radio; returns "true" if
                  checked by default and "false" if not checked.

Methods
click   Simulates a user-click on the referenced checkbox.

Event Handling
The onClick event handler may be attached to radio objects by using the handler as
an argument inside the radio's own <INPUT> tag:

```
<INPUT TYPE="checkbox" NAME="checkbox1" onClick="doThis()">
```

> **WARNING** Since radio objects do not (and cannot) have their own
> individual names, you can't assign a subroutine to a radio button, or use
> the <SCRIPT> tag's FOR and EVENT arguments on its behalf, because
> both procedures require the object to have a unique name:
>
> ```
> sub ObjectName_ProcessingEvent
> ```

Reset Object
Term: reset
Example Syntax:
```
document.forms(0).elements(9)
'ninth element in the array, which is a reset button

document.forms(0).theReset
'refers to reset button whose name is "theReset"
```

Reset is one of the fourth-tier objects in the VBScript Object Hierarchy. It is the
child of the form object, the grandchild of the document object, and the great-
grandchild of the window object. An instance of the reset object is created for every
<INPUT> tag in the current document whose TYPE is "reset."

All of the reset objects in a document are indexed along with all other form elements in the elements array. Elements are positioned in this array in the order that
their tags appear in the parent form. In this example, the reset button on
"thisForm" is actually the fifth element in the elements array:

```
<FORM NAME="thisForm">

<INPUT TYPE="password"> 'document.thisForm.elements(0)
<INPUT TYPE="button">    'document.thisForm.elements(1)
```

```
<TEXTAREA ROW=2 COL=20>  'document.thisForm.elements(2)
<INPUT TYPE="submit">     'document.thisForm.elements(3)
<INPUT TYPE="reset">      'document.thisForm.elements(4)
```

```
</FORM>
```

Since all form elements, regardless of type, appear together in the elements array, using this array to reference your subordinate form objects is not very intuitive. You'll find it more expedient to name your reset button (and all other form objects), so you can refer to it by name in your scripts.

```
<FORM NAME="thisForm">
```

```
<INPUT TYPE="reset" NAME="theReset" VALUE="Clear Form">
```

```
</FORM>
```

If you are referring to a reset button from within its own <INPUT> tag, you don't need to include any reference to the document and form objects. The following tag creates a reset button that says "Clear Form." Clicking the "Clear Form" button changes its displayed name to "Clear Again."

```
<INPUT TYPE="reset" NAME="theReset" VALUE="Clear Form" onClick="theReset.value =
'Clear Again'">
```

Properties

form	Gets the forms array position of the reset button's parent form.
name	Sets or gets the name of the reset button defined by the <INPUT> tag's NAME argument.
value	Sets or gets the display name of the reset button defined by the <INPUT> tag's VALUE argument.

Methods

click	Simulates a user-click on the referenced reset button.

Event Handling

The onClick event handler may be attached to reset objects using the <SCRIPT> tag's EVENT and FOR arguments, or by creating a subroutine that references the object and the handling event, or by using the handler as an argument inside the object's own <INPUT> tag. When using the first two methods, you can dispense with the document and form reference, and simply use the object's name.

```
<SCRIPT LANGUAGE="VBScript" FOR="theReset" EVENT="onClick()">

    -- OR --

sub theReset_onClick()

    -- OR --

<INPUT TYPE="reset" NAME="theReset" VALUE="Clear Me" onClick="doThis()">
```

Script Object

Script is one of the third-tier objects in the VBScript Object Hierarchy. The placement of a script object within a document can affect the relationships of other objects. For instance, under ordinary circumstances, a button object on a form is referenced using a pathname that leads from its grandparent object (the document) through its parent object (the form) to the object itself (the button):

```
document.formName.buttonName
```

However, if you place a script that calls the button anywhere between that button's <FORM> tags, you can dispense with the hierarchical formalities and simply refer to it as:

```
buttonName
```

You can place a script inside a form by enclosing it in <SCRIPT> tags, but it is generally considered a better, more orderly coding strategy to place <SCRIPT> tags in the <HEAD> of your document. This is especially important as future browsers come on board with VBScript, since these browsers may process HTML documents differently than Internet Explorer. Placing <SCRIPT> tags in the <HEAD> of a document is safer in general, since all browsers load the <HEAD> portion of a document before loading its <BODY>. This placement policy eliminates the possibility that a user might take an action on the page (while it's still loading), and the browser won't be able to find a referenced script (because it's not yet loaded).

Another, less risky way to attach a script object to a form is to place it inside a form element tag, as an answer to an event handler argument. From this scripting vantage point, you can also informally address the form's elements:

```
<INPUT TYPE="button" NAME="myButton" VALUE="Hello"
onClick="myButton.value='Good-bye'">
```

Properties
className, docHeight, docLeft, docTop, docWidth, parentElement, sourceIndex, tagName, event, for, id, in, language, library, title

Select Object
Term: select
Example Syntax:
```
document.thisForm.elements(3)
' fourth element in array, which is also a select object

document.thisForm.select1
' a select object in the referenced form named "select1"
```

Select is one of the fourth-tier objects in the VBScript Object Hierarchy. It is the child of the form object, the grandchild of the document object, and the great-grandchild of the window object. An instance of the hidden object is created for every <SELECT> tag in the current document.

All of the select objects in a document are indexed along with all other form elements in the elements array. Elements are positioned in this array in the order that their tags appear in the parent form. In this example, a select object on "thisForm" is actually the third element in the elements array:

```
<FORM NAME-"thisForm">

<INPUT TYPE="password"> 'document.thisForm.elements(0)
<INPUT TYPE="button">   'document.thisForm.elements(1)
<SELECT SIZE=2>         'document.thisForm.elements(2)
<OPTION>                'document.thisForm.elements(2).options(0)
<OPTION>                'document.thisForm.elements(2).options(1)
</SELECT>               'counted in the array by its opening tag

</FORM>
```

Since all form elements, regardless of type, appear together in the elements array, using this array to reference your subordinate form objects is not very intuitive. You'll find it more expedient to name your select objects (and all other form objects), so you can refer to them by name in your scripts.

```
<FORM NAME="thisForm">

<SELECT SIZE=1 NAME="OSType">

<OPTION>Windows 95
```

```
<OPTION>Macintosh
<OPTION>UNIX

</SELECT>

</FORM>
```

Naming the select object in the example script just shown allows you to use that name to refer to that select object in other scripts:

```
document.thisForm.OSType
```

If you are referring to a select object from within its own <SELECT> tag, you don't need to include any reference to the document and form objects, as shown in the following script (whose results appear in Figure 4.7):

```
<SELECT SIZE=2 NAME="OSType"

onChange="if (OSType.selectedIndex = 0) then

    alert ('Congratulations! You are a Windows User.')
```

Figure 4.7 Different alerts are displayed, depending on the option chosen from the Select object.

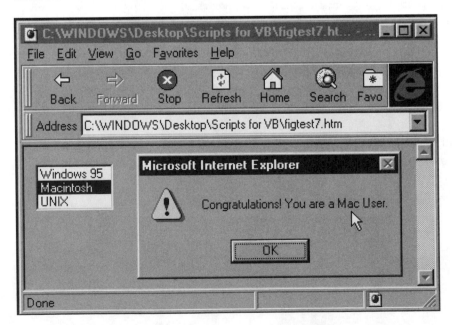

```
elseif (OSType.selectedIndex = 1) then

        alert ('Congratulations! You are a Mac User.')

else

    alert ('Congratulations! You are a UNIX User.')

end if">
```

> **TIP** Internet Explorer currently has some trouble processing quoted strings inside handler argument/answer pairs. Since HTML requires double quotes around answers that are literal strings, any quoted strings in your handler's answering script must take single quotes (as discussed in Chapter 3). While this problem is intermittent, it occurred in testing the Select object example script. The single-quoted strings inside the alert method's parens (the "Congratulations" messages) caused Internet Explorer to choke (return an error). If you have trouble with a similarly structured script, you can declare a global variable, transfer each quoted string from the handler's answering script to its associated variable, then use the name of the variable in its place. Here's how the Select object script was rewritten to work around this interpreter problem:
>
> ```
> <HTML>
> <HEAD>
> <SCRIPT LANGUAGE="VBScript">
>
> DIM msg1, msg2, msg3
>
> msg1 = "Congratulations! You are a Windows User."
> msg2 = "Congratulations! You are a Mac User."
> msg3 = "Congratulations! You are a UNIX User."
>
> </SCRIPT>
> </HEAD>
> <BODY>
> <FORM>
>
> <SELECT SIZE=3 NAME="OSType"
>
> onChange="if (OSType.selectedIndex = 0) then
>
>     alert (msg1)
>
> elseif (OSType.selectedIndex = 1) then
> ```

```
    alert (msg2)

else

    alert (msg3)

end if">

<OPTION>Windows 95
<OPTION>Macintosh
<OPTION>UNIX

</SELECT>
</FORM>
</BODY>
</HTML>
```

Properties

name	Sets or gets the name of the select object defined by the <SELECT> tag's NAME argument.
length	The number of options assigned to the specified select object.
defaultSelected	Sets or Gets the default option.
selectedIndex	Sets or Gets the selected option; if multiple options are selected, returns first selected option.
options array	An array of the select object's associated options.

Methods

blur	Removes the application focus from the specified select object, as if the user moved away from it.
focus	Sets the application focus to the specified select object, as if the user clicked and held the mouse down.

Event Handling

The onChange, onBlur, and onFocus event handlers may be attached to select objects using the <SCRIPT> tag's EVENT and FOR arguments, or by creating a subroutine that references the object and the handling event, or by using the handler as an argument inside the object's own <INPUT> tag. When using the first two methods, you can dispense with the document and form reference, and simply use the object's name.

```
<SCRIPT LANGUAGE="VBScript" FOR="theChoices" EVENT="onClick()">

    -- OR --

sub theChoices_onClick()

    -- OR --

<SELECT NAME="theReset" onClick="doThis()">
```

Selection Object
Term: `selection`
Example Syntax:
```
document.selection
'refers to submit button whose name is "submitButton "
```

Selection is one of the third-tier objects in the VBScript Object Hierarchy. It is the child of the document object, and the grandchild of the window object. It returns a string representing any currently selected text in a cascading style sheet page.

Properties
type

Methods
clear, empty, createRange

Event Handling
Selection objects have no built-in Event Handlers.

Submit Object
Term: `submit`
Example Syntax:
```
document.forms(0).elements(8)
'eighth element in the array, which is a submit button

document.forms(0).submitButton
'refers to submit button whose name is "submitButton "
```

Submit is one of the fourth-tier objects in the VBScript Object Hierarchy. It is the child of the form object, the grandchild of the document object, and the great-grandchild of the window object. An instance of the submit object is created for every <INPUT> tag in the current document whose TYPE is "submit."

All of the submit objects in a document are indexed along with all other form elements in the elements array. Elements are positioned in this array in the order that their tags appear in the parent form. In this example, the "Submit" button on "thisForm" is also the fourth element in the elements array:

```
<FORM NAME="thisForm">


<INPUT TYPE="password">  'document.thisForm.elements(0)
<INPUT TYPE="button">     'document.thisForm.elements(1)
<TEXTAREA ROW=2 COL=20>  'document.thisForm.elements(2)
<INPUT TYPE="submit">     'document.thisForm.elements(3)


</FORM>
```

Since the submit object creates a button used to submit the form to the server, there is usually only one instance of a "Submit" button per form. You might, however, create multiple "Submit" buttons for the user to click, depending on submission type. For instance, you might create an order form with one "Submit" button for placing an order, and another for simply requesting information. Then, you could provide separate VBScripting for each type of submission.

```
<FORM NAME="thisForm">

<INPUT TYPE="submit" NAME="Order" VALUE="Submit Order" onClick="doOrder()">

<INPUT TYPE="submit" NAME="Info" VALUE="Request Info" onClick="doInfo()">

</FORM>
```

Giving names to the multiple "Submit" buttons in the preceding example script allows you to use those names to refer to the buttons elsewhere:

```
document.thisForm.Order
document.thisForm.Info
```

If you are referring to a "Submit" button from within its own <INPUT> tag, you don't need to include any reference to the document and form objects:

```
<INPUT TYPE="submit" NAME=" Order" VALUE="Submit Order" onClick="Order.value =
'Thanks!'">
```

Properties

form   Gets the forms array position of the "Submit" button's parent form.

name   Sets or gets the name of the submit object defined by the <INPUT> tag's NAME argument.

value   Sets or gets the display name of the "Submit" button defined by the <INPUT> tag's VALUE argument.

Methods

click   Simulates a user-click on the referenced "Submit" button.

Event Handling

The onClick event handler may be attached to submit objects using the <SCRIPT> tag's EVENT and FOR arguments, or by creating a subroutine that references the object and the handling event, or by using the handler as an argument inside the object's own <INPUT> tag. When using the first two methods, you can dispense with the document and form reference, and simply use the object's name.

```
<SCRIPT LANGUAGE="VBScript" FOR="theSubmit" EVENT="onClick()">

    -- OR --

sub theSubmit_onClick()

    -- OR --

<INPUT TYPE="submit" NAME=" theSubmit" VALUE="Submit Order" onClick="doThis()">
```

> **TIP** If you want to display your own (or someone else's) icon instead of the browser's built-in icon for the submit object, you can answer "image" to the TYPE argument, and use the SRC and ALIGN arguments to point to the source picture file, and determine its alignment on the page. In this instance, you'd dispense with the VALUE argument, since its answer won't be displayed. In its stead, you should be sure that your artwork provides either a display name for the button or some other visual cue to its purpose.
>
> ```
> <INPUT TYPE="image" SRC="this.gif" ALIGN="left" NAME="Order">
> ```

Text Object

Term: text
Example Syntax:

```
document.thisForm.elements(2)
' third element in the array, which is also a text field

document.thisForm.Address
' a field in the referenced form named "Address"
```

Text is one of the fourth-tier objects in the VBScript Object Hierarchy. It is the child of the form object, the grandchild of the document object, and the great-grandchild of the window object. An instance of the text object is created for every <INPUT> tag in the current document whose TYPE is "text."

All of the text objects in a document are indexed along with all other form elements in the elements array. Elements are positioned in this array in the order that their tags appear in the parent form. In this example, the text objects on "thisForm" are actually the first and fifth elements in the elements array:

```
<FORM NAME="thisForm">

<INPUT TYPE="text">    'document.thisForm.elements(0)
<INPUT TYPE="button"> 'document.thisForm.elements(1)
<INPUT TYPE="radio">   'document.thisForm.elements(2)
<INPUT TYPE="radio">   'document.thisForm.elements(3)
<INPUT TYPE="text">    'document.thisForm.elements(4)

</FORM>
```

Since all form elements, regardless of type, appear together in the elements array, using this array to reference your subordinate form objects is not very intuitive. You'll find it more expedient to name your text fields (and all other form objects), so you can refer to them by name in your scripts.

```
<FORM NAME="thisForm">

<INPUT TYPE="text" NAME="Name">
<INPUT TYPE="text" NAME="Address">
<INPUT TYPE="text" NAME="Phone">

</FORM>
```

Giving names to the text fields in the preceding example script allows you to use those names to refer to those fields in other scripts:

```
document.thisForm.Name
document.thisForm.Address
document.thisForm.Phone
```

If you are referring to a field from within its own <INPUT> tag, you don't need to include any reference to the document and form objects. (The results of the following script are shown in Figure 4.8.)

```
<INPUT TYPE="text" NAME="Address"

onBlur="if Address.value = '' then

    alert ('Please type your address into this field.')

end if">
```

Figure 4.8 If the user clicks or tabs out of the Address field, and the field is still empty, an alert advises the user to type an address into the field. (In a real-life page, you should provide a wider field.)

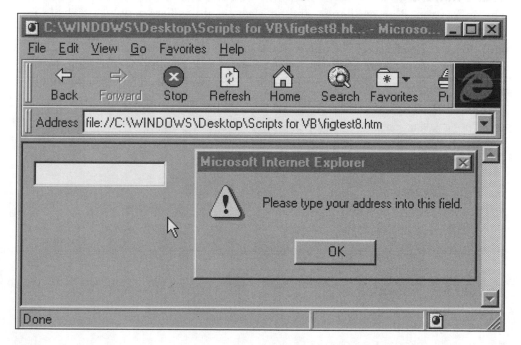

Properties

form	Gets the forms array position of the text field's parent form.
name	Sets or gets the name of the text field defined by the <INPUT> tag's NAME argument.
value	Sets or gets the contents of the text field.
defaultValue	Sets default contents, or gets default contents defined by the <INPUT> tag's VALUE argument.

Methods

focus	Sets the application focus to the specified field, as if the user clicked it.
blur	Removes the application focus from the specified field, as if the user left it.
select	Highlights the contents of the specified field, as if the user manually selected the text.

Event Handling

The onFocus, onBlur, onChange, and onSelect event handlers may be attached to text fields using the <SCRIPT> tag's EVENT and FOR arguments, or by creating a subroutine that references the object and handling event, or by using any of these handlers as an argument inside the object's own <INPUT> tag. When using the first two methods, you can dispense with the document and form reference and simply use the object's name.

```
<SCRIPT LANGUAGE="VBScript" FOR="thisField" EVENT="onFocus">

    -- OR --

sub thisField_onFocus

    -- OR --

<INPUT TYPE="text" NAME="thisField" onFocus="doThis()">
```

Textarea Object

Term: textarea
Example Syntax:
```
document.thisForm.elements(2)
' third element in array, which is also a textarea field
```

```
document.thisForm.Comments
' a textarea field in the referenced form named "Comments"
```

Textarea is one of the fourth-tier objects in the VBScript Object Hierarchy. It is the child of the form object, the grandchild of the document object, and the great-grandchild of the window object. An instance of the textarea object is created for every <TEXTAREA> tag in the current document.

All of the textarea objects (or multiple-line fields) in a document are indexed along with all other form elements in the elements array. Elements are positioned in this array in the order that their tags appear in the parent form. In this example, the textarea object on "thisForm" is actually the fourth element in the elements array:

```
<FORM NAME="thisForm">


<INPUT TYPE="text">        'document.thisForm.elements(0)
<INPUT TYPE="button">      'document.thisForm.elements(1)
<INPUT TYPE="radio">       'document.thisForm.elements(2)
<TEXTAREA ROWS=4 COLS=20>  'document.thisForm.elements(3)
<INPUT TYPE="text">        'document.thisForm.elements(4)


</FORM>
```

Since all form elements, regardless of type, appear together in the elements array, using this array to reference your subordinate form objects is not very intuitive. You'll find it more expedient to name your textareas (and all other form objects), so you can refer to them by name in your scripts.

```
<FORM NAME="thisForm">

<TEXTAREA ROWS=4 COLS=20 NAME="Comments">

</FORM>
```

Naming the textarea object in the preceding example script allows you to use that name to refer to that textarea in other scripts:

```
document.thisForm.Comments
```

If you are referring to a textarea from within its own <TEXTAREA> tag, you don't need to include any reference to the document and form objects. (The results of the following script are shown in Figure 4.9.)

```
<TEXTAREA NAME="Comments"

onChange="if Comments.value <> '' then

    alert ('Thank you for your comments.')

end if">
```

Properties

form   Gets the forms array position of the textarea's parent form.

name   Sets or gets the name of the textarea defined by the <TEXTAREA>
              tag's NAME argument.

value   Sets or gets the contents of the textarea.

defaultValue Sets default contents, or gets the default contents defined between
              the <TEXTAREA></TEXTAREA> tags.

**Figure 4.9 If the user clicks or tabs out of the Address field after
making changes to that field, and the field is NOT empty, an alert
thanks the user for the comments.**

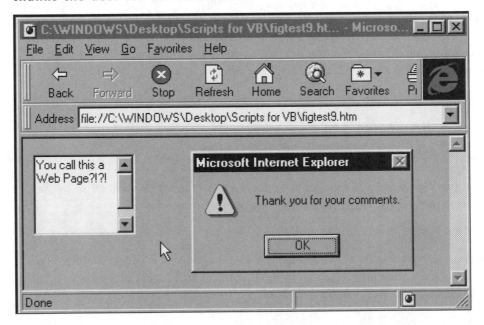

Methods

focus — Sets the application focus to the specified textarea, as if the user clicked it.

blur — Removes the application focus from the specified textarea, as if the user left it.

select — Highlights the contents of the specified textarea field, as if the user manually selected its text.

Event Handling

The onFocus, onBlur, onChange, and onSelect event handlers may be attached to textarea fields using the <SCRIPT> tag's EVENT and FOR arguments, or by creating a subroutine that references the object and handling event, or by using any of these handlers as an argument inside the object's own <INPUT> tag. When using the first two methods, you can dispense with the document and form reference and simply use the object's name.

```
<SCRIPT LANGUAGE="VBScript" FOR="thisArea" EVENT="onFocus">

    -- OR --

sub thisArea_onFocus

    -- OR --

<TEXTAREA NAME="thisArea" onFocus="doThis()">
```

TextRange Object

Term: textRange
Example Syntax:
```
document.thisForm.elements(2)
' third element in the array, which is also a text field

document.thisForm.Address
' a field in the referenced form named "Address"
```

TextRange is not included in the VBScript Object Hierarchy. It represents the entire stream of text that is fed to the browser as the HTML script for that page.

Properties

text, htmlText, end, start, htmlSelText

Methods

queryCommandSupported, queryCommandIndeterm, duplicate, inRange, isEqual, scrollIntoView, collapse, expand, move, moveEnd, moveStart, setRange, select, parentElement, commonParentElement, execCommand, queryCommandEnabled, queryCommandText, isEmbed, queryCommandState, pasteHTML

Event Handling

The textRange object accepts no events.

Visual Object

Term: visual

Example Syntax: visual.colorDepth 'returns bit-depth of the current screen

Visual is one of the second-tier objects in the VBScript Object Hierarchy and, as such, is also considered a property of the window object. The visual object houses information about the current monitor. Only one visual object exists at any given time for the browser, and you can access it by simply using its object name:

```
visual
```

You can use the visual object to discover, for instance, whether your current visitor has a color monitor:

```
<SCRIPT LANGUAGE="VBScript">
<!--
sub isColor()

    if visual.colorDepth > 2 then

        navigate("colorpages.htm")

    else

        navigate("bwpages.htm")

    end if

end sub
-->
</SCRIPT>
```

Properties

bufferDepth	Gets the code name of the current browser.
colorDepth	Gets the bit-depth of the current monitor.
hres	Gets the horizontal resolution of the current monitor.
vres	Gets the vertical resolution of the current monitor.

Methods and Event Handling

The visual object has no assigned Methods or Event Handlers.

Window Object

Term: `window`

Example Syntax:

```
window.open        'opens a new window

self.location      'the URL of the current window's document
```

Window refers to the top-level object in the VBScript Object Hierarchy. It belongs to the browser, which automatically creates this object by simply opening a window. A separate window object is created for each window the browser opens.

You may reference your currently open windows in VBScript using any of the aforementioned syntax formats. The keyword "self" is an alternative term used to refer to the window containing the executing script. When referring to the executing script's window, however, scripters ordinarily use the third format, which doesn't explicitly reference the window object at all. When you use this latter format (referring, say, to the alert() method without using the term "window"), the executing script assumes you are calling its resident window.

To access a foreign window (that doesn't contain the executing script), you can use the term "top" (to refer to the topmost window in a frameset), or "parent" (to refer to the window that created the current window).

Your scripts can only access windows created by those scripts, or that contain your scripted documents. To access one of your windows that is neither the top window in a frameset nor the parent to a window you've created, you'll need to call that window by name. Of course, you can only do so if you give the window a name when you create it.

> **TIP** If you routinely name your windows, you'll always have the option of calling any window's script from scripts in other windows.

There are three ways to name your windows:

1. You can pass an answer to the open method's target argument:

```
newWindow = window.open("http://www.me.com/this.htm","thisWindow")
```

2. You can provide an answer to the <FRAME> tag's NAME argument when creating a frameset:

```
<FRAMESET ROWS="25%,75%">
  <FRAME NAME="FirstFrame" SRC="First.htm">
  <FRAME NAME="SecondFrame" SRC="Second.htm">
</FRAMESET>
```

3. You can provide an answer to the <ANCHOR> tag's TARGET argument:

```
<A HREF="Order.htm" TARGET="OrderWindow">
```

If for any reason you fail to name a window when you create it, you can name it "on-the-fly" by placing this statement into any script:

```
name = "[newName]"
```

The problem with this method of naming is that the window's new name only exists for the current page's script. Scripts executed from other windows won't be able to use its new name to refer to the window that is named "on-the-fly."

```
Dim windName
name = "newName"
windName = name
```

Once a window has a valid name, you can access that name using the window name property. For example, if you place this script in the <HEAD> of an HTML page, it'll generate an Alert dialog containing the new name of the window displaying the page (see Figure 4.10):

```
<SCRIPT LANGUAGE="VBScript">

Dim windName
name = "newName"
windName = name

alert(name)

</SCRIPT>
```

Figure 4.10 This Alert dialog displays the name of the current window as soon as it loads the page containing its script.

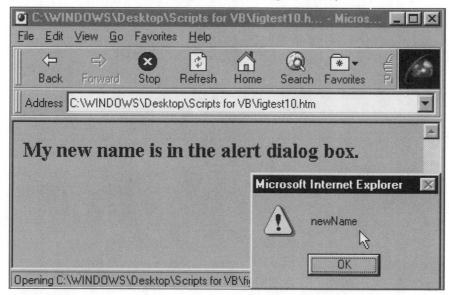

Properties

closed	Returns "true" if the referenced window is closed.
defaultStatus	Sets the default message to be displayed in the Status Bar of the referenced window.
document	The document on display in the referenced window.
frames	Gets the frames array for the referenced window.
history	Gets the history list for the referenced window.
location	The URL of the document in the referenced window.
name	The name of the script's resident window.
navigator	The current browser application.
opener	The window that opened the current window; or, if none, the current window.
parent	The window that created the current window; or, if none, the current window.
self	The current window.
top	The topmost window in a frameset; or, if none, the current window.
status	Sets a message to be displayed in the Status Bar of the referenced window.

Methods

alert	Opens an Alert dialog above the referenced window.
blur	Causes the referenced element to lose the document focus.
focus	Set the document focus to the referenced element.
clearTimeout	Stops the execution of SetTimeout.
close	Closes the referenced window.
confirm	Opens a Confirmation dialog above the referenced window.
fireOnLoad	Sends the load event.
fireOnUnload	Sends the unload event.
item	Gets the ordinal position or the name of the requested element.
navigate	Loads the document of a specified URL into the referenced window.
open	Creates a new browser window.
prompt	Opens a User-prompt dialog above the referenced window.
scroll	Gets the current value of the document's scroll property.
setTimeout	Sets a timer to call a function after a specified number of milliseconds.
showModalDialog	Displays an HTML dialog.

Event Handling

You can attach the onLoad, onUnload, onFocus, onBlur, and onHelp event handlers to window objects via the <BODY> and <FRAMESET> tags. The following script contained within the <BODY> opens the Alert dialog shown in Figure 4.11 as soon as the page is loaded into the browser window:

```
<BODY onLoad="alert('Here I am!')">
```

You can also attach the onUnload event to the window using the <SCRIPT> tag's EVENT and FOR arguments, or by creating a subroutine that references the window (by name, or by window, if it's the current window) and its handling event.

```
<SCRIPT LANGUAGE="VBScript" FOR="window" EVENT="onUnload">

    -- OR --

sub window_onUnload
```

Figure 4.11 This Alert dialog is opened above the browser's display window by the onLoad handler script in the page's <BODY> tag.

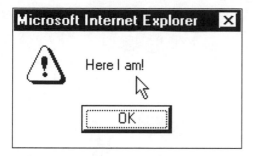

What's Next?

With the general arsenal of VBScript objects well in hand, the next chapter provides additional information on the type, contents, and use of the object properties described in this chapter. Included are some of the additional properties made available as a result of the dynamic HTML model. Many of the property descriptions include example scripts and tips for using the object.property relationship to its fullest in your own code.

5

Object Properties

With the advent of DHTML came the addition of almost 200 new properties to the VBScript lexicon. Many of these new properties were listed with their associated objects in Chapter 4's descriptions of each Object in the VBScript Object Hierarchy. To further your knowledge of the use of these properties, this chapter presents a detailed look at many of the VBScript properties, including its spelling, use, example syntax, and short example scripts (as needed).

> **W W W** For a complete list of all of the properties that are now exposed to the VBScript engine, check Microsoft's online documentation at:
>
> www.microsoft.com/workshop/author/dynhtml/

The Built-In Properties of VBScript Objects

For easy reference, the VBScript Properties that are presented in this chapter are organized in alphabetical order; not according to the Objects they support. The latter approach would be doubly difficult since (as you may have already noted in your review of Chapter 4) many Properties are assigned to multiple Objects. For instance, the Name property is assigned to almost every member of the Object Hierarchy. For this reason, each Property definition in this chapter also includes a list of its assigned Objects, as well as any variable information regarding the use of that Property with different Objects.

As you learned in Chapter 2, Properties behave very much like variables. Both are virtual containers created in your computer's memory to hold specified *values* (pieces of information). When you invoke a built-in Property for a given Object (e.g., Name), it reveals information regarding a characteristic of that Object (in this example, its name). Using the property feature of objects, you can retrieve (or, in some cases, set) object characteristics by simply using the name of the property and its associated object:

```
object.property
```

Like static variables, some Property values are set in stone and cannot be changed. Such Properties are described in this Chapter as *read-only*, which means you can only "get" its associated value. Other Properties behave more like nonstatic variables, and can be changed by scripting actions. Properties with this capacity are described as *read-write*, which means you can "get" or "set" its associated value using VBScript.

Even before Microsoft and Netscape put the word "dynamic" into HTML, most VBScript and JavaScript objects were already the work of an HTML tag whose arguments became that object's properties (or, in some cases, methods). With DHTML's exposure of virtually every tag in the HTML specification came an explosion of additional properties. In every case, however, these properties are merely the original tag's arguments; and, in every case, they may be referenced in your VBScripts by attaching the target argument to its tag's name or pseudonym:

```
<IMG ID="thisImg" BORDER=0 SRC="this.gif">
alert thisImg.src      ' presents "this.gif" in an alert dialog box
```

Thus, to know the new DHTML properties, you only need to know your HTML—or refer to Microsoft's online reference of HTML tags and attributes supported by Internet Explorer.

W W W   Internet Explorer's HTML documentation may be found at:

www.microsoft.com/workshop/author/newhtml/default.htm

Action Property

Term: action

Example Syntax:

`document.formName.action 'URL that receives the submitted form`

Type: read-write

Assigned Objects: form

The action property gets or sets the answer to the <FORM> tag's ACTION argument, which is the URL of the server application that receives the submitted form.

```
document.forms(0).action = "http://www.this.com/bin/procOrder.cgi"
'sets the form's action address to a cgi script called "procOrder," in the "bin"
directory on the "www.this.com" server
```

```
ACTION="mailto:mjmara@onr.com?subject=Order"
```

> **TIP** If you're looking for very simple forms processing, you don't need a server-side application to process the submitted form. Instead, you can set a "mailto:" address for the action property, and a "text/plain" MIME type for the encoding property (see "Encoding" definition). Together, these two settings cause the form to be sent as an e-mail message to the specified online address:
>
> ```
> document.forms(0).action = "mailto:mjmara@onr.com?subject=Order"
> document.forms(0).encoding = "text/plain"
> ```

ALinkColor Property

Term: aLinkColor

Example Syntax:

`document.aLinkColor`
`'display color of active links in the current document`

Type: read-write

Assigned Objects: document.

The aLinkColor property gets or sets the color used to display clicked-and-held hypertext links in the current document. A *clicked-and-held link* is one that the user has clicked and not yet released (i.e., continues to hold the mouse button down on). As long as the mouse button remains down on the link, the link is considered active. Some browsers support an active link state in order to give users additional, visual feedback on their clicking activities. (Internet Explorer does *not* support active links.) For browsers that support active links, the aLinkColor can be set using any of the allowed color literals listed in Appendix B, or using the hexadecimal equivalent of the desired color.

```
document.aLinkColor = "green"

-OR-

document.aLinkColor = "008000" 'also evaluates to green
```

The following script displays the hexadecimal equivalent of the document's currently set active link color in an alert dialog when the page is loaded into the browser:

```
<BODY onLoad="alert(document.aLinkColor)">
```

> **N O T E** Active links are not supported in the current version of Internet Explorer, but Microsoft includes the aLinkColor property in the VBScript language ". . . for compatibility reasons." Presumably this is so the aLinkColor property can be used in scripting pages for VBScript-aware browsers that *do* support active links. Plus, it provides for the possibility that future versions of Internet Explorer may support active links.

AppCodeName Property

Term: appCodeName

Example Syntax:

```
navigator.appCodeName
' returns the code name of the browser-in-use
```

Type: read-write

Assigned Objects: navigator

The appName property returns a string that represents the name of the underlying body of code that supports the current browser application. Both Internet Explorer and Netscape Navigator support the Navigator object, and the appName property for both VBScript and JavaScript.

```
navigator.appCodeName
' returns "Mozilla" for Internet Explorer and Netscape Navigator
```

> **W A R N I N G**   At first glance, this may seem like an excellent property to use to discover if the current browser client is either Internet Explorer or Netscape Navigator. You may have tuned your site especially for these two browsers—and the fact that both are based on NCSA Mosaic code (Netscape is based directly on the Mosaic code; Internet Explorer is based on the revised, Spyglass version) could be a way to distinguish the two from the maddening crowd. Problem is, NCSA Mosaic code (codenamed "Mozilla," obviously) is available for licensing to all comers. Thus, the appCodeName alone is not enough to insure that your visitor is traveling with IE or Navigator.

AppName Property

Term: appName
Example Syntax:
```
navigator.appName
' returns the application name of the browser-in-use
```
Type: read-write
Assigned Objects: navigator

The appName property returns a string that represents the name of the current browser, embedded into the application by its developers. Both Internet Explorer and Netscape Navigator support the Navigator object, and the appName property for both VBScript and JavaScript.

```
navigator.appName
' returns "Microsoft Internet Explorer" for Internet Explorer and "Netscape" for
Netscape Navigator
```

AppVersion Property

Term: appVersion
Example Syntax:
```
navigator.appVersion
' returns the current version of the browser-in-use
```
Type: read-write
Assigned Objects: navigator

The appVersion property returns a string that represents the version of the current browser, embedded into the application by its developers. Both Internet Explorer and Netscape Navigator support the Navigator object, and the appVersion property for both VBScript and JavaScript.

```
navigator.appName
' returns " 2.0(compatible;MSIE 3.01;Windows95)" for Internet Explorer 3 for
Windows 95; and "3.0 (Macintosh;1;68k)" for Netscape Navigator 3 for 68K Macs
```

Checked Property

Term: checked
Example Syntax:
```
document.forms(0).checkbox1.checked
'the checked status of checkbox1
```
Type: read-write
Assigned Objects: checkbox, radio

The checked property gets or sets the checked status of the referenced object. This property returns a 0 (zero) when the object is unchecked, and a 1 (one) when the object is checked.

```
<INPUT TYPE="checkbox" NAME="Yes">
```

```
forms(1).Yes.checked        'returns 1 if checkbox is selected, 0 if not
forms(1).Yes.checked = 1  'selects the checkbox
```

Cookie Property

Term: cookie
Example Syntax:
```
document.cookie
'server-specific contents of the current client's cookie text file
```
Type: read-write
Assigned Objects: document

The cookie property gets or sets a specially formatted string in a text file (created and maintained by the browser on the client's machine expressly for the purpose of holding this data). Microsoft's cookie property for Internet Explorer conforms to Netscape's preliminary specification (now a de facto standard) for setting "Persistent Client State HTTP Cookies."

W W W   You can review Netscape's Cookie spec for yourself at:

home.netscape.com/newsref/std/cookie_spec.html

The Netscape spec was originally written to describe how CGIs (server helper applications conforming to the Common Gateway Interface) could save and retrieve small bits of information to and from its visiting clients. To set a cookie (i.e., place it into the current client's cookie text file), you must provide the browser with a string of text that is formatted like this:

```
[cookieName]=[cookieValue]
```

In the expression just shown, "cookieName" represents the name of the cookie, and "cookieValue" represents the actual data you want to save. The name/value information that is saved in a cookie is like the name/value properties of a field. The name of the field is its unique identifier (and usually also a clue to its contents), and the value is its actual contents. Similarly, the name of the cookie separates it from other cookies (and may be used to describe its contents); and the value is the actual data that the cookie is meant to house.

Here's an example that saves "rosedaniels" (a string typed by the current user into a field called "myNick") as a "nickname" cookie, so that it may be retrieved each time the user reconnects to the server, and used to automatically log the user in:

```
cookieName = "nickname"
'places "nickname" into variable "cookieName"

userNick = document.forms(0).myNick.value
'places "rosedaniels" (typed into field "myNick") into variable "userName"

document.cookie = cookieName & "=" & userNick
' concatenates and saves the string "nickname=rosedaniels" to the cookie file
```

Since this cookie string contains no expiration date, it will automatically expire at the end of the session (which makes it virtually useless for its purpose). Cookies may not be saved forever on the client's machine, however, so if you want the cookie to persist beyond the current session you must set an expiration date, using the following format (which requires a Greenwich Mean Time date):

```
[cookieName]=[cookieValue];expires=[DD-MMM-YY] GMT
```

Here's how to set the current example cookie to expire on December 1, 1999:

```
document.cookie = cookieName & "=" & userNick & ";expires=" & "01-Dec-99 GMT"
'saves the string "nickname=rosedaniels;expires=01-Dec-99 GMT" to the cookie
'file
```

There is no guarantee that your cookie will actually persist until its expiration date, since current browser cookie files only support a total of 300 cookies per client machine. Once the client's file reaches its limit, the browser begins deleting the older cookies to make way for new cookies. Every time a new cookie slot is needed, the cookie with the oldest placement date gets the boot.

In addition to *name*, *value*, and *expires*, you can also designate the *domain* for which the cookie is valid (defaults to the domain of the page that set the cookie), a URL *path* to a subset of pages for which the cookie is valid (defaults to the path of the page that set the cookie), and a *secure* parameter which, if present, only transmits the cookie if the channel is secure (defaults to false).

```
[cookieName]=[cookieValue];expires=[date];domain=[given.domain];path=/[given.url]
;secure
```

The Netscape spec allows each server or domain to place up to 20 cookies in a single client file, so you can set multiple cookies using the semicolon delimiter:

```
[cookieName]=[cookieValue];[cookieName]=[cookieValue]; ...
```

-OR-

```
[cookieName]=[cookieValue];expires=[date];
[cookieName]=[cookieValue];expires=[date]; ...
```

-OR-

```
[cookieName]=[cookieValue];expires=[date];path=/[this.url];
[cookieName]=[cookieValue];secure; ...
```

Retrieving cookies is more complicated that setting cookies, although the first step is simply to request the document.cookie itself. The returned string, however, contains all of the cookies in the client's current file that have been set from your server (or domain). To find any individual cookie in the string, you must write a parser routine (lines of code that search the string for the substring you seek) that looks for the named cookie (cookieName) and its associated value (=cookieValue). An excellent, fully commented parsing routine has been written by Microsoft for this purpose, which you can review, and copy, from the Microsoft Web server.

W W W   Microsoft's cookie explanations and examples are at:

www.microsoft.com/vbscript/us/samples/cookies/extcookie.htm

The Cookie Controversy

Not everyone thinks cookies are such a good idea. The controversial process of inserting information (however benign) into a file on the user's hard drive is the subject of much discussion, and many flames, across the Internet.

By default, the current version of Internet Explorer is set to detect incoming cookies, giving the user a chance to accept or reject the cookie at will. This popular solution to the cookie dilemma may or may not be adopted by other browsers, although some solution is likely to be included in any browser worth its salt.

If you're the conscientious type, you may want to ask permission to come aboard before launching a cookie on a client's machine. Here's one way to do so:

```
if confirm("Can a cookie containing your user nickname be saved to
your machine?") then

    [cookie code]

end if
```

DefaultChecked Property

Term: `defaultChecked`

Example Syntax: `document.forms(0).checkbox1.defaultChecked`
`'the default selection status of checkbox1`

Type: read-write

Assigned Objects: checkbox, radio

The defaultChecked property gets or sets the default selection status of the referenced object. This property returns "false" when the object is unchecked by default:

```
<INPUT TYPE="checkbox" NAME="Yes">

forms(1).Yes.defaultChecked
'returns false, since checkbox is not selected by default
```

This property returns "true" when the object is checked by default:

```
<INPUT TYPE="checkbox" NAME="Yes" CHECKED>

forms(1).Yes.defaultChecked
'returns true, since checkbox is selected by default
```

DefaultValue Property

Term: `defaultValue`
Example Syntax:
`document.forms(0).text1.defaultValue`
`'the object's default text, if any`
Type: read-write
Assigned Objects: password, text, textarea

The defaultValue property gets or sets the default text string to be displayed by the referenced object.

```
<INPUT TYPE="text" NAME="Name" VALUE="Type your name here.">
<INPUT TYPE="password" NAME="Pword">


forms(1).elements(0).value        'returns "Type your name here."

forms(1).elements(1).value = "Type your password here."
'puts the string "Type your password here" into the password object named
"Pword"
```

Encoding Property

Term: `encoding`
Example Syntax:
`document.formName.encoding`
`'the submitted form's designated MIME type`
Type: read-write
Assigned Objects: form

The encoding property gets or sets the answer to the <FORM> tag's ENCTYPE argument, which is the MIME type to be used in formatting the submitted order. If no MIME type is specified, text/html is used.

```
document.forms(0).encoding = "text/plain"
'sets the MIME type of the formatted form information to plain text
```

FgColor Property

Term: `fgColor`
Example Syntax: `document.fgColor 'current document's foreground color`
Type: read-write
Assigned Objects: document

The fgColor property gets or sets the foreground color of the current document, the color used to display non-hypertext text (also definable by the <BODY> tag's TEXT argument). The foreground color can be set using any of the allowed color literals listed in Appendix B, or using the hexadecimal equivalent of the desired color.

```
document.fgColor = "beige"

-OR-

document.fgColor = "F5F5DC" 'also evaluates to beige
```

The following script displays the hexadecimal equivalent of the document's currently set foreground text color in an alert dialog when the page is loaded into the browser:

```
<BODY onLoad="alert(document.bgColor)">
```

Hash Property

Term: hash
Example Syntax:
```
location.hash
' hash portion of the URL of the window's current document
```
Type: read-only
Assigned Objects: location, links

The hash property returns the #string portion of the URL of the associated object. #string represents a string at the end of the URL, that is preceded by a # symbol. This string is used to point to an <ANCHOR> whose NAME argument is answered by the same string:

```
<A HREF-"http://www.this.com:1000/thisFolder/this.htm#thisString">

-REFERS TO-

<A NAME="thisString">

document.links(0).hash 'returns "#thisString" for the above example link
```

> **N O T E** If there is no hash string in the referenced URL, the hash property returns # all by itself.

Host Property

Term: host
Example Syntax:
```
location.host
' host portion of the URL of the window's current document
```
Type: read-only
Assigned Objects: location, links

The host property returns the hostname and hostport portion of the URL of the associated object:

```
<A HREF="http://www.this.com:1000/thisFolder/this.htm">
```

```
document.links(0).host 'returns "www.this.com:1000" for the above example link
```

Hostname Property

Term: hostname

Example Syntax:

```
location.hostname
' hostname portion of the URL of the window's current document
```

Type: read-only

Assigned Objects: location, links

The "hostname" property returns the hostname portion of the URL of the associated object:

```
<A HREF="http://www.this.com:1000/thisFolder/this.htm">
```

```
document.links(0).hostname 'returns "www.this.com" for the above example link
```

Href Property

Term: href

Example Syntax: location.href   ' URL of the window's current document

Type: read-only

Assigned Objects: location, links

The href property returns the complete URL of the associated object:

```
<A HREF="http://www.this.com:1000/thisFolder/this.htm">
```

```
document.links(0).href 'returns "http://www.this.com:1000/thisFolder/this.htm"
for the above example link
```

LastModified Property

Term: lastModified

Example Syntax:

```
document.lastModified
' returns date that the current    document was last modified
```

Type: read-only

Assigned Objects: document

The lastModified property returns a string containing the date that the document was last modified (see Figure 5.1).

```
<BODY onLoad="alert(lastModified)">
```

Figure 5.1 An onLoad handler in the <BODY> tag displays an alert containing the date the page was last modified.

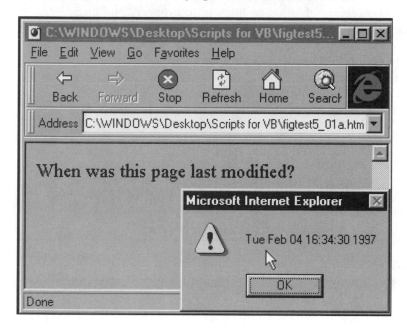

NOTE Since the returned text string is formatted as a proper date string, VBScript automatically converts it to a Date subtype.

Length Property

Term: length
Example Syntax:
```
document.links.length
' total number of items in the links array
```
Type: read-only
Assigned Objects: all arrays (including anchors, elements, frames, forms, links, options), history

The length property returns an integer specifying the number of items in the referenced array.

```
<INPUT TYPE="button" NAME="button1">   'array(0)
<INPUT TYPE="text">                    'array(1)
<INPUT TYPE="password" NAME="Pword">   'array(2)

forms.length 'returns "3"
```

> **WARNING** The length property always counts from 1, while built-in array objects always count from 0. It is very important to remember this discrepancy in numbering when using the length property and array positions together in a script. For instance, if you want to repeat a series of actions for each object in an array—and you use the length property to determine the total number of items in that array—you must subtract 1 from the length to get the last object's position in the array. In the preceding example, forms.length equals 3, but the position of the last object in the forms array is 2, or forms.length-1.

> **TIP** Although the history object operates in all other regards as an array object (its main purpose being to provide an indexed array of the current pages in the browser's history list), it is not considered an array. It's only real departure from array object behavior, however, is the fact that it counts its items from 1 instead of 0. Thus, it is not necessary to compensate for a 0 base when counting history pages.

LinkColor Property

Term: linkColor

Example Syntax:

```
document.linkColor
' display color for hypertext links in the current document
```

Type: read-write

Assigned Objects: document

The linkColor property gets or sets the color used to display hypertext links in the current document. Link colors can be set using any of the allowed color literals listed in Appendix B, or using the hexadecimal equivalent of the desired color.

```
document.linkColor = "blue"

-OR-

document.linkColor = "0000FF" 'also evaluates to blue
```

The following script displays the hexadecimal equivalent of the document's currently set link color in an alert dialog when the page is loaded into the browser:

```
<BODY onLoad="alert(document.linkColor)">
```

Method Property

Term: method

Example Syntax: document.formName.method   ' the form's submission method

> **NOTE** The *aLinkColor, linkColor, vLinkColor, bgColor,* and *fgColor* properties may all be expressed as a hexidecimal equivalent. A hexidecimal equivalent is a string of six characters representing an RGB (monitor-based) color value. The first two chars represent the amount of RED in the color; the second two chars represent the amount of GREEN; and the last two represent the amount of BLUE. Since hex references are not the same as regular alphanumeric references, you can't depend on these char-pairs to tell you how much red, green, or blue is in a color. You simply have to know the hexidecimal value of the color you want to use. Consult Appendix B for a list of more than 100 RGB color values and their hexidecimal equivalents.

> **TIP** If you see a color you like on another page, view its source code to discover the color's name or hexidecimal equivalent. If you have trouble locating this information within the page's source, copy the source file to your system, then place an "alert(document.*theColorProperty*)" script into the page to display the named property's RGB color value in an alert dialog (as shown in Figure 5.2). You can also use the hexidecimal equivalents in Appendix B to come up with your own color values. Mix and match the RGB hex-pairs shown in the Appendix, or try your own number or letter combos. Feed the resulting six-char hex string to the browser when the page is loaded to see if it returns an error, or a color you like:

```
<BODY onLoad="document.linkColor = "ANYHEX">
```

Type: read-write
Assigned Objects: form

The method property gets or sets the answer to the <FORM> tag's METHOD argument, which is the method to be used in formatting the submitted order. Currently, there are only two possible answers to the METHOD argument:

- **GET:** Appends the collected form data to the ACTION argument's URL, and sends it to the server—just as the browser would send any URL generated by clicking an anchor. This method is limited to 4K of passed data.

- **POST:** Sends the collected form data as an HTTP post transaction, which supports unlimited data.

```
document.forms(0).method = "post"
'sets the submission method of the current form to "post"
```

Figure 5.2 The RGB value of the currently set link color appears in an alert when the page is loaded.

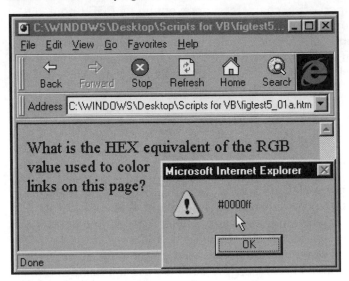

Name Property

Term: name
Example Syntax: frames(1).name   ' name of the second frame in a frameset
Type: read-write (except for the anchors object, which is read-only).
Assigned Objects: anchors, frames, windows, all objects in the elements array
(except radio buttons)

The name property returns the answer to the NAME argument within the parent tag of the referenced object, or "null" if no NAME answer exists.

```
<INPUT TYPE="button" NAME="button1">
<INPUT TYPE="text">
<INPUT TYPE="password" NAME="Pword">

forms(0).elements(2).name  ' returns "Pword"

forms(0).elements(1).name  ' returns "null"
```

The name property can also be used to name (or change the name of) an object.

```
<INPUT TYPE="button" NAME="button1">
<INPUT TYPE="text">

elements(1).name = "address"  'sets the text object's name to "address"
```

Opener Property

Term: opener
Example Syntax:
```
opener.name 'name of the window that opened the current window
```
Type: read-only
Assigned Objects: window, frame

The opener property returns the window object that opened the current window.

```
DIM theWind
theWind = opener.name
'places the name of the window that opened the current window into a variable
'named "theWind"
```

Parent Property

Term: parent
Example Syntax:
```
parent.status
'text in the status bar of the current frame's containing window
```
Type: read-only
Assigned Objects: window, frame

The parent property returns the window object that contains the current frame.

```
DIM theWind
theWind = opener.name
theWind = parent.name
'places the name of the window that contains the current frameset into variable
'named "theWind"
```

Pathname Property

Term: pathname
Example Syntax:
```
location.pathname
' path portion of the URL of the window's current document
```
Type: read-only
Assigned Objects: location, links

The pathname property returns the document path portion of the URL of the associated object:

```
<A HREF="http://www.this.com:1000/thisFolder/this.htm">
```

```
document.links(0).pathname
'returns "/thisFolder/this.htm" for the above example link
```

> **N O T E**   The port property always returns "" for URL's whose protocol is "file."

Port Property

Term: port
Example Syntax:
```
location.port  'port portion of the URL of the window's current document
```
Type: read-only
Assigned Objects: location, links

The port property returns the port portion of the URL of the associated object:

```
<A HREF="http://www.this.com:1000/thisFolder/this.htm">
```

```
document.links(0).port  ' returns ":1000" for the above example link
```

> **N O T E**   The port property always returns "" for URL's whose protocol is "file."

Protocol Property

Term: protocol
Example Syntax:
```
location.protocol
' protocol portion of the URL of the window's current document
```
Type: read-only
Assigned Objects: location, links

The protocol property returns the protocol portion of the URL of the associated object:

```
<A HREF="http://www.this.com:1000/thisFolder/this.htm">
```

```
document.links(0).protocol  ' returns "http:" for the above example link
```

Referrer Property

Term: referrer
Example Syntax: `document.referrer  ' the URL of the referring page`
Type: read-only
Assigned Objects: document

The referrer property returns a string containing the URL of the document that referred your current visitor to your page.

The referrer may be a page of your own, or it may be any other page on the Web that contains a hypertext link to your page. If there is no referrer (the user arrived at your page through other means; perhaps it's a saved Favorite or Bookmark), document.referrer returns "null."

If the value of document. referrer is not "null," the following if statement places the referring URL into a previously declared variable called saveRef.

```
if (document.referrer <> null) then
    saveRef = document.refer
end if
```

Search Property

Term: search
Example Syntax:
```
location.search
' port portion of the URL of the window's current document
```
Type: read-only
Assigned Objects: location, links

The search property returns the search portion of the URL of the associated object, if specified. If none is specified, this property returns "null."

```
<A HREF="http://www.this.com:1000/thisFolder/this.htm?string">

document.links(0).search  ' returns "?string" for the above example link
```

SelectedIndex Property

Term: selectedIndex
Example Syntax: document.forms(0).select1.selectedIndex
```
            'the option array position of the selected option
```
Type: read-only
Assigned Objects: select

The selectedIndex property returns an integer representing the currently selected option's position in the options array.

```
<SELECT SIZE=1 NAME="choices">

        <OPTION VALUE=1>First Choice    'choices.options(0) Selected --->
        <OPTION VALUE=2>Second Choice   'choices.options(1)
        <OPTION VALUE=3>Third Choice    'choices.options(2)

</SELECT>

document.forms(0).choices.selectedIndex  ' returns 1
```

Self Property

Term: self
Example Syntax: self.status   ' text in the current window's status bar
Type: read-only
Assigned Objects: window, frame

The self property is another way of referring to the current window.

```
theWind = self.name   ' places the name of the current window into theWind
theWind = name        ' places the name of the current window into theWind
```

Status Property

Term: status
Example Syntax:

```
status
'text in the current window's status bar

parent.status
'text in the status bar of the current frame's parent window
```

Type: read-write
Assigned Objects: window, frames

The status property gets or sets the text displayed in the referenced window's Status Bar.

> **TIP** You can display your own message in the Status Bar of any available window by simply naming it in your script, and assigning the desired string using the "=" assignment operator (discussed in Chapter 10). The following line of script places the assigned string in the Status Bar of the window that opened the current window:
>
> ```
> opener.status = "Thanks for the memory!"
> ```

Target Property

Term: target
Example Syntax:

```
document.formName.target
' window that receives the results of the form submission
```

Type: read-write
Assigned Objects: form, link

The target property gets or sets the answer to the <FORM> or <ANCHOR> tag's TARGET argument, which is the name of the window that will display the results of the form submission process, or that will display the link's assigned URL.

```
document.forms(0).target = "newWind"
'sets the name of the window that displays the form results to "newWind," and
'causes the response to the form submission to display in that window
```

```
document.links(0).target = "_blank"
'sets the name of the window that displays the form results to "blank," and
'causes the link's referenced document to display in that window
```

Title Property

Term: `title`
Example Syntax: `document.title   ' the title of the current document`
Type: read-only
Assigned Objects: document

The title property returns a string representing the text inserted between the referenced document's <TITLE> tags.

Top Property

Term: `top`
Example Syntax: `top.status   ' text in the current window's status bar`
Type: read-only
Assigned Objects: window, frame

The top property refers to the topmost window in a frameset; or the window that houses all of the related frames.

```
theWind = top.name
' places the name of the topmost window in the current frameset into a variable
' named "theWind"
```

userAgent Property

Term: `userAgent`
Example Syntax:
```
navigator.userAgent
' returns all available information regarding the browser-in-use
```
Type: read-write
Assigned Objects: navigator

The userAgent property returns a string that represents the code name and version of the current browser (for Netscape Navigator), and the code name, application name, and version (for Internet Explorer). In essence, this string contains all (or almost all) of the identification information embedded into the application by its developers. Both Internet Explorer and Netscape Navigator support the Navigator object, and the userAgent property for both VBScript and JavaScript.

```
navigator.appName
' returns " Mozilla/2.0(compatible;MSIE 3.01;Windows95)" for Internet Explorer 3
' for Windows 95; and "Mozilla (3.0 Macintosh;1;68k)" for Netscape Navigator 3
' for 68K Macs
```

Value Property

Term: value
Example Syntax:
```
document.form1.button1.value
'the value of the referenced button
```
Type: read-write
Assigned Objects: elements array (except for the Select object), options array

The value property returns the answer to the VALUE argument within the parent tag of the referenced object.

```
<INPUT TYPE="button" NAME="button1" VALUE="Cliok">
<INPUT TYPE="text"NAME="field1">
<INPUT TYPE="password" NAME="Pword">

buttonVal = forms(1).elements(0).value
' puts the string "Click" into the ButtonVal variable

forms(1).elements(1).value = "Hello"
' puts the string "Hello" into the text field named "field1"
```

As noted earlier, the Select object has no value property of its own. However, its subordinate options *do* allow this property, as shown in the following script, which causes an alert to display the value of any selected option (see Figure 5.3).

```
<HTML>
<HEAD>
<SCRIPT LANGUAGE="VBScript">

sub showOptVal()


alert(document.forms(0).choices.options(document.forms(0).choices.selectedIndex).
value)

end sub

</SCRIPT>
</HEAD>
<BODY>
```

```
<FORM>
<SELECT SIZE=1 NAME="choices" onChange="showOptVal">

    <OPTION VALUE="1">1st Choice
    <OPTION VALUE="2">2nd Choice
    <OPTION VALUE="3">3rd Choice

</SELECT>
</form>
</BODY>
</HTML>
```

VLinkColor Property

Term: vLinkColor

Example Syntax:

```
document.vLinkColor
' display color for visited hypertext links in the current document
```

Type: read-write

Assigned Objects: document

The vLinkColor property gets or sets the color used to display previously clicked, or visited, hypertext links in the current document. The color of visited links can be set using any of the allowed color literals listed in Appendix B, or using the hexadecimal equivalent of the desired color.

Figure 5.3 An alert displays the value of any option the user selects.

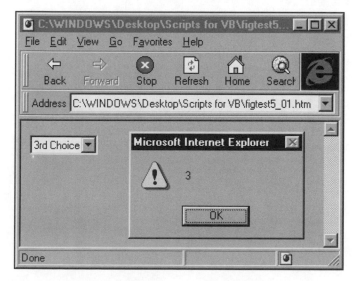

```
document.vLinkColor = "red"

-OR-

document.vLinkColor = "008000" 'also evaluates to red
```

The following script displays the hexadecimal equivalent of the document's currently set visited link color in an alert dialog when the page is loaded into the browser:

```
<BODY onLoad="alert(document.vLinkColor)">
```

What's Next?

The sampling of property descriptions and examples in this chapter should provide you with a solid basis for implementing any object property in VBScript. Short definitions of individual properties not directly addressed in this chapter may be found on the Microsoft DHTML documentation page (listed at the beginning of this chapter).

The next chapter takes a close-up look at the methods used by the objects presented in Chapter 4. Unlike this chapter, only a relatively small cadre of new methods resulted from the DHTML-ization of Internet Explorer, and all of them are covered in Chapter 6.

6

Object Methods

hapter 5 provided detailed descriptions of some of the available
VBScript properties; some of which had already been briefly described in
Chapter 4. Due to the large number of properties now assigned to objects,
Chapter 5 only addressed a representative sampling of properties. This chapter, however, provides definitions, spelling, syntax, and, in many instances,
example scripts for all of the built-in VBScript Methods documented to date
by Microsoft; including those methods introduced with the DHTML object
model.

The Built-In Methods of VBScript Objects

For easy reference, VBScript's built-in Methods are presented here in alphabetical order; not according to the Objects they support. Like Properties,
many Methods are assigned to multiple Objects. For instance, the click()
method is assigned to several form element objects, such as buttons, checkboxes, and submit and reset objects. For this reason, each Method definition
in this chapter also includes a list of its assigned Objects, as well as any variable information regarding the use of that Method with different Objects.

From earlier chapter discussions, you already know that built-in Methods are made up of one or more operations that you (the programmer) would commonly like to perform upon the associated object(s). The document object's write() method, for instance, allows you to write text and/or HTML code to a page from an internal VBScript. Other methods provide similar built-in procedures for their objects, allowing you to instigate that procedure by simply using the name of the method and its calling object:

```
object.method(arg1,arg2...)
```

Use of Parentheses with Methods

Chapter 3 introduced a set of rules (derived through testing) regarding the use of parentheses to enclose method and function arguments within procedures. As noted in that chapter, enclosing parentheses *are* acceptable for script-level code (code that is not contained in a sub or function statement), and are even sometimes required inside procedures (if used, say, within an if statement). Given the complexity of these conditions, you might find it helpful to review the conventions used for displaying method syntax in this chapter's example scripts:

1. All "Example Syntax" items display a set of enclosing parenthesis for arguments, because this format makes the method string much more readable; especially for methods that take several arguments.

2. Additional one-line scripting examples are also displayed with arguments in a set of enclosing parenthesis, both for readability and because these examples are not shown as belonging to a procedure.

3. Methods referenced within the introductory line of a procedure-based control statement (for instance, as part of an "if" statement's assigned condition), or within a variable assignment statement, display the enclosing parenthesis because their absence results in an "expected)" error.

4. Full scripting examples that show methods in use within a procedure, however, forego the enclosing parenthesis, even though the VBScript interpreter often executes procedure-based methods just fine when parentheses *are* included.

In general, any time you see a method reference with a set of enclosing parenthesis inside a procedure, it is because the failure to include the parenthesis returned an error in the latest version of Internet Explorer tested. If you find that you are receiving errors in your own (or in these) scripts—even when following what appears to be the proper method syntax for the current scripting situation—it may be that your version of Internet Explorer has been updated with new rules. By all means, lose or use the parenthesis as the interpreter dictates.

Add Method
Term: add(*element*,[*n*])
Example Syntax:
```
selectObj.options.add(thisOption,2)
' places a new member in the third index position in the referenced select
' object's options array, using text stored in a variable named thisOption
```
Assigned Objects: area, options, select

The "add" method takes any string that represents an appropriate object type, and adds it to the referenced collection. The element argument (which represents the object to add) is required. An optional number may also be passed to place the object into that index position in the array.

Alert Method
Term: alert(*textString*)
Example Syntax:
```
alert("Hello, World!")
' displays the text "Hello, World!" in an alert dialog box
```
Assigned Objects: window

The "alert" method takes any text string (or any expression that evaluates to a text string) as its only argument. It displays this string in a standard VBScript user alert dialog box along with a single "OK" button (shown in Figure 6.1).

Theoretically, the textString argument is optional, since the alert dialog box is still presented if you fail to provide this string. Practically speaking, however, it is required—since there's no purpose to displaying an alert with the default string "<undefined>."

Any time you place a literal text string directly into any method's parenthesis, you must enclose it in quotes. If you use variables or the properties of other objects that evaluate to a text string, the quotes are not used.

```
alert("Welcome to my Website.") ' literal text strings must be quoted

myVariable = "Welcome to my Website."
alert(myVariable)
' expressions that evaluate to text strings are not quoted
```

If any portion of a concatenated string is literal, that portion must be enclosed in quotes. In the following example, the alert string is created by concatenating "myVariable" with the contents of a text field, and then adding a period (literal) at the end of the sentence. For the script to be successful, that period must be enclosed in quotes (as shown):

```
<HTML>
<HEAD>
```

```
<SCRIPT LANGUAGE="VBScript">

sub text1_onBlur()

    DIM myVariable
    myVariable = "Welcome to my Web site, "

    alert myVariable & document.forms(0).text1.value & "."

end sub

</SCRIPT>
</HEAD>
<BODY>
<FORM>
<INPUT TYPE="text" NAME="text1">
</FORM>
</BODY>
```

Since the alert() method belongs to the top-level window object, you needn't include any reference to that object if you want the alert to appear above the current window. To bring another window forward, and then show the alert, you must attach the alert() method to the target window object:

```
windowName.alert("Here's another window for you.")
```

The alert() method's single "OK" button gives the user only one possible response. To give the user more choices, or to collect unique user feedback, use the confirm() or prompt() methods, as appropriate.

Back Method

Term: back(*number*)
Example Syntax:
```
history.back(2)
' browses back two pages in the current history list
```
Assigned Objects: history

This method is used to change the displayed document in the referenced window. If no object reference is used with this method, the current window is assumed. This method takes one argument which is a number (or an expression that evaluates to a number) that represents the position of the target document in the user's history list.

```
parent.history.back(1)
' displays the page listed in the parent window's history right before the page
currently displayed in that window
```

Figure 6.1 The alert dialog displays a message it created by stringing together a variable container, an object property (the value of the displayed text field), and a literal string (a period).

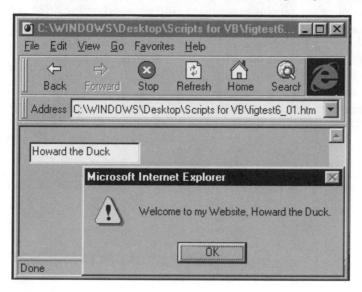

Blur Method

Term: blur()

Example Syntax:

```
document.thisForm.myField.blur()
' removes focus from the referenced field
```

Assigned Objects: select, text, textarea

The blur method is an event simulation method. It sends an onBlur event to the referenced field, as if a user physically clicked or tabbed into its referenced field or list object. It takes no arguments.

The blur() method takes no arguments.

The following script sends a "blur to the Change field when the user clicks the "Hello" button, causing the contents of the field to become the displayed name of the "Hello" button (see Figures 6.2 and 6.3):

```
<HTML>
<HEAD>

<SCRIPT LANGUAGE="VBScript">

sub hello_onClick()
```

> **TIP** The blur event is only sent to the referenced object if that object is the current document focus, as evidenced (for example) by the text insertion cursor appearing inside a field. If you send this event to an object without focus, it never receives the event, and scripted actions do not execute. If you are counting on the execution of these actions, then you must be sure to set up the situation to ensure that the target object is also the current focus. One easy way to do this is to send the focus event before you send the blur event. If the object already has the document focus, there's no harm done. The object simply won't receive the first event sent (focus), but it will receive the second event (blur).

```
document.forms(0).change.focus ' ensures that the field has focus
document.forms(0).change.blur

end sub

</SCRIPT>
</HEAD>
<BODY>
<FORM>
<CENTER>

<INPUT TYPE="button" NAME="hello" VALUE="Hello">
<p>
<INPUT TYPE="text" SIZE=10 NAME="change"
onBlur="hello.value = change.value">

</CENTER>
</FORM>
</BODY>
</HTML>
```

Clear Method

Term: `clear()`

Example Syntax:

```
document.clear()
' clears the document's display
```

Assigned Objects: document

The "clear" method removes all displayed HTML from the referenced document object, so that the page appears empty. It must be used in conjunction with the document.close() method, or the browser continues to exhibit the system "wait" cursor until the user clicks the browser's "Stop" button.

Figure 6.2 When this page is first loaded, a "Hello" button and an empty field appear.

Figure 6.3 Whatever the user types into the empty field becomes the displayed name of the "Hello" button, whether the user physically leaves the field, or simply clicks the "Hello" button.

The clear() method takes no arguments.

When the user clicks the "Empty Page" button generated by this example script (see Figure 6.4), the page is emptied as shown in Figure 6.5:

```
<HTML>
<HEAD>
```

```
<SCRIPT LANGUAGE="VBScript">

sub theButton_onClick()

    document.clear
    document.close

end sub

</SCRIPT>
</HEAD>
<BODY>

This is an example of how the clear() method can be used to empty the current
page display.

<FORM>

<p><INPUT TYPE="button" NAME="theButton" VALUE="Empty Page">

</FORM>
</BODY>
```

Figure 6.4 When the user clicks the "Empty Page" button on this page, the page is emptied—as shown in Figure 6.5.

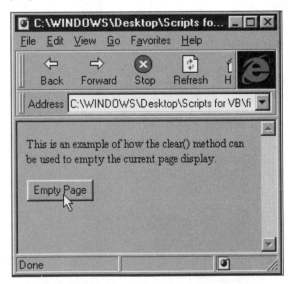

Figure 6.5 The empty page.

ClearTimeout Method

Term: clearTimeout(*setTimeoutID*)

Example Syntax:

```
clearTimeout(thisTimer)
' stops the activities of the setTimeout() method whose ID is "thisTimer"
```

Assigned Objects: window

The clearTimeout method is used to stop the setTimeout() method from continuing to call its referenced procedure. It takes only one argument, which is the ID of the target setTimeout() script.

```
thisGuy setTimeout("Call some_proc()",100,"VBScript")
clearTimeout(thisGuy)
' stops the execution of the "thisGuy" setTimeout() script
```

The following example creates a form with a text field that displays a "0," and a Start and Stop button. Clicking the Start button causes the setTimeout() method to repeatedly call theTimer() procedure in 1-second intervals. Each call to theTimer() adds a "1" to the Elapsed Seconds field, providing the user with a visual review of the passing seconds. Clicking the "Stop" button stops theTimer() from adding any more seconds to the field, and reinitializes the field with "0" so it can count elapsed again, if the user reclicks the "Start" button (see Figure 6.6).

```
<HTML>
<HEAD>
```

```
<SCRIPT LANGUAGE="VBScript">

DIM myTimer

sub Start_onClick()

    Call theTimer()

end sub

sub theTimer()

    document.forms(0).Seconds.value = document.forms(0).Seconds.value+1
    myTimer = setTimeout("Call theTimer()",1000,"VBScript")

end sub

sub Stop_onClick()

    clearTimeout myTimer
    document.forms(0).Seconds.value = 0

end sub

</SCRIPT>
</HEAD>
<BODY>
<FORM>

<b>Elapsed Seconds</b>:
<INPUT TYPE="text" SIZE=2 NAME="Seconds" VALUE="0">
<INPUT TYPE="button" NAME="Start" VALUE="Start">
<INPUT TYPE="button" NAME="Stop" VALUE="Stop">

</FORM>
</BODY>

sub Start_onClick()

    document.forms(0).Seconds.value = 0
    Call theTimer()
```

**Figure 6.6 When the user clicks the "Stop" button, the setTimeout()
activities ar halted, and the value of the "Elapsed Seconds" field is
reset to 0.**

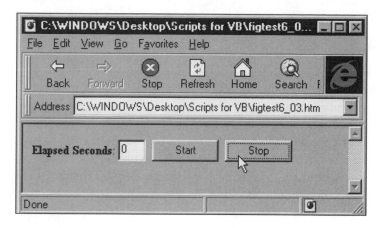

```
end sub

sub theTimer()

    document.forms(0).Seconds.value = document.forms(0).Seconds.value+1
    myTimer = setTimeout("Call theTimer()",1000,"VBScript")

end sub

sub Stop_onClick()

    clearTimeout myTimer

end sub
```

TIP If you want to leave the total elapsed seconds on display in the
field after the user clicks "Stop"but also want the counter to begin from
0 if the user reclicks the "Start" button—move the line of script that sets
the value of the field back to "0" from the bottom of the Stop_onClick()
sub statement to the top of the Start-onClick() sub statement. Then, the
user can click "Stop" without updating the field. As soon as the user
clicks "Start" again, however, the field's value is reset to "0."

Click Method

Term: click()
Example Syntax:
```
document.thisForm.myButton.click()
' sends a click to the referenced button
```
Assigned Objects: button, reset, submit, checkbox, radio

The click method is an event simulation method. It sends at least part of the onClick event to the referenced button, as if a user physically clicked the button. The click() method takes no arguments.

Although the following script does indeed send a click to the target button, causing the button to be visibly depressed in Internet Explorer, this scripted click does not cause the button's internal onClick script to execute. If it had, the displayed name of the "Hello" button would be changed to the contents of the "change" field whenever a user clicks or tabs out of the field.

```
<HTML>
<HEAD>

<SCRIPT LANGUAGE="VBScript">

sub change_onBlur()

    document.forms(0).hello.click

end sub

</SCRIPT>
</HEAD>
<BODY>
<FORM>

<INPUT TYPE="button" NAME="hello" VALUE="Hello" onClick="hello.value =
change.value">
<INPUT TYPE="text" SIZE=10 NAME="change">

</FORM>
</BODY>
```

Close Method

Term: close()
Example Syntax: close()   ' closes the current window

> **TIP** There *are* instances where simply sending a click to a target field can be useful. You could, for example, turn radio buttons or checkbox buttons on and off at will by sending clicks—although you couldn't execute their internal onClick scripts. Perhaps future versions of Internet Explorer will enhance the operation of this method to include this functionality.

```
document.close()
```
`' closes a previously opened document output stream`
Assigned Objects: window, document

The name of this method is the same for both the document and window objects, but its behavior depends upon its calling object.

As a Window Method

The close method is used to close the referenced window object. If no window reference is used, the current window is assumed. This method takes no arguments.

```
parent.close()   ' closes the current window's parent
```

As a Document Method

The close method is used to close a document output stream that was previously opened via the document.open() method, and writes the text generated since invoking the open() method to the document. It is used in conjunction with the document.open, and document.write/writeLn methods, and is virtually unusable except as a closing mechanism for the document's open() and write() methods.

The close() method takes no arguments.

```
document.open()
document.write("Any string of valid HTML supported by the browser.")
document.close()
```

Collapse Method

Term: `collapse([start])`
Example Syntax:
```
document.all.div1.collapse(0)
```
`' creates an empty range at the end of the textRange`
Assigned Objects: body, button, div, marquee, td, textarea, th

The collapse method lets you create an empty range at the beginning or end of the current textRange object. The optional start argument may be passed a 0 to start at the end of the range, or a –1 to start at the beginning.

CommonParentElement Method

Term: commonParentElement(*char*)

Example Syntax:

```
theParent = document.all.div1.commonParentElement()
' puts the parent of the reference range object into theParent variable
```

Assigned Objects: body, button, div, marquee, td, textarea, th

The commonParentElement method returns the common parent, shared by all of the characters in the range object. It takes no arguments.

Confirm Method

Term: confirm(*textString*)

Example Syntax:

```
confirm("Do you want to play a game?")
' displays the text "Do you want to play a game?" in a confirmation dialog box,
with an OK and Cancel button
```

Assigned Objects: window

The confirm method takes any text string (or any expression that evaluates to a text string) as its only argument. It displays this string in a standard VBScript confirmation dialog box with an "OK" and "Cancel" button (shown in Figure 6.7).

As with the alert() method, the confirm() method's textString argument is theoretically optional, and the confirmation dialog box is still presented if you fail to provide this string. Again, for all practical purposes, the argument is required—since there's no purpose in asking the user to confirm the default string <undefined>.

Any time you place a literal text string directly between any method's enclosing parenthesis, you must enclose that text string in quotes. If you use variables or the properties of other objects that evaluate to a text string, the quotes are not used.

```
confirm("Are you ready to order this product?")
' literal text strings must be quoted

myVariable = "Are you ready to order this product?"
confirm(myVariable)
' expressions that evaluate to text strings are not quoted
```

The confirm() method is used whenever you want to offer the user a "Yes/No" choice. This method returns "true" if the user clicks the **OK** button, and "false" if the user clicks the **Cancel** button.

```
<HTML>
<HEAD>

<SCRIPT LANGUAGE="VBScript">
```

```
sub theButton_onClick()

    if (confirm("Are you ready to order this product?")) then

    navigate "orderForm.htm"

    end if

end sub

</SCRIPT>
</HEAD>
<BODY>
<FORM>
```

```
Click this button if you think this sounds like a <INPUT TYPE="button"
NAME="theButton" VALUE="Great Product">
```

```
</FORM>
</BODY>
```

Since the confirm() method belongs to the top-level window object, you needn't include any reference to that object if you want the confirmation to appear above the current window. To bring another window forward, and then show the confirmation, you must attach the confirm() method to the target window object:

```
windowName.confirm("Are you ready to order this product?")
```

Contains Method

Term: contains(*element*)
Example Syntax:
```
document.thisForm.myField.focus()
' sets the document focus to the referenced field
```
Assigned Objects: all object collections (or arrays)

The contains method returns "true" if the passed answer to its element argument is an alias to an element in the named object collection, and "false" if it is not. The following script returns "true" in an alert dialog box when the script's resident document is loaded into the browser window.

```
sub window_onLoad()

    DIM one,two
```

Figure 6.7 When the "Great Product" button is clicked, this dialog asks whether the user is ready to order the product. If the user clicks OK, an Order Form page is loaded into the current window. If the user clicks Cancel, the user remains on the current page.

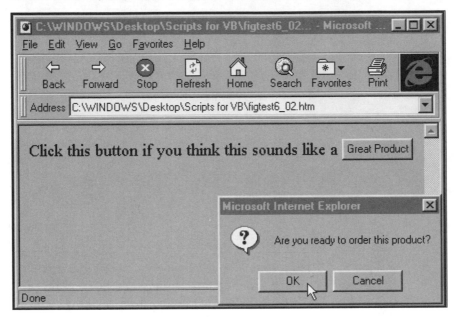

```
SET one = document.forms(0)
SET two = document.forms(0).elements(0)

alert one.contains(two)
```

```
end sub
```

CreateElement Method

Term: createElement(*tag*)
Example Syntax:
```
document.selectObj.createElement(option)
' creates a new option tag for the referenced select object
```
Assigned Objects: area, options, select

The createElement method takes any string that represents an appropriate HTML tag, and adds it to the referenced array (or collection).

CreateRange Method

Term: createRange()
Example Syntax: alert document.selection.createRange()

```
' displays the range of the current selection in an alert
```
Assigned Objects: selection

The createRange method returns the contents of the current selection object as a range. It takes no arguments.

CreateTextRange Method

Term: createTextRange(*start*,[*end*])

Example Syntax:

```
alert document.all.div1.createTextRange()
' displays the range of the text enclosed by a <DIV> tag's whose ID is "div1"
' in an alert
```

Assigned Objects: body, button, div, marquee, td, textarea, th

The createTextRange method returns the contents of the current selection as a range, from the point in the range designated by your answer to the begin argument, to the end of the range (or, to the point designated by your answer to the optional end argument).

Duplicate Method

Term: duplicate()

Example Syntax:

```
alert document.all.div1.duplicate()
'duplicates the current textRange
```

Assigned Objects: body, button, div, marquee, td, textarea, th

The duplicate method returns a duplicate of the current textRange. It takes no arguments.

ElementFromPoint Method

Term: elementFromPoint(*x*,*y*)

Example Syntax:

```
sub document_onClick()
alert document.elementFromPoint(150,200).id
end sub
'when the document receives a click event, an alert displays the id of the
'element (tag) that sits 150 pixels from the left of the window, and 200 pixels
'from the top of the window
```

Assigned Objects: document

The elementFromPoint method takes any two strings that represent horizontal and vertical screen coordinates (respectively) in pixels.

Empty Method

Term: empty()

Example Syntax:

```
sub document_onClick()
alert document.elementFromPoint(150,200).id
end sub
```

```
'when the document receives a click event, an alert displays the id of the
'element (tag) that sits 150 pixels from the left of the window, and 200 pixels
'from the top of the window
```
Assigned Objects: selection

The empty method deselects the current selection (contained in the selection object), sets the selection type to "HTMLSelectionNone," and sets the selection object's item property to "null." It takes no arguments.

ExecuteCommand Method
Term: executeCommand(*command*,[*value*,*boolean*])
Example Syntax:
```
theQuery = document.body.executeCommand(2)
'executes query #2, and returns "true" to theQuery variable if execution is
'successful, and "false" if not
```
Assigned Objects: document, body, button, div, marquee, td, textarea, th

The executeCommand method executes the passed command or query over the current selection or textRange object, and returns "true" if the operation is successful, and "false" if it is not successful. Its required command argument is answered with the number of the command or query. Its optional value argument may be answered using any variant containing the value to assign to the query or command. Its final optional argument may be answered "true" (the default) or "false," indicating whether a UI display is necessary.

Expand Method
Term: expand(*unit*)
Example Syntax:
```
document.all.div1.collapse(2)
'moves one word in the current range
```
Assigned Objects: body, button, div, marquee, td, textarea, th

The expand method lets you expand the current textRange object. The unit argument may be passed a 1 to expand the range by a character, 2 to expand it by a word, 3 to expand it by a sentence, and 6 to expand it by a story.

Focus Method
Term: focus()
Example Syntax:
```
document.thisForm.myField.focus()
'sets the document focus to the referenced field
```
Assigned Objects: a, applet, body, button, checkbox, embed, frame, frameset, iframe, img, object, select, text, textarea, window

The focus method is an event simulation method. It sends an onFocus event to the referenced object, as if a user physically clicked or tabbed into its referenced field or list. For the object to receive the focus event, it must be currently out of focus, meaning, for instance, that the text insertion cursor cannot be in a target field. The focus() method takes no arguments.

The following script switches focus to the Change field by moving the text cursor into it, but it doesn't cause its internal onFocus script to execute. If it did, a user could click the "Copy" button to copy the contents of the first field into the second field.

```
<HTML>
<HEAD>

<SCRIPT LANGUAGE="VBScript">

sub copy_onClick()

    document.forms(0).text2.focus

end sub

</SCRIPT>
</HEAD>
<BODY>

<FORM>

<INPUT TYPE="button" NAME="copy" VALUE="Copy">
<INPUT TYPE="text" SIZE=10 NAME="text1">
<INPUT TYPE="text" SIZE=10 NAME="text2"
onFocus="text2.value = text1.value">

</FORM>
</BODY>
</HTML>
```

> **T I P** There *are* instances where simply placing the text cursor into a target field can be useful. You could, for example, override Internet Explorer's normal tabbing sequence and instigate your own. This is an admittedly limited use, however, compared to what you could accomplish if this method invoked a field's internal onFocus script. Perhaps future versions of Internet Explorer will enhance the operation of this method to include this functionality.

Forward Method

Term: forward(*number*)

Example Syntax:

```
history.forward(2) ' browses forward two pages in the current history list
```

Assigned Objects: history

The forward method is used to change the displayed document in the referenced window. If no object reference is used with this method, the current window is assumed. This method takes one argument, which is a number (or an expression that evaluates to a number) that represents the position of the target document in the user's history list.

```
parent.history.forward(1)
' displays the page listed in the parent window's history right after the page
' currently displayed in that window
```

GetMember Method

Term: getMember(*property*)

Example Syntax:

```
sub document_onClick()
alert document.body.getMember(bgColor)
end sub
' when the document receives a click event, an alert displays the current value
' of the document bgColor property
```

Assigned Objects: all HTML tags

The getMember method returns the current value of the property passed to it for the reference object. The property argument must be the VBScript name for a valid property for the referenced HTML object.

Go Method

Term: go(*number*)

Example Syntax:

```
history.go(2) ' browses to the second page in the current history list
```

Assigned Objects: history

The go method is used to change the displayed document in the referenced window. If no object reference is used with this method, the current window is assumed. This method takes one argument, which is a number (or an expression that evaluates to a number) that represents the position of the target document in the user's history list.

```
history.go(history.length)
' displays the last page listed in the current window's history list
```

InRange Method

Term: inRange(*compare*)

Example Syntax:

```
document.all.div1.inRange(document.all.body)
' returns "true" since the referenced <DIV> tag must be inside the current
' <BODY>
```

Assigned Objects: body, button, div, marquee, td, textarea, th

The inRange method returns "true" if the specified range is within or equal to the current range object, and "false" if it is not. The required compare argument is answered with the range object to which the referenced range is to be compared.

IsEqual Method

Term: isEqual(*compare*)

Example Syntax:

```
document.all.div1.isEqual(document.all.body)
' returns "false" since the referenced <DIV> tag's is smaller than that of the
' <BODY> tag
```

Assigned Objects: body, button, div, marquee, td, textarea, th

The isEqual method returns "true" if the specified range is equal to the current range object, and "false" if it is not. The required compare argument is answered with the range object to which the referenced range is to be compared.

Item Method

Term: item(*index*,[*subindex*])

Example Syntax:

```
theElement = document.all.item(0)
' places the opening <HTML> tag into theElement variable, since it is always
' first in the document's all collection
```

Assigned Objects: all, anchors, applets, areas, elements, embeds, frames, forms, images, links, plugins, scripts, window

The item method returns the element or collection at the index position specified by the answer to the index argument. The index argument is answered with a number specifying a position in a collection. The subindex argument is used when the element in the position specified by the first argument is the member of a subcollection.

```
theElement = document.all.item(6,0)
' if the seventh item in the all collection is a <FORM> tag, the 0 answer to
' the subindex argument causes the item() method to return the first element in
' the form
```

Move Method

Term: move(*unit*,[*count*])

Example Syntax:

```
newRange = document.all.div1.move(2,-1)
' moves one word to the left in the current range, and returns the number of
' units moved to the newRange variable
```

Assigned Objects: body, button, div, marquee, td, textarea, th

The move method lets you move the current textRange object. The unit argument may be passed a 1 to move the range by a character, 2 to move it by a word, 3 to move it by a sentence, and 6 to move it by a story. The optional count argument tells the method how many units to move; a positive number moves the range to the right, a negative number moves it to the left. The default is 1.

MoveEnd Method

Term: moveEnd(*unit*,[*count*])

Example Syntax:

```
newRange = document.all.div1.moveEnd(2,-1)
' shrinks the end of the range one word to the left, and returns the number of
' units moved to the newRange variable
```

Assigned Objects: body, button, div, marquee, td, textarea, th

The moveEnd method lets you shrink or expand the current textRange object from the end of that range. The unit argument may be passed a 1 to move the range by a character, 2 to move it by a word, 3 to move it by a sentence, and 6 to move it by a story. The optional count argument tells the method how many units to move; a positive number expands the end of the range, a negative number shrinks the end of the range. The default is 1.

MoveStart Method

Term: moveStart(*unit*,[*count*])

Example Syntax:

```
newRange = document.all.div1.moveStart(2,-1)
' grows the start of the range one word to the left, and returns the number of
' units moved to the newRange variable
```

Assigned Objects: body, button, div, marquee, td, textarea, th

The moveStart method lets you shrink or expand the current textRange object from the beginning of that range. The unit argument may be passed a 1 to move the range by a character, 2 to move it by a word, 3 to move it by a sentence, and 6 to move it by a story. The optional count argument tells the method how many units to move; a positive number shrinks the start of the range, a negative number expands the start of the range. The default is 1.

Move Method

Term: move(*unit*,[*count*])

Example Syntax:

```
newRange = document.all.div1.move(2,-1)
' moves one word to the left in the current range, and returns an integer
' representing the new range
```

Assigned Objects: body, button, div, marquee, td, textarea, th

The move method lets you move the current textRange object. The unit argument may be passed a 1 to expand the range by a character, 2 to expand it by a word, 3 to expand it by a sentence, and 6 to expand it by a story. The optional count argument tells the method how many units to move; a positive number moves the range to the right, a negative number moves it to the left. The default is 1.

Navigate Method

Term: navigate(*url*)

Example Syntax:

```
parent.navigate("http://www.microsoft.com/vbscript")
' displays Microsoft's VBScript Home Page in the current window's parent window
```

Assigned Objects: window

The navigate method is used to change the displayed document in the referenced window. If no object reference is used with this method, the current window is assumed. This method take one argument, which is a string (or an expression that evaluates to a string) that represents the URL of the target document.

```
parent.navigate(window.location)
' displays the current window's document in the parent window as well
```

Open Method

Term: window.open(*url*,*target*,"part=[*yes/no*],part=[*yes/no*]…","size=[*pixels*],size=[*pixels*]…

Example Syntax:

```
open("http://www.my.com/my.htm","thisWind","toolbar=no")
' creates a new window called "thisWind" without a toolbar, then displays the
' page represented by the passed URL

document.open
' clears current document, and opens a new document stream
```

Assigned Objects: window, document

The name of this method is the same for both the document and window objects, but its behavior depends upon its calling object.

As a Window Method

The open method is used to open a new window, or to bring an existing window forward. It takes four types of arguments:

1. The URL argument is any text string or expression that evaluates to a proper URL. The answer to the URL argument determines the address of the page to be displayed in the target window. This argument is required, although you can answer it with the empty literal ("") to open an empty target window. If you pass an answer to the URL argument that cannot be resolved as a proper document address, an empty target window is opened.

```
open("")   ' opens a new empty window
```

> **TIP** Only windows opened from scripts receive default names from the browser. Windows that are opened by the Internet Explorer application (such as the startup window, or any window opened via File > New Window) have no name. You can name these windows on-the-fly, however, by executing the following line of script from a page in the target window: name = "windowName." If you use the unique name of a currently open window with the open() method, nothing happens. If you use the generic name of a currently open window (such as parent), the operation is successful (assuming everything else in your script is correct). The failure of the script to operate when unique names are used may or may not be a bug. Microsoft's documentation is not clear about this. but such operations clearly fail in current versions of Internet Explorer.

```
open("","newWindow")   ' opens a new empty window named "newWindow"

open("this.htm","")    ' opens a new browser-named window displaying
"this.htm"
```

2. The target argument is any text string or expression that evaluates to a text string. If window.open() or open() is used, this text string is used to name a new window for the open() method to create. If another window is referenced by this method (such as parent.open()), this string is used to name (or rename) the parent window (which becomes the target of the open() method). This argument is optional; but, if you skip it—or pass empty ("") to it—the browser creates its own name for the window (which is something weird like w_i_n_d_o_w0 or w_i_n_d_o_w1, etc., for Internet Explorer). Use the window.name property to discover the exact string used by your browser.

3. The part argument is actually an argument group that may contain up to seven sub-arguments that take "yes" or "no" for an answer. Any number of these sub-arguments can be listed within the argument string in any order desired, as long as its sub-argument label is present. To include any member

of this argument group in your open() method string, you must provide at
least a placeholder answer for the URL and target arguments (which the
open() method expects to precede the part argument group).

```
open("","","toolbar=no")
' opens an empty browser-named window without a toolbar

open("","","toolbar=no,status=no,menubar=no")
' opens an empty browser-named window without a toolbar, status bar,
' or menu bar
open("toolbar=no")
' interprets "toolbar=no" as an improper URL, and opens an empty
' browser-named window

open("this.htm","toolbar=no")
' opens a new window named "toolbar=no," displaying this.htm
```

a. The toolbar argument determines whether or not the browser's toolbar is
displayed on the target window.

b. The location argument determines whether or not the browser's location
field is displayed on the target window. (This appears to be a Netscape
Navigator item only. It is not currently applicable to Internet Explorer, whose
Address field is considered, by the browser, to be part of its toolbar item.)

c. The directories argument determines whether or not the browser's
"Directory" buttons are displayed on the target window. (This appears to
be a Netscape Navigator item only. It is not currently applicable to Internet
Explorer.)

d. The status argument determines whether or not the browser's Status Bar is
displayed on the target window. If this argument is not declared, it defaults
to "Yes," and the item is displayed.

e. The menubar argument determines whether or not the browser's Menubar
is displayed on the target window. If this argument is not declared, it
defaults to "Yes," and the item is displayed.

f. The scrollbars argument determines whether or not the browser's scrollbars
are displayed on the target window.

g. The resizable argument determines whether or not the browser's toolbar is
displayed on the target window. (This appears to be inoperable for the current version of Internet Explorer.)

4. The size argument is also an argument group which may contain up to four
sub-arguments. Size arguments take an integer representing "number of pixels" for an answer. Any number of these sub-arguments can be listed within
the argument string in any order desired, as long as its sub-argument label is

> ## Undocumented Features of the Window.open() Method?
>
> Microsoft's published VBScript language guides do not clearly document whether the window.open() method requires that a part argument string precede the size argument. It may be that these two optional argument strings may be passed in either order (as long as their respective argument strings contain proper internal labels, and that there are placeholders present for the URL and target arguments). Although I suspect that this hypothesis is *supposed to be true*, it has not been possible to test it, because current versions of Internet Explorer don't appear to allow the setting of both a window's part properties *and* size properties in the same open() method call.
>
> Although it is not the purpose of this book to report interpreter bugs that may well be fixed by the time you read these words, it is difficult to avoid occasional exceptions (such as the previous tip). Especially when a language element behaves in an unexpected way that *might reflect its intended behavior*. However, in the absence of any documentation from Microsoft verifying this particular behavior, I suspect this a bug that may soon be fixed, if not in your current version, then in a future update.
>
> ```
> open("","","width=200,height=200")
> ' opens an empty browser-named window 200 pixels wide and 200 pixels high
> ```

present. To include any member of this argument group in your open() method string, you must provide at least a placeholder answer for the URL and target arguments (which the open() method expects to precede the size argument group).

a. The width argument determines the new window's width in pixels.

b. The height argument determines the new window's height in pixels.

c. The top argument determines the number of pixels between the top of the screen and the top of the window.

d. The top argument determines the number of pixels between the left side of the screen and the left side of the window.

(See Figure 6.8.)

```
<HTML>
<HEAD>

<SCRIPT LANGUAGE="VBScript">

sub theButton_onClick()

    open window.location,"myWind","toolbar=no,status=no"
```

```
end sub

</SCRIPT>
</HEAD>
<BODY>
<FORM>

I would like to see this button in a   <INPUT TYPE="button"
NAME="theButton" VALUE="New Window">

</FORM>
</BODY>
```

Since the open() method belongs to the top-level window object, you needn't include any reference to that object if you create a new window from the current window. To use the open() method to open another window (instead of creating a new one):

```
windowName.prompt("How many widgets do you want to order?")
```

Figure 6.8 When the user clicks the "New Window" button in the first window, a new window (sans Status and Toolbars) presents the same button in its document display field.

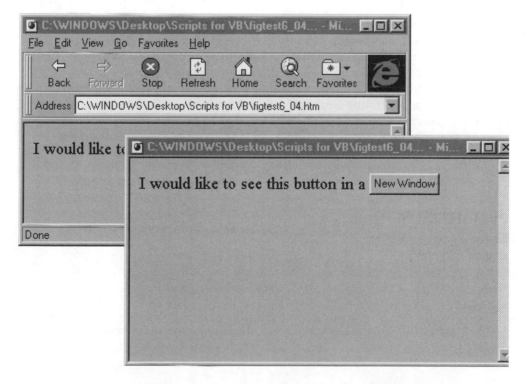

As a Document Method

The open method is used to open a new document output stream, in preparation for a new HTML string to be written to the document using one of the document object's write methods. The document stream is then closed by the document.close() method.

The document.open() method takes no arguments.

```
document.open()
document.write("Any string of valid HTML supported by the browser.")
document.close()
```

ParentElement Method

Term: parentElement(*char*)

Example Syntax:

```
theParent = document.all.div1.parentElement(12)
' puts the parent of the reference range character into theParent variable
```

Assigned Objects: body, button, div, marquee, td, textarea, th

The parentElement method returns the parent of the range character specified by the answer to the char argument, which takes a number representing a character position in a string.

> **WARNING** This method cannot be used alone, but must be followed by at least one document.write() or document.writeLn() statement. If used by itself, this method "hangs" the interpreter, which is now waiting endlessly for a follow-up instruction. In current versions, the interpreter doesn't respond to the browser's "Stop" button, and Windows users must resort to Control-Alt-Delete to open the End Task dialog, and force the browser to quit. If document.open is used without an ending document.close() statement, the interpreter also "hangs," but allows you to recover by clicking its "Stop" button.

PasteHTMLMethod

Term: pasteHTML(*HTMLstring*)

Example Syntax:

```
document.all.div1.parentElement("<TEXTAREA>New Text</TEXTAREA>")
' pastes the new textarea into the refrenced range object
```

Assigned Objects: body, button, div, marquee, td, textarea, th

The pasteHMTL method pastes the HTML string into the referenced range object.

Prompt Method

Term: prompt(*textString,fieldString*)

Example Syntax:

```
prompt("Please type your name:")
' displays the text " Please type your name:" in a prompt dialog box, with an
' input field, and an OK and Cancel button
```

Assigned Objects: window.

The prompt method takes any text string (or any expression that evaluates to a text string) as its first argument. It displays this string in a standard VBScript prompt dialog box with an "OK" and "Cancel" button, and a user input field (shown in Figure 6.9). Like the alert() and confirm() methods before it, if you do not provide a string for this argument, <undefined> is used as the prompt message.

The prompt() method also takes a text string as its second argument, allowing you to place a default response into the prompt dialog box's user input field, to save the user some typing (or to persuade the user to respond to the prompt in a particular way). The default field string argument is optional. If you don't provide this string, <undefined> is placed into the field. If you prefer the field to be empty, pass the empty literal as an answer to this argument:

```
prompt("How many widgets do you want to order?","")
```

Any time you place a literal text string directly between any method's enclosing parenthesis, you must enclose it in quotes. If you use variables or the properties of other objects that evaluate to a text string, the quotes are not used.

```
prompt("How many widgets do you want to order?","Make it 100.")
' literal text strings must be quoted

myVariable1 = "How many widgets do you want to order?"
myVariable2 = "Make it 100."
prompt(myVariable1,myVariable2)
' expressions that evaluate to text strings are not quoted
```

The prompt() method is used whenever you need unique feedback from the user. For this purpose, the prompt dialog box provides an editable field into which the user may type any short response to the displayed prompt message. This method returns the contents of the input field if the user clicks the "OK" button, and "" if the user clicks the "Cancel" button.

```
<HTML>
<HEAD>

<SCRIPT LANGUAGE="VBScript">
```

```
DIM numOrdered

sub theButton_onClick()

    numOrdered = prompt("How many widgets do you want to order?","none")

    if (numOrdered = "") or (numOrdered = "none")   then

        alert "Sorry you didn't want any widgets."

    else

        alert "Thank you for ordering " & numOrdered & " widgets."

    end if

end sub

</SCRIPT>
</HEAD>
<BODY>
<FORM>

I would like to <INPUT TYPE="button" NAME="theButton" VALUE="Order Widgets">

</FORM>
</BODY>
```

> **TIP** The previous example shows how to assign the same script response to two different "false" result strings from the prompt() method—which is a handy technique to know. In essence, this script tells the browser to present the "Sorry" alert (see Figure 6.10 versus Figure 6.11) if the user clicks Cancel (which returns the ""string), *or* if the user leaves the word "none" in the field and clicks OK (which returns the "none" string). While there are many instances where you'll need to allow different return values to execute the same response to a "false" condition, this particular example script could also have been written to assign the same value ("") to both false results. Following is a rewritten version of the same script that assigns "" to the default prompt string. This causes the prompt() method to return the same "" string whether the user clicks Cancel or OK. Now the if statement only needs to allow

for one return string to execute its false condition—regardless of
whether the user clicks Cancel, or the "OK" button while the input field
is empty:

```
sub theButton_onClick()

    numOrdered = prompt("How many widgets do you want to order?","")

    if (numOrdered = "") then

        alert "Sorry you didn't want any widgets."

    else

        alert "Thank you for ordering " & numOrdered & " widgets."

    end if

end sub
```

**Figure 6.9 When the user clicks the "Order Widgets" button, the "How
many do you want..." prompt appears.**

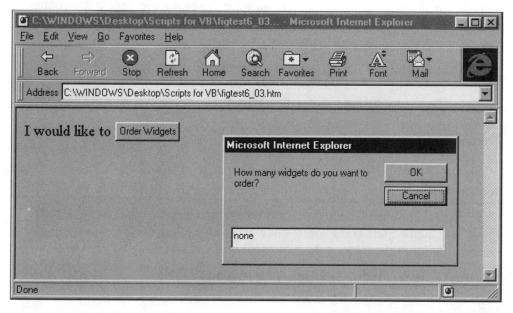

Figure 6.10 If the user clicks the "Cancel" button—or the "OK" button while "none" is still in the field—the "Sorry" alert appears.

Figure 6.11 If the user types something else into the field and clicks the "OK" button, the "Thank you" alert appears.

Since the prompt() method belongs to the top-level window object, you needn't include any reference to that object if you want the prompt to appear above the current window. To bring another window forward, and then show the prompt, you must attach the prompt() method to the target window object:

```
windowName.prompt("How many widgets do you want to order?")
```

QueryCommandEnabled Method

Term: queryCommandEnabled(*command*)

Example Syntax:

```
isEnabled = document.body.queryCommandEnabled(2)
' returns "true" if query #2 is available
```

Assigned Objects: body, button, div, document, marquee, td, textarea, th

The queryCommandEnabled method returns "true" if the passed command or query is available, and "false" if it is not. Its required command argument is answered with the number of the command or query.

QueryCommandIndeterm Method

Term: queryCommandIndeterm(*command*)

Example Syntax:

```
isIndeterm = document.body.queryCommandIndeterm(2)
' returns "true" if it cannot be determined whether query #2 is available
```

Assigned Objects: body, button, div, document, marquee, td, textarea, th

The queryCommandIndeterm method returns "true" if the passed command or query is in an indeterminate, and "false" if it is not. Its required command argument is answered with the number of the command or query.

QueryCommandState Method

Term: queryCommandState(*command*)

Example Syntax:

```
theState = document.body.queryCommandState(2)
' returns "true" if query #2 is available, "false" if not, and "null" if
' indeterminate
```

Assigned Objects: body, button, div, document, marquee, td, textarea, th

The queryCommandState method returns the state of the passed command or query. Its required command argument is answered with the number of the command or query.

QueryCommandSupported Method

Term: queryCommandSupported(*command*)

Example Syntax:

```
isOn = document.body.queryCommandSupported(2)
' returns "true" if query #2 is turned on
```

Assigned Objects: body, button, div, document, marquee, td, textarea, th

The queryCommandSupported method returns "true" if the passed command or query is turned on, and "false" if it is turned off. Its required command argument is answered with the number of the command or query.

QueryCommandText Method

Term: queryCommandText(*command*)

Example Syntax:

```
theQuery = document.body.queryCommandText(2)
' returns a text string associated with query #2
```

Assigned Objects: body, button, div, document, marquee, td, textarea, th

The queryCommandText method returns the associated text string that describes the passed command or query. Its required command argument is answered with the number of the command or query.

RangeFromElement Method

Term: rangeFromElement(*theElement*)

Example Syntax:

```
theRange = document.rangeFromElement(document.all(12))
' if the 13th element in the all collection is a textRange object, it puts the
' textRange into theRange variable
```

Assigned Objects: document

The rangeFromElement method locates the passed element, and returns it as a textRange object. If the element is not found, or if it does not support the textRange object, "null" is returned.

Reload Method

Term: `reload()`

Example Syntax:

```
sub window_onDblClick()
        location.reload()
end sub
' reloads the current page whenever the user double-clicks anywhere in the
' window
```

Assigned Objects: location

The reload method reloads the current location object (Web page) into the current window.

Remove Method

Term: `remove(index)`

Example Syntax:

```
alert document.all.remove(12)
' removes the 13th member of the all collection
```

Assigned Objects: areas, script, select, options

The remove method removes the member of the collection that occupies the index position represented by the number passed to this method's index argument.

RemoveMember Method

Term: `removeMember()`

Example Syntax:

```
sub document_onClick()
        document.all.div1()
end sub
' when the document receives a click event, the referenced tag is removed from
' the document
```

Assigned Objects: all HTML tags

The removeMember method removes the referenced HTML object from the page.

Replace Method

Term: `replace(url)`

Example Syntax:

```
sub window_onDblClick()
        location.replace("new.htm")
end sub
```

```
' replaces the current page with "new.htm" when the user double-clicks anywhere
' in the window
```
Assigned Objects: location

The replace method replaces the current location object (Web page) with the Web page passed to it in the form of a URL, in answer to its url argument.

Reset Method
Term: reset()
Example Syntax:
```
document.thisForm.reset()
' resets the referenced form
```
Assigned Objects: form

The reset method is an event simulation method. It coerces the resetting of a form, without requiring the user to click a formal "Reset" button. The reset() method takes no arguments.

Scroll Method
Term: scroll(*x,y*)
Example Syntax:
```
window.scroll(125,200)
' scrolls the object(s) at the specified x,y coordinates into view
```
Assigned Objects: window

The scroll method is an event simulation method. It scrolls the window view to include the area of the page that is defined by the screen pixels (numbers) passed to the x, and y arguments, without requiring the user to manipulate the scroll.

ScrollIntoView Method
Term: scrollIntoView(*start*)
Example Syntax:
```
document.all.div1.scroll(false)
' scrolls to the end of the visible objects created by the <DIV> tag whose ID
' is "div1"
```
Assigned Objects: all HTML tags

The scrollIntoView method is an event simulation method. It scrolls the window view to include the range of visible objects presented by the referenced HTML object. The answer to the start argument must be "true" to scroll to the start of the range, and "false" to scroll to its end.

Select Method
Term: select()
Example Syntax:
```
document.thisForm.myField.select()
```

```
' selects the contents of the referenced field
```
Assigned Objects: password, text, textarea

The select method is an event simulation method. It sends a select event to the referenced field, as if a user physically highlighted the contents of that field. For the field to receive the select event, it must contain text. The select() method takes no arguments.

The following script selects the contents of the second text field whenever the user tabs or clicks into it (see Figure 6.12):

```
<HTML>
<HEAD>

<SCRIPT LANGUAGE="VBScript">

</SCRIPT>
</HEAD>
<BODY>

<FORM>
<CENTER>

<INPUT TYPE="text" SIZE=15 NAME="text1" VALUE="Tab to next field.">
<INPUT TYPE="text" SIZE=10 NAME="text2" VALUE="Type here."
onFocus="text2.select()">

</CENTER>
</FORM>
</BODY>
</HTML>
```

Figure 6.12 When this page is first loaded, its first text field automatically receives the document focus. When the user tabs from this field into the second field, the contents of the second field are automatically selected.

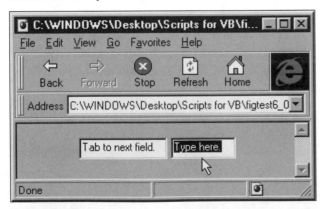

SetMember Method
Term: setMember(*value,property*)
Example Syntax:
```
sub document_onClick()
        document.body.setMember("red",bgColor)
end sub
' when the document receives a click event, the document bgColor property is set
' to red
```
Assigned Objects: all HTML tags

The setMember method sets the value of the passed property according to the answer given to its value argument. The value argument must receive a valid setting for the passed property. The property argument must be a valid property for the referenced object.

SetTimeout Method
Term: setTimeout(*action,milliseconds,language*)
Example Syntax:
```
myTimer = setTimeout("Call doProc()",60000,"VBScript")
' sets the language to "VBScript," and causes a procedure named "doProc()" to
' execute its statements once a minute
```
Assigned Objects: window

This method is used to incrementally repeat a given procedure. When used without an object reference, it sets its timeout activities for the current window. To use this method to time activities in another window, you must reference that window when invoking this method:

```
myTimer = parent.setTimeout("Call doProc()",60000,"VBScript")
' performs its timer services for the current window's parent
```

The setTimeout() method is often used to create timers for games, tests, or other time-based user activities on a Web page. It takes three arguments, all of which are required. The first argument is any expression that evaluates to a scripted procedure or object method that defines the action that the method should repeat. The second argument is any number or expression that evaluates to a number that designates the number of milliseconds the interpreter should wait between executions. The third argument tells the browser the scripting language in use and (for the current version of Internet Explorer) appears to be necessary to the proper operation of the code, even when that code is enclosed within a <SCRIPT> tag that already identifies VBScript as the current language.

In addition to processing its passed procedure, this method also returns its ID string—which comes in handy for the clearTimeout() methods which requires this string to stop the setTimeout() method from repeatedly calling its action script. (See ClearTimeout Method for details.)

The follow example creates a form with a text field that displays a "0," and a "Start" and "Stop" button. Clicking the "Start" button causes the setTimeout() method to repeatedly call theTimer() procedure in 1-second intervals (see Figure 6.13). Each call to theTimer() adds a "1" to the Elapsed Seconds field, providing the user with a visual review of the passing seconds.

```
<HTML>
<HEAD>

<SCRIPT LANGUAGE="VBScript">

DIM myTimer

sub Start_onClick()

    Call theTimer()

end sub

sub theTimer()

    document.forms(0).Seconds.value = document.forms(0).Seconds.value+1
    myTimer = setTimeout("Call theTimer()",1000,"VBScript")

end sub

sub Stop_onClick()

    clearTimeout myTimer
    document.forms(0).Seconds.value = 0

end sub

</SCRIPT>
</HEAD>
<BODY>
<FORM>

<b>Elapsed Seconds</b>:
<INPUT TYPE="text" SIZE=2 NAME="Seconds" VALUE="0">
<INPUT TYPE="button" NAME="Start" VALUE="Start">
<INPUT TYPE="button" NAME="Stop" VALUE="Stop">

</FORM>
</BODY>
```

Figure 6.13 When the user clicks the "Start" button, the timer script begins counting the seconds in the "Elapsed Seconds" field. (See the ClearTimeout Method for a discussion of the "Stop" button.)

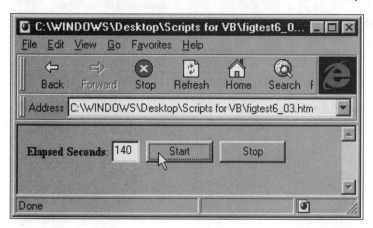

SetTimeout() Anomalies

Microsoft's VBScript documentation of the setTimeout() method provides this example script:

```
MyID = setTimeout ("Button1.Click",100).
```

However, this line of script did not work in the version of Internet Explorer used with this book for two reasons:

1. It was necessary to answer the language argument to get this method to work—which could point to a bug in the interpreter (since Microsoft's documenter obviously believed the argument to be optional). It may also be that the language argument is actually required (which is the assumption made in this book, since setTimeout() wouldn't work otherwise). This assumption seems sensible, since the JavaScript version of setTimeout() is implemented a little differently than the VBScript version. Given the fact that Internet Explorer interprets both, it may need to know which language is in use.

2. This script's answer to the action argument (a direct reference to the button object's click() method) failed to start the timer process.

The solution to the first problem is simple: pass an answer to the setTimeout() method's language argument. This is good coding practice

210

anyway (especially since additional scripting languages are in the making as you read this).

The second problem is also simply solved. If your version of Internet Explorer (or other VBScript-aware application) has trouble executing this method using only a procedure name or object.method reference, use the Call statement to coerce the method into doing its job (as shown in the previous example).

ShowModalDialog Method
Term: showModalDialog(*url*,[*args*],[*features*])
Example Syntax:
```
window.showModalDialog("notice.htm")
' displays the "notice.htm" document in a modal dialog
```
Assigned Objects: window

The showModalDialog displays the passed HTML document in a modal dialog box. The required url argument must be answered with a proper url to an existing HTML document. Its optional args argument lets you specify arguments to display; and the optional features argument lets you set window dressing parameters (toolbar, etc.). See Window Open Method.

Start Method
Term: start()
Example Syntax:
```
document.all.marquee1.start()
' starts scrolling the contents of the referenced marquee
```
Assigned Objects: marquee

The start method is used to start the scrolling of the referenced marquee's contents. It takes no arguments.

StartPainting Method
Term: startPainting(*mlsecs*)
Example Syntax:
```
document.all.marquee1.startPainting(200)
' starts painting the contents of the referenced marquee using the referenced
number of millseconds for its transition
```
Assigned Objects: button, checkbox, div, img, marquee, object, password, radio, table, td, text, textarea, th

The startPainting method is used to paint the element using a custom transition defined by the number of milliseconds dictated by the answer (a number) to the mlsecs argument. Passing 0 to this argument removes the existing transition and resumes normal painting. This method requires a transition object that supports IViewTransition and IViewTransitionSite.

Stop Method

Term: stop()
Example Syntax:

```
document.all.marquee1.stop()
' stops scrolling the contents of the referenced marquee
```

Assigned Objects: marquee

The stop method is used to stop the scrolling of the referenced marquee's contents. It takes no arguments.

StopPainting Method

Term: stopPainting(*transition*)
Example Syntax:

```
document.all.marquee1.stopPainting(transObj)
' stops painting scrolling the contents of the referenced marquee
```

Assigned Objects: button, checkbox, div, img, marquee, object, password, radio, table, td, text, textarea, th

The stopPainting method is used to stop painting the referenced element using the custom transition defined by the transition argument. This method requires a transition object that supports IViewTransition and IViewTransitionSite.

Submit Method

Term: submit()
Example Syntax:

```
document.thisForm.submit()
' submits the referenced form
```

Assigned Objects: form

The submit method is an event simulation method. It coerces the submission of a form, without requiring the user to click a formal "Submit" button. The submit() method takes no arguments.

When the user clicks or tab out of the "Name" field generated by this example script, the contents of that field are automatically submitted as part of the Subject string for an e-mail message to the address given in the answer to the <FORM> tag's ACTION argument (see Figure 6.14):

```
<HTML>
<HEAD>

<SCRIPT LANGUAGE="VBScript">

sub nameField_onBlur()

    document.myForm.submit

end sub
```

```
</SCRIPT>
</HEAD>
<BODY>

<FORM NAME="myForm" ACTION="mailto:mjmara@onr.com?subject=Order"
ENCTYPE="text/plain">

<b>Name:</b><INPUT TYPE="text" NAME="nameField">

</FORM>
</BODY>
</HTML>
```

Tags Method

Term: tags(*tag*)

Example Syntax:

```
SET theScripts = document.all.tags("script")
```

Figure 6.14 When the user clicks or tabs out of the name field, its contents are e-mailed to the address in the ACTION argument.

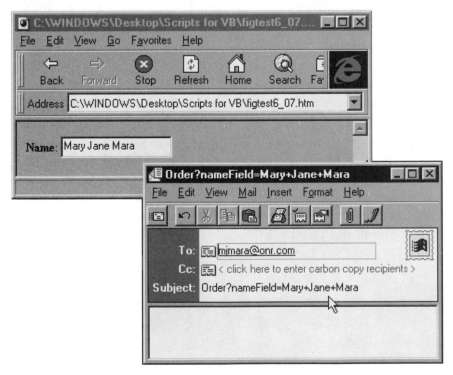

```
' sets theScripts variable to a collection of all <SCRIPT> tags in the current
' document
```
Assigned Objects: all, anchors, applets, areas, elements, embeds, frames, forms, images, links, plugins, scripts

The tags method returns a collection of the elements belonging to the tag specified by the answer to the tag argument. The following script returns "div1" (the ID of the second <DIV> tag) in an alert:

```
<HTML>
<HEAD>
<SCRIPT LANGUAGE="VBScript">

DIM theElements

sub document_onClick()

    SET theElements = document.all.tags("div")
    alert theElements(1).id

end sub

</SCRIPT>
</HEAD>
<BODY>
<DIV ID="div1">This is the first line of text</DIV>
<DIV ID="div2">This is the second line of text</DIV>
<DIV ID="div3">This is the third line of text</DIV>

</BODY>
</HTML>
```

Write Method

Term: write(*htmlString*)
Example Syntax:
```
document.write("<b>This is new text for the current document.</b>")
' writes the passed string of HTML to the current document.
```
Assigned Objects: document

The "write" method is used to dynamically generate HTML for display in the current page or in a new document. This method takes only one argument, which is a string (or any expression that evaluates to a string) of proper HTML. Simple text with no HTML tags is acceptable, and is placed on the page as paragraph text.

To write to the current document, you must invoke the write() method at parse time. This means, that the document.write() method must be called as the page is loading into the browser. This occurs when you call the write() method (or a procedure that references this method) from an "onLoad" handler (perhaps in the <BODY> tag of your page), or from an inline script (see Figure 6.15):

```
<HTML>
<HEAD>
</HEAD>

<BODY>

This is an example of an inline script that dynamically generates HTML for display in a specific location on the current page.

<SCRIPT LANGUAGE="VBScript">

document.write("<p><b>This text was placed in this spot on the current page by the document.write method.</b>")

</SCRIPT>

<p>All of the rest of the text on this page was generated by its base HTML script.

</BODY>
</HTML>
```

Why Write Additional HTML to the Current Document?

At first glance, it may seem futile to use the document.write() method to add HTML lines to the current document. Since you can only perform this operation on the current document at parse time (as the document is being loaded into the browser), the same page display results as if you simply included the document.write() string in your regular HTML code. Why bother?

Even during document load, however, it is possible to gather unique information about your current visitor, such as browser in use, previously stored cookie data, or (if you're using VBScript on the server side) server-provided update information (see Figure 6.16). Other information you can gather at parse time includes document.referrer (the URL of the page that sent the user to the current page) and document.lastModified (the document's last modification date).

This is some of the information you can obtain at parse time that you won't already know when you're writing the base HTML for a page. After gathering this info, you can use the document.write() method to insert and display it in the current page, as does this example script:

```
<HTML>
<HEAD>
</HEAD>
<BODY>

Welcome to my Web site.

<p>I see that you are using the

<SCRIPT LANGUAGE="VBScript">

document.write("<b>" & navigator.appName & "</b>")

</SCRIPT>

browser.

<p>Good choice!

</BODY>
</HTML>
```

To rewrite the current document (clear all of the existing HTML items from the page and display a completely new version of the page), you must invoke the write() method *after* parse time. This means, that the document.write() method *cannot* be called as the page is loading into the browser. Scripts that use the document.write() method to totally regenerate the page must be invoked by a user-generated event occurring after the page is fully loaded and on view in the browser window.

The following example script presents explanatory text and a button when the page is first loaded into the browser. However, when the user clicks the "Revise Page" button, this information disappears, and is replaced by a single, bolded sentence (see Figures 6.17 and 6.18):

Figure 6.15 The bolded lines on this page were inserted by an inline script containing a document.write() statement.

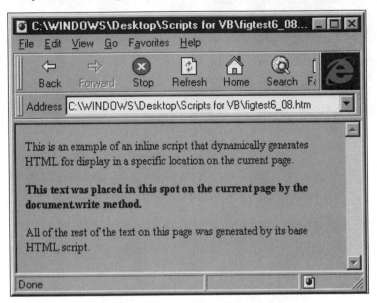

Figure 6.16 The bolded name of the browser in use was inserted during parse time using document.write() in an inline script.

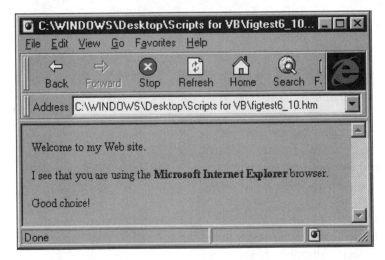

> **TIP** Keep in mind that VBScript is a "safe" subset of the Visual Basic
> language. Because of this, it is not possible for VBScript to overwrite
> any file, including your HTML files. When VBScript's document.write()
> methods are used to clear the current page display and display new
> HTML items, the new HTML exists only in the browser's memory. The
> window's current location object continues to be the URL to your origi-
> nal HTML file. Thus, if the user clicks the "Refresh" button to reload the
> page, the original HTML document is reparsed and redisplayed—not
> your document.write() statements dynamically-generated HTML.

```
<HTML>
<HEAD>

<SCRIPT LANGUAGE="VBScript">

sub theButton_onClick()

    document.open()
    document.write("<p><b>The document.write() method was used, after parse
time, to replace all of the previous information on this page with this single
sentence.</b>")
    document.close()

end sub

</SCRIPT>
</HEAD>
<BODY>

This is an example of a document.write() statement that clears the current page,
then dynamically generates HTML to display new information on that page.
<p>
Scripts that perform this type of writing action are usually set up to execute
after parse time, in response to some user action like the clicking of this
button:

<FORM>

<p><INPUT TYPE="button" NAME="theButton" VALUE="Revise Page">

</FORM>
</BODY>
```

Figure 6.17 When the page is initially loaded into the browser, it displays this information.

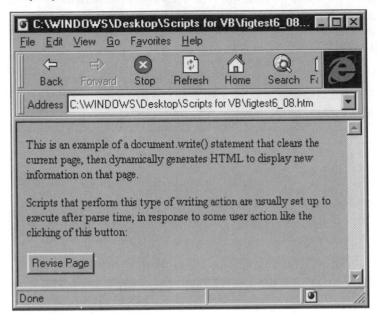

WriteLn Method

Term: writeLn(*htmlString*)

Example Syntax:

```
document.writeLn("<PRE>This is a single line of text.</PRE>")
' writes the passed string of HTML and a newline character to the current
' document.
```

Assigned Objects: document

The writeLn method behaves exactly as the document.write() method, with the exception that it tacks a "newline" character to the end of its passed HTML string. Like the write() method, writeLn() is used to dynamically generate HTML for display in the current page or in a new document. This method takes only one argument, which is a string (or any expression that evaluates to a string) of proper HTML. Simple text with no HTML tags is acceptable, and is placed on the page as paragraph text.

To write new, separated lines to the current document, you must invoke the writeLn() method at parse time (as discussed in the Write Method section).

Figure 6.18 When the "Revise Page" button is clicked, the previously displayed information disappears, replaced by this single, bolded sentence.

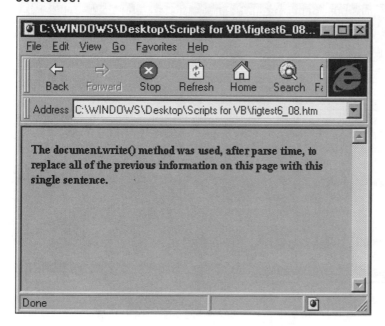

For all practical purposes, this method's passed HTML string must be enclosed in <PRE> tags, since this is the only HTML tag (for now) that recognizes the new-line character. If you pass the string without enclosing it in <PRE> tags, the writeLn() method behaves exactly as document.write() (see Figure 6.19).

```
<HTML>
<HEAD>
</HEAD>
<BODY>

This is an example of an inline script that inserts two separate lines of text
into the current document using the document.writeLn() method.

<SCRIPT LANGUAGE="VBScript">

document.writeLn("<PRE><b>This is the first new line of text.</b></PRE>")
document.writeLn("<PRE><b>This is the second new line of text.</b></PRE>")

</SCRIPT>
```

Figure 6.19 The bolded lines on this page were inserted by an inline script containing a document.write() statement.

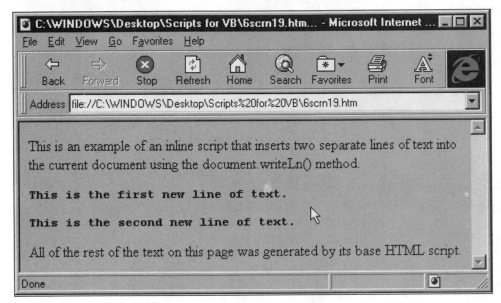

```
<p>All of the rest of the text on this page was generated by its base HTML
script.

</BODY>
</HTML>
```

To rewrite the current document (clear all of the existing HTML items from the page, and display a completely new version of the page), you must invoke the writeLn() method *after* parse time. Scripts that use the document.writeLn() method to totally regenerate the page must be invoked by a user-generated event occurring after the page is fully loaded and on view in the browser window (see the Write Method section for an example).

ZOrder Method

Term: zOrder(*pos*)

Example Syntax:

```
document.all(12).zOrder(0)
' places the referenced object in the front of the document, at the top of the
' z-index or in the top layer
```

Assigned Objects: button, checkbox, div, img, marquee, object, password, radio, select, table, td, text, textarea, th

The zOrder method is used to set the z-index of the referenced object in fixed layout regions. If the number 0 is passed to the pos argument, the object is sent to the front.

What's Next?

Now that you've fully reviewed the objects, properties, and methods at your disposal, events are next on the agenda. There are more events available for your use in VBScript than ever before, thanks to the new Document Object Model. Moreover, there are new ways to work with events using the Object Hierarchy. Chapter 7 presents all of the VBScript events—new and old—and reviews the new concept of event bubbling.

7

Event Handlers

Chapters 4 through 6 provided explanations, tips, and example scripts for VBScript's built-in Objects, many of its associated Properties, and all of its attached Methods. Yet, even with all these language elements at your fingertips, nothing happens in a VBScript until some recognized event (like the user clicking a button) starts the ball rolling (or the event bubbling, as they say in DHTML). On rare occasions, this event can even be triggered by the browser, for example, when it displays a default page on startup, causing the *load* event to fire. Most events, however, are ultimately instigated by the user who, for the most part, has total control over which events do and do not fire while your scripted page is on display in the user's browser window. The keyword here is *user*'s. Note the critical use of the possessive in this term; it is the *user's* window, not yours.

Once your page *is* displayed in a given browser, however, you're (probably) assured of at least two events firing during its session lifetime (the period of time the page remains on display in that browser): the initial load event, fired when the document is first loaded into the window; and the unload event, fired when the user ultimately moves to another document, or quits the browser application. Beyond that, death and taxes are the only other inevitables.

However, when the load and unload events *are* fired (or when the user deigns to take an action on your page that results in the firing of another recognized event), you can make the most of it by attaching a scripted "browser to-do list" to the object that fired the event, or to an appropriate parent object that sits above the target object in the hierarchy and (thanks to the introduction of DHTML) has the right to process events for its children.

Scripts are attached to an appropriate object and a designated event by an *event handler*, so-called because it is set up to handle that event—in other words, pass a set of scripting actions to the browser when that event is fired by the object attached to the handler, or by a child of that object for whom the event is both valid and targeted. (The latter process is described in a moment.)

If you want certain scripting actions to take place when a particular button is clicked (thereby firing the *click* event), then you can attach the *onClick* event handler, and its handling script, directly to that button using one of the three event-attachment methods discussed in Chapter 1:

1. You can include the event handler as an argument within the target object's HTML tag, along with an answering script:

```
<INPUT TYPE="button" NAME=thisButton onClick="doThis('thing')">
```

2. You can combine the name of the target object with the name of the event handler in the opening line of a *sub* statement:

```
sub thisButton_onClick()
```

3. You can include the FOR and EVENT arguments in the <SCRIPT> tag:

```
<SCRIPT LANGUAGE="VBScript" FOR="thisButton" EVENT="onClick()">
```

Chapter 4's Object definitions include whether or not the object takes events and, if so, *which* events. The definition for each object that takes events also notes which of the aforementioned attachment methods are valid for that object (for instance, not every object may be attached to its event via a sub statement). Check that chapter reference if you are unsure of the valid attachment formats for a given object.

New Way to Process Events

With the introduction of DHTML in Internet Explorer 4—and the consequent expansion of the HTML Object Model—there are not only additional events that you can intercept in your scripts, but a new way of processing those events for your objects and object collections. You can now attach events to a parent object, and create a centralized routine (script) for processing that event for all of that object's children—with branches that dictate the behavior of the script for various object types.

The following sub statement, for instance, intercepts *any* click event on the entire page, and allows you to create a central script for processing those clicks. Using conditional and repeat control structures, you could create a single, compact script that would respond one way if an <INPUT TYPE="button"> object is clicked, and another way if an <A HREF> object is clicked. When the click event occurs, it *bubbles up* the hierarchy to the document object, where it is *trapped* by this sub statement:

```
sub document_onClick
```

Another example use of event bubbling is this sub statement that captures the change event fired by any element in a form named *thisForm* that supports that event:

```
sub thisForm_onChange
```

You could also use the previous sub to trap the blur event for the form's elements, or you could use the window object to trap the blur event for all of the appropriate form elements within multiple forms on the page:

```
sub window_onBlur
```

A handy bit of additional scripting that allows you to quickly discover the actual object that fired the event makes use of the event object's srcElement property:

```
theTarget = window.event.srcElement
```

When this statement is used in conjunction with a parental script that traps an event, you can really fine-tune your page's response to that event. Event bubbling may be canceled by setting the event object's cancelBubble property to "false."

The VBScript Event Handlers

Like all of the other chapters in Part II of this book, VBScript's Event Handlers are presented here in alphabetical order, not according to their associated Objects. Like Properties and Methods, Event Handlers are also assigned to multiple Objects. For instance, the onBlur() event is assigned to multiple form element objects, including password, text, and textarea objects. For this reason, each Event Handler definition in this chapter also includes a list of its assigned Objects, as well as any variable information regarding the use of that Handler with different Objects.

onAbort Handler

Term: onAbort()

Example Syntax:

```
<IMG SRC="this.gif" onAbort="alert('Sorry you don't want to see this image.'">
' presents the alert message if the user performs an abortive action before the
' image is through loading
```

Assigned Objects: img

The onAbort event handler intercepts the *abort* event when its attached image is prevented from fully loading. This happens, for instance, whenever a user clicks the browser's "Stop" button or a hypertext link on the page before the image is finished loading.

The following example script is executed if the user performs an action that causes the abort event to fire for the attached image object.

```
<HTML>
<HEAD>

<SCRIPT LANGUAGE="VBScript">

sub mapImage_onAbort()

    alert "The current image isn't finished loading. It contains links to other
documents that won't be available to you without the full display of this image.
If you'd like to access these links, just reload the page."

</SCRIPT>
</HEAD>
<BODY>

<IMG SRC="map.gif" ID="mapImage">

</BODY>
</HTML>
```

onAfterUpdate Handler

Term: onAfterUpdate()

Example Syntax:

```
<INPUT TYPE="password" NAME="pword"
onBeforeUpdate()="confirm('Are you sure you want to change your password?')"
```

```
onAfterUpdate="alert 'Your password has been changed.'">
' advises the user that the password has been changed.
```
Assigned Objects: a, applet, area, body, button, checkbox, div, document, embed, img, marquee, object, password, radio, reset, select, submit, table, td, text, textarea, th

The onAfterUpdate event handler must be fired following an onBeforeUpdate event resulting in a change to the element's contained data. Both events are only valid for the page if data binding is active.

> **N O T E** Data binding refers to the fact that you can now bind data on a server to tables or controls that appear in a Web page. See Chapter 16 for a VBScript example that uses data binding.

onBeforeUpdate Handler
Term: onBeforeUpdate(*canCancel*)
Example Syntax:
```
<INPUT TYPE="password" NAME="pword"
onBeforeUpdate()="confirm('Are you sure you want to change your password?')">
onAfterUpdate="alert 'Your password has been changed.'">
' confirms the user's desire to change the password before completing the
' operation.
```
Assigned Objects: a, applet, area, body, button, checkbox, div, document, embed, img, marquee, object, password, radio, reset, select, submit, table, td, text, textarea, th

The onBeforeUpdate event handler is fired before the transfer of data from the element to the server, as soon as the element loses focus (or the page is unloaded), if the element has changed its value since it received the document focus. A Boolean value may be passed to the onBeforeUpdate handler, specifying whether the event can be canceled. This event is only valid for the page if data binding is active.

onBlur Handler
Term: onBlur()
Example Syntax:
```
<INPUT TYPE="textarea" onBlur="doThis('thing')">
' executes a procedure named "doThis()" whenever a text field named "textObject"
' loses the document focus
```
Assigned Objects: a, applet, area, body, button, checkbox, div, embed, frame, frameset, iframe, img, object, radio, select, submit, text, textarea, window

The onBlur event handler intercepts the *blur* event when its attached object loses the document focus. This happens, for instance, whenever a user clicks or tabs out of a text field that previously held the text insertion cursor. It can also result from the execution of the object's blur() method by an internal script.

The following example script is executed when the blur event is fired by a text object named *nameFld*. The object fires this event when the user clicks or tabs out of the *Name* field, causing a confirmation dialog to ask if the name typed into the field is correct. Clicking "OK" simply allows the browser's natural tab sequence to move focus into the *Phone* field. Clicking "Cancel" selects the contents of the Name field (if any), so the user can retype the information (see Figure 7.1).

```
<HTML>
<HEAD>

<SCRIPT LANGUAGE="VBScript">

sub nameFld_onBlur()

    DIM theName

    theName = document.forms(0).nameFld.value

    if (confirm ("Is your name " & theName & "?") = false then

        document.forms(0).nameFld.select

    end if

end sub

</SCRIPT>
</HEAD>
<BODY>
<FORM>

<b>
Name: <INPUT TYPE="text" NAME="nameFld">
<p>
Phone: <INPUT TYPE="text" NAME="phoneFld">
</b>

</FORM>
</BODY>
</HTML>
```

Figure 7.1 The user is asked to confirm the information in the Name field. Clicking "Cancel" selects the contents of the Name field, so the user can retype the information; and clicking "OK" moves focus to the Phone field.

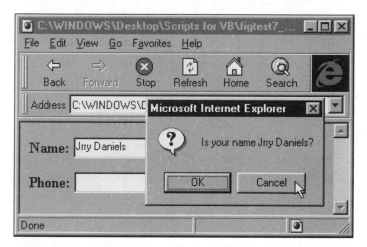

onBounce Handler

Term: onBounce(*side*)

Example Syntax: <MARQUEE BEHAVIOR="Alternate" onBounce(left)="doThis('thing')">
' executes a procedure named "doThis()" whenever the contents of the <MARQUEE>
' reach the left side

Assigned Objects: marquee

The *onBounce* event handler intercepts the *bounce* event when its marquee object's behavior is set to alternate, and the contents of the marquee reaches the specified side. The side parameter of this argument returns *right*, *left*, *top*, or *bottom*, depending on the side that fired the bounce event.

The following script is executed whenever the scrolling text bounces off of the left or right sides of the page, and causes the background of the text to alternate between white and yellow:

```
<HTML>
<HEAD>
<SCRIPT LANGUAGE="VBScript">

sub theMarq_onBounce()
```

```
    if theMarq.bgColor = "white" then

        theMarq.bgColor = "yellow"

    else

        theMarq.bgColor = "white"

    end if


end sub

</SCRIPT>
</HEAD>
<BODY>

<MARQUEE ID="theMarq" BEHAVIOR=ALTERNATE>
This is scrolling text.
</MARQUEE>

</BODY>
</HTML>
```

onChange Handler

Term: onChange()

Example Syntax:

```
<SELECT onChange="doThis('thing')">
' executes a procedure named "doThis()" whenever the user selects a new item
' from the referenced select object's list
```

Assigned Objects: checkbox, radio, select, text, textarea

The *onChange* event handler intercepts the *change* event when its attached object loses the document focus *and its value has changed*. This happens, for instance, whenever a user clicks or tabs out of a text field after typing new data into the field, or erasing existing data.

The following example script is executed when the *change* event is fired by a select object named *selectList*. The object fires this event when the user selects a new option from its list, returning an alert that tells the user if the answer is right or wrong (see Figures 7.2 and 7.3).

```
<HTML>
<HEAD>
```

```
<SCRIPT LANGUAGE="VBScript">

sub selectList_onChange()

    DIM bool,opt

    opt = document.forms(0).selectList.selectedIndex
    bool = document.forms(0).selectList.options(opt).value

    alert "You've selected the " & bool & " answer."

end sub

</SCRIPT>
</HEAD>
<BODY>
<FORM>

<b>Who was the first to sign the Declaration of Independence?</b>

<SELECT NAME="selectList">

<OPTION VALUE="Wrong"> John Quincy Adams
<OPTION VALUE="Right"> John Hancock
<OPTION VALUE="Wrong"> Sally Jesse Raphael
<OPTION VALUE="Wrong"> Thomas Jefferson

</SELECT>

</FORM>
</BODY>
</HTML>
```

onClick Handler

Term: onClick()

Example Syntax:

```
<INPUT TYPE="radio" onClick="doThis('thing')">
' executes a procedure named "doThis()" whenever the user clicks the referenced
' radio button
```

Assigned Objects: a, address, applet, area, b, big, blockquote, body, button, caption, center, checkbox, cite, code, col, dd, dfn, dir, div, dl, document, dt, em, embed, font, frameset, h1-6, i, img, kbd, label, li, listing, map, marquee, menu, object, ol, p, plaintext, password, pre, radio, s, samp, select, small, span, strike, strong, sub, submit, sup, table, tbody, td, text, textarea, tfoot, th, thead, tr, tt, u, ul, var, xmp

Figure 7.2 When the user selects a new name from this list, the change event is fired, and the select object's onChange event handler script is executed.

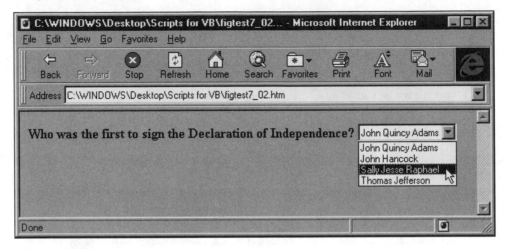

The onClick event handler intercepts the *click* event when its attached object is clicked by the user. It can also result from the execution of the object's click() method by an internal script.

Figure 7.3 If the user's new choice is anyone other than "John Hancock," the alert dialog displays a "wrong answer" message.

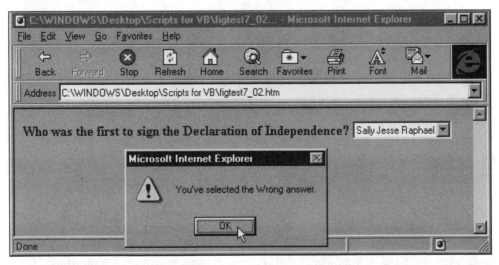

The following example script is executed when the *click* event is fired by a button named *Answer*. The object fires this event when the user clicks its generated button, returning an alert that tells the user if the answer is right or wrong (see Figures 7.4 and 7.5).

```
<HTML>
<HEAD>
<SCRIPT LANGUAGE="VBScript">

DIM theAns
theAns = "<h1><CENTER>None. It's a<br>HARDWARE<br>problem.</CENTER></h1>"

</SCRIPT>
</HEAD>
<BODY>
<FORM>
<CENTER>

<h2>How many programmers does it take to screw in a light bulb?</h2>
<p>
<INPUT TYPE="button" NAME="Answer" VALUE="I GIVE UP"
onClick="document.open()
        document.write(theAns)
        document.close()">

</CENTER>
</FORM>
</BODY>
</HTML>
```

> **TIP** There is an alternate way to implicitly attach an onClick event handler to a link object. You simply answer its HREF argument with a script instead of a URL. The bad news is, VBScript does not (yet) recognize scripts used in place of URLs. The good news is, you can still use this method with Internet Explorer if you limit yourself to calling a single VBScript function (either built-in or do-it-yourself), using this format:
>
> ```
> <A HREF="javascript:vbFunctionName(args)">
> ```

onDblClick Handler

Term: onDblClick()

Figure 7.4 When the user click the "I Give Up" button, the click event is fired, and the button's onClick event handler script is executed.

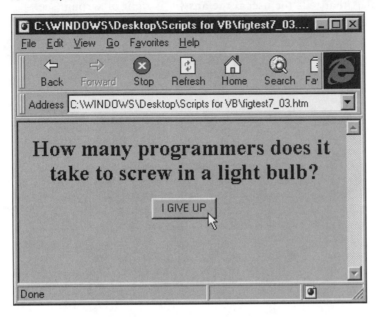

Figure 7.5 The onClick event handler script writes new HTML to the page.

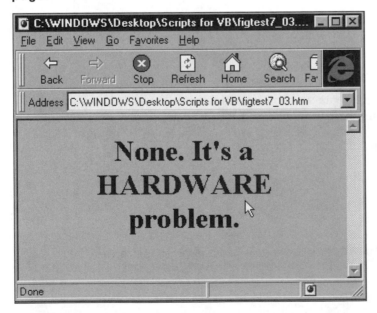

Example Syntax:
```
<INPUT TYPE="radio" onDblClick="doThis('thing')">
' executes a procedure named "doThis()" whenever the user double-clicks the
' referenced radio button
```
Assigned Objects: a, address, applet, area, b, big, blockquote, body, button, caption, center, checkbox, cite, code, col, dd, dfn, dir, div, dl, document, dt, em, embed, font, frameset, h1-6, i, img, kbd, label, li, listing, map, marquee, menu, object, ol, p, plaintext, password, pre, radio, s, samp, select, small, span, strike, strong, sub, submit, sup, table, tbody, td, text, textarea, tfoot, th, thead, tr, tt, u, ul, var, xmp

The *onDblClick* event handler intercepts the *dblclick* event when its attached object is clicked twice by the user within the time limit specified by the system's double-click speed setting.

onError Handler
Term: onError()
Example Syntax:
```
<IMG SRC="this.gif" onError="alert('This image didn't load properly.')">
' presents the alert message informing the user that the image failed to load
```
Assigned Objects: img

The *onError* event handler returns the *error* event when its attached image fails to load due to a browser, system, or network error.

onFinish Handler
Term: onFinish()
Example Syntax:
```
<MARQUEE LOOP=5 onFinish()="doThis('thing')">
' executes a procedure named "doThis()" after the contents of the <MARQUEE> have
' scrolled five times
```
Assigned Objects: marquee.

The *onFinish* event handler returns the *finish* event when the contents of the attached marquee have scrolled for the designated number of loops.

onFocus Handler
Term: onFocus()
Example Syntax:
```
<INPUT TYPE="textarea" onFocus="doThis('thing')">
' executes a procedure named "doThis()" whenever a text field named "textObject"
' receives the document focus
```
Assigned Objects: a, applet, area, body, button, checkbox, div, embed, frame, frameset, iframe, img, object, password, radio, select, submit, text, textarea, window

The *onFocus* event handler intercepts the *focus* event when its attached object receives the document focus. This happens, for instance, whenever a user clicks or tabs into a text field that previously held the text insertion cursor. It can also result from the execution of the object's focus() method by an internal script.

The following example script is executed when the focus event is fired by a text object named *birthDay*. The object fires this event when the user tabs (or clicks) from the *Name* field into the *Date of Birth* field, causing an alert dialog to instruct the user in the proper date format to use for the field (see Figure 7.6).

```
<HTML>
<HEAD>
<SCRIPT LANGUAGE="VBScript">

sub birthDay_onFocus()

    alert "Please type your date of birth in this format: MM/DD/YY. Thank you."

end sub

</SCRIPT>
</HEAD>
<BODY>
<FORM>

<b>
Name: <INPUT TYPE="text" NAME="Name">
Date of Birth: <INPUT TYPE="text" NAME="birthDay">
</b>

</FORM>
</BODY>
</HTML>
```

onHelp Handler

Term: onHelp()

Example Syntax:

```
sub document_onHelp()
' attaches the help event to the document object
```

Assigned Objects: a, address, applet, area, b, big, blockquote, body, button, caption, center, checkbox, cite, code, col, dd, dfn, dir, div, dl, document, dt, em, embed, font, frameset, h1-6, i, img, kbd, label, li, listing, map, marquee, menu, object, ol, p, plaintext, password, pre, radio, s, samp, select, small, span, strike, strong, sub, submit, sup, table, tbody, td, text, textarea, tfoot, th, thead, tr, tt, u, ul, var, xmp

Figure 7.6 As soon as the Date of Birth field receives the focus event, its handling script issues an instruction alert before the user begins typing in the field.

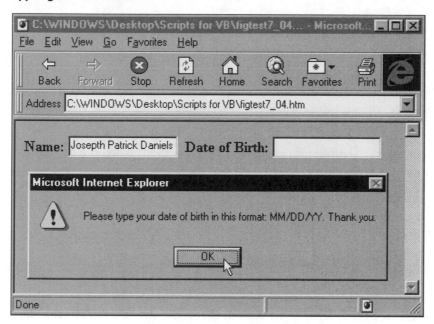

The onHelp event handler intercepts the *help* event when the user clicks the keyboard's F1 key, or the browser's "Help" button.

onKeyDown Handler

Term: onKeyDown(*shift*)
Example Syntax:

```
sub document_onKeyDown(shift)
        alert shift
end sub
' presents an alert containing 1 when the user depresses the Shift key
```

Assigned Objects: a, applet, area, body, button, checkbox, div, document, embed, img, map, marquee, object, password, radio, select, submit, td, text, textarea, th, thead

The *onKeyDown* event handler intercepts the *keyDown* event when the user presses the shift, control, or alt key on the keyboard. The shift parameter returns 1 if the shift key is pressed, 2 if the control key is pressed, 4 if the alt key is pressed, and 0 if any other key is pressed.

onKeyPress Handler

Term: onKeyPress()
Example Syntax:

```
sub document_onKeyPress()
      alert window.event.keyCode
end sub
' presents an alert when the user presses a key, containing the ASCII code for
' that key
```

Assigned Objects: a, applet, area, body, button, checkbox, div, document, embed, img, map, marquee, object, password, radio, select, submit, td, text, textarea, th, thead

The *onKeyPress* event handler intercepts the *keyPress* event when the user clicks any key on the keyboard.

onKeyUp Handler

Term: onKeyUp(*shift*)
Example Syntax:

```
sub document_onKeyUp(shift)
      alert shift
end sub
' presents an alert containing 1 when the user depresses the Shift key
```

Assigned Objects: a, applet, area, body, button, checkbox, div, document, embed, img, map, marquee, object, password, radio, select, submit, td, text, textarea, th, thead

The onKeyUp event handler intercepts the *keyUp* event when the user presses the shift, control, or alt key on the keyboard. The shift parameter returns 1 if the shift key is pressed, 2 if the control key is pressed, 4 if the alt key is pressed, and 0 if any other key is pressed.

onLoad Handler

Term: onLoad()
Example Syntax:

```
<BODY onLoad="doThis('thing')">
' executes a procedure named "doThis()" whenever the document is loaded into the
' window
```

Assigned Objects: applet, embed, frame, img, object, window

The *onLoad* event handler intercepts the *load* event whenever its attached page is loaded or refreshed in a VBScript-aware browser window. If you've got a script that's valid for the load event, you can attach it to an onLoad event handler in the <BODY> tag of your document or a sub statement that attaches the event to the window:

```
sub window_onLoad()
```

You can also let a statement stand alone (outside of any control structure) in a <SCRIPT>, and that statement will execute as soon as the <SCRIPT> tag is loaded by the browser. The following example script is executed when the load event is fired from the document's <BODY> tag, causing an alert dialog to instruct the user in the proper date format to use for the field. Note that the surfDate variable is declared (dimensioned) as soon as the <SCRIPT> is loaded (see Figure 7.7).

```
<HTML>
<HEAD>

<SCRIPT LANGUAGE="VBScript">

DIM surfDate
surfDate = date

</SCRIPT>
</HEAD>
<BODY onLoad="alert ('Thanks for stopping by at ' & surfDate & '.')">

The HTML that the document is set up to display appears here.

</BODY>
</HTML>
```

onMouseDown Handler

Term: onMouseDown(*x,y,shift,button*)

Example Syntax:

```
<A HREF="this.htm" onMouseDown(x,y,shift,button)="doThis('thing')">
' executes a procedure named "doThis()" whenever the mouse pointer is over the
' referenced link, and one of the mouse buttons is depressed
```

Assigned Objects: a, address, applet, area, b, big, blockquote, body, button, caption, center, checkbox, cite, code, col, dd, dfn, dir, div, dl, document, dt, em, embed, font, frameset, h1-6, i, img, kbd, label, li, listing, map, marquee, menu, object, ol, password, p, plaintext, pre, radio, s, samp, select, small, span, strike, strong, sub, submit, sup, table, tbody, td, text, textarea, tfoot, th, thead, tr, tt, u, ul, var, xmp

Figure 7.7 As soon as this page is loaded, it displays an alert generated by the onLoad event handler script in its <BODY> tag.

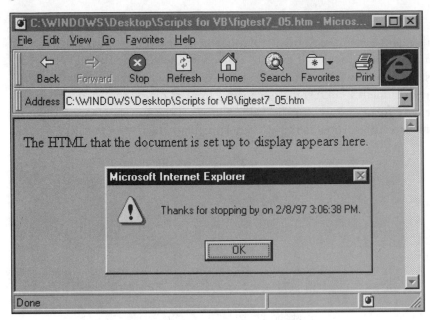

The onMouseDown event handler intercepts the *mouseDown* event when the mouse pointer is over an appropriate object, and one of the mouse buttons is pressed down. This event also provides the horizontal (x) and vertical (y) coordinates of the mouse pointer when the event was fired, whether the shift, control, or alt key was depressed, and which mouse button was down during the event. The shift parameter returns 1 if the shift key is pressed, 2 if the control key is pressed, 4 if the alt key is pressed, and 0 if any other key is pressed.

onMouseMove Handler

Term: onMouseMove(x,y,shift,button)

Example Syntax:

```
<A HREF="this.htm" onMouseMove(x,y,shift,button)="doThis('thing')">
' executes a procedure named "doThis()" whenever the mouse's pointer is moves
' over the referenced link
```

Assigned Objects: a, address, applet, area, b, big, blockquote, body, button, caption, center, checkbox, cite, code, col, dd, dfn, dir, div, dl, document, dt, em, embed, font, frameset, h1-6, i, img, kbd, label, li, listing, map, marquee, menu, object, ol, password, p, plaintext, pre, radio, s, samp, select, small, span, strike, strong, sub, submit, sup, table, tbody, td, text, textarea, tfoot, th, thead, tr, tt, u, ul, var, xmp

The *onMouseMove* event handler intercepts the *mouseMove* event when the mouse pointer moves over an appropriate object. This event also provides the horizontal (x) and vertical (y) coordinates of the mouse pointer when the event was fired, whether the shift, control, or alt key was depressed, and which mouse button (if any) was down during the mouseMove event. The shift parameter returns 1 if the shift key is pressed, 2 if the control key is pressed, 4 if the alt key is pressed, and 0 if any other key is pressed.

See Chapter 15 for example "drag 'n drop" scripts that use the onMouseMove event handler.

onMouseOut Handler

Term: onMouseOut()

Example Syntax:

```
<A HREF="this.htm" onMouseOut="doThis('thing')">
' executes a procedure named "doThis()" whenever the mouse's pointer moves
' outside the referenced link
```

Assigned Objects: a, address, applet, area, b, big, blockquote, body, button, caption, center, checkbox, cite, code, col, dd, dfn, dir, div, dl, document, dt, em, embed, font, frameset, h1-6, i, img, kbd, label, li, listing, map, marquee, menu, object, ol, password, p, plaintext, pre, radio, s, samp, select, small, span, strike, strong, sub, submit, sup, table, tbody, td, text, textarea, tfoot, th, thead, tr, tt, u, ul, var, xmp

The *onMouseOut* event handler intercepts the *mouseOut* event when the mouse pointer mouse outside of the screen space of an appropriate object.

onMouseOver Handler

Term: onMouseOver()

Example Syntax:

```
<A HREF="this.htm" onMouseOver="doThis('thing')">
' executes a procedure named "doThis()" whenever the mouse's pointer is placed
' over the referenced link
```

Assigned Objects: a, address, applet, area, b, big, blockquote, body, button, caption, center, checkbox, cite, code, col, dd, dfn, dir, div, dl, document, dt, em, embed, font, frameset, h1-6, i, img, kbd, label, li, listing, map, marquee, menu, object, ol, password, p, plaintext, pre, radio, s, samp, select, small, span, strike, strong, sub, submit, sup, table, tbody, td, text, textarea, tfoot, th, thead, tr, tt, u, ul, var, xmp

The *onMouseOver* event handler intercepts the *mouseOver* event when an appropriate object is under the mouse pointer.

The following example script is executed when the mouseOver event is fired by the second link in the document. The link fires this event when the user places the mouse pointer over its enclosed hyperlink text, causing a friendly alert dialog to say "hello" (see Figure 7.8).

```
<HTML>
<HEAD>
</HEAD>
<BODY>

Nothing happens when you place the mouse pointer over <A HREF="this.htm">this
link</A>.<p>
But an alert dialog appears when you place the mouse pointer over <A
HREF="thisOther.htm" onMouseOver="alert 'If you value your life, DO NOT CLICK
THIS LINK!'">this other link</A>.

</BODY>
</HTML>
```

Figure 7.8 As soon as the second hypertext link on this page receives the mouseOver event, its handling script issues a warning alert to the user.

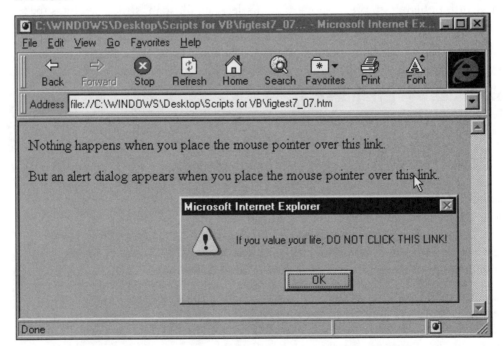

> **WARNING** In a real script, you should think twice before causing an alert dialog to open every time the mouse pointer moves over a link. A scripting action of this kind can be very annoying, because it prevents the user from ever clicking the underlying link. Each time the user approaches the link, the warning alert appears. Since VBScript alerts, confirms, and prompts are all application-modal (no other activity can take place in the browser while the dialog box is open), the user must click the alert away before doing anything else. If, after dealing with the alert, the user moves the pointer back over the link, the pesky alert appears *again*—and so on, ad nauseum. If you want to provide the user with information about a link before it's clicked (and its page is loaded), you can put up a confirmation dialog and provide an if-then-else script that allows the user to click "OK" and go to the link's page, or to Cancel and *not* go there. If the user clicks "OK," you can use the following script to take the user to the target page:
>
> ```
> url = "document.links(arrayPosition).href" ' use the actual array posi-
> tion
> navigate(url)
> ```

onMouseUp Handler

Term: onMouseUp(x,y,shift,button)

Example Syntax:

```
<A HREF="this.htm" onMouseUp(x,y,shift,button)="doThis('thing')">
' executes a procedure named "doThis()" whenever the mouse pointer is over the
' referenced link, and one of the mouse buttons is depressed, then released
```

Assigned Objects: a, address, applet, area, b, big, blockquote, body, button, caption, center, checkbox, cite, code, col, dd, dfn, dir, div, dl, document, dt, em, embed, font, frameset, h1-6, i, img, kbd, label, li, listing, map, marquee, menu, object, ol, password, p, plaintext, pre, radio, s, samp, select, small, span, strike, strong, sub, submit, sup, table, tbody, td, text, textarea, tfoot, th, thead, tr, tt, u, ul, var, xmp

The *onMouseUp* event handler intercepts the *mouseUp* event when the mouse pointer is over an appropriate object, and one of its buttons is pressed and released. This event also provides the horizontal (x) and vertical (y) coordinates of the mouse pointer when the event was fired, whether the shift, control, or alt key was depressed, and which mouse button was down during the event. The shift parameter returns 1 if the shift key is pressed, 2 if the control key is pressed, 4 if the alt key is pressed, and 0 if any other key is pressed.

> **T I P** The various and mouse- and click-generated events are executed
> in the following sequence: mouseover, mouseMove, mouseOut; and
> mouseDown, mouseUp, click, dblClick (and mouseUp again after the
> second click).

onReadyStateChange Handler

Term: onReadyStateChange()

Example Syntax:

```
sub document_onReadyStateChange()
' attaches the readyStateChange event to all appropriate objects on the page
```

Assigned Objects: applet, document, embed, img, object, script.

The *onReadyStateChange* event handler intercepts the *readyStateChange* event
when an attached element changes to the loaded state (i.e., is fully loaded into the
current page; or browser window, in the case of the document object).

onReset Handler

Term: onReset()

Example Syntax:

```
<FORM onReset="doThis('thing')">
' executes a procedure named "doThis()" when the form's reset button is clicked
```

Assigned Objects: form

The *onReset* event handler intercepts the *reset* event when its attached form is
reset. This happens, for instance, whenever a user clicks a *Reset* button on that form.
It can also result from the execution of the form's reset() method by an internal script.

onSelect Handler

Term: onSelect()

Example Syntax:

```
<TEXTAREA onSelect="doThis()">Select this text.</TEXTAREA>
' executes a procedure named "doThis()" as soon as the user begins to select
' the text
```

Assigned Objects: text, textarea

The *onSelect* event handler intercepts the *select* event as soon as the user selects
it containing text. This event fires continuously as the user clicks and drags the cursor across the text.

onStart Handler

Term: onStart()

Example Syntax:

```
<MARQUEE BEHAVIOR="Alternate" onBounce(left)="doThis('thing')
onStart()="doThat()">
' executes a procedure named "doThat()" as soon as the marquee bounces (and
```

```
' after the onBounce handler executes)
```
Assigned Objects: marquee

The *onStart* event handler intercepts the *start* event each time a marquee loops to begin a new scroll of its contents; or, if the behavior is set to alternate, whenever the scrolling text bounces.

onSubmit Handler

Term: onSubmit()

Example Syntax:

```
<FORM onSubmit="doThis('thing')">
' executes a procedure named "doThis()" when the form is submitted
```

Assigned Objects: form.

The *onSubmit* event handler intercepts the *submit* event when its attached form is submitted. This happens, for instance, whenever a user clicks a "Submit" button on that form. It can also result from the execution of the form's submit() method by an internal script.

The following example script is executed when the submit event is fired by a submit object named *submitIt*. The object fires this event when the user clicks the form's "Submit" button, causing the form's internal onSubmit event handler script to bring up an alert dialog thanking the user for the submission (see Figure 7.9).

```
<HTML>
<HEAD>
</HEAD>
<BODY>

<FORM onSubmit="alert('Thanks for the information. Have a nice day!')">

<b><PRE>

Name:  <INPUT TYPE="text" NAME="Name">
Grade: <INPUT TYPE="text" NAME="Grade">
<HR>
<INPUT TYPE="submit" NAME="submitIt">

</b></PRE>

</FORM>
</BODY>
</HTML>
```

onUnload Handler

Term: onUnload()

Example Syntax:

```
<BODY onUnload="doThis('thing')">
' executes a procedure named "doThis()" whenever the document is unloaded from
' the window
```

Assigned Objects: applet, embed, frame, img, object, window

The *onUnload* event handler intercepts the *unload* event whenever its attached page is unloaded from a VBScript-aware browser window. Like the onLoad event, you can attach a script to an onUnload event handler in the <BODY> tag of your document, or a sub statement that attaches the event to the window:

```
sub window_onUnload()
```

Figure 7.9 Clicking the "Submit" button causes the form's onSubmit handler to execute—then allows the browser to proceed with its internal submission process.

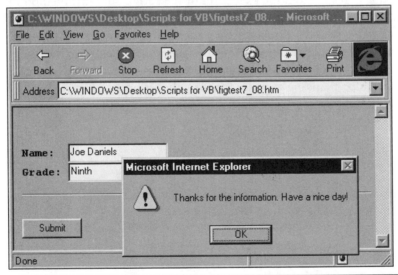

TIP Using normal scripting procedures like the previous example won't allow you to interfere with the browser's submission process. However, there is a tricky little technique that you can use to prevent the submission of a form if a function (that you've written) returns "false." This script attaches the onSubmit event handler to the form object in an unusual way. If this statement returns "true," the form is submitted. If it returns "false," it is not submitted. This is a handy device for validating the information in a form. If your function finds the information valid, it can return "true." If not, it can return "false" and stop the browser from submitting useless information to your server.

```
document.thisForm.onSubmit = return myFunction()
```

The following example script is executed when the unload event is fired from the document's <BODY> tag, causing a subroutine to check the status of two variables and present an alert if the *Name* field's value is not empty, but the form has not been submitted (see Figure 7.10):

```
<HTML>
<HEAD>
<SCRIPT LANGUAGE="VBScript">

DIM filled,submitted
submitted = false

sub byeBye()

    filled = document.forms(0).elements(0).value

    if (submitted = false) then

        if (filled <> empty) then

            alert "Come back! You haven't submitted the form."

        end if

    end if

end sub

</SCRIPT>
</HEAD>
<BODY onUnload="byeBye()">

<FORM onSubmit="submitted = true">

Name: <INPUT TYPE="text">
<INPUT TYPE="submit">

<FORM>
</BODY>
</HTML>
```

Figure 7.10 If the user fills in the Name field, but unloads the page without submitting the form, this alert is presented.

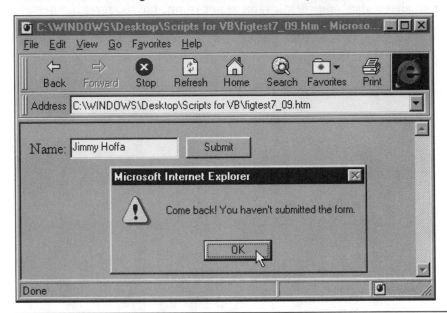

NOTE In the previous example, the "submitted" variable is globally declared, then immediately initialized as "false." If the user clicks the "Submit" button (invoking the form's onSubmit handler), this variable's contents are changed to "true." This is how the script knows whether or not the user has submitted the form. Like the submitted variable, the filled variable is also a tracking device. It tracks whether or not the user inputs data into the Name field. It is also initialized with the current value of the Name field, whichstarts out as empty, but may be filled by the time the user unloads the page. Unlike the submitted variable, this variable is initialized inside the sub statement, because the script only needs to know the value of the field when the unload event is fired.

What's Next?

Now that you've absorbed all the objects, methods, and many of the properties in the VBScript lexicon, you're ready to move on to the more general language elements that are not directly attached to any object. The first category of general language terms is covered in the next chapter, which addresses VBScript's built-in functions. Like user-created functions and subroutines, these built-in code blocks bring a great deal of extra power to the VBScript table—and are well worth the time it takes to review them.

Functions and
Constants

VBScript offers numerous built-in functions that allow you to discover and/or manipulate a variety of environmentally defined values in your scripts, including values made available to you through:

- The current page, and other pages in a frameset (if any).

- Any page whose URL is known or derived through available scripting devices.

- Any input into the page made by the user or through user-driven choices or events.

- The current browser and its open windows and displayed pages (if opened and displayed by your script).

- Limited parts of the user's system, such as the cookie text file, or the system date and time functions.

VBScript also provides dozens of predefined constants (values that never change) to help you fine-tune your implementation of functions and their results—including your own user-defined functions.

The VBScript Functions and Constants

For the most part, VBScript's Functions are presented in this chapter in alphabetical order, with the exception of the Date functions. Since scripts that manipulate dates often involve multiple date and time operations, all date- or time-related functions are grouped together under a single entry called *Date and Time Functions*. In addition to the convenience this grouping offers the veteran scripter, it also helps the beginner, who—not knowing the name of a particular date function—would otherwise be forced to page through this whole section to find it.

> **NOTE** The cDate(), formatDateTime(), and isDate() functions are listed separately, since these functions either convert or confirm a value as a date subtype, but do not manipulate the date or time, per se. In addition, each belongs to its own subgroup of functions that accomplish similar ends. The cDate() function is one of several conversion functions (such as cBool and cInt), and is therefore listed under "C" with the rest of its subtype convertor group. Ditto for formatDateTime(), listed under "F" with all the other formatting functions; and isDate(), listed under "I" with all the other is*DataType* functions.

Each function definition includes example syntax, usage, and example scripts, as needed. Also included are tables of constants for applicable functions. The only group of constants that do not belong to an explicit function is *Color Constants*, which appears by itself within the alphabetic list of functions as separate entries.

If a function takes an argument, an italicized description of the type of answer the function requires for each appears in the *Term* listing. Optional arguments are enclosed in brackets "[ ]." The vertical line (pipe) symbol "|" is used between exclusionary arguments to signify the word "or," meaning that one *or* the other argument type may be passed, but not both.

Use of Parentheses with Functions

The conventions used in this chapter for displaying function syntax in the example scripts are the same as those used in Chapter 6 for displaying method syntax. They are repeated herein because of their complexity. As noted in Chapter 3, enclosing parentheses are acceptable for script level code (code that is not contained in a sub or function statement), and are even sometimes required inside procedures (if used, say, within an *if* statement).

1. All *Example Syntax* items display enclosing parentheses for arguments because this format makes the function string much more readable, especially for functions that take several arguments.

2. Additional one-line scripting examples are also displayed with arguments in enclosing parentheses, both for readability and because these examples are not shown as belonging to a procedure.

3. Functions referenced within the introductory line of a procedure-based control statement (for instance, as part of an if statement's assigned condition), or within a variable assignment statement, display the enclosing parentheses because their absence results in an *expected* error.

4. Full scripting examples that show functions in use within a procedure, however, forego the enclosing parentheses—even though the VBScript interpreter often executes procedure-based functions just fine when parentheses *are* included.

In general, any time you see a function reference with enclosing parentheses inside a procedure, it is because the failure to include the parentheses returned an error in the latest version of Internet Explorer tested. If you find that you are receiving errors in your own (or in these) scripts—even when following what appears to be the proper function syntax for the current scripting situation—it may be that your version of Internet Explorer has been updated with new rules. By all means, lose or use the parentheses as the interpreter dictates.

Abs Function

Term: abs(*number*)
Example Syntax:

```
absValue = abs(thisField.value)
' places the absolute value of any number typed into a field named "thisField"
' into a variable named "absValue"
```

The *abs* function returns the absolute value of its passed number. It takes only one argument, which is the number passed to it, which can be an actual number or any expression that evaluates to a number.

The absolute value of a number is the number without regard to its sign, or to beginning or ending zeros. Thus, the abs() function is often used to remove the negative operator from a number, or to remove unnecessary zeros:

```
absValue = abs(-02.2050) ' returns "2.205"
```

If the answer to the abs() number argument evaluates to empty, a zero is returned. If it evaluates to null, null is returned.

Array Function

Term: array([*element1,element2,element...*])
Example Syntax:

```
DIM prodCats
prodCats = array("Toys","Electronics","Housewares")
' creates a one-dimensional array with 3 product categories
```

The *array* function may be used to create 1-dimensional arrays in variant variables. Although the argument limit for this function is not published, in testing it took more than 60 arguments without difficulty. You can try passing it more arguments and, if you get an error, you'll know you've gone too far.

Each answer passed to the array() function is (or represents) an item to occupy the same array position as its answer occupies in the argument list. In the preceding example, a string literal containing "Toys" is the first element in a new array called *prodCats*, the second element is "Electronics," and the third element is "Housewares."

As always, arrays begin counting from zero. So, when the prodCats array variable is queried for its contents, the following answers results:

```
prodCats(0) returns "Toys"
prodCats(1) returns "Electronics"
prodCats(2) returns "Housewares"
```

If no arguments are passed, the array() function creates a zero-length array.

Asc Function

Term: asc(*string*)

Example Syntax:

```
asc("& friends")
' returns "38" which is the ASCII value of the ampersand character
```

The *asc* function returns the decimal ASCII value of the first char in its passed string. It takes only one argument, which is the string passed to it, which can be a quoted literal string, any expression that evaluates to a string, or a number.

```
asc(7) ' returns 55
```

> **TIP** Use this variation of the asc() function to get the first byte, instead of the first char, of a string: **ascB**(*string*). The **ascW**(*string*) variation is also available for deriving the wide character code (Unicode) of the first char in the passed string.

If the answer to the asc() string argument evaluates to empty or null, an error results.

Atn Function

Term:

```
atn(number)
```

Example Syntax: atn(lenAdj * lenHyp)
```
' multiplies the contents of "lenAdj" by the contents of "lenHyp", and returns
' the corresponding angle
```

The *atn* function returns the arc tangent (the corresponding angle) of the passed number, which represents the ratio of two sides of a right triangle. It takes only one argument, the number passed to it, which can be an actual number or any expression that evaluates to a number. The range of the function result is from –pi/2 to pi/2 (in radians).

> **TIP** To convert the atn() function's result to degrees, multiply the returned radians by 180/pi.

CBool Function

Term: cBool(*number*)

Example Syntax:

```
alert cBool(17)
' returns "true" in an alert dialog
```

The *cBool* function is a datatype conversion function. It converts a number to a Boolean subtype. It takes only one argument, which is the number passed to it, which can be an actual number, or any expression that evaluates to a number.

If the answer to the cBool() function's number argument evaluates to 0 or empty, "false" is returned. If the number evaluates to anything else, including a negative number, "true" is returned. You can use this conversion function to set up a script that follows one path if a numeric value is 0, and another if it is not 0.

The following two statements are exact equivalents. The first only executes its actions if theNum does not contain 0. The second only executes its actions if cBool(theNum) returns "true"—which only happens if theNum is not 0.

```
if (theNum <> 0) then     ' executes if theNum does not equal 0
if (cBool(theNum)) then   ' executes if cBool() returns true
```

CByte Function

Term: cByte(*number*)

Example Syntax:

```
alert cByte(25*10)
' returns "250" as a byte subtype
```

The *cByte* function is a datatype conversion function. It converts a number to a byte subtype. It takes only one argument, which is the number passed to it, which can be any number from 0 to 255, or any expression that evaluates to a number that is within this range. Larger numbers and negative numbers return an error. The empty keyword returns a 0.

The returned value is the same as the integer value of the passed number, but the interpreter now sees this number as a byte subtype, forcing operations that would normally be performed in currency, integer, double- or single-precision arithmetic into byte arithmetic.

The value range for byte subtypes is: 0–255

This function performs internally aware conversions, including the correct interpretation of thousand and decimal separators, according to the current computer's local settings.

CCur Function

Term: cCur(*number*)

Example Syntax:

```
alert cCur(10.5)
' returns "10.5" as a currency subtype
```

The *cCur* function is a datatype conversion function. It converts a number to a currency subtype. It takes only one argument, which is the number passed to it, which can be an actual number, or any expression that evaluates to a number.

The returned value is the same as the integer value of the passed number, but the interpreter now sees this number as a currency subtype, forcing operations that would normally be performed in integer, double- or single-precision arithmetic into currency arithmetic.

The value range for currency subtypes is: –922,337,203,685,477.5808 to 922,337,203,685,477.5807.

This function performs internally aware conversions, including the correct interpretation of thousand and decimal separators, according to the current computer's local settings.

CDate Function

Term: cDate(*datestring*)

Example Syntax:

```
alert cDate(121796)
' returns "12/17/96" in an alert dialog, for computer systems set to U.S. date
' format
```

The *cDate* function is a datatype conversion function. It converts any properly formatted string to a date subtype. It takes only one argument, which is the number passed to it, which can be an actual number, or any expression that evaluates to a number.

VBScript stores dates and times as real numbers. Any whole number portion converts to a date, and any fractional portion converts to a time component, starting at midnight. cDate() is used to convert string or other date literals into this format. The order of day, month, and year is determined by the local settings on the user's system, but its correct display is entirely dependent on whether or not the date is provided in the correct date format.

The cDate() function is typically used after the isDate() function has determined if the target string can be converted to a date or time.

```
if isDate(theDate) then

    cDate(theDate)

end if

' turns "theDate" into a date subtype, if it's a properly formatted date string
```

CDbl Function
Term: cDbl(*number*)
Example Syntax:
```
alert cDbl(10.502)
' returns "10.502" as a double subtype
```

The *cDbl* function is a datatype conversion function. It converts a number to a double subtype. It takes only one argument, which is the number passed to it, which can be an actual number, or any expression that evaluates to a number.

The returned value is the same as the integer value of the passed number, but the interpreter now sees this number as a double subtype, forcing operations that would normally be performed in currency, integer, or single-precision arithmetic into double-precision arithmetic.

The value range for double subtypes is: $-1.79769313486232E308$ to $-4.94065645841247E-324$ for negative values; and $4.94065645841247E-324$ to $1.79769313486232E308$ for positive values.

This function performs internally aware conversions, including the correct interpretation of thousand and decimal separators, according to the current computer's local settings.

Chr Function
Term: chr(*ascii*)
Example Syntax:
```
textArea.value = "Hello." & chr(13) & chr(10) "How are you?"
' Types "Hello." on the first line of the referenced textarea object, types a
' carriage return and a line feed, then types "How are you?" on the second line
```

The *chr* function returns the character value of the ASCII code number passed to it. It takes only one argument, which is a number from 0 to 255, or an expression that evaluates to a number in that range.

If the answer to the asc() string argument evaluates to empty, empty is returned. If it evaluates to null, an error results.

In the preceding example, the results of the two chr() operations cause a carriage return and a line feed (respectively) to be typed into the field (see Figure 8.1). This is not the only way that you can force a new line to be typed by a script. You can also use the vbNewLine constant (found in the chr() constant list that follows Figure 8.1). The great thing about using this constant is that it constructs the new-line character according to the current platform, which varies from Windows, to Macintosh, to UNIX.

The chr() Functions constants are listed here:

Constant	Value	Character
vbCr	chr(13)	Carriage return
vbCrLf	chr(13) & chr(10)	Carriage return
vbFormFeed	chr(12)	Carriage return
vbLf	chr(10)	Carriage return
vbNewLine	chr(13)& chr(10)or chr(10)	Platform-specific newline
vbNullChar	chr(0)	Empty or no char
vbNullString	0 string	Empty or no char
vbTab	chr(9)	Tab
vbVerticalTab c	hr(11)	Vertical Tab*

*This character value is not used in Windows or Mac.

CInt Function

Term: cInt(*number*)
Example Syntax:
```
alert cInt(10.502)
' returns "11" as an integer subtype
```

The *cInt* function is a datatype conversion function. It converts a number to an integer subtype. It takes only one argument, which is the number passed to it, which can be an actual number, or any expression that evaluates to a number. The cInt() function returns the passed value rounded to the nearest integer, rounding up for numbers whose decimal values are more than .5, and down for values that are less than .5. However, whenever the decimal value is exactly .5, cInt() rounds to the nearest *even* number:

```
alert cInt(10.500) ' returns "10" as an integer subtype
alert cInt(11.500) ' returns "12" as an integer subtype
```

Figure 8.1 Two separate lines are typed into the textarea field when the user clicks out, thanks to the chr() functions ability to translate its passed number into a carriage return and a line feed.

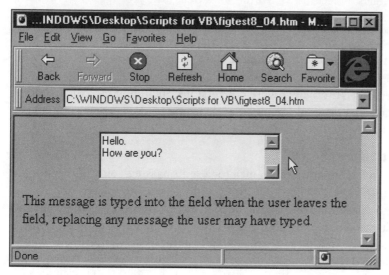

The returned value is now seen by the interpreter as an integer subtype, forcing operations that would normally be performed in currency, single-, or double-precision arithmetic into integer arithmetic.

The value range for integer subtypes is: –32,768 to 32,767. If you pass it a number outside this range, an error results. To convert longer numbers, use the cLng() function.

This function performs internally aware conversions, including the correct interpretation of thousand and decimal separators, according to the current computer's locale settings.

CLng Function

Term: cLng(*number*)
Example Syntax:

```
alert cLng(1237810.502)
' returns "1237811" as an long subtype
```

The *cLng* function is a datatype conversion function. It converts a number to a long subtype. It takes only one argument, which is the number passed to it, which can be an actual number, or any expression that evaluates to a number. The cLng() function behaves the same as the cInt() function, returning the passed value rounded to the nearest long number, rounding down for numbers whose decimal value is less than .5, and rounding up for numbers whose decimal values are more than .5. However, like cInt(), cLng() rounds any number whose decimal value is exactly .5 to the nearest *even* number.

```
alert cLng(1237810.500) ' returns "1237810" as a long subtype
alert cLng(1237811.500) ' returns "1237811" as a long subtype
```

The difference between cInt() and cLng() are that they return two different datatypes (integer and long, respectively), and cLng() supports a much broader value range of –2,147,483,648 to 2,147,483,647.

This function performs internally aware conversions, including the correct interpretation of thousand and decimal separators, according to the current computer's local settings.

Color Constants

VBScript offers the following constant names for use in passing color information around in your scripts, to set background, foreground, text, and link colors. At the time of testing, these constants were a little quirky. For example, both the constant name vbRed, and its shorthand hex equivalent (&hFF) evaluated to greenish blue on the monitor tested, not red. On the other hand, simply passing the string *"red"* resulted in a brilliant red.

All of the actual colors shown in the list following the script may be derived by passing the color's name as a literal string:

```
document.bgColor = "yellow"
' at the time of testing, this line of script worked better than the vbYellow
' constant or its hex value
```

The Color constants are:

Constant	Value	Description
vbBlack	&h00	black
vbRed	&hFF	red
vbGreen	&hFF00	green
vbYellow	&hFFFF	yellow
vbBlue	&hFF0000	blue
vbMagenta	&hFF00FF	magenta
vbCyan	&hFFFF00	cyan
vbWhite	&hFFFFFF	white

Cos Function

Term: cos(*number*)

Example Syntax:

```
cos(theAngle)
' takes the angle passed to it by the variable "theAngle" and returns the ratio
' of its two sides
```

The *cos* function returns the cosine (the ratio of two sides of a right triangle) of the passed number (which represents an angle of the right triangle). It takes only one argument, which is the number passed to it, which can be an actual number, or any expression that evaluates to a number.

> **TIP** To convert the cos() function's result to degrees, multiply the returned radians by 180/pi.

The ratio is the length of the side adjacent the angle divided by the length of the hypotenuse. The range of the function result is from –1 to 1 (in radians).

CSng Function

Term: cSng(*number*)

Example Syntax:

```
alert cSng(10.502) ' returns "10.502" as a single subtype
```

The *cSng* function is a datatype conversion function. It converts a number to a single subtype. It takes only one argument, which is the number passed to it, which can be an actual number, or any expression that evaluates to a number.

The returned value is the same as the integer value of the passed number, but the interpreter now sees this number as a single subtype, forcing operations that would normally be performed in currency or integer arithmetic into single-precision arithmetic, a more internationally aware standard.

The value range for single subtypes is: –3.402823E38 to –1.401298E-45 for negative values; and 1.401298E-45 to 3.402823E38 for positive values.

CStr Function

Term: cStr(*expression*)

Example Syntax:

```
alert cStr(25*10) ' returns "250" as a string subtype
```

The *cStr* function is a datatype conversion function. It converts the value of any expression to a byte subtype. It takes only one argument, which is the expression passed to it.

The returned value may appear to be the same as the value of the passed expression, but the interpreter now sees this value as a string subtype, as follows:

For Value	Cstr() Returns
Boolean	A "true" or "false" string
Date	A date string in the current system's short-date format
Null	A runtime error
Empty	The quoted empty string ""
Error	An error string containing the word error, and the error number
Number	A number string

The length of a string may range from 0 to over 2 billion characters, which should be long enough for any scripting purpose!

Date and Time Functions

VBScript provides a collection of functions for manipulating date and time strings. For quick reference, all of these functions are listed in alphabetical order in the following table. Entries into this table that require further explanation appear in bold, and are expanded upon in the section following the table.

The DateAdd() interval constants are as follows:

Function	Arguments	Syntax	Results	Comments
date current	none	*theDate* = date	theDate = current date	places just the date into "theDate" variable
dateAdd	interval,num,date, [firstDayOfWk], [firstWkOfYr]	dateAdd ("m",1,"3/15/97")	4/15/97	adds 1 month to passed date
dateDiff	interval,fromDate, toDate,[firstDay OfWk], [firstWk OfYr]	dateDiff("yyyy", "3/17/82", "2/12/97")	15	returns number of years from 3/17/82 to 2/12/97
datePart	interval,date	datePart ("d","3/17/82")	17	returns requested part of date
dateSerial	yr,mon,day	dateSerial(48,3,28)	3/28/48	Pass all 4-digits for non-20th c. years

Function	Arguments	Syntax	Results	Comments
dateValue	dateTime|date|time	dateValue ("12/2/97 15:23:29")	12/2/97	returns date portion as a date subtype
day	date	day("12/2/97")	2	returns day portion of passed date
hour	dateTime|date|time	hour ("12/2/97 15:23:29")	15	returns hour portion of passed date/ time
minute	date	minute ("12/2/97 15:23:29")	23	returns minute portion of passed date/ time
month	date	month("12/2/97")	12	returns month portion of passed date
now	none	*theDate* = now	theDate = current date/time	places the current date and time into "the Date" variable
second	date ("12/2/97 15:23:29") date/time	second portion of passed	29	returns seconds
time	none	*theTime* = time current time	theTime = time into "theTime"	places just the current variable
timeSerial	hr,min,sec	TimeSerial(12,34,22)	12:34:22 PM	returns the string as a date subtype
timeValue	dateTime|date|time	timeValue ("12/2/97 15:23:29")	3:23:29 PM	returns time portion as a date subtype
weekday	date[firstDayOfWk] ("2/2/97",vbMonday)	weekday	3	given day is a Wed., 3rd day of week, if week begins w/Mon.

Continued

Function	Arguments	Syntax	Results	Comments
year	date	year("12/2/97")	1997	returns the year portion of date

The *dateAdd()* function adds a designated interval of time to a given date string. It takes three required arguments, the first of which is a VBScript constant that defines the *interval* (month, day, etc.). The second argument is the *number* of intervals to add (1, 2, etc.). The last argument is the *datestring* to which the interval is added. The interval constants available for use with this function are shown in the list of interval constants, at the end of the "Date and Time Functions" section.

> **TIP** You can use the dateAdd() function to subtract a specified interval from a date by answering its number argument with a negative number:
>
> ```
> dateAdd("m",-1,"3,15,97")
> ' subtracts 1 month from the passed date, and returns 2/15/97
> ```

The *dateDiff()* function returns the difference in time between two passed dates. It takes three required arguments, the first of which is a VBScript constant that defines the *interval* (month, day, etc.). The second argument is the *fromDate*, and the third argument is the *toDate*. The function then determines how many of the passed intervals have occurred from the fromDate to the toDate.

The dateDiff() function also takes two optional arguments: *firstDayOfWeek* and *firstWeekOfYear*, in that order. If you want to answer the firstWeekOfYear argument, you must pass an answer to firstDayOfWeek as well. If these arguments are not answered, the dateDiff() function assumes Sunday for the first argument, and the week of January 1 for the second argument. If you want the function to consider a week beginning with another day, or use another value for the first week of the year, use the constants presented in the interval constants list in this section. The "day of the week" constants, and the "first day of the year" constants are also listed in this section. All three lists are at the end of the "Date and Time Functions" section.

Valid Date Strings

VBScript's Date and Time functions can only be performed on valid date and time strings.

Strings are considered dates when they evaluate to any acceptable date format, from January 1, 100, to December 31, 9999. The date functions recognize the order for month, day, and year according to the short date format on the current computer system. If year is omitted, the current system setting for year is assumed.

You can force a string to be recognized as a VBScript date literal by enclosing it with pound signs: #1/12/95#. If the string is ambiguous (the numbers for month and day are interchangable), it is interpreted according to the date format used by the current system. Thus, #1/12/95# is interpreted by most U.S. computers as January 12, 1995. If it is input (into a field perhaps) as a European date format (day before month)—and meant to convey December 1, 1995—its interpretation will be wrong. Unambiguous dates, however, are correctly interpreted, regardless of the format used by the current computer. For instance, the interpreter correctly views #15/2/97# as February 15, 1997, even on a U.S.-based computer, because it knows that there is no 15th month.

Valid date strings can also include a time, either to the right of the date, or all by itself. Time strings are colon-separated hours, minutes, and seconds: 02:15:35. If a 12-hour clock is used, a space followed by AM or PM is added to the string: 02:15:35 PM. Time values are evaluated, however, based on the 24-hour (military) clock, regardless of the format of the passed time string. The hour() function, for instance, returns "14" as the hour represented in the "02:15:35 PM" string. Hours passed to the timeSerial() function are considered to be 24-hour clock numbers, so that timeSerial(1,15,22) returns 1:15:22 AM. You must pass "13" for the hour if you want the hour to be treated as 1:00 PM.

TIP The timeSerial() function takes 1–24 for its hour arguments, –60 for its minutes argument, and 1–60 for its seconds arguments. However, by passing it a minus or plus value, you can actually add or subtract hours, minutes, or seconds from the current time:

```
theTime = time
theHour = hour(theTime)
theMin = minute(theTime)
theSecs = second(theTime)
alert timeSerial(theHour,theMin-5,theTime)
' subtracts ten minutes from the current time; if the current time is
' 3:25:15 PM, this script returns 3:15:15 PM
```

The following list shows the interval constants:

Constant	Value
yyyy	year
q	quarter
m	month
y	day of year
d	day
w	weekday
h	hour
m	minute
s	second

> **TIP** *Although "m" is the constant assigned to the "minute" interval in the current VBScript documentation, someone obviously made a boo-boo. You can't use the exact same constant twice, and "m" is already reserved for month. If you need to manipulate minutes, use the second constant (s) and pass the number of minutes times 60 to the number argument.
>
> ```
> dateAdd("s",120,"12:15:04 PM")
> ' adds 120 seconds (or 2 minutes) to the passed time, and returns 12:17:04 PM
> ```

The Day of Week constants follow:

Constant	Value	Description
vbUseSystem	0	Use National Language Support API setting
vbSunday	1	Sunday
vbMonday	2	Monday
vbTuesday	3	Tuesday
vbWednesday	4	Wednesday
vbThursday	5	Thursday
vbFriday	6	Friday
vbSaturday	7	Saturday

Here are the First Week of Year constants:

Constant	Value	Description
vbUseSystem	0	Use National Language Support API setting
vbFirstJan1	1	Starts with week in which Jan 1 occurs
vbFirstFourDays	2	Starts with the week that has at least four days in the new year
vbFirstFullWeek	3	Starts with the first full week of the new year

Exp Function

Term: exp(*number*)

Example Syntax:

```
alert exp(9)
' displays the alert message "8103.08392757539," which is 2.71281828459045⁹
```

The *exp* function returns the value of Euler's constant, raised to the power of the passed number. It takes only one argument, which is the number passed to it, which can be an actual number, or any expression that evaluates to a number.

Euler's constant is 2.71281828459045, the base of all natural logarithms. The exp() function uses this constant as a base and the passed number as the exponent to perform an exponentiation operation.

If the answer to the exp() number argument evaluates to empty or zero, a "1" is returned. If it evaluates to null, null is returned.

> **TIP** If you need to perform other math operations using Euler's constant, pass "1" to the exp() function to return the constant by itself, and place it into a constant of your own (created with the const statement). Then, you can use your own const in subsequent expressions instead of typing (let alone remembering) this lengthy number.

```
const eConst = exp(1)
' places Euler's constant "2.71281828459045" into "eConst"
```

Filter Function

Term: filter(*arrayVariable*,*searchString*,[*include*],[*compare*])

Example Syntax:

```
nameArray = split("J.J.J.Smith",".")
lastName = filter(nameArray,"J",false)
' split() creates a four-element array called "nameArray,"
' filter() excludes all "J" elements, and returns the "lastName" array, whose
' single element contains "Smith"
```

The *filter* function searches for a designated string in the passed array, and—by default—returns a new, zero-based array containing only those elements that matched the search string. It takes two required arguments, which are the name of an array, and a string to search for in that array.

The filter() function also takes two optional arguments. This first optional argument is the include argument that is answered with "true" if you want the new array to include all the elements that *matched* the search string; and "false" if you want the new array to contain only those elements that *did not match* the search string. If the include argument is omitted, the include value defaults to true. The second optional argument is *compareType*, which takes a comparison constant that designates the comparison type to use in evaluating substrings. The VBScript comparison constants are shown in the list at the end of this section.

The following script splits a string of comma-delimited numbers into a six-element array, and populates each element in that array with its corresponding number substring. The filter() function is then used to filter out the two occurrences of the number "11."

```
thisVar = "2,11,75,19,11,95"
newArray = split(thisVar,",")

' "newArray" is created with six, populated elements: 2, 11, 75, 19, 11, and 95

shortArray = filter(newArray,"11",false)

' "shortArray" is created by excluding all elements containing "11" from
' "newArray," resulting in a four-element array, whose elements and values are:

shortArray(0) = 2
shortArray(1) = 75
shortArray(2) = 19
shortArray(3) = 95

alert shortArray(2)

' an alert displays the number "19"
```

The Comparison constants are listed here:

Constant	Value	Description
vbBinaryCompare	0	Performs a binary comparison
vbTextCompare	1	Performs a string comparison
vbDatabaseCompare	2	Performs a comparison against information contained in a database

Fix Function

Term: `fix(number)`
Example Syntax:
```
alert fix(10.502)
' displays "10" in an alert dialog box
```

The *fix* function returns the integer portion of any number passed to it (the whole number sans any fractional value). It takes only one argument, which is the number passed to it, which can be an actual number, or any expression that evaluates to a number.

The fix() function returns the passed value without its fractional portion, and without performing any rounding operations:

```
alert fix(10.2) ' returns "10"
alert fix(-10.9) ' returns "-10"
```

FormatCurrency Function

Term: `formatCurrency(number,[digitsAfterDec],[leadingDigit],[parenNegNum],[group])`
Example Syntax:
```
formatCurrency(23.085)
' returns "$23.09" on computers set to American currency
```

The *formatCurrency* function formats a passed number to reflect the currency format setting of the local computer system. It takes one required argument, which is the number to be formatted, which can be an actual number, or any expression that evaluates to a number.

The formatCurrency() function also takes four optional arguments. The first optional argument's answer tells the interpreter how many digits to display to the right of the decimal. The last three take a tristate value: true, false, or current computer's default. These optional arguments tell the interpreter whether to display leading zeros for fractional values, whether to parenthesize negative values, and whether to group numbers using the local computer's group delimiter.

If you answer one optional argument, you must answer any other optional argument(s) that precedes it. For instance, if you answer the parenNegNum arguments, you must pass a placeholder answer to the digitsAfterDec and leadingDigits arguments as well.

Answers to the tristate arguments must be expressed with the Tristate constants shown here:

Constant	Value	Description
tristateTrue	−1	True
tristateFalse	0	False
tristateUseDefault	−2	Use local computer default

FormatDateTime Function

Term: `formatDateTime(date,[format])`

Example Syntax:

```
formatDateTime(13/12/96)
' returns "12/13/96" on computers set to American date display standards
```

The *formatDateTime* function formats a passed date to reflect the date format setting of the local computer system. It takes one required argument, which is the date to be formatted.

The formatDateTime() function also takes one optional argument that indicates the type of date and/or time format to be used:

```
formatDateTime(13/12/96,vbLongDate)
' returns "Sunday, December 13, 1996" on computers set to American date display
' standards
```

Answers to the format argument must be expressed with the Format constants shown in the following list. If no answer is passed, vbGeneralDate is used.

Constant	Value	Description
vbGeneralDate	0	Uses short date and long time
vbLongDate	1	Uses local computer's long date format
vbShortDate	2	Uses local computer's short date format
vbLongTime	3	Uses local computer's long time format
vbShortTime	4	Uses local computer's short time format

FormatNumber Function

Term: `formatNumber(number,[digitsAfterDec],[leadingDigit],`
`[parenNegNum],[group])`

Example Syntax:

```
formatNumber(1028.278,3)
' returns "1,028.278" on computers set to American number format
```

The *formatNumber* function formats a passed number to reflect the number format setting of the local computer system. It takes one required argument, which is the number to be formatted, which can be an actual number, or any expression that evaluates to a number.

The formatNumber() function also takes four optional arguments. The first optional argument's answer tells the interpreter how many digits to display to the right of the decimal. The last three take a tristate value: true, false or current computer's default. These optional arguments tell the interpreter whether to display leading zeros for fractional values, whether to parenthesize negative values, and whether to group numbers using the local computer's group delimiter.

If you answer one optional argument, you must answer any other optional argument(s) that precedes it. For instance, if you answer the parenNegNum arguments, you must pass a placeholder answer to the digitsAfterDec and leadingDigits arguments, as well.

Answers to the tristate arguments must be expressed with the Tristate constants shown here:

Constant	Value	Description
tristateTrue	−1	True
tristateFalse	0	False
tristateUseDefault	−2	Use local computer default

FormatPercent Function

Term: formatPercent(*number*,[*digitsAfterDec*],[*leadingDigit*], [*parenNegNum*],[*group*])

Example Syntax:
```
formatNumber(1028.278,3)
' returns "102,827.800%"
```

The *formatPercent* function multiplies a passed number by 100, and displays it with a trailing %. It takes one required argument, which is the number to be formatted, which can be an actual number, or any expression that evaluates to a number.

The formatPercent() function also takes four optional arguments. The first optional argument's answer tells the interpreter how many digits to display to the right of the decimal. The last three take a tristate value: true, false or current computer's default. These optional arguments tell the interpreter whether to display leading zeros for fractional values, whether to parenthesize negative values, and whether to group numbers using the local computer's group delimiter.

If you answer one optional argument, you must answer any other optional argument(s) that precedes it. For instance, if you answer the parenNegNum arguments, you must pass a placeholder answer to the digitsAfterDec and leadingDigits arguments, as well.

Answers to the tristate arguments must be expressed with the Tristate constants shown in the following list:

Constant	Value	Description
tristateTrue	−1	True
tristateFalse	0	False
tristateUseDefault	−2	Use local computer default

Hex Function

Term: hex(*number*)
Example Syntax:

```
alert hex(10.502)
' displays "B" in an alert dialog box, which is the hex value of "11"
```

The *hex* function returns the hexadecimal value of any number passed to it. If the number contains a fraction, it is first rounded to the nearest whole number. It takes only one argument, the number passed to it, which can be an actual number, or any expression that evaluates to a number.

Int Function

Term: int(*number*)
Example Syntax: `alert int(10.502) ' returns "10"`

The *int* function returns the integer portion of any number passed to it (the whole number sans any fractional value). It takes only one argument, which is the number passed to it, which can be an actual number, or any expression that evaluates to a number.

The int() function treats positive numbers in exactly the same way as the fix() function treats them, returning the passed value without its fractional portion, and without performing any rounding operations:

```
alert int(10.2) ' returns "10"
```

The difference between the int() function and the fix() function lies in the way that the int() function treats negative numbers. Instead of simply removing the fractional portion of a passed number, and returning its integer alone, it rounds down to the next integer along the negative number line, regardless of the fractional value passed:

```
alert int(-10.9) ' returns "-11"
alert int(-10.1) ' returns "-11"
```

InputBox Function

Term: inputBox(*message*,[*title*],[*defaultInput*],[*left*],[*top*],[*helpFile*], [*context*])

Example Syntax:

```
input("This is my message.","This is My Box")
' displays an input dialog box titled "This is My Box," with the message "This
' is my message."
```

The *inputBox* function creates a prompt dialog box that allows the user to input an answer string, and click an "OK" or "Cancel" button. It takes only one required argument, which is the message to be displayed in the box.

The inputBox() function also takes six additional optional arguments:

Argument	Answer Type	Description
title	string	Used as the title of the dialog box
defaultInput	string	Used as default text in the user's input field; if absent, defaults to empty
left	number	Specifies the number of twips between left side of screen and left side of dialog box
top	number	Specifies the number of twips between top of screen and top of dialog box
helpFile	string	name of help file for context-sensitive help
context	number	topic number assigned to the help file by author; required if helpFile argument is answered

TIP The input box message is divided into paragraphs by passing the VBScript character constants for carriage return and line feed (see bolded items) to the *val* function in the example script.

```
<HTML>
<HEAD>
<SCRIPT LANGUAGE="VBScript">

DIM val

val = "Welcome to my custom dialog box." & vbCrLf & vbLf & "I cre-
ated it using the inputBox() function. How do you like it?" & vbCrLf
& vbLf & "If you need to give the user more button choices, you can
use the msgBox() function. However, the message box version doesn't
provide a user input field." & vbCrLf & vbLf & "Tell me which type
of dialog you use most."

</SCRIPT>
</HEAD>
<BODY>
<FORM>

<INPUT TYPE="button" NAME="theButton"
VALUE="Click Me" onClick="inputBox val,'My Dialog','',1860,1880">

</FORM>
</BODY>
</HTML>
```

A twip is a unit of measurement that approximates to 1/1440 of an inch, or 1/567 of a centimeter. If the left and top arguments are not specified, a default position that varies according to screen size is used.

The following script creates and displays the input box shown in Figure 8.2, when the user clicks a "Click" button.

InStr Function

Term: inStr([*startNum*],firstString,secondString,[*compareType*])

Example Syntax:

```
thisString = "Hello"
thatString = "e"
inStr(thisString,thatString) ' returns "2"
```

The *inStr* function searches the first string passed to it to see if it contains the second string, searching from left to right. It takes two required arguments, which

Figure 8.2 The left and top twips passed to the inputBox() function give the resulting input dialog box a unique position on the screen.

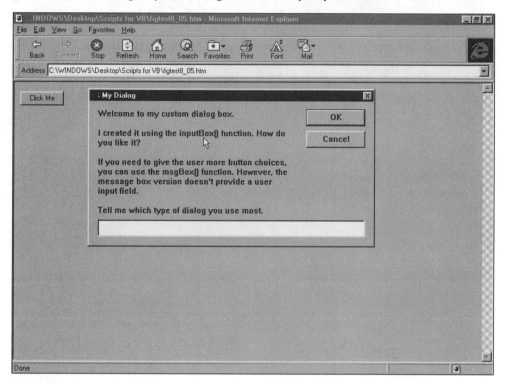

are the string to search (which is passed first), and the string to find (which is passed second).

The inStr() function also takes two optional arguments. The first optional argument (which actually comes at the very beginning of the argument list) is *startNum*, which takes a number that indicates where to begin the search in the first string. The second optional argument (which comes at the end of the argument list) is *compareType* which takes a comparison constant that designates the comparison type to use in the search. The VBScript comparison constants are shown in the list at the end of this section.

If the startNum argument is omitted, inStr() begins searching for the second string at position 1, which is the first char in the first string. If the comparison argument is answered, the startNum argument becomes required. Check out the warning in this section for another situation that requires the startNum argument.

> **WARNING** For some reason, the VBScript developers decided to depart from the rule that required arguments must precede optional arguments in an argument list. The inStr() function actually takes an optional argument as its *very first argument*, followed by the function's two required arguments. This means you can theoretically omit the startNum argument, and just pass the two required strings. This works fine in IE4, and it also works in IE3 *if the strings contain text*. However, if the strings are actually numbers, omitting the startNum argument can be a real problem. VBScript interprets the first passed numeric string (which is supposed to answer the first string argument) as an answer to the startNum argument. Thus, in the following example, inStr() returns a 0 (even though the second string clearly appears in the first string) when the optional startNum argument is omitted. To fix the problem, the startNum argument is included, even though the default starting position of 1 is desired.
>
> ```
> val = 14
> val2 = 4
> inStr(val,val2) ' returns "0"
> inStr(1,val,val2) ' returns 2, indicating that "4" is found in the
> second position of the "val" string
> ```

If the second string is not found in the first string, a 0 is returned. If the string is found, a number representing the position of the first character of the search string is returned.

```
DIM val,val2
val = "This is the first string."
val2 = "string"
inStr(val,val2) ' returns "19," which is the position that the first char in
' "val2" (the "s" in string) holds in "val"
```

InStrRev Function

Term: inStrRev(*firstString*,*secondString*,[*startNum*],[*compareType*])
Example Syntax:
```
thisString = "Hello"
thatString = "e"
inStrRev(thisString,thatString) ' returns "2"
```

The *inStrRev* function searches the first string passed to it to see if it contains the second string. It takes two required arguments, which are the string to search (which is passed first) and the string to find (which is passed second).

There are only two differences between inStrRev() and the inStr() function. The inStrRev() function searches from right to left (the reverse of inStr()).

The second difference is its argument structure, which adopts the rule that required arguments precede optional arguments. Accordingly, the inStrRev() function takes two optional arguments *that both follow the required arguments*. The first optional argument is *startNum*, which takes a number that indicates where to begin the search in the first string. The second optional argument is *compareType* which takes a comparison constant that designates the comparison type to use in the search. The VBScript comparison constants are shown in the list at the end of this section.

> **TIP** If you are searching a large block of text for some string, and you know that the string is positioned closer to the end of the text block than it is to the start of the block, use inStrRev(). Since this function begins its search at the end of the block, it can find the string faster than inStr() (always assuming that the string *is* in the block).

If the startNum argument is omitted, inStr() begins searching for the second string at position −1, which is the last char in the first string. If the comparison argument is answered, the startNum argument becomes required.

If the second string is not found in the first string, a 0 is returned. If the string is found, a number representing the position of the first character of the search string is returned.

```
DIM val,val2
val = "This is the first string."
val2 = "string"
inStrRev(val,val2)
' searching from the very end of the string, it quickly returns "19,"
' which is the position that the first char in "val2" (the "s" in string)
' holds in "val"
```

The Comparison constants are as follows:

Constant	Value	Description
vbBinaryCompare	0	Performs a binary comparison
vbTextCompare	1	Performs a string comparison
vbDatabaseCompare	2	Performs a comparison against information contained in a database

IsArray Function

Term: isArray(*variableName*)

Example Syntax:

```
alert isArray(thisVariable)
' alert message is "true" if "thisVariable" is an array variable, and "false" if
' it is not
```

The *isArray* function tests the variable container passed to it to see if it contains an array. It takes one required argument, which is the name of the variable or any other variable or VBScript container that points to the variable (i.e., contains its name).

If the passed variable is an array variable, the isArray() function returns "true"; if not, it returns "false."

```
DIM val
val = array(1,2,3)
alert isArray(val) ' returns "true"
```

```
DIM val
val = "1,2,3"
alert isArray(val) ' returns "false"
```

Use the isArray() function to test the data subtype of your variables before attempting to perform operations requiring an array variable, *if there is any possibility that the variable no longer points to a valid array.*

IsDate Function

Term: isDate(*variableName*)

Example Syntax:

```
alert isDate(thisVariable)
' alert message is "true" if "thisVariable" is an array variable, and "false" if
' it is not
```

The *isDate* function tests the variable container passed to it to see if it contains a valid date or time. It takes one required argument, which is the name of the variable date container, or any expression that points to that variable.

If the passed variable contains a valid date or time string, the isDate() function returns "true"; if not, it returns "false."

```
DIM val
val = now
alert isDate(val) ' returns "true"
```

```
DIM val
val = "now"
alert isDate(val) ' returns "false"
```

Use the isDate() function to test the data subtype of your variables before attempting to perform date or time operations on a variable, *if there is any possibility that the variable might not contain a valid date or time string.*

IsEmpty Function

Term: isEmpty(*variableName*)

Example Syntax:

```
alert isEmpty(thisVariable)
' alert message is "true" if "thisVariable" is empty, and "false" if it is not
```

> **WARNING** Don't expect the isEmpty() function to check for the empty literal (""), or an empty field value (which translates to ""). The isEmpty() function returns "false" for both of these conditions, because it is looking for the empty value, and the empty value only.

The *isEmpty* function tests the variable container passed to it to see if it is empty. It takes one required argument, which is the name of the variable date container, or any expression that points to that variable.

A variable is empty if it has been declared but not initialized (not yet passed any data), or if the keyword *empty* has been actively placed into it. If the passed variable meets either of these empty conditions, the isEmpty() function returns "true"; if not, it returns "false."

```
DIM val
alert isEmpty(val) ' returns "true"

DIM val
val = "This is a valid string."
alert isEmpty() ' returns "false"
```

IsNull Function

Term: isNull(*variableName*)

Example Syntax:

```
alert isNull(thisVariable)
' alert message is "true" if "thisVariable" contains invalid data, and "false"
' if it does not
```

The *isNull* function tests the variable container passed to it to see if it contains a valid VBScript value. It takes one required argument, which is the name of the variable date container, or any expression that points to that variable.

A variable is *not* null simply because it has not been initialized (passed any data). Uninitialized variables are empty. A variable is only null if invalid data has been passed to it, because of environmental conditions or an error elsewhere in the code, or if the keyword "null" has been actively placed into it. If the passed variable meets either of these null conditions, the isNull() function returns "true"; if not, it returns "false."

```
DIM val
val = "null"
alert isNull(val) ' returns "true"

DIM val
val = "This is a valid string."
alert isNull(val) ' returns "false"
```

IsNumeric Function

Term: `isNumeric(variableName)`

Example Syntax:

```
alert isNumeric(thisVariable)
' alert message is "true" if "thisVariable" evaluates to a number, and "false"
' if it does not
```

> **WARNING** If the variable passed to isNumeric() is an expression containing multiple data subtypes (such as a number string that contains a comma), isNumeric() returns "false," even if the contents of the variable begin with a number.

The *isNumeric* function tests the variable container passed to it to see if it evaluates to a valid number. It takes one required argument, which is the name of the variable container, or any expression that points to that variable.

If the passed variable contains a valid number, the isNumeric() function returns "true"; if not, it returns "false."

```
DIM val
val = now
alert isDate(val) ' returns "true"

DIM val
val = "now"
alert isDate() ' returns "false"
```

IsObject Function

Term: isObject(*variableName*)

Example Syntax:

```
alert isArray(thisVariable)
' alert message is "true" if "thisVariable" is an object variable, and "false"
' if it is not
```

The *isObject* function tests the variable passed to it to see if it is an object variable. It takes one required argument, which is the name of the variable or any other variable or VBScript container that points to the variable (i.e., contains its name).

If the passed variable is an object variable, the isArray() function returns "true"; if not, it returns "false."

```
DIM val
SET val = document.forms(0).thisField
alert isObject(val) ' returns "true"

DIM val
val = "thisField"
alert isObject(val) ' returns "false"
```

Use the isObject() function to test the data subtype of your variables before attempting to perform operations requiring an object variable, *if there is any possibility that the object variable has been set back to nothing*—either by a scripting action, or by VBScript itself.

Join Function

Term: join(*arrayVariable*,[*delimiter*])

Example Syntax:

```
join(thisArray)
' joins the contents of each element in the array in a list, and returns the list
```

The *join* function returns a list of all of the contents in the named array, in order of its elements from left to right. It takes one required argument, which is the name of the target array variable. It also takes one optional argument, which is the delimiter to use between each item in the list. If no delimiter is passed, then a space is placed between the contents of each element.

The following script uses the join() function to create a comma-delimited list of the information that the user types into the four text fields (see Figure 8.3):

```
<HTML>
<HEAD>
</HEAD>
<BODY>
```

```
<FORM>

<INPUT TYPE="button" NAME="theButton" VALUE="Show List">
<br><b><pre>
First Name:     <INPUT TYPE="text" NAME="fname">
Last Name:      <INPUT TYPE="text" NAME="lname">
<hr>
Email Address: <INPUT TYPE="text" NAME="email">
Telephone:      <INPUT TYPE="text" NAME="phone">
</b></pre>

<SCRIPT LANGUAGE="VBScript" FOR="theButton" EVENT="onClick">

DIM myArray(3)
myArray(0) = fname.value
myArray(1) = lname.value
myArray(2) = email.value
myArray(3) = phone.value
```

Figure 8.3 When the "Show List" button is clicked, an alert displays the text typed into the four fields, in a comma-delimited list.

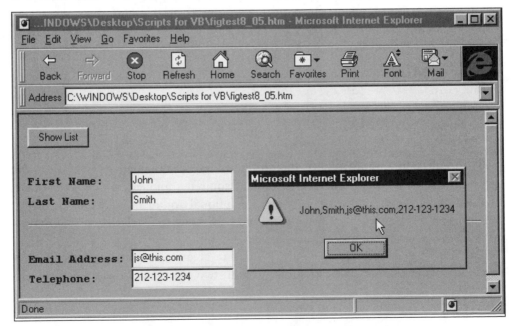

```
alert join(myArray,",")

</SCRIPT>

</FORM>
</BODY>
</HTML>
```

LBound Function

Term: LBound(*arrayVariable*,[*dimension*])
Example Syntax:

```
LBound(thisArray)
' returns the index position of the lowest element in "thisArray"
```

The *lBound* function returns the index position of the lowest (or first) element in the named array. It takes one required argument, which is the name of the target array variable. It also takes one optional argument, which is the target dimension. The dimension argument is only necessary if your target is a *not the first dimension* in a multidimensional array. You can forget this argument for 1-dimensional arrays, or if you're only looking at the first dimension in a multidimensional array. In the absence of any answer to the dimension argument, the function defaults to the first dimension in the array anyway.

The lBound() function is invariably used in conjunction with the uBound() function to determine the size of an array's dimension when that size is unknown (as it might be if user actions are dictating the resizing of a dynamic array)—or if your script might access scripts written by other authors. For a zero-based array containing three element—0, 1, and 2—you might write the following script:

```
arraySize = lBound(myArray) + uBound(myArray) + 1
```

This is virtually the same as saying:

```
arraySize = 0 + 2 + 1 ' places 3 into "arraySize"
```

LCase Function

Term: LCase(*string*)
Example Syntax: lCase("HELLO") ' returns "hello"

The *lCase* function converts any letters contained in its passed string to lower case (if necessary). It takes a text string (or any expression that evaluates to a text string) as its only argument, and that argument is required.

> **TIP** If a passed expression evaluates to a number, not only is no error
> generated—but the expression is evaluated, and its result is returned:
>
> ```
> theString = 2+2+2
> lCase(theString)
> ' returns "6"
> ```

Left Function

Term: left(*string*,*number*)

Example Syntax: left("good-bye",4) ' returns "good"

The *left* function returns the designated number of characters from the left-hand side of the passed string. It takes two required arguments: a string (or any expression that evaluates to a string), and a number (or any expression that evaluates to a number). The answer to the number argument tells the interpreter how many characters to return.

The interpreter begins counting from the leftmost char in the string, up to the number given, then returns the resulting string. If the number indicated is higher than the number of chars in the passed string, then the complete string is returned. If the number expression passed evaluates to 0, then a 0-length (or empty) string is returned.

Len Function

Term: len(*string*)

Example Syntax: len("hello") ' returns "5"

The *len* function returns the number of characters in the passed string. It takes a string (or any expression that evaluates to a string) as its single, required argument.

Log Function

Term: log(*number*)

Example Syntax:
```
log(2)
' returns "0.693147180559945" which is 2/2.71281828459045
```

The *log* function returns the natural logarithm of the passed number to the base "e" (Euler's constant). It takes only one argument, which is the number passed to it, which can be an actual number, or any expression that evaluates to a number.

Euler's constant is 2.71281828459045, the base of all natural logarithms. The log() function uses this constant as a base to determine the natural logarithm of the passed number.

If the answer to the log() number argument evaluates to empty or zero, a "1" is returned. If it evaluates to null, null is returned.

> **TIP** You can change the base of the log() function's calculation by dividing the results of to log() operations. For example, you can use the following function to calculate a base-10 logarithm. Just pass the target number (whose base-10 logarithm you wish to calculate) as an answer to the log10() function's *num* argument.
>
> ```
> function log10(num)
>     log10 = log(num) / log(10)
> end function
> ```

LTrim Function

Term: lTrim(*string*)

Example Syntax: lTrim(" hello") ' returns "hello"

The *lTrim* function strips spaces (if any) from the left-hand side of the passed string. It takes a string (or any expression that evaluates to a string) as its only required argument.

The lTrim() function is often used in conjunction with the rTrim() function to remove the beginning and ending spaces in a passed string. To remove all of the spaces in a string, see the trim() function.

```
theString = " and the beat goes on… "
theString = lTrim(theString) ' puts "and the beat goes on… " into "theString"
theString = rTrim(theString) ' puts "and the beat goes on…" into "theString"
```

MsgBox Function

Term: msgBox(*message*,[*buttonGroup*],[*title*],[*helpFile*],[*context*])

Example Syntax:
```
msgBox("This is my message.","This is My Box")
' displays a non-input, dialog box titled "This is My Box," with the message
' "This is my message."
```

The *msgBox* function creates a confirmation dialog box that presents a message that asks the user to make a choice, and a variable number and type of buttons to click in response. It takes only one required argument, which is the message to be displayed in the box.

The msgBox() function also takes four additional optional arguments:

Argument	Answer Type	Description
buttonGroup	constant|number	Displays the specified button group; if none is specified, displays an OK button
title	string	Used as the title of the dialog box
helpFile	string	name of help file for context-sensitive help
context	number	topic number assigned to the help file by author; required if helpFile argument is answered

> **TIP** Your answer to the msgBox() function's buttonGroup argument can be a button group constant, an icon constant, a button default constant—or it can be the total numeric value of up to four options; one from each of the four msgBox() constant types. Using the latter strategy, the following example script answers "4387" to the buttonGroup argument. This number is derived from adding the values of the following constants (one from each constant group): vbYesNoCancel (3) + vbQuestion (32) + vbDefaultButton2 (256) + vbSystemModal (4096). Note that you can only add *one option* from each constant group. See the lists at the end of this section for names and values of all possible msgBox() constants for each constant type.

When the user clicks a "Click Me" button, the following script creates and displays the custom message dialog box shown in Figure 8.4. The resulting dialog box is system modal with a Question icon—and "Yes," "No," and "Cancel" buttons. The second button (No) is designated as the default, which is automatically selected if the user hits the Return or Enter key.

```
<HTML>
<HEAD>
<SCRIPT LANGUAGE="VBScript">

DIM val

val = "Welcome to my custom dialog box." & vbCrLf & vbLf & "You have to respond
to it, or it will dog you in other applications." & vbCrLf & vbLf & "Isn't it
Cool?"
```

```
</SCRIPT>
</HEAD>
<BODY>
<FORM>

<INPUT TYPE="button" NAME="theButton" VALUE=" Click Me "
onClick="msgBox val,4387,'My Message'">

</FORM>
</BODY>
</HTML>
```

Figure 8.4 Because it has been set to "system modal," this dialog follows the user into other applications until one of its buttons is clicked. The default button for this annoying dialog is "No."

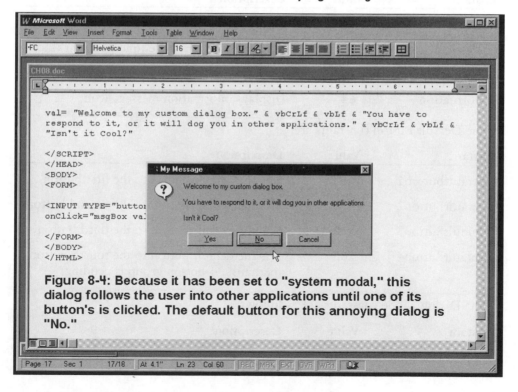

Figure 8-4: Because it has been set to "system modal," this dialog follows the user into other applications until one of its button's is clicked. The default button for this annoying dialog is "No."

The msgBox() constants are as follows:

Constant	Value	Description
vbOKOnly	0	Displays a single OK button; this is the default
vbOKCancel	1	Displays OK and Cancel buttons
vbAbortRetryIgnore	2	Displays Abort, Retry, and Ignore buttons
vbYesNoCancel	3	Displays Yes, No, and Cancel buttons
vbYesNo	4	Displays Yes and No buttons
vbRetryCancel	5	Displays Retry and Cancel buttons

The Icon constants are listed here:

Constant	Value	Description
vbCritical	16	Displays critical message icon
vbQuestion	32	Displays query message (question mark) icon
vbExclamation	48	Displays exclamation point (warning) icon
vbInformation	64	Displays information message icon

The Default Button constants are:

Constant	Value	Description
vbDefaultButton1	0	Sets the default button to the first button
vbDefaultButton2	256	Sets the default button to the second button
vbDefaultButton3	512	Sets the default button to the third button
vbDefaultButton4	768	Sets the default button to the fourth button (perhaps a 4-button group is pending)

The Dialog Mode constants are as follows:

Constant	Value	Description
vbApplicationModal	0	User must respond before continuing work in application
vbSystemModal	4096	User must respond before continuing work anywhere in system

The Button Results constants are:

Constant	Value	Description
vbOK	1	Value returned when the "OK" button is clicked
vbCancel	2	Value returned when the "Cancel" button is clicked
vbAbort	3	Value returned when the "Abort" button is clicked
vbRetry	4	Value returned when the "Retry" button is clicked
vbIgnore	5	Value returned when the "Ignore" button is clicked
vbYes	6	Value returned when the "Yes" button is clicked
vbNo	7	Value returned when the "No" button is clicked

Mid Function

Term: `mid(string,fromNumber,[numberReturned])`
Example Syntax: `mid("hello",2,2) ' returns "el"`

The *mid* function returns the section of the passed string designated by fromNumber and numberReturned. It takes two required arguments: a string (or any expression that evaluates to a string), and a number designating the char position with which the mid() function should begin. It takes an optional argument that is also a number, designating the total number of characters to return.

```
theDate = "Monday, Jan. 15, 1997"
mid(theDate,9,7) ' extracts 7 characters—beginning from the 9th char in the
                 ' string—to return "Jan. 15"
```

Oct Function

Term: `oct(number)`
Example Syntax:
```
alert oct(9)
' displays "11" in an alert dialog box, which is octal equivalent of the
' decimal-based number "9"
```

The *oct* function returns the octal value of any number passed to it. If the number contains a fraction, it is first rounded to the nearest whole number. It takes only one argument, which is the number passed to it, which can be an actual number, or any expression that evaluates to a number.

Replace Function

Term: `replace(`*`firstString,secondString,thirdString,`*`[`*`startNum`*`],[`*`count`*`],` `[`*`compareType`*`])`

Example Syntax:
```
thisString = "ha-ha-ho-ho"
thatString = "ho"
replace(thisString,thatString,"ha")
' returns "ha-ha-ha-ha"
```

The *replace* function searches the first string passed to it to see if it contains the second string; then it replaces the second string with the third string. It takes three required arguments, which are the string to search (passed first), the string to find (passed second), and the replacement string (passed third).

The replace() function also takes three optional arguments. The first optional argument is *startNum*, which takes a number that indicates where to begin the search in the first string. The second optional argument is *count*, which indicates how many times to perform the replacement in the string. The third optional argument is *compareType*, which takes a comparison constant that designates the comparison type to use in the search. The VBScript comparison constants are shown in the list at the end of this section.

If the startNum argument is omitted, replacement() begins searching for the second string at position 1, which is the first char in the first string. If the comparison argument is answered, the startNum and count arguments are required.

If the second string is not found in the first string, a 0 is returned. If the string is found, the replacement operation is performed according to the number passed to the count argument. If the count argument is not answered, the replace() function performs all possible replacements. Three replacement operations are shown for the following three strings:

```
thisString = "ha-ha-ho-ho"
thatString = "ho"
otherString = "ha"
```

The first replacement operation starts searching for *thatString* at the first character in *thisString*, because the startNum argument is 1. It replaces the first instance of thatString, but not the second, because the count argument is only 1:

```
replace(thisString,thatString,otherString,1,1)
' returns "ha-ha-ha-ho"
```

The second replacement operation starts searching for thatString at the fourth character in thisString, because the startNum argument is 4. It replaces the first instance of thatString, but not the second, because the count argument is still only 1. It returns the corrected string, starting with the fourth character in the original string:

```
replace(thisString,thatString,otherString,4,1)
' returns "ha-ha-ho"
```

The third replacement operation starts searching for thatString at the fourth character in thisString, because the startNum argument is 4. It replaces *every* instance of thatString, because the count argument is omitted. It returns the corrected string, starting with the fourth character in the original string:

```
replace(thisString,thatString,otherString,4)
' returns "ha-ha-ha"
```

The Comparison constants are as follows:

Constant	Value	Description
vbBinaryCompare	0	Performs a binary comparison
vbTextCompare	1	Performs a string comparison
vbDatabaseCompare	2	Performs a comparison against information contained in a database

Right Function

Term: right(*string,number*)

Example Syntax: right("good-bye",3) ' returns "bye"

The *right* function returns the designated number of characters from the right-hand side of the passed string. It takes two required arguments: a string (or any expression that evaluates to a string), and a number (or any expression that evaluates to a number). The answer to the number argument tells the interpreter how many characters to return.

The interpreter begins counting from the right-most char in the string, up to the number given, then returns the resulting string. If the number indicated is higher than the number of chars in the passed string, then the complete string is returned. If the number expression passed evaluates to 0, then a 0-length (or empty) string is returned.

Rnd Function

Term: rnd([*zeroValue*])

Example Syntax:

```
rnd()
' returns a unique number each time the function is run in a given session
```

The *rnd* function uses a mathematical formula to generate a unique—and very long—number each time its script is run in a given session. It takes one optional argument, which is a seed number that it uses to mathematically calculate a random number each time the function is executed. If no number is passed to this argument, it uses its own internal seed for the calculation.

The random value returned by the rnd() function is always greater than zero, but never greater than one. Although its random generator routine often results in numbers that appeared to be greater than one, (including the example script shown in the sidebar whose first returned value is 1.414126E-02), these seemingly higher numbers are actually using scientific notation. In the case of our example number (1.414126E-02) the E-02 is another way of showing a number whose absolute value would require you to move the decimal two (02) places to the left. Pass this number to the abs() function, and it'll return 0.01414126—a value that is less than one.

> **TIP** It is recommended that the rnd() function be used in conjunction with the randomize statement (discussed in Chapter 9), to produce the necessary seed number and, thereby, increase the randomness of subsequently generated numbers. It was difficult to tell in tests whether this strategy really made any difference, since rnd() seemed to behave exactly the same regardless of the absence or presence of a randomize statement. Nevertheless, it is always a good idea to follow the advice of the development team when it comes to using their product. The seeming lack of effectiveness of the randomize/rnd() combo may be a result of poor documentation regarding its use; or there could be a bug in either the randomize statement or the rnd() function. In any event, the problem could soon be fixed (it may be fixed—or the documentation improved—by the time you read this); and, meanwhile, the randomize statement did not appear to help or hinder the process of generating random numbers.

Round Function

Term: round(*number*,[*decimals*])

Example Syntax: round(1.56789,3) ' returns "1.568"

The *round* function returns the passed number rounded to the designated number of decimals. It takes a number (or any expression that evaluates to a number) as its only required argument. It also takes one optional argument, which is the number of decimal places to allow in the result. If this argument is omitted, only whole numbers are returned.

Eccentricities of the Rnd() Function

The numbers generated by the rnd() function are not actually random, but rather "psuedo" random numbers. Though based on a complex mathematical formula, rnd() generates the exact same set of numbers, in the same order, in every session.

In a test, the following script was set up to run whenever a button on its page was clicked:

```
randomize(2)
alert rnd()
```

After each click, a freshly generated random number was presented in an alert. Clicking the button three times caused the following three numbers to appear (one at a time) in three successive alerts:

```
1.414126E-02
0.9312817
0.7110189
```

When the page was refreshed, the button was clicked three more times, resulting in the display of *the same three numbers*—one right after the other, in the same order. When the browser was exited, relaunched, and the page reloaded, the same three numbers were generated again, in the same order. Given this behavior—and depending on the purpose of your generator—you may want to pass it a new seed number (upon which to base its calculation) each time a new session is opened, so that it doesn't always repeat the same procession of numbers.

RTrim Function

Term: rTrim(*string*)

Example Syntax: rTrim("hello ") ' returns "hello"

The *rTrim* function strips spaces (if any) from the right-hand side of the passed string. It takes a string (or any expression that evaluates to a string) as its only argument, and that argument is required.

The rtrim() function is often used in conjunction with the lTrim() function to remove the beginning and ending spaces in a passed string. To remove all of the spaces in a string, see the trim() function.

```
theString = " and the beat goes on… "
theString = rTrim(theString) ' puts " and the beat goes on…" into "theString"
theString = lTrim(theString) ' puts "and the beat goes on…" into "theString"
```

ScriptEngine Function

Term: `scriptEngine()`

Example Syntax:

```
scriptEngine()
' returns "VBScript" or "JScript" depending on engine in use
```

The *scriptEngine* function returns the name of the current scripting engine. It takes no arguments, and returns "VBScript," "JScript," or "VBA" for Visual Basic for Applications.

ScriptEngineBuildVersion Function

Term: `scriptEngineBuildVersion()`

Example Syntax:

```
scriptEngineBuildVersion()
' returns the build version of the current scripting engine
```

The *scriptEngineBuildVersion* function returns the build version number of the current scripting engine. It takes no arguments.

ScriptEngineMajor|MinorVersion Function

Term: `scriptEngineMajorVersion()`
`scriptEngineMinorVersion()`

Example Syntax:

```
scriptEngineMajorVersion()
' returns the major portion of the version number of the current scripting engine

scriptEngineMinorVersion()
' returns the minor portion of the version number of the current scripting engine
```

The *scriptEngineMajorVersion* and *scriptEngineMinorVersion* functions return the major and minor portions (respectively) of the version number for the current scripting engine. These functions take no arguments.

The major version number refers to the number(s) to left of the current full version number's decimal. The minor version number refers to the number(s) to right of the decimal Thus, for version 1.5, the major version number is 1, and the minor version number is 5. Use a script like this to obtain the complete version number:

```
theVersion = scriptEngineMajorVersion() & "." & scriptEngineMinorVersion()
' puts "2.2" into "theVersion" for the 2.2 version of VBScript
```

Sgn Function

Term: `sgn(number)`

Example Syntax: `sgn(-12)  ' returns "-1"`

The *sgn* function returns 1, 0, or –1, depending on the sign of the passed number. It takes a number (or any expression that evaluates to a number) as its only argument, and that argument is required.

The sgn() function is used to determine whether the passed value is a positive number, a negative number, or zero. If the number is positive, the sgn() function returns 1; if it is negative, it returns –1; if it is zero, it returns 0.

```
theNumber = -2*-2
sgn(theNumber) ' returns 1, since -2 times -2 = 4


theNumber = -2+2
sgn(theNumber) ' returns 0, since -2 + 2 = 0


theNumber = -2-2
sgn(theNumber) ' returns -1, since -2 - 2 = -4
```

Sin Function

Term: `sin(number)`
Example Syntax:

```
sin(theAngle)
' takes the angle passed to it by the variable "theAngle" and returns the ratio
' of its two sides
```

The *sin* function returns the sine (the ratio of two sides of a right triangle) of the passed number (which represents an angle of the right triangle). It takes only one argument, which is the number passed to it, which can be an actual number, or any expression that evaluates to a number.

> **TIP** To convert the sin() function's result to degrees, multiply the returned radians by 180/pi.

The ratio is the length of the side opposite the angle divided by the length of the hypotenuse. The range of the function result is from –1 to 1 (in radians).

Space Function

Term: `space(number)`
Example Syntax: `spaceVar = space(3)  ' puts three spaces into "spaceVar"`

The *space* function puts the number of spaces specified by its number argument into a container (such as a variable, or a text field). It takes only one argument, which is the number passed to it, which can be an actual number, or any expression that evaluates to a number. This argument is required.

The following script populates three variables, then concatenates the three variables into a fourth variable—and an alert presents the result. The second variable, string2, contains five space characters—causing a big gap to appear between the "WARNING" and "Do Not Push..." strings (see Figure 8.5).

```
string1= "WARNING"
string2= space(5)
string3= "Do Not Push the Click Button!"
thisString = string1&string2&string3
alert thisString
```

The space() function can also be used to string together data collected in fields on a form, and redisplay it in another field, with spaces wherever needed. This function is especially useful for displaying columns of data in what looks like a tabbed table. These kinds of formatting operation are the primary purpose of this function.

Split Function

Term: split(*subStrings*,[*delimiter*],[*count*],[*compare*])
Example Syntax:
```
nameArray = split("John Jacob Jingleheimer Smith")
' creates a four-element array called "nameArray," and populates it with the
' four, space-delimited names passed to the function
```

The *split* function breaks a string of substrings that share a common delimiter (divider) into a populated array. It takes only one required argument, which is a string of commonly delimited substrings, which can be the actual substrings (as shown in the Example Syntax), or any expression that evaluates to those substrings.

The split() function also takes three optional arguments. This first optional argument is the delimiter that divides the substrings. If the delimiter argument is omitted, the default delimiter—space—is used (which makes it easy to create an array of all the words in a block of text). The second optional argument is *count*,

Figure 8.5 Five spaces were placed between the word "WARNING" and the "Do Not Push..." message, courtesy of the space() function.

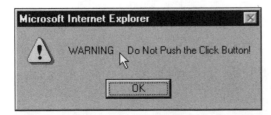

which indicates the number of substrings to return. If the count argument is omitted, all substrings are returned. The third optional argument is *compareType,* which takes a comparison constant that designates the comparison type to use in evaluating substrings. The VBScript comparison constants are shown in the list at the end of this section.

The following script separates a date string—which is actually a combination of three, forward-slash delimited substrings—into a three-element array, and populates each element in that array with its corresponding date substring.

```
thisVar = "2/11/95"
newArray = split (thisVar,"/")

' this script creates a "newArray" from the "/" delimited date in "thisVar"
' "newArray" automatically contains the following three, populated elements:
            newArray(0) = 2
            newArray(1) = 11
            newArray(2) = 95

alert newArray(2)

' an alert displays the data contained in the 3rd element in "newArray," which
is "95"
```

The Comparison constants are:

Constant	Value	Description
vbBinaryCompare	0	Performs a binary comparison
vbTextCompare	1	Performs a string comparison
vbDatabaseCompare	2	Performs a comparison against information contained in a database

Sqr Function

Term: sqr(*number*)
Example Syntax: sqr(900) ' returns "30"

The *sqr* function returns the real square root of the passed number, which must be a positive number. It takes this number (or any expression that evaluates to a number) as its only argument, and that argument is required.

StrComp Function

Term: `strComp(firstString,secondString,[compare])`
Example Syntax: `strComp(900,200) ' returns "1"`

The *strComp* function performs a binary comparison of two passed strings. It takes these two strings (or any two expressions that evaluate to strings) as its two required arguments. It takes an optional compare argument which, when answered with "1," changes the binary comparison to a character comparison.

The strComp() function returns 1 if the first string value is greater than that of the second string; it returns –1 if the second string value is greater than that of the first string; and it returns 0 if the values of the strings are the same.

```
strComp(300,200) ' returns "1"
strComp(200,300) ' returns "-1"
strComp(300,300) ' returns "0"
```

String Function

Term: `string(number,character)`
Example Syntax: `string(10,"/") ' returns "//////////"`

The *string* function creates a string that repeats a passed *character* for the designated *number* of times. It takes two required arguments, which are a number (or any expression that evaluates to a number), and the target character (or an expression that evaluates to that character) to repeat.

> **TIP** The answer to the character argument can be a target character's ASCII number. For instance, you can create a string that contains carriage returns by answering the string() function's character argument with "13" (the ASCII number for a carriage return). Then, you can concatenate your "return" string with other strings to type text, followed by hard returns, into an alert, confirm, or prompt dialog (see Figure 8.6):
>
> ```
> myReturns = string(2,13) ' puts two hard returns into "myReturns"
> alert("Hello:" & myReturns & "How are you today?")
> ```

strReverse Function

Term: `strReverse(string)`
Example Syntax: `strReverse("hello") ' returns "olleh"`

Figure 8.6 Two returns are placed between "Hello" and "How are you..." using the string() function.

The *strReverse* function takes the string that is passed to it, and reverses the order of its characters. It takes the passed string (or any expression that evaluates to a string) as its only argument, and that argument is required.

Tan Function

Term: tan(*number*)

Example Syntax:

```
tan(theAngle)
' returns the ratio of two sides of a right triangle, which is the side
' opposite the passed angle divided the side adjacent to the passed angle
```

The *tan* function returns the tangent (the ratio of two sides of a right triangle) of the passed number (which represents an angle expressed in radians). It takes only one argument, which is the number passed to it, which can be an actual number, or any expression that evaluates to a number.

The ratio is the length of the side opposite the angle divided by the length of the side adjacent to the angle.

> **TIP** To convert the tan() function's result to degrees, multiply the returned radians by 180/pi.

TypeName Function

Term: typeName(*variableName*)

Example Syntax:

```
thisVar = #12/11/95#
if (typeName(thisVar) = date) then
    alert "This is a date."
end if
```

The *typeName* function returns the subtype of the passed variable. It takes only one argument, which is the name of the variable passed to it, or any expression that points to that variable.

The actual value returned is the name of the subtype as listed in the Value column)of the following list of Subtype Name constants.

Value	Description
Empty	uninitialized variable
Null	invalid data
Integer	integer
Long	long integer
Single	single-precision floating-point number
Double	double-precision floating-point number
Currency	currency
Date	date
String	string
Object	generic object
Error	error
Boolean	True or False
Decimal	decimaled number
Unknown	unknown object type
Byte	byte value
Nothing	object variable with nothing in it
<object type>	actual name of an object

UBound Function

Term: uBound(*arrayVariable*,[*dimension*])
Example Syntax:
```
uBound(thisArray)
' returns the index position of the highest element in "thisArray"
```

The *uBound* function returns the index position of the highest (or last) element in the named array. It takes one required argument, which is the name of the target array variable. It also takes one optional argument, which is the target dimension. The dimension argument is only necessary if your target is *not the first dimension* in a multidimensional array. You can forget this argument for 1-dimensional arrays, or if you're only looking at the first dimension in a multidimensional array. In the absence of any answer to the dimension argument, the function defaults to the first dimension in the array anyway.

The uBound() function is invariably used in conjunction with the lBound() function to determine the size of an array's dimension when that size is unknown (as it might be if user actions are dictating the resizing of a dynamic array), or if your script might access scripts written by other authors. For a zero-based array containing three elements—0, 1, and 2—you might write the following script:

```
arraySize = lBound(myArray) + uBound(myArray) + 1
```

This is virtually the same as saying:

```
arraySize = 0 + 2 + 1 ' places 3 into "arraySize"
```

UCase Function

Term: uCase(*string*)
Example Syntax: uCase("hello") ' returns "HELLO"

The *uCase* function converts any letters contained in its passed string to upper case (if necessary). It takes a text string (or any expression that evaluates to a text string) as its only argument, and that argument is required.

TIP If a passed expression evaluates to a number, not only is no error generated, but the expression is evaluated, and its result is returned. If it evaluates to a VBScript keyword (such as "true" or "false"), that keyword is returned in uppercase. Although keywords are normally returned in lowercase, since VBScript is not case-sensitive, uppercasing keywords does not affect VBScript's interpretation of that keyword.

```
theString = 2+2+2
uCase(theString)
' returns "6"

theString = 2+2+2
if (theString = 6) then
    theString = true
end if
uCase(theString)
' returns "TRUE"
```

VarType Function

Term: varType(*variableName*)

Example Syntax:

```
thisVar = #12/11/95#
if (varType(thisVar) = vbDate) then
     alert "This is a date."
end if
```

The *varType* function returns the subtype of the passed variable. It takes only one argument, which is the name of the variable passed to it, or any expression that points to that variable.

The actual value returned is the appropriate number (listed in the Value column in the Data Subtype Constants listed here). You can use this number value, or the displayed constant name in your scripts (as shown in the Example Syntax).

The Data Subtype constants are as follows:

Constant	Value	Description
vbEmpty	0	empty
vbNull	1	null
vbInteger	2	integer
vbLong	3	long integer
vbSingle	4	single-precision floating-point number
vbDouble	5	double-precision floating-point number
vbCurrency	6	currency
vbDate	7	date
vbString	8	string
vbObject	9	automation object
vbError	10	error
vbBoolean	11	Boolean
vbVariant	12	variants (used only with arrays of variants)
vbDataObject	13	data-access object
vbByte	17	byte
vbArray	8192	array

What's Next?

As you can see, the VBScript allows you to leverage the power of an impressive library of built-in functions, letting you do everything from manipulating dates and times, to performing sophisticated mathematical operations, to reformatting and revising strings of text, to constructing your own arrays, to presenting unique question and answer dialogs, and beyond. You may never use some of the functions presented in this chapter, and others you may use only rarely. But there are nevertheless many that you'll call upon regularly to help you make short work of complex tasks.

In Chapter 9, you'll discover ways to further maximize the use of the functions in this chapter—as well as all the objects, properties, methods presented in the three preceding chapters—through the strategic implementation of the control structures and statements provided by the VBScript environment.

Statements

If Objects and their Properties and Methods, along with VBScript's built-in Functions, are the building blocks of your code, *Statements* provide the framework. It is through the strategic use of VBScript's Statements that you are able to dictate to the interpreter how, when, and under what circumstances actions are executed within your scripts. Because the ultimate goal is process control, structuring code is more commonly referred to as controlling program flow (also discussed in Chapters 2 and 3).

Controlling Program Flow

The built-in VBScript Statements are the first tools to turn to once you've decided what needs to happen on the page when targeted events are fired by designated objects. These statements are the defined control structures you have at your disposal for declaring variables, writing unique procedures, setting up *if-then-else* conditionals, and formulating intelligent repeat loops (among other things).

VBScript's Statements are presented in this chapter in alphabetical order. Like the preceding chapters in this part of the book, each Statement definition includes example syntax, usage, and example scripts, as needed.

Call Statement

Term: `call procedure(args)`
Example Syntax:
```
onClick="Call thisSub()"
' causes a subroutine named "thisSub()" to execute
```

The *call* statement is used to invoke the execution of a procedure you've written, either in the form of a sub or function. The call statement is followed by the name of the sub or function. If the procedure takes arguments, you must enclose its argument list in parentheses whenever the call statement is used.

The following example uses the call statement to pass a text string to a subroutine called "myProc" when a button named "thisButton" is clicked, causing an alert to display the message "This button has been clicked" (see Figure 9.1).

```
<HTML>
<HEAD>
<SCRIPT LANGUAGE="VBScript">

sub myProc(myArg)

    alert(myArg)

end sub

</SCRIPT>
</HEAD>
```

Figure 9.1 Clicking the Click Me button passes the displayed alert message to the myProc sub.

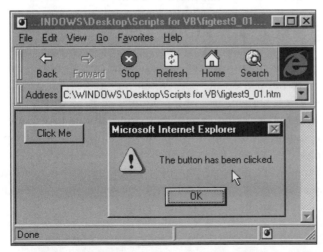

```
<BODY>
<FORM>
<INPUT TYPE="button" NAME="thisButton" VALUE="Click Me" onClick="call
myProc('The button has been clicked.')">
</FORM>
</BODY>
</HTML>
```

When using the call statement to invoke a sub or function, you must follow the procedure's name with enclosing parentheses. You can also invoke internal routines without using the call statement by simply naming the target sub or function. In these instances, you may be able to forego the parentheses unless otherwise required by the script. (See Chapter 3 for a discussion of when to use parentheses.) The alternative syntax is:

```
onClick="myProc 'This button has been clicked.'">
```

> **TIP** Even though the word "call" is not always necessary, if you have trouble getting a routine to run from somewhere in your script, add a little muscle to your script by adding "call" to your statement. It coerces the calling process.

Const Statement

Term: const [*constantName*] = [*value*]
Example Syntax:
```
const lowAgeLimit = 18
' creates a constant named "lowAgeLimit" that represents the number 18
```

The *const* statement is used to create aliases to constant values whose names are then used in your scripts instead of the actual value. A constant's assigned value must be actual and not derived. In other words, you cannot assign a variable, a user-defined function, or an expression that contains an operator to a constant. You can only assign literal values, such as "Hello," a formatted date string (the string *itself*, not a function that derives the string), or a number (as shown in the preceding example).

The following script creates a *ceiling* constant with a value of 100. When the user leaves the field on the form, if that field's value is greater than 100, the alert is presented (see Figure 9.2).

```
<HTML>
<HEAD>
<SCRIPT LANGUAGE="VBScript">

const ceiling = 100
```

```
sub checkAmt(amt)

    if (amt > ceiling) then

        alert ("You have exceeded the $" & ceiling & ".00 spending limit.")

    end if

end sub

</SCRIPT>

</HEAD>
<BODY>
<CENTER>
<FORM>
Total: $<INPUT TYPE="text" VALUE="100" NAME="theText"
onBlur="checkAmt(theText.value)">
</FORM>
</CENTER>
</BODY>
```

Figure 9.2 An alert informs the user that the amount in the Total field exceeds the current spending limit, which is represented by the ceiling constant.

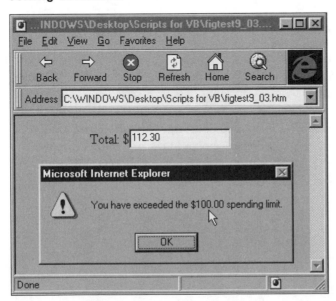

Why Use a Constant Instead of the Value It Represents?

At first glance, it may seem a little simple-minded to type the word "ceiling" in a script instead of just typing "100," which is a shorter string and says exactly what you mean. If you are only going to refer to a value once (or even twice) in a script, you would be going a little overboard by declaring it as a constant. The purpose of the const statement, however, is to allow you to create an alias to a value that you'll be referring to frequently in a script, and possibly in other scripts that access that script.

In the preceding example, a spending limit is declared in the ceiling constant. What if you created several scripts that referred back to that spending limit, then decided to change the limit? To reflect that change throughout your entire scripting environment, all you have to do is change it in one place: in the line of script where you assigned the value to the ceiling constant.

Conversely, if you had used the actual number "100" throughout your script, you'd have to search and replace every occurrence. If outside scripts referred to the constant, you might even miss a few references, which could really cause havoc in your application. This is the kind of nightmare housekeeping chore that the const statement allows you to avoid.

By default, constants declared at the script level (outside of any sub or function statement) are *public*. This means that they are accessible to the scripts in other pages (as in a frameset, for instance) or to VBScripted pages on the server (called *active server pages* or *.asp documents*). You can *lock* any script-level constant so that it is only accessible from other parts of its resident script by declaring the variable as *private*.

```
PRIVATE const [myPrivateConst] = [value]
```

> **TIP** Inside procedures (subs or functions) constants are always private, and this status cannot be changed. So if you want to publicize a constant, you must create it at the script level.

Dim Statement

Term: dim [variable1],[variable2],[variable...]

Example Syntax:

```
DIM thisVar,thatVar
' declares two variables named "thisVar" and "thatVar"
```

The *dim* statement (which is short for dimension) is used to declare a name for a variable, and to allocate memory space for storage of that name and the variable's subsequent contents.

The *scope* of the variable (the portion of the script for which it is valid) is determined by the placement of the dim statement. When the dim statement is placed inside a procedural control structure (sub or function), any associated variable becomes a *local variable*. This means that the names and contents of the variable are only valid *for that procedure*. If a local variable is referred to elsewhere in a script (outside the scope of its resident procedure), it is treated like an *undeclared* new, empty variable.

If *option explicit* has been declared in the script, any variable appearing outside of its procedural venue is still treated like an undeclared variable—which produces an error in option explicit mode. This is because an option explicit declaration forces you to formally declare all of your variables.

```
<SCRIPT LANGUAGE="VBScript">


OPTION EXPLICIT

sub myProc()

    DIM myVar


end sub



</SCRIPT>
```

```
' sets the script to option explicit mode, and declares "myVar" as a local
' variable within myProc().if referred to outside of myProc(), "myVar" returns an
' error—unless redeclared using dim, redim, public, or private
```

If the dim statement is placed at the script level (outside of any controlling structure, such as in the first line following the <SCRIPT> tag), any associated variable becomes a *global variable*, whose scope is valid *for all of the current scripts* (including scripts that interact in a frameset).

```
<SCRIPT LANGUAGE="VBScript">
DIM myVar ' declares "myVar" as a global variable
```

> **WARNING** You can use the same name over and over again for local variables appearing in different procedures, so that the variable means something different in each procedure. This may seem like a confusing way to script, but there are times when it actually makes good scripting sense to do so (see the "Global versus Local Variables" sidebar in Chapter 12 for a discussion of why). However, you cannot use the same name for a global *and* a local variable, since a global variable, by definition, means the same thing to every statement that accesses it throughout the entire scripting environment. Placing your scripts in option explicit mode is a dandy way to avoid this and other variable naming conflicts.

When a variable is first declared, it automatically has a value of 0 if used in its pristine state for numeric or Boolean operations, or a value of "" for string operations. If you want the variable to begin life with another value, or to represent another data subtype, you must initialize it with appropriate data after declaring it:

```
DIM myDate
myDate = now
' puts the current date into "myDate" as soon as it is declared, making it into a
' properly formatted date variable that may be used with any VBScript date
' functions
```

You can also use the dim statement to create your own array by declaring an *array variable*, and passing its dimension data in parentheses. Passing numbers in the parentheses results in a static array whose dimensions cannot be programmatically changed.

```
DIM myArray1(2)
' creates a one-dimensional static array with 3 index items

DIM myArray2(2,4)
' creates a multi-dimensional static array with 3 columns and 5 rows (counting
' from 0)
```

Passing empty parentheses results in a dynamic array which can be redimensioned over and over again, at any time, in your script. (See the "Redim Statement" section for information on redimensioning an array.)

```
DIM dyArray()
' creates a one-dimensional static array with 3 index items
```

> **WARNING** Don't forget that each number you pass to an array variable represents a zero-based counter. Passing 2 creates an index of 3 items, passing 9 creates an index of 10 items, and so on.

By default, all global variables are public, meaning that they are accessible to the scripts in other pages (as in a frameset, for instance) or to VBScripted pages on the server (called active server pages or .asp documents). Although it did not appear to work in the version of Internet Explorer tested, VBScript is supposed to allow you to *lock* any global variable (even an array variable) so that it is only accessible from other parts of its resident script by declaring the variable as private. If you declare private globals in this way, you may want to explicitly declare your public globals as well, so you can see at a glance which are public and which are private. Following this convention for all globals (when mixing private and public in the same script) helps to ensure that globals that you intended to keep private aren't accidentally made public.

```
PRIVATE myPrivateVariable
PUBLIC myPublicVariable
```

Do Until Statement

Term: do **until** [*condition*]
        [*statements*]
     loop

Example Syntax:
```
do until thisField <> "Please type here."
    document.bgColor = "magenta"
    document.bgColor = "cyan"
loop
```

Alternative Syntax:
```
do
    document.bgColor = "magenta"
    document.bgColor = "cyan"
loop until thisField <> "Please type here."
```

```
' either format causes the background to flash between the two colors until the
' user types something else into "thisField"
```

The *do until* statement is a repeat loop control structure that instructs the browser to execute its enclosed statements *until its passed condition becomes true*. Do until statements may be nested.

The following snippet creates a field that counts to 10 by placing the contents of a previously declared variable named "thisNum" into a form field called "count10." The do until loop continues to run this script until thisNum equals 11.

```
do until thisNum <> 11


    document.forms(0).count10.value = thisNum
    thisNum = thisNum + 1


loop
```

> **NOTE** The first iteration of the loop in this example places 0 into the Counting field, and adds 1 to thisNum. The next iteration places 1 into the field, then raises the value of thisNum to 2. So, at the beginning of each loop, the value in thisNum is always 1 greater than the value displayed in the field. Thus, when 10 is finally placed into the field, thisNum equals 11, and the loop stops executing.

Do While Statement
Term:
```
do while [condition]
    [statements]
loop
```
Example Syntax:
```
do while thisField = "Please type here."
    document.bgColor = "magenta"
    document.bgColor = "cyan"
loop
```
Alternative Syntax:
```
do
    document.bgColor = "magenta"
    document.bgColor = "cyan"
loop while thisField = "Please type here."


' either format causes the background to flash between the two colors as long
' as "Please type here." remains in "thisField"
```

The *do while* statement is a repeat loop control structure that instructs the browser to execute its enclosed statements *as long as its passed condition remains true*.

The following snippet is a revision of the *do until* statement example. It also creates a field that counts to 10 by placing the contents of a previously declared variable named "thisNum" into a form field called "count10." However, the do until loop continues to execute *until* thisNum *does* equal 11.

```
do while thisNum <> 11


    document.forms(0).count10.value = thisNum
    thisNum = thisNum + 1


loop
```

> **N O T E** It is also possible to perform do while loops using the *while...wend* syntax familiar to programmers from other languages:
>
> ```
>         while [condition}
>             [statements]
>         wend
> ```
>
> However, even the VBScript development team recommends using the do while control structure instead, since it does everything while...wend does, plus takes the critically important *exit do* statement. Word is, Microsoft may be phasing out while...wend anyway.

Erase Statement

Term: `erase array1,array2,array…`

Example Syntax:

```
erase staticArray
' reinitializes all of the array's elements
erase dynamicArray
' reinitializes all of the array's elements, and deallocates
' its storage space in memory
```

The *erase* statement empties every element in its passed array. Static arrays are reinitialized as follows:

Static Array Type	Erase Results
Number Array	Sets each element to 0
String Array	Sets each element to a zero-length ("") string
Object Array	Sets each element to nothing (see definition of *nothing* keyword in Chapter 10)

Dynamic arrays are completely erased from the system's memory and must be restored to memory (using the *redim* statement) before your scripts can refer to them again.

Exit Do Statement

Term:

```
do until [condition]
    [statements]
    if ([condition]) then exit do
loop
```

Example Syntax:

```
do until thisField <> "Please type here."
    document.bgColor = "magenta"
    document.bgColor = "cyan"
    thisNum = thisNum + 1
    if (thisNum = 100) then exit do
loop
' causes the background to flash between the two colors until the user types
' something else into "thisField," or until "thisNum" equals 100
```

The *exit do* statement allows you to stop the execution of a do loop before its own halt condition is met. It is best used in conjunction with an *if* conditional (as shown in Example Syntax) to stop the action of the script if a secondary condition is met before the do loop's primary halt condition.

When the script is halted, control is transferred to the statement immediately following *loop*. If there are no statements after loop, no further action is executed.

TIP It is always prudent to provide an exit do statement in any script that might otherwise never meet its halt condition. The preceding script is a good example of a potentially endless loop. To fix this problem, the do until/exit do statements are used together to cause the page to flash between two vibrant colors for a set period of time. If at any time the user types new data into the referenced field, the screen stops flashing. However, if the user fails to type anything into the field before the value of thisNum reaches 100, the exit do statement stops the flashing anyway. Without the exit do statement, this script's halt condition might never be met.

Exit For Statement

Term:

```
for [counter] = [start] to [finish] step [increment]
    [statements]
    if ([condition]) then exit for
next
```

Example Syntax:

```
for thisNum = 1 to 100 step 1
    document.bgColor = "magenta"
    document.bgColor = "cyan"
    if (document.forms(0).stop.checked = true) then exit for
next
' causes the background to flash between colors 100 times, unless the user
' clicks a checkbox named "Stop" before thisNum reaches 100
```

The *exit for* statement allows you to stop the execution of a *for* loop before the value of its counting variable equals its *finish* value. The exit for statement may also be used in a *for each* loop, to stop its execution before the script's actions have been executed on all of the elements in its referenced array, or all of the objects in its referenced collection.

The exit for statement is best used in conjunction with an if conditional (as shown in Example Syntax) to stop the action of the script if a secondary condition is met before the loop's finish condition—or before all of the items in its group have been affected.

When a for or for each script is halted, control is transferred to the statement immediately following *next*. If there are no statements after next, no further action is executed.

Exit Function Statement

Term:

```
function functionName(arg1,arg2,arg…)
    [statements]
    functionName = [returnedValue]
    exit function
end function
```

Example Syntax:

```
function addAmts(amt1,amt2)
    if (amt1 = "" or amt2 = "") then
        exit function
```

```
    else
        addAmts = 0 + amt1 + amt2
    end if
    end function
' exits the function if either passed argument is ""
```

The *exit function* statement allows you to stop the execution of a function at any time. It is best used in conjunction with an if conditional (as shown in Example Syntax) to stop the action of the script if certain conditions of the function aren't met.

When the script is halted, control is returned to the statement that called the function, although no value is returned.

The Example Syntax script shows a function that adds the amounts passed to it. However, if the values passed are found to contain the empty string literal " "— since it is useless to perform the addition—the function is exited. See "Function Statement" for a related scripting example.

Exit Sub Statement

Term:

```
sub procedureName(arg1,arg2,arg...)
    [statements]
    exit sub


end sub
```

Example Syntax:

```
sub addAmts(amt1,amt2)
    if (amt1 = "" or amt2 = "") then
        exit sub
    else
        addAmts = 0 + amt1 + amt2
    end sub
' exits the sub if either passed argument is ""
```

The *exit sub* statement allows you to stop the execution of a subroutine at any time. It is best used in conjunction with an if conditional (as shown in Example Syntax) to stop the action of the script if certain conditions of the sub aren't met.

When the script is halted, control is returned to the statement that called the sub.

The Example Syntax script shows a sub that adds the amounts passed to it. However, if the values passed are found to contain the empty string literal " "— since it is useless to perform the addition—the sub is exited. See "Sub Statement" for a related scripting example.

For Statement

Term:

```
for [counter] = [start] to [finish] step [increment]
    [statements]
next
```

Example Syntax:

```
for thisNum = 1 to 100 step 1
    document.bgColor = "magenta"    document.bgColor = "cyan"
next
' causes the background to flash between colors 100 times
```

The *for* statement is a repeat loop control structure that instructs the browser to execute its enclosed statements *for a designated number of times.* The number of loops is set by creating a variable that contains the current count (thisNum in the Example Syntax script), and passes the interpreter a start number and a finish number.

The *step* clause takes any integer (or expression that evaluates to an integer) that is not 0, and can be a positive or negative number. The step amount automatically adds itself to the counter variable each time the loop reiterates. If the step amount is a positive number, the value of the counter is raised by the number passed to step. If it is negative, it is lowered. The step clause is optional and, if you omit it, defaults to 1.

```
for theCounter = 1 to 100
    theCounter = theCounter + 1

' adds 1 to theCounter on each iteration
```

The following script presents a "Click Me to Select All Checkboxes" button on a page with five checkboxes (see Figure 9.3). The for statement is used to incrementally check any box that is not yet selected. When the last box is checked, the loop ends. To show how this control structure may be set up to count down, instead of up, this script checks the last box (furthest right) on the page first, and moves left from there, using a step amount of –1.

```
<HTML>
<HEAD>
<SCRIPT LANGUAGE="VBScript" FOR="theButton" EVENT="onClick()">

DIM i,theBoxNum
theBoxNum = document.forms(1).elements.length
```

```
for i = theBoxNum-1 to 0 step -1

    if (document.forms(1).elements(i).checked = false) then

        document.forms(1).elements(i).checked = true

    end if

next

</SCRIPT>
</HEAD>
<BODY>

<FORM>

<INPUT TYPE="button" NAME="theButton"
VALUE="  Click Me to Select All Checkboxes   ">

</FORM>
<P>
<FORM>

<INPUT type="checkbox">Item 0
<INPUT type="checkbox">Item 1
<INPUT type="checkbox">Item 2
<INPUT type="checkbox">Item 3
<INPUT type="checkbox">Item 4

<FORM>
</BODY>
</HTML>
```

NOTE Two forms objects were created in the preceding script, so that the Click Me... button would not be counted in the elements array that contained the checkboxes. However, if the button belonged to the same form as the boxes, it would have been possible to begin the counter at theBoxNum without subtracting 1.

Figure 9.3 Clicking the button executes a for statement that selects all the checkboxes.

> **TIP** Let this script serve as a reminder that *arrays* count from 0, but the *array length property* counts from 1. In this example, the length of the elements array is used to get the starting number of this script. However, since the total number of items in the array is 5—and yet, there is no element whose index position is 5—1 is subtracted from this total to arrive at the highest number in the array, which is 4.

For Each Statement

Term:

```
for each [element/object] in [array/collection]
    [statements]
    next [element]
```

Example Syntax:

```
for each theFlds in elements
    if (theFlds.value = empty) then
```

```
        alert ("You have not filled in all the fields.")
        exit for
    end if
next elements
' checks all the elements in a form to see if any are empty; if so, the loop is
' exited and an alert issued
```

The *for each* statement is a repeat loop control structure that instructs the browser to execute its enclosed statements *for each member of a designated group*. The group can be the elements in an array, or the objects in a collection. The element name must be a variant variable that references the element. The object name can be a variant or object variable, or a specific OLE automation object variable.

> **TIP** When you use the Array() function to create an array, it returns a variant variable containing that array.

Function Statement
Term:
```
function functionName(arg1,arg2,arg…)
    [statements]
    functionName = [returnedValue]
end function
```
Example Syntax:
```
function addAmts(amt1,amt2,amt3)
    addAmts = amt1+amt2+amt3
end function
' adds the numbers passed to the arguments "amt1," "amt2," and "amt3," and
' returns the total
```

The *function* statement is a procedural control structure that executes its statements *and returns a value* to the script that called it. The function's value is returned by assigning that value to the function using its own name.

Functions cannot be nested.

The Example Syntax script assigns the total of the three passed amounts to addAmts(), which is the function's name. Whenever addAmts() is called from anywhere else in the script, it returns the total of those three amounts. Here's a script that uses the addAmts() function to add the values that a user types into three fields, and place the total into a fourth field (see Figure 9.4):

```
<HTML>
<HEAD>
```

```
<SCRIPT LANGUAGE="VBScript">

function addAmts(amt1,amt2,amt3)

    addAmts = 0+amt1+amt2+amt3

end function

</SCRIPT>
</HEAD>
<BODY>
<CENTER>
<FORM>
<INPUT TYPE="text" NAME="first"><p>
<INPUT TYPE="text" NAME="second"><p>
<INPUT TYPE="text" NAME="third"><p>

<INPUT TYPE="button" VALUE=" Calculate Total "
onClick="total.value = addAmts(first.value,second.value,third.value)">

<p><INPUT TYPE="text" NAME="total"><p>

</FORM>
</CENTER>
</BODY>
</HTML>
```

> **TIP** Did you notice the 0 that was added to the addition string used in this script? This is a handy little trick you can use to "coerce" the data subtype of a variable, function, or object property. In the current example, the information typed into the fields is considered a *string value*. Even though the *addition operator* is used (+), a *concatenation operation* results when the amt argument values are added together alone. It is both a blessing and a curse that the + operator behaves as an Arithmetic Operator or Concatenation Operator according to the first char value passed to it. If the first char is string data, it concatenates. In our example, a zero is passed before the argument variables to force the + operator to perform as an arithmetic operator. Of course, this operation would ultimately fail if the string values in amt1, amt2, and amt3 are not recognizable numbers.

Figure 9.4 Clicking the Calculate Total button executes a function statement that places the total of the top fields into the bottom field.

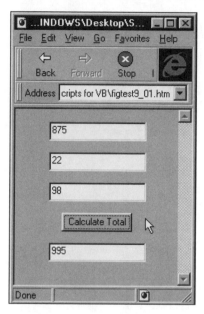

By default, all functions are public, meaning that they are accessible to the scripts in other pages (as in a frameset, for instance) or to VBScripted pages on the server (called active server pages or .asp documents). However, you can *lock* any function so that it is only accessible from other parts of its resident script by declaring the function as private. If you declare private functions in this way, you may want to explicitly declare your public functions as well, so you can see at a glance which are public and which are private. Following this convention for all functions (when mixing private and public in the same script) helps to ensure that functions that you intended to keep private aren't accidentally made public.

```
PRIVATE function addAmts(amt1,amt2,amt3)
PUBLIC function subtractAmts(amt1,amt2,amt3)
```

If Statement
Term:

```
if [condition] then [statement] else [alternateStatement]
```

```
     -OR-
```

```
if [condition] then
```

```
        [statements]

else

    [statements]

end if

    -OR-

if [condition] then

    [statements]

elseif [condition] then

    [statements]

end if
```

Example Syntax:
```
if (birthDay = now) then alert("Today is my birthday.")
```

' displays the alert message if the date string in a variable called "birthDay" matches the current date

```
if (thisField.value = "") then

    alert("Please fill in the field.")

else

    alert("Thank you for filling in the field.")

end if
```

' displays the first alert message if "thisField" is empty, or the second alert message if "thisField" is not empty

```
if (thisField.value = "Type here.") then

    alert("Please fill in the field.")

elseif (thisField.value = "") then
```

```
    alert("There is nothing in the field.")

else

    alert("Thank you for filling in the field.")

end if

' displays the first alert message if "thisField" contains "Type here.", the
' second alert message if "thisField" is empty, or the third alert message if
' "thisField" is not empty
```

The if statement is a *decision control statement*, allowing you to set up statement branches that execute according to current conditions in the script, the browser, and the page.

The simplest if statements only have one statement list that executes if the condition is met, or does not execute if the condition is *not* met. If the statement is very short, it can be placed on one line, like the Example Syntax script that only displays its alert message on your birthday.

> **TIP** In the continuing saga on the use or non-use of parentheses: You don't have to use enclosing parentheses around the passed if condition. They are used here because VBScript doesn't care. Since they are required in JavaScript and also make it easier to read the if statements, they are used here for the latter reason. Many of the examples throughout this reference section also incorporate the parentheses around the if statement's passed conditions. Many of the examples in the rest of the book, however, do not. The scripts usually work using either syntax, so whether you use parens your own scripts should depend on whether they make the code more readable for you.

A more complex if statement has at least two *branches* and an *else* clause. If the condition is met, one statement branch executes; if not, the other branch executes— like the Example Syntax script that displays one message if its reference field is empty, and another if it is not. One way or another, one of the script's branches is going to execute.

> **WARNING** You can have multiple elseifs in a single if statement, but you can only have one else clause. Once you place an else clause in an if statement, you cannot place any elseifs after it.

An if statement that requires multiple conditions can make use of the elseif clause, which can be passed a second condition. The Example Syntax script that displays one of three alerts is a good example of how this clause is used.

On Error Resume Next Statement

Term: on error resume next

Example Syntax:

```
sub doCalc()
    on error resume next
    theScore = document.thisForm.ansFld.value * 10
    theName = document.thisForm.nameFld.value
    alert "Your score is " & theScore & "," & theName

end sub
```

The *on error resume next* statement causes a script to continue executing if one or more of its internal statements results in an error. In the Example Syntax script shown, if the mathematical expression used to populate theScore variable returns an error, the rest of the script still runs, without presenting the user with a VBScript error dialog. Of course, if theScore statement is in error, then the alert will read "Your score is <undefined>, [theName]." To find out how to recover from such errors, see Chapter 14's discussion of Error Handling. Also, check out the description of the Err object in Chapter 4.

Randomize Statement

Term: randomize [*number*]

Example Syntax:

```
randomize numField.value
rnd()
' initializes the rnd() function with the seed value represented by the number
' typed into a field named "numField"
```

The *randomize* statement is used in conjunction with rnd(), to initialize that function's random number generator. See "Rnd Function" in Chapter 8 for details.

Redim Statement

Term: redim [*arrayVar1(dim1,dim2,dim...)*], [*arrayVar1(dim1,dim2,dim...)*]

Example Syntax:

```
DIM thisArray()
' declares a dynamic array

REDIM thisArray(2)
thisArray(0) = "Item 1": thisArray(1) = "Item 2"
' redimensions thisArray() to contain two items
```

The *redim* statement (which is short for *redimension*) is used to allocate memory to a dynamic array, and assign its dimensions (up to 60 are allowed). Dynamic arrays are declared using the dim statement and empty parentheses (as shown in Example Syntax).

Dynamic arrays make more sense when their dimensions are set by variables, whose values (by definition) vary according to scripted conditions and environmental (the application's environment, that is) circumstances.

```
REDIM thisArray(itemsOrdered)
' redimensions thisArray() to contain a number of items eqiuvalent to the number
' of products ordered by the current customer
```

Rem Statement

Term: rem explanatory comments

Example Syntax: REM lets you include non-executing remarks in your code

The *rem* statement (which is short for *remarks*) is used to preface explanatory comments typed into your code *that you do not want the interpreter to execute.* When the rem statement precedes a line in a script, the interpreter skips all of the information on that line (i.e., everything typed to the right of the rem statement):

```
REDIM thisArray(itemsOrdered)
REM redimensions thisArray()
```

If you want to use the rem statement within a line of code, you must type a colon first:

> **TIP** You can also use the single quote/apostrophe symbol (') instead of the rem statement, as all example scripts in this book do. This saves a little typing, looks a little clearner, and allows comments within lines of script without a chaparoning colon.

```
REDIM thisArray(itemsOrdered):REM redimensions thisArray()
```

If you want to write more than one line (or partial line) of comments, you must precede each new line with its own rem statement.

Special words or symbols are reserved by every programming language (including HTML) for use in hiding typed explanations of the code from its interpreter. The rem allows you to document your code for greater comprehension for yourself (when you return to it weeks later), and anyone else who may work with you or otherwise make use of it.

Select Case Statement

Term:

```
select case [test]
    case [possibleAns1,possibleAns2,…]
    case [possibleAltAns1,possibleAltAns2,…]
    case else

end select
```

Example Syntax:

```
select case theWinner
    case play1,play2,play3

        alert("The winner is Team One!")

    case play4,play5,play6

        alert("The winner is Team Two!")

    case else

        alert("It's a tie!")

end select

' if the value of "theWinner" is the same as the value "play1," "play2," or
' "play3," the first alert is returned

' if the value matches "play4," "play5," or "play6," the second alert is
' returned

' if none of the values match, the third alert is returned
```

The *select case* statement is a decision control statement similar to the if statement. Like the if statement, the select statement allows you to set up statement branches that execute according to current conditions in the script, the browser, and the page. Its beauty lies in its compactness, since it allows you to script less and accomplish more.

In the preceding example, six players of a scripted game are divided into two teams. Although the scripting example doesn't show it, imagine that each player is defined by one of the *play* variables. The players on the first team are play1, play2, and play3. The players on the second team are play4, play5, and play6. Each player's score is placed into that player's associated play variable. At the end of the game, the play variable that contains the highest number for each team is checked against the highest number for the other team. If one number is higher than the other, the play variable that contributed the high number is placed into a variable named "theWinner." If the number matched, no number is placed into theWinner.

In the script segment shown, a select statement is then used to determine if the contents of theWinner match the contents of any of the play variable in the first case clause. If so, an alert announces that the first team wins. If not, the second case clause is checked against theWinner. If a match is found, an alert announces that the second team wins. If no match is found, the case else clause is executed, and an alert declares a tie.

Set Statement

Term: set [*objectVariable*] = [*object*]

Example Syntax:

```
SET theBrowser = window.navigator
' places the navigator object into a variable named "theBrowser"
```

The *set* statement is used to create an object variable whose name, for all scripting purposes, becomes synonymous with the object itself, and can be used in place of its formal reference string.

```
DIM theField
SET theField = document.forms(0).elements(5)
' declares a variable named "theField," then sets it to the referenced form
' object
```

> **TIP** If you use several variables for the same object, or several object variables, it's good coding practice to set these variables back to nothing when you're done with them. By this action, you release memory and system resources that were temporarily allocated to the object variable. If you fail to reset these variables to nothing, the system eventually does it for you, as soon as the object variable goes out of scope (i.e., its referencing script is no longer executing).

```
SET theField = nothing ' removes the form object from "theField"
```

Sub Statement

Term:

sub *procedureName*(*arg1*,*arg2*,*arg...*)
    [*statements*]

end sub

Example Syntax:

```
sub addAmts(amt1,amt2,amt3)
    theTotal = amt1+amt2+amt3
    alert(theTotal)

end sub
```

```
' adds the numbers passed to the arguments "amt1," "amt2," and "amt3," and dis
' plays as alert containing the total
```

The *sub* statement is a procedural control structure that executes its statements *but does not return a value* to the script that called it. Scripting operations that result from the execution of a sub statement must be listed within that sub statement, with one exception. Although you can't pass any data to it (except by populating a global variable or an object property), you *can* fire an event from a sub statement by attaching a method to an object that executes its event handler script.

```
onBlur="call sub theProc(theFld.value)"

sub theProc(newAmt)

    totalAmt = newAmt
    theButton.click

end sub

onClick="theButton.value = totalAmt"
```

```
' when the user leaves "theFld," its value is sent as an answer to theProc()
' sub procedure's newAmt argument

' theProc() puts newAmt into a previously-declared global variable named
' totalAmt, and sends the click event to "theButton"
```

```
' "theButton" OnClick handler changes the displayed name of the button to the
' value contained in "totalAmt"
```

You can pass data *to* a sub statement easily enough, as long as the sub is written to allow arguments.

```
sub theSub(string)


    alert(string)

end sub

call theSub("Hello")

' sends "Hello" to the string argument, causing "Hello" to appear in the
' subsequently displayed alert
```

Sub statements cannot be nested.

Here's a variation on the example script used for the function statement. As with the function script, clicking the Calculate Total button calls the addAmts() sub, and passes the value of the first three fields to answer its three arguments. Also like the function script, the sub adds the three numbers (starting with 0, to get the + operator to behave as an arithmetic operator, and not a concatenator).

Instead of returning the resulting total to the calling button script, and letting that script set the value of the total field, this script sets the value of the field from within the sub itself.

```
<HTML>
<HEAD>
<SCRIPT LANGUAGE="VBScript">

DIM theTotal

sub addAmts(amt1,amt2,amt3)

    document.forms(0).total.value = 0+amt1+amt2+amt3

end sub

</SCRIPT>
</HEAD>
```

```
<BODY>
<CENTER>
<FORM>
<INPUT TYPE="text" NAME="first"><p>
<INPUT TYPE="text" NAME="second"><p>
<INPUT TYPE="text" NAME="third"><p>

<INPUT TYPE="button" VALUE=" Calculate Total "
onClick="call addAmts(first.value,second.value,third.value)">

<p><INPUT TYPE="text" NAME="total"><p>

</FORM>
</CENTER>
</BODY>
</HTML>
```

By default, all sub statements are public, meaning that they are accessible to the scripts in other pages (as in a frameset, for instance) or to VBScripted pages on the server (called active server pages or .asp documents). However, you can *lock* any sub procedure so that it is only accessible from other parts of its resident script by declaring the sub as *private*. If you declare private subs in this way, you may want to explicitly declare your public subs as well, so you can see at a glance which are public and which are private. Following this convention for all subs (when mixing private and public in the same script) helps to ensure that subs that you intended to keep private aren't accidentally made public.

```
PRIVATE sub addAmts(amt1,amt2,amt3)
PUBLIC sub subtractAmts(amt1,amt2,amt3)
```

A sub statement may also be written as an event handler. In such instances, the sub's name becomes a combination of the name of the target object, and the name of the associated event. When that event is fired by the referenced object, the sub routine executes:

```
sub thisButton_onClick()
  [statements]
end sub
' executes its statements when a button named "thisButton" is clicked
```

What's Next?

Through the concerted use of some or all of the statements and structures presented in this chapter, you can certainly exert a firm control over the flow of events, the use of built-in functions, and the objects, methods, and properties invoked within your pages. All that's left are the *Operators* and *Keywords* that serve as grist for the construction of the simple-to-complex expressions needed to arrive at the data that must pass through your carefully crafted statements and control structures, and ultimately drive the execution of your scripts.

10

Operators and Keywords

Operators and *Keywords* are specialized tools that you can use to put the final, expert touches on your code. These critical language elements provide the material for constructing the simple-to-complex expressions used to solidify your control over what happens in your Web page. Some form of expression appears in almost every line of code written in every language, allowing programmers to accomplish a multitude of tasks; much of which—in the VBScript/Web page environment—centers on passing necessary information to objects that need it (such as text to a field on the page), or to the interpreter (such as a Boolean value dictating which if-then-else action to execute).

The VBScript Operators and Keywords

VBScript's built-in Operators and Keywords are used (respectively) to create expressions and to represent standard expressed values that the interpreter recognizes. These language elements work side by side to help your scripts discover needed information, and interpret it properly. Thus, they are presented together in this chapter, in alphabetical order by name or, (in the case of Operators), by operation name, followed by operator symbol. As with the other chapters in this part of the book, each item definition includes example syntax, usage, and example scripts, as needed.

Addition Operator

Term: [*number*] + [*number*]

Example Syntax: `theTotal = 1+1 ' puts 2 into a variable named "theTotal"`

The + operator is an Arithmetic Operator, and is best used to add numeric values together. However, you can also use it to concatenate strings—which it will only do if both of its *addends* (the numbers or expressions that sit on either side) evaluate to string subtypes.

If one of the + operator's addends evaluates to a valid number, and the other to empty, the operation treats the empty expression as a 0, and returns the valid number by itself. If both expressions evaluate to empty, the operation returns 0. If one or both expressions evaluate to null, the operation returns null.

`true + false ' adds -1 to 0, resulting in -1`

> **NOTE** Expressions that evaluate to *true* are treated as –1, and expressions that evaluated to *false* are treated as 0.

> **TIP** It is a good coding practice to limit the use of the add operator to arithmetic operations, and use the concatenation operator to tie together strings of data. This makes your code easier to read, since you'll know that the + sign invariably means that an arithmetic operation is intended. Then, if you get a concatenated string, you know that something is wrong with one or both of its addend expressions.

And Operator

Term: [*condition*] and [*condition*]

Example Syntax:

```
isTrue = (2+2=4) and (1+2=3)
' puts true into a variable named "isTrue"
```

The *and* operator is a Logical Conjunction Operator, used to determine if the conditions that enclose it are *both true*. If either or both conditions are false, the operation results in false.

1st Condition Is	2nd Condition Is	and Returns
true	true	true
false	false	false
false	true	false
true	false	false

> **TIP** It is also possible for the and operation to return a null value, if either or both of its enclosing conditions is null. If you are setting up a conditional script—and it's possible that one of your conditional expressions could return null—be sure your script provides for true, false, *and null* alternatives.

The and operator also moonlights as a *bit-wise comparison operator*, meaning that you can use it to compare bits that occur in the same position in the results of two numeric expressions, allowing you to set the corresponding bits according to this truth table:

1st Bit Is: AND	2nd Bit Is	Result Is
1	1	1
0	0	0
0	1	0
1	0	0

Concatenation Operator

Term: [*string*] & [*string*]
Example Syntax:

```
alert("Hello, " & document.forms(0).nameFld.value & ".")
' if "John" is typed into the field called "nameFld," displays this alert:
' "Hello, John."
```

The & operator is the Concatenation Operator, used to join two text strings together. If either of the concatenator's enclosing expressions is not a string, it is converted to a string subtype and joined to the results of the other expression.

```
2 & " days ago"
' 2 is converted from an integer to a string, and joined to the " days ago"
' string to produce: "2 days ago"
```

If one of the expressions enclosing the concatenator evaluates to a string, but the other evaluates to null or empty, the true string expression is returned by itself. (The other expression is treated as a zero-length string.) If *both* enclosing expressions evaluates to null, null is returned.

> **NOTE** The & operator does not provide spaces between expressed strings. You must provide the needed ending or starting spaces yourself, just as you must provide every other character in your strings.

Division Operators

Term: [*number*] / [*number*] -OR- [*number*] \ [*number*]

Example Syntax:

```
floatNum = 12.50/5
' puts 2.50 into a variable named " floatNum"

noFloatNum = 12.50/5
' puts 2 into a variable named "noFloatNum"
```

   VBScript provides two division operators: one for floating point division, and one for non-floating point (or integer) division.

About the Floating Point Division Operator

The / operator is an Arithmetic Operator, used to divide the number to its left by the number to its right and return a *floating point number*.

   If one of the / operator's dividend expressions evaluates to a valid number, and its divisor evaluates to empty, the divisor is treated as a 0, and vice versa. If one or both expressions evaluate to null, the operation returns null.

> **NOTE** Expressions that evaluate to true are treated as –1, and expressions that evaluated to false are treated as 0.
>
> ```
> true + false ' adds -1 to 0, resulting in -1
> ```

About the Integer Division Operator

The \ operator is an Arithmetic Operator, used to divide the number to its left by the number to its right and return an integer value. This operator behaves in all respects like the floating point division operator, except that it returns only integer values, rounding the result down 1 if the remainder is 5 or less, and up one if the remainder is greater than 5.

> **WARNING** When using either division operator, if both expressions evaluate to empty, you may receive a runtime error.

Does Not Equal Operator

Term: [expression] <> [expression]

Example Syntax: if (thisValue <> thatValue) then

```
' executes the script if the contents of "thisValue" are different from the con
' tents of "thatValue"
```

The <> operator is a Comparison Operator, used to determine if its enclosing expressions represent different values. For instance, if one of its expressions is empty, and the other one contains the text string "Hello," then the <> operation is true.

```
if (document.forms(0).field1.value <> empty) then
' returns true, and executes its script if the referenced field contains some
' text
```

Empty Keyword

Term: [*operationResult*] = empty
Example Syntax:

```
thisVar = empty
' puts the empty keyword into a variable named "thisVar"
```

The *empty keyword* may be passed to a variable or object container (such as a field) to empty its contents. If can also be used to describe an empty container.

```
if (document.forms(0).field1.value = empty) then
' returns true if the referenced field contains no text
```

You can also use the literal string "" as an alternative to the empty keyword.

> **WARNING** If you wish to use a keyword for its intended purpose, don't surround it in quotes or the browser will interpret it as a string literal comprised of the letters e-m-p-t-y. One the other hand, if you want to use one of the system's reserved keywords in a script, you must enclose it in quotes to keep the interpreter from handling it as the system's keyword. However, it's generally a bad idea to use strings that are identical to the system's reserved keywords. It's not only confusing, but bugs could result.

Equals Operator

Term: [*expression*] = [*expression*] -OR- [*variable*] = [*expression*]
Example Syntax:

```
if (thisValue = thatValue) then
' executes the script if the contents of "thisValue" are the same as the con
' tents of "thatValue"
```

The = operator is a Comparison Operator, used to determine if its enclosing expressions represent the exact same value, regardless of data subtype. For instance, if the two expressions result in the same text string, the = operation is true.

```
if (document.forms(0).field1.value = empty) then
' returns true, and executes its script if the referenced field contains no text
```

The = operator also doubles as an Assignment Operator, and is used to place values into variables:

```
theField = document.forms(0).field1.value
' places the contents of the referenced field into a variable named "theFeld"
```

Equivalence Operator

Term: [*condition*] eqv [*condition*]

Example Syntax:

```
isSame = (2+2=7) and (1+2=12)
' puts true into a variable named "isSame"
```

The *eqv* operator is a Logical Equivalence Operator, used to determine if the conditions that enclose it are either *both true* or *both false*. If the true/false results of the conditions do not match (one is true, and one is false), the operation results in false.

1st Condition Is	2nd Condition Is	eqv Returns
true	true	true
false	false	true
false	true	false
true	false	false

> **TIP** Like its and operator counterpart, it is also possible for the eqv operation to return a null value, if either or both of its enclosing conditions are null. So make sure any conditional scripts that use this operator provide true, false, *and null* alternatives.

The eqv operator, like and, can also be used compare bits that occur in the same position in the results of two numeric expressions, allowing you to set the corresponding bits according to a truth table that is slightly different from the truth table for the and operator. (Remember, the and operator is looking for a *true-only* condition, whereas the eqv operator is looking for a *same* condition.)

1st Bit Is: AND	2nd Bit Is	Result Is
0	0	1
1	1	1
0	1	0
1	0	0

Exponent Operator

Term: [*number*] ^ [*number*]

Example Syntax: theTotal = 2^2 ' puts 4 into a variable named "theTotal"

The ^ operator is an Arithmetic Operator, used to raise the number to its left to the power represented by the number to its right.

If multiple exponentiation operations are performed in a single parenthetical expression, the ^ operator is evaluated from left to right, as the browser encounters it.

```
3^2^2 ' evaluated as 3^2, then 9^2, resulting in 81
```

If the exponent value is empty, or if both enclosing values are empty, a 1 is returned. If the value representing the number to be raised is empty, a 0 is returned. If either value is null, the operation returns null.

Microsoft says that the exponentiation operation can be executed upon negative numbers as long as the value for the exponent is an integer. For all practical purposes, this obviously holds true for positive numbers as well, since, in any circumstance where one of the ^ operator's enclosing expressions is not a valid number, a true exponentiation cannot result.

False Keyword

Term: if (condition = false) then

Example Syntax:
```
boolVal = 1+1=3
' puts the false keyword into a variable named "boolVal"
```

The *false* keyword is returned whenever a Boolean expression evaluates to false. You can assign the false keyword to a variable by directly placing it into that variable, or by assigning an expression that evaluates to false to that variable:

```
isOK = false
' initializes the variable with a false value
```

```
if (10*10=200) then
' returns false, and executes the script
```

You can also use the number 0 as an alternative to the false keyword, which is the actual result of a false evaluation. The interpreter recognizes both as a false condition.

Greater Than Operator

Term: [*number*] > [*number*]

Example Syntax:
```
if (thisValue > thatValue) then
' executes the script if the contents of "thisValue" evaluate to a higher number
' than the contents of "thatValue"
```

The > operator is an Comparison Operator, used to determine if the number on its left is higher in value than the number on its right.

```
if (12 > 10) then
' returns true and executes the script

if (12 > 13) then
' returns false and does not execute the script
```

> **TIP** You can use the equals and greater than operators together if you want to test and see if the number to the left of the operators is greater than or equal to the number to the left:
>
> ```
> if (12 => theNumber) then
> ' returns true if "theNumber" is 12 or less, and false if it's higher than
> 12
> ```

Implication Operator

Term: [condition] imp [condition]
Example Syntax:
```
isSame = (2+2=7) and (1+2=12)
' puts true into a variable named "isSame"
```

The *imp* operator is a Logical Implication Operator. This operator returns true, false, or null according to the circumstances shown in the following table:

1st Condition Is	2nd Condition Is	Imp Returns
true	true	true
false	true	true
false	false	true
false	null	true
null	true	true
true	false	false
true	null	null
null	false	null
null	null	null

As with the and eqv operators, the imp operator can be used to compare bits that occur in the same position in the results of two numeric expressions, allowing you to set the corresponding bits according to this truth table:

1st Bit Is: AND	2nd Bit Is	Result Is
0	0	1
0	1	1
1	1	1
1	0	0

Is Operator

Term: [object] is [object]
Example Syntax:

```
isSameObj = this and that
' puts true into a variable named "isSameObj" if this and that are variable
' references to the same object
```

The *is* operator is a Comparison Operator, used to determine if its enclosing expressions refer to the same object. Its enclosing expressions usually compare a variable that has been set to the target object using the *set* statement, to either the object itself or to another variable reference to that object.

```
SET windowDoc = location
windowDoc is location
' returns true because the variable named "windowDoc" is now identical to the
' window's location object in the eyes of the browser
```

> **N O T E** You cannot simply assign an object to a variable container in the same way that you assign values. When objects are involved, you must use the set statement, or the is operation returns an error:
>
> ```
> windowDoc = location
> windowDoc is location
> ' results in a runtime error
> ```

Less Than Operator

Term: [number] < [number]
Example Syntax:

```
if (thisValue < thatValue) then
' executes the script if the contents of "thisValue" evaluate to a lower number
' than the contents of "thatValue"
```

The < operator is a Comparison Operator, used to determine if the number on its left is lower in value than the number on its right.

```
if (12 < 13) then
' returns true and executes the script

if (12 < 10) then
' returns false and does not execute the script
```

> **TIP** You can use the equals and greater than operators together if you want to test and see if the number to the left of the operators is greater than or equal to the number to the left:
>
> ```
> if (12 =< theNumber) then
> ' returns true if "theNumber" is 12 or higher, and false if it's less than
> 12
> ```

Modulus Operator

Term: [*number*] mod [*number*]

Example Syntax:

```
theRemainder = 13 mod 5
' puts 3 into a variable named "theRemainder"
```

The *mod* operator is an Arithmetic Operator, used to divide its enclosing numbers and return only the remainder (if any). The remainder value is returned as an integer, with floating point number rounded down if 5 or less, and up if greater than 5.

> **TIP** The mod operator is a popular programmer's tool used in many languages to determine whether an unknown number is odd or even—which is sometimes useful knowledge in games and other applications. You simply divide the unknown number (passed to your operator in a variable, probably) by 2. If the result is 0, the unknown number is odd; if the result is anything else, it is even. Be sure to verify that the variable contains an integer, and is not null or empty, before you perform the mod operation, or your results will be unreliable.

Multiplication Operator

Term: [*number*] * [*number*]

Example Syntax: theTotal = 10*10 ' puts 100 into a variable named "theTotal"

The * operator is an Arithmetic Operator, used to multiply two numeric values.

If one of the * operator's enclosing expressions evaluates to a valid number, and the other to empty, the operation treats the empty expression as a 0, and returns the valid number by itself. If both expressions evaluate to empty, the operation returns 0. If one or both expressions evaluate to null, the operation returns null.

> **N O T E** Expressions that evaluate to true are treated as –1, and expressions that evaluated to false are treated as 0.
>
> ```
> true * 2 ' multiplies -1 by 2, resulting in -2
> ```

Negation Operator

Term: [*number*] - [*number*] -OR- - [*number*]

Example Syntax: theTotal = 10-1 ' puts 9 into a variable named "theTotal"

The - operator is an Arithmetic Operator, used to subtract the number to its right from the number to its left. It is also used without a *minuend* (left-hand number) to simply negate the number (or expression) to its right.

When used in subtraction operations, if one of the - operator's enclosing expressions evaluates to empty, the operation treats the empty expression as a 0, and returns the result accordingly. If both expressions evaluate to empty, the operation returns 0. If one or both expressions evaluate to null, the operation returns null.

> **N O T E** Expressions that evaluate to true are treated as –1, and expressions that evaluated to false are treated as 0.
>
> ```
> true - 2 ' subtracts 2 from -1, resulting in -3
> ```

Not Operator

Term: not [*expression*]

Example Syntax:

```
not(1+2=3)
' changes the "true" value of the expression to "false"
```

The *not* operator is a Logical Negation Operator that evaluates the expression passed to it, then returns the opposite Boolean value. Its passed expression must evaluate to a true or false, or an error results.

The not operator can also be used to invert the bits values of any variable, allowing you to set the corresponding bit according to this truth table:

Bit Is	Not Value Is
0	1
1	0

Nothing Keyword

Term: set [*objectVariable*] = nothing

Example Syntax:

```
SET thisObj = nothing
' removes a previously placed object from an object variable
```

The *nothing* keyword is used to remove an object from a variable to which it was previously assigned using the set statement:

```
SET isObj = document.forms(0).elements(0)
' makes the "isObj" variable exactly equivalent to the referenced form element

SET isObj = nothing
' removes the form element from "isObj"
```

> **WARNING** If you set several object variables to the same object, setting them back to nothing when you're done is advisable. Object variables take up memory and use system resources. If you keep too many "alive" during a session, it could create problems on the user's system. If you don't do your own housekeeping here, the system will set them back for you when the variables are no longer in scope (their associated script has finished executing).

Null Keyword

Term: [*operationResult*] = null

Example Syntax:

```
if (thisNum * thatNum = null) then
' returns true, and executes the script
```

The *null* keyword is returned when the results of any operation, or the contents of any variable, are invalid.

> **TIP** Whether by accident or design, this keyword is not always returned when it's expected. If you have a script that's looking for a null result, and it just isn't happening for you, you may be getting empty back instead. Try switching your script to that keyword and see if it helps. Other options to try are 0 or –1.

Or Operators

Term: [*condition*] or [*condition*] -OR- [*condition*] xor [*condition*]
Example Syntax:

```
isTrue = (2+2=4) or (1+2=8) ' puts true into a variable named "isTrue"
```

VBScript provides two *or* operators–one is *inclusive* and the other is *exclusive*.

About the Inclusion Or Operator

The *or* is a Logical Disjunction Operator, used to determine if *either one* of the conditions that enclose it is true. This operation is inclusive because it allows for any instance of a true result—and only results in false if *both* conditions are false.

1st Condition Is	2nd Condition Is	or Returns
true	true	true
false	true	true
true	false	true
false	false	false

The or operator is also a bit-wise comparison operator, meaning that you can use it to compare bits that occur in the same position in the results of two numeric expressions, allowing you to set the corresponding bits according to this truth table:

1st Bit Is: And	2nd Bit Is:	Result Is:
1	1	1
0	1	1
1	0	1
0	0	0

About the Exclusion Or Operator

The *xor* is also a Logical Disjunction Operator. However, it is used to determine if *one but not both* of the conditions that enclose it is true. This operation is exclusive because it only allows one of its conditions to be true. If both are true, it returns false.

1st Condition Is	2nd Condition Is	xor Returns
false	true	true
true	false	true

1st Condition Is	2nd Condition Is	xor Returns
true	true	false
false	false	false

The xor operator performs its bit-wise comparisons according to this truth table:

1st Bit Is: And	2nd Bit Is:	Result Is:
0	1	1
1	0	1
1	1	0
0	0	0

> **TIP** It is also possible for the or operators to return a null value, if either or both of its enclosing conditions are null. Make sure conditional scripts provide true, false, *and null* alternatives.

Preserve Keyword

Term: `REDIM Preserve myArray(number)`

Example Syntax:

```
REDIM myArray(25)
...
REDIM Preserve myArray(50)
' resizes "myArray" to 50, while preserving the contents of its original 25
' elements
```

The *preserve* keyword is used to resize a dynamic array without losing the contents of its previously populated elements. In the Example Syntax, for instance, a dynamic array was originally redimensioned (using redim) to contain 25 elements. Later in the script, it is resized to 50 elements—but data previously stored in any of the first 25 elements remains intact, thanks to the use of the preserve keyword.

> **WARNING** When downsizing a dynamic array, be aware that the preserve keyword only protects the contents of the remaining elements, not the elements that are no longer in the array's range. For instance, if myArray is resized from 25 elements to 20 elements, any data previously stored in the last five elements (which, for a zero-based array, is actually elements 20, 21, 22, 23, and 24) is irretrievably lost.

True Keyword

Term: `if (condition = true) then`

Example Syntax:

```
boolVal = 1+1=2
' puts the true keyword into a variable named "boolVal"
```

The *true* keyword is returned whenever a Boolean expression evaluates to true. You can assign the true keyword to a variable by directly placing it into that variable, or by assigning an expression that evaluates to true to that variable:

```
isOK = true
' initializes the variable with a true value
if (10*10=100) then
' returns true, and executes the script
```

You can also use the number –1 as an alternative to the true keyword, which is the actual result of a true evaluation. The interpreter recognizes both as a true condition.

Operator Precedence

When expressions contain multiple operators, Arithmetic operations are always executed first, regardless of where they occur in the expression statement. Concatenation operations (&) are executed next, followed by Comparison operations—with Logical operations bringing up the rear.

Tables 9.1 through 9.3 show the order of precedence used to evaluate complex expressions within operator class. The Concatenation type does not have a table because its only operator is &, which is first, last, and always in its class. (Just remember that concatenation follows arithmetic operations, and takes precedence over comparison and logical operations.) The operation listed at the top of each table is performed first, the operation below it is performed next, and the operation listed at the bottom of each table comes last in the order of precedence for its operation type.

Table 9.1 Order of Precedence for Arithmetic Operators

Operator	Operation
^	Exponentiation
-	Unary Negation
*	Multiplication

Continued

Table 9.1 *Continued*

Operator	Operation
/	Floating Point Division
\	Integer Division
Mod	Modulus
+	Addition
-	Subtraction

N O T E Multiplication and Division operations actually occupy the same precedence level within Arithmetic operations, as do Addition and Subtraction. Whenever these operation pairs occur in the same expression, each separate operation is performed in order of its appearance in the expression statement, from left to right.

Table 9.2 Order of Precedence for Comparison Operators

Operator	Operation
=	Equal to
<>	Not Equal to
<	Less Than
>	Greater Than
<=	Less Than or Equal to
>=	Greather Than or Equal to
is	Object Equivalence

Table 9.3 Order of Precedence for Logical Operators

Operator	Operation
not	Logical Negation
and	Logical Conjunction
or	Logical Disjunction
xor	Logical Exclusion
eqv	Logical Equivalence
imp	Logical Implication

What's Next?

You've reached the end of the glossary portion of this book. If you were patient enough to wade through the bulk of its reference material, you'll be amply rewarded by the ease with which you'll slip into the tutorials presented in Part III. If you are already well-versed in VBScript, you may consider the lessons in Part III too elementary, and opt to move on to the advanced scripting in Part IV. However, although the lessons in this part of the book are, indeed, aimed at the intermediate scripter, even an advanced user may benefit from a quick perusal of the chapter tutorials. You'll find scripting tips and advanced technical advice woven throughout each seemingly simple example.

The first chapter in Part III, for instance, provides a tutorial for creating the "Easy Reader" page for youngsters. At first glance, this page may appear to be the soul of simplicity, but it nevertheless provides a thorough, real-world review of how and when to use inline scripting techniques, and get big returns on relatively small code investments.

Part Three
VBScript in the
Real World

Part III of the *VBScript Sourcebook* consists entirely of Web page production tutorials. This means that all of the example scripts in Chapters 11 through 13 culminate in a document combining all of each chapter's scripts into a *real-world* Web page example. In addition to reading the chapter text on how these Web pages were composed—and how and why the various scripts work—the actual pages can be loaded from the companion Web site (www.wiley.com/compbooks/mara) into your browser, then viewed, revised, and reviewed, either as you read each chapter, or at your leisure.

The ultimate goal of Part III of the book is to provide you with real-world examples of how and why you might employ some of the scripting concepts and techniques that were presented in Part I, and further illuminated through Part II's reference material. Chapter 14 (the final chapter in this part of the book) veers from the working Web page format in order to teach you tricks that veteran programmers use to debug code, as well as some specific techniques and tools to use in debugging VBScripts.

Scripting the
Behavior of
Built-In Objects

This chapter presents the "Easy Reader" Web page, which consists of several VBScript modules pieced together to create a Web-based "educational playscape" whose mission is to advance the reading skills of 6-to-9 year-olds who are already basic readers. The tutorial focus of the chapter, and its Web page example, is on creating simple scripts that take maximum advantage of VBScript's built-in objects, properties, methods, and arrays. There are no user-created subs or functions used in this page; only simply scripted control structures, and standalone lines of code. As an added bonus, working with the Easy Reader Web page also provides real-world experience in scripting inline code (introduced in Chapter 3), to be executed at strategic points within the page as soon as the page is loaded into the browser.

Overview of the Easy Reader Page

The purpose of the "Easy Reader" Web page is to provide several interactive GUI elements to engage the interest of early readers. In order to "play" with these interactive elements, the young browser must read his or her way through some fairly sophisticated (for this user) instructions. It's a simple page meant to make reading fun, but challenging. If you have a child, or work with children who'd enjoy a page like this, you can have a lot of fun—and learn a lot in the process—by expanding the existing elements, or adding your own interactive elements to this page, or to other connected pages. If you have the time and talent to graphically enhance the page as well, you could build this virtual "playscape" into an enchanting visual as well as educational experience for precocious young readers.

The focus here and now, however, is the supporting scripts that power the Easy Reader page. Before delving into the details of how these underlying scripts work, you'll need an overview of how the page itself works. One of the fastest ways of obtaining such an overview is to take a visual walk through the page by reviewing Figures 11.1 through 11.7 and their captions—or, better yet, by downloading the page from the companion Web site and playing with it in your Internet Explorer browser as you read through the chapter.

W W W The Easy Reader Page is in the Chapter 11 link on the companion Web site, www.wiley.com/compbooks/mara. To use this page on your local system, be sure to download the entire folder, then load easyReader.htm into the browser.

Figure 11.1 As soon as the Easy Reader page is loaded into the browser, a prompt dialog box asks for the user's name.

Figure 11.2 When the user finishes with the first prompt, a second prompt asks for the user's age.

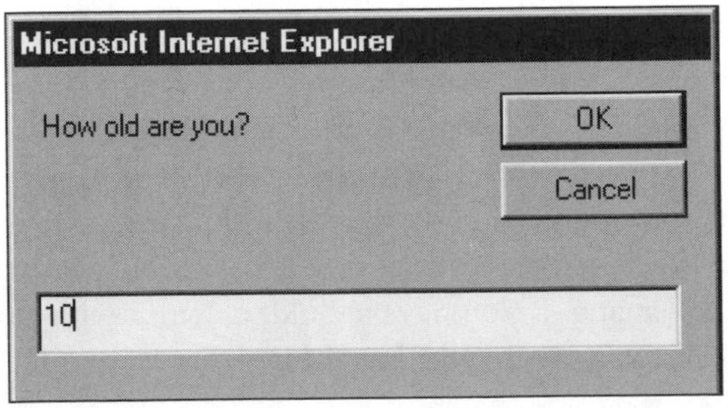

Figure 11.3 If the user is younger than 6, or older than 9, an alert appears.

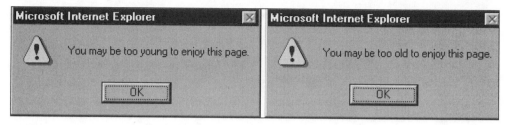

Figure 11.4 Using the information gathered through the first two prompts, the user's name and age are woven into the instructions that appear throughout the page.

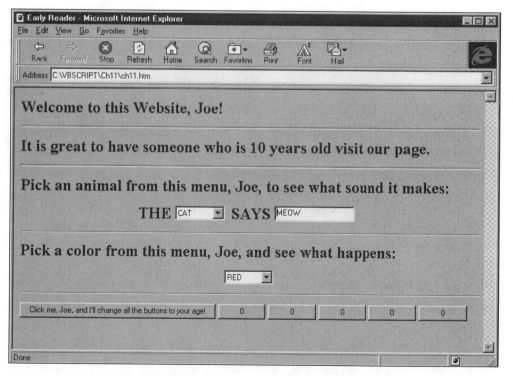

Figure 11.5 When the user picks an animal from the Animals menu, the sound that the animal makes is placed into the adjoining field.

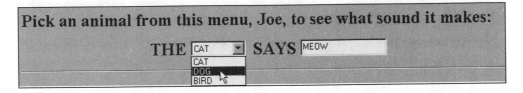

Figure 11.6 When the user picks a color from the Colors menu, either the background of the page—or the text on the page—becomes that color.

Pick a color from this menu, Joe, and see what happens:

WHITE

Figure 11.7 When the user clicks the Click Me button, the row of buttons on the right display the user's age, and the status field on the window presents a congratulatory message.

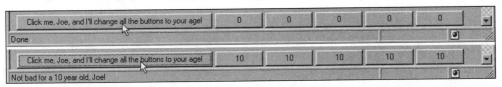

The Easy Reader Scripts

Now that you have an overview of how the Easy Reader page works, let's break it down into its individual scripting components, and examine each component in detail. The Easy Reader page is made up of five basic script segments, each of which accomplishes a set of related tasks:

- Segment 1 gathers information through the opening prompts.
- Segment 2 uses the gathered information to dynamically generate parts of the page.
- Segment 3 sets up and runs the Animal Sounds game.
- Segment 4 sets up and runs the Colors game.
- Segment 5 sets up and runs the Buttons game.

Segment 1: Opening Prompts

The first script segment appears between <SCRIPT> tags in the <HEAD> section of the document. Since none of the lines in this script are explicitly attached to any object/event, or housed inside any procedure (sub or function), the entire script simply executes as soon as the page is loaded. In other words, scripts like this, which are not specifically attached to any other event, are attached to the onLoad event by default.

```
<HEAD>

<TITLE>Easy Reader</TITLE>

<SCRIPT LANGUAGE="VBScript">

DIM g_theName,g_theAge
g_theName = prompt("What is your name?","")
g_theAge = prompt("How old are you?","")

if g_theAge < 6 then

    alert "You may be too young to enjoy this page."

elseif g_theAge > 9 then

    alert "You may be too old to enjoy this page."

end if

</SCRIPT>

</HEAD>
```

The first line of this script creates global variables to house the user's name and age information, and make that information available to all of the other scripts on the page.

```
DIM g_theName,g_theAge
```

The next two lines invoke the window object's *prompt* method (shown in Figures 11.1 and 11.2). The first prompt statement receives "What is your name?" as an answer to its first argument (which defines the message to use inside the prompt), and an empty string ("") as an answer to its second argument. The empty literal is used to clear out the editable field where the user is expected to type an answer. If no answer is passed to this second argument, <undefined> appears in this field.

```
g_theName = prompt("What is your name?","")
```

> **TIP** In a variation of this script, you could pass "Type your name here" as the answer to the prompt method's second argument. This would give the user a helpful instruction, and also requires additional reading.

The second prompt statement receives a string asking for the user's age, and the empty literal:

```
g_theAge = prompt("How old are you?","")
```

The two prompt method statements are followed by an *if-then-elseif* control structure, used to discover whether the child is too young or too old for the page. The *if* and *elseif* conditions use the *less than* (<) and *greater than* (>) operators—along with the two global variables (now populated by the user's response to the two prompts)—to discover whether the child is younger than 6 or older than 9.

```
if g_theAge < 6 then

    alert "You may be too young to enjoy this page."

elseif g_theAge > 9 then

    alert "You may be too old to enjoy this page."

end if
```

If either condition is met (the if condition that checks to see if the age is less than 6, or the elseif condition that checks to see if the age is greater than 9), then—before the page is loaded—an alert informs the child (or the attending adult) that he or she may be too young or too old for the page. If the user is within the 6–9 age range, however, neither condition executes, and the page is simply loaded.

As you can see, the if-elseif structure is useful for testing for and reacting to two or more conditions—while not reacting at all to a final, unspoken condition. If the unspoken condition is true, scripts written in this way result either in nothing happening or (if more scripting actions follow the if statement), the execution of the remainder of the script. In the case of the current example, remaining scripts execute.

Segment 2: Dynamic Page Generation

The second script is enclosed by <SCRIPT> tags placed in the <BODY> section of the document. You'll recall from Chapter 3 that scripts placed within the <BODY> of a document—but not attached to any scriptable tag (such as a button or a link)—are called *inline* scripts. Although you can place scripted procedures (subs or functions) within the <BODY> of a document, earlier chapters have already discussed why the <HEAD> section of the document may be the most effective location for user-created procedures that are called by other scripts within the page. However, if code is meant to actually execute at the point of its page location—like an inline image is meant to appear in the page at its tag location—inline scripting may not only be the *best* way, but the *only* way the script will work.

In the case of the current example, which uses *the document.writeLn* method to dynamically generate text that includes the user's name and age information, inline scripting is the only way to accomplish the task. When the document.writeLn method is applied to the current (and not a new) window, *its enclosing script must appear at the place in the HTML script where the text is to be generated*. This is a built-in behavior of both the document.writeLn and *document.write* methods.

```
<BODY>

<h2>Welcome to this Website,

<SCRIPT LANGUAGE-"VBScript">

document.writeLn(g_theName & "!<HR SIZE=3>")

document.writeLn("It is great to have someone who is " & g_theAge & " years old
visit our page.<HR SIZE=3>")

document.writeLn("Pick an animal from this menu, " & g_theName & ", to see what
sound it makes:")

</SCRIPT>
```

Accordingly, the second script module in the Easy Reader page, which makes use of the document.writeLn method to weave the name and age of the user into the text presented at the top of the page, is placed at the point in that page where the text is needs to appear. The result is the display of the following message:

> *Welcome to this Web site, [username]! It is great to have someone who is [user-age] years old visit our page. Pick an animal from this menu, [username], to see what sound it makes.*

Also included in the script that creates these lines are <HR> tags for creating size-3 horizontal lines on the page. The ability to accept strings that include HTML is a built-in behavior of the *write* and *writeLn* methods.

When the page first loads, the initial script in the <HEAD> of the document executes first—causing the appropriate prompts and alerts to appear as soon as the page is loaded—but *before* the <BODY> portion of the page is displayed. So the user sees—and fills in—these dialogs before the rest of the page is built. As part of its scripted tasks, segment 1 populates two global variables with the name and age that the user types into the opening prompts. After the first script is done executing, this global information remains available to the document.writeLn script, which uses the appropriate variable to include the user's name or age in its passed string.

The writeLn method is used because, unlike the document.write method, it automatically places a newline character at the end of the passed string (which the browser interprets as a <BR> tag). The strings passed to each of the writeLn statements in this script use the concatenation operator (&) to piece together string literals and the information housed in the global variables *g_theName* and *g_theAge*.

```
document.writeLn(g_theName & "!<HR SIZE=3>")
```

```
document.writeLn("It is great to have someone who is " & g_theAge & " years old
visit our page.<HR SIZE=3>")
```

```
document.writeLn("Pick an animal from this menu, " & g_theName & ", to see what
sound it makes:")
```

In the current example, the first line of HTML to be presented on the page is placed above the <SCRIPT> that weaves the remaining HTML—just to show you that you can do it this way. You could also have included the opening line in the string passed to the first document.writeLn statement:

```
document.writeLn("<h2>Welcome to this Website, " & g_theName & "!<HR SIZE=3>")
```

> **TIP** The & operator does not place any spaces between the items it concatenates. Remember this when you're building sentences using quoted strings along with data containers, and be sure to include the necessary spaces (and needed punctuation) before or after the concatenated items in your quoted strings.

write versus *writeLn*

You can also create multiple lines on a page with the *document.write* method by passing a concatenated string that includes the <BR> tag. In fact, in the current example, you wouldn't even need the <BR> tag to create the new line, since the appearance of the <HR> tag at the end of each section of text creates a new line by default when it draws the horizontal rule.

The following document.write statement, for instance, would generate a page exactly like the one generated by the example script's three document.writeLn statements:

```
document.write(g_theName & "!<HR SIZE=3>" & "It is great to have
someone who is " & g_theAge & " years old visit our page.<HR SIZE=3>"
& "Pick an animal from this menu, " & g_theName & ", to see what
sound it makes:")
```

The reason why the writeLn method is used instead of the write method in the current example is because it makes the code easier to read. Compare the script preceding this paragraph to the script following it, and decide for yourself which one is more immediately scrutable. Given the brevity of the generated text, it certainly takes no discernible additional time for the interpreter to execute and display the results of the longer script.

```
document.writeLn(g_theName & "!<HR SIZE=3>")
```

```
document.writeLn("It is great to have someone who is " & g_theAge & "
years old visit our page.<HR SIZE=3>")
```

```
document.writeLn("Pick an animal from this menu, " & g_theName & ",
to see what sound it makes:")
```

In addition to making the code much more readable, the writeLn method also comes in handy when you want to generate longer strings of HTML on-the-fly (either in the currently loading page, or in a page to be displayed in another window). This is because there is a limit to the size of the string that may be passed to the write method. Current documentation doesn't reveal what this limit is, but you'll know when you reach it, because either the passed HTML won't be displayed or you'll get a VBScript error. If so, you can switch to the writeLn method, and feed the string to the interpreter in smaller, more pallatable bytes (OK, bad pun).

For more information on the write, writeLn, and writeBlankLn methods, see the associated section in Chapter 6.

Segment 3: The Animal Sounds Game

The third segment is passed as the answer to an *onChange* argument inside the document's first set of <SELECT> tags. These <SELECT> tags, and their enclosed <OPTION> tags, generate the *animals* menu, followed by an <INPUT> tag that generates the *sound* field. The onChange script attached to the animals <SELECT> tag uses a *select case* statement to place the sound of the animal that is chosen from the menu into the sound field, as soon as the user makes that choice. When the page is loaded, the first item on the menu—CAT—is selected by default; so, the sound tag receives an initializing value of "MEOW" to match that menu choice.

```
<FORM>

<CENTER>

THE

<SELECT NAME="animals"
onChange="select case animals.selectedIndex

    case 0

        sound.value = 'MEOW'

    case 1

        sound.value = 'RUFF'

    case 2

        sound.value = 'TWEET'

end select">

<OPTION>CAT
<OPTION>DOG
<OPTION>BIRD

</SELECT>

 SAYS
```

```
<INPUT TYPE=text NAME='sound' VALUE='MEOW'>
```

```
</CENTER>
```

The condition passed to the select case statement is an expression that returns the options array position of the currently selected item in the animals menu. The selectedIndex property of the select object is used to determine this array position. Since the script appears inside the <FORM> tags that enclose the target select object, its simple name is used (without any reference to the parent document.form objects).

```
select case animals.selectedIndex
```

Having provided a means of identifying the current animal selection (by using its array position), the control structure's internal case statements provide instructions for the browser on the action to take for each of the possible selections. If the first item in the menu (and therefore, in the options array) is selected, then the selectedIndex property is going to return a 0. If the second item is selected, a 1 is returned. If the third item is selected, a 2 is returned. Thus, three cases must be provided for:

```
case 0, case 1, & case 2
```

In every case, the required action is the same: to place a quoted string into the sound field, via its value property. The only thing that changes from case to case is the string itself, which in every case represents the sound made by the selected animal:

```
case 0

    sound.value = 'MEOW'

case 1

    sound.value = 'RUFF'

case 2

    sound.value = 'TWEET'
```

While the first script segment is executed as soon as the page is loaded, and the second is executed as soon as the first segment's prompts and alerts are clicked away, this script segment is not executed until and unless the user selects an item from the animals menu. When this happens, the *change* event is fired, thus executing the onChange script inside the animals selection object.

> **NOTE** Even if the user clicks the animals menu and selects the first item (which is ostensibly already selected), the change event is still fired, and the onChange script executed. In the current example, this isn't visually apparent. However, if you added an extra statement to the case 0 response—invoking, say, the alert method to appear with some message—you could load the page, select the first item on this menu, and receive the alert.

> **WARNING** If a page contains only tag-attached scripts, but no <SCRIPT> tags to specify VBScript as the current LANGUAGE, the IE Interpreter defaults to JavaScript (JScript, actually). This is not a problem for VBScripts that conform to JavaScript syntax (such as one-liners that invoke a universal method—and include parentheses after the method name). However, if you placed the current *select case* script all by itself in a page, attached to the example *select* object by the *onChange* event handler, it would return an error because JavaScript doesn't provide for the select case control structure. Documentationon the Microsoft site indicates that you can avoid this error—and still use VBScript-specific code (like this select case script) all by itself into a document—if you add a LANGUAGE argument to the page's <BODY> tag, and answer it with VBScript. This fix actually doesn't work in current versions of Internet Explorer. However, you *can* include empty <SCRIPT> tags somewhere in the document to initialize the VBScript interpreter to recognize your tag-attached select case (or any other VBScript-specific) script:

```
<HEAD>
<SCRIPT LANGUAGE="VBScript">
</SCRIPT>
</HEAD>
```

Segment 4: The Color Game

The fourth segment is actually composed of two modules. The first module is a lone document.write statement enclosed between <SCRIPT> tags, and executed during page-load (along with Segment 2's document.writeLn script) as soon as the user disposes of the opening prompts and alerts.

```
<SCRIPT LANGUAGE="VBScript">

document.write("<HR>Pick a color from this menu, " & g_theName & ", and see what
happens:  ")

</SCRIPT>
</h2>
```

The result of this script is the display of a horizontal rule, followed by another line of text that uses the & operator to include the name of the current user (via the global variable g_theName, populated by the opening prompts script) in the displayed text:

"Pick a color from this menu, [username], and see what happens: "

This script has been placed so far down the page because, as previously noted, a document.write script that writes to the current page *must* appear at the actual point in the page where you want the resulting HTML string displayed. You may have noted that the script segment just shown ends with a header 2 closing tag. If you review the previous document.writeLn script (Segment 2), you'll see that this portion of the page *begins* with the header 2 opening tag. All of the HTML text that is written between these opening and closing tags is displayed using the current browser's header 2 font—whether that text is generated by standard HTML, or by VBScript.

The second script module in this segment is passed as the answer to an onChange argument inside the second set of <SELECT> tags, which generate the *colors* menu. Like the Animal Sounds script, the onChange script attached to the colors <SELECT> tag uses a *select case* statement. In this script, however, the selection of an item from the colors menu changes either the background color of the page, or the color of the page's foreground text.

```
<CENTER>
<SELECT NAME="colors"

onChange="select case colors.selectedIndex

    case 0

        document.bgColor = 'red'

    case 1

        document.fgColor = 'blue'
```

```
      case 2

          document.bgColor = 'green'

      case 3

          document.fgColor = 'yellow'

      case 4

          document.bgColor = 'white'

      case 5

          document.fgColor = 'black'

      case 6

          document.bgColor = 'gray'

end select">

<OPTION>RED
<OPTION>BLUE
<OPTION>GREEN
<OPTION>YELLOW
<OPTION>WHITE
<OPTION>BLACK
<OPTION>GRAY

</SELECT>
</CENTER>
<HR>
```

Like the Animal Sounds script, the condition passed to the select case statement in this script is also an expression that returns the options array position of the currently selected item in the colors menu, using the selectedIndex property of the select object:

```
select case colors.selectedIndex
```

The enclosed case statements in the script tell the browser which action to take in every possible case—of which there are 7, numbered from 0 to 6. In the even-numbered cases (including 0), the *bgColor* property of the document object is changed to the color currently selected in the colors menu. In the odd-numbered cases, the *fgColor* property of the document object (its displayed text) is changed to the currently selected color. Some interesting color combinations may result.

```
case 0

    document.bgColor = 'red'

case 1

    document.fgColor = 'blue'

case 2

    document.bgColor = 'green'

case 3

    document.fgColor = 'yellow'

case 4

    document.bgColor = 'white'

case 5

    document.fgColor = 'black'

case 6

    document.bgColor = 'gray'
```

> **TIP** As you can see in the Colors script example, simple colors may be designated by common names rather than hexidecimal equivalents. When working with colors, you might try this procedure first. If you don't like the shade or intensity of the resulting color (and many simple colors *are* dark or intense), then you can scout around for the hexidecimal equivalent of a more acceptable shade or level of brightness. See Appendix B for a hex list of some of the available colors.

Segment 5: The Button Game

The fifth and final segment of script in the Easy Reader page can also be broken into two modules. The first is an answer to an *onClick* argument inside the *counter* button's <INPUT> tag:

```
<INPUT TYPE="button" NAME="counter" VALUE=" Click me, please, and I'll change
all the buttons to your age! "
onClick="DIM i

for i = 4 to elements.length-1

    elements(i).value = g_theAge

next

status = 'Not bad for a ' & g_theAge & ' year old, ' & g_theName & '!'">

<INPUT TYPE="button" VALUE=0>
<INPUT TYPE="button" VALUE=0>
<INPUT TYPE="button" VALUE=0>
<INPUT TYPE="button" VALUE=0>
<INPUT TYPE="button" VALUE=0>

</FORM>
```

The onClick script creates a local variable called *i*, then sends this variable through a counting repeat loop that changes the displayed name of elements 4 through 8 in the current <FORM> object's elements array. These are the five buttons that initially display a 0 (shown in Figure 11.7). The number 4 is hard-coded (typed as is) into the for statement's conditional expression, because only buttons with an initializing VALUE of 0 are included in the current action, and the first 0-value button in the form is number 4 in the elements array. The ending number in the condition is calculated by subtracting 1 from the length of the elements array, to allow for the fact that the length is calculated from 1, while array items are numbered from 0.

```
for i = 4 to elements.length-1
```

Using the length property of the elements array to calculate the array position of the last item to be affected by the repeat loop is a "softer" coding approach than force-feeding it a set number. By contrast, this approach allows you to add to or subtract from the loop's target group of 0-value buttons without rewriting this script. However, this approach *doesn't* allow for the addition of other types of elements to the end (or to the beginning) of the form.

> **TIP** It is possible to further soft-code the counting loop's condition, so that you don't have to rewrite the script if you add elements to the beginning or end of the form. All you have to do is create a separate form object (by providing a separate set of enclosing <FORM> tags) to house the counter button and its associated 0-value buttons. With the new form object in place, you can rewrite the previously illustrated conditional expression using the opening number of 1 (since the counter button takes the 0 position in the array), along with the length-1 expression to calculate the ending number in the condition. With this new page format you can add or subtract 0-value buttons at will, as well as add or subtract other form elements above or below this script—as long as you don't place new form elements inside the repeat loop script's <FORM> tags.

Each time the counting repeat loop executes, it changes the value (or displayed name) of one of the 0-value buttons to the number contained in the global variable "g_theAge." The first time the repeat loop executes, i = 4. When it encounters the *next* statement, it automatically adds 1 to i, causing the next iteration of the property-setting statement to execute for elements(5), and so forth.

```
elements(i).value = g_theAge
```

> **NOTE** Remember, if you want the *next* statement to increment your counting variable by more than 1, you must use the *step* keyword. The following statement would change every other button's name to the user's age:
>
> ```
> for i = 1 to elements.length-1 step 2
> ```

When the repeat loop is done executing for every one of the target elements (4 to 8), the last line of the onClick script changes the contents of the window's status property to:

"Not bad for a [userage] year old, [username]!"

Since this statement is meant to execute upon the status property of the *current* window, it isn't necessary to reference the window object (window.status) in the script:

```
status = 'Not bad for a ' & g_theAge & ' year old, ' & g_theName & '!'
```

The second part of Segment 5 is another statement that executes during page-load, after the opening prompts, document.write, and document.writeLn scripts. It is a single line of code of that simply assigns a new value (display name) to the counter button itself.

```
<SCRIPT LANGUAGE="VBScript">

document.forms(0).counter.value = " Click me, " & g_theName & ", and I'll change
all the buttons to your age! "

</SCRIPT>
```

As simple as this script is, it nevertheless performs a little fancy footwork. First of all, any script that executes during page-load and references a page element *must* be placed below that element's HTML tag, because it relies on the existence of that element to execute without error. If, for instance, the current script appeared *before* the counter button's <INPUT> tag in the base HTML document, VBScript would return an error, claiming that the named object has no value property. What it really means is, the object doesn't exist.

In addition to properly placing the script, you also have to trick the Interpreter into creating a counter button that is wide enough to house the long, concatenated string that this script assigns to its value property. This is accomplished by using almost the same string as the answer to the tag's VALUE argument. The word "please" is used in place of the name (which, hopefully, won't be much longer than that word).

```
VALUE=" Click me, please, and I'll change all the buttons to your age! "
```

This initializing string appears so very briefly as the button's name, that it's too fast for the naked eye to see on all but perhaps the doggiest systems. It is nevertheless long enough to overwrite the browser's natural tendency to create a skinny little button showing only a small portion of the passed string. You may have noticed that both the initial VALUE string, and the new string assigned to the button's value property also include opening and closing spaces. If you don't include enclosing spaces in your button value strings, the frame of the button will appear flush against the opening and closing letters in your string; not an aesthetically pleasing arrangement.

Putting the Easy Reader Page Together

There's not much more involved in putting the Easy Reader page together than simply placing the five segments, one right after the other, into a single document. If you reviewed the segment discussions and explanations in the previous section, you should be able to actually "read" the full script, and get a good sense of how the pieces fit and work together as cooperating units in a single Web page.

The Full Script

```
<HTML>
<HEAD>

<TITLE>Easy Reader</TITLE>

<SCRIPT LANGUAGE="VBScript">

DIM g_theName,g_theAge
g_theName = prompt("What is your name?","")
g_theAge = prompt("How old are you?","")

if g_theAge < 5 then

    alert "You may be too young to enjoy this page."

elseif g_theAge > 8 then

    alert "You may be too old to enjoy this page."

end if

</SCRIPT>

</HEAD>

<BODY>

<h2>Welcome to this Website,

<SCRIPT LANGUAGE="VBScript">

document.writeLn(g_theName & "!<HR SIZE=3>")

document.writeLn("It is great to have someone who is " & g_theAge & " years old
visit our page.<HR SIZE=3>")
```

```
document.writeLn("Pick an animal from this menu, " & g_theName & ", to see what
sound it makes:")

</SCRIPT>

<FORM>

<CENTER>

THE

<SELECT NAME="animals"
onChange="select case animals.selectedIndex

case 0

    sound.value = 'MEOW'

case 1

    sound.value = 'RUFF'

case 2

    sound.value = 'TWEET'

end select">

<OPTION>CAT
<OPTION>DOG
<OPTION>BIRD

</SELECT>

 SAYS

<INPUT TYPE=text NAME='sound' VALUE='MEOW'>
</CENTER>

<SCRIPT LANGUAGE="VBScript">
```

```
document.write("<HR>Pick a color from this menu, " & g_theName & ", and see what
happens:  ")

</SCRIPT>

</h2>
<CENTER>
<SELECT NAME="colors"

onChange="select case colors.selectedIndex

case 0

    document.bgColor = 'red'

case 1

    document.fgColor = 'blue'

case 2

    document.bgColor = 'green'

case 3

    document.fgColor = 'yellow'

case 4

    document.bgColor = 'white'

case 5

    document.fgColor = 'black'

case 6

    document.bgColor = 'gray'

end select">

<OPTION>RED
```

```
<OPTION>BLUE
<OPTION>GREEN
<OPTION>YELLOW
<OPTION>WHITE
<OPTION>BLACK
<OPTION>GRAY

</SELECT>
</CENTER>
<HR>

<INPUT TYPE="button" NAME="counter" VALUE=" Click me, please, and I'll change
all the buttons to your age! "
onClick="DIM i

for i = 4 to elements.length-1

    elements(i).value = g_theAge

next

status = 'Not bad for a ' & g_theAge & ' year old, ' & g_theName & '!'">

<INPUT TYPE="button" VALUE=0>
<INPUT TYPE="button" VALUE=0>
<INPUT TYPE="button" VALUE=0>
<INPUT TYPE="button" VALUE=0>
<INPUT TYPE="button" VALUE=0>

<SCRIPT LANGUAGE="VBScript">

document.forms(0).counter.value = " Click me, " & g_theName & ", and I'll change
all the buttons to your age! "

</SCRIPT>

</FORM>
</BODY>
</HTML>
```

What's Next?

Now that you've glimpsed what may be done using only built-in VBScript objects, properties, methods, and arrays within simple control structures and inline code segments, Chapter 12 picks up the pace, moving into slightly more complex script construction techniques.

Chapter 12, *Writing Your Own Procedures*, explores the creation of your own subs and functions, and how these user-created procedures may be set up to interact with each other, and with other scripts in a page.

Writing Your Own
Procedures

This chapter's lesson focuses on performing field and form-level validations with VBScript. The example Membership Application page consists of several VBScript modules pieced together to create a self-validating form that checks for valid data in format-specific fields, and prevents form submission unless all required fields on the form are filled. Validation takes place on two levels: *field-level validation* and *form-level validation.*

Field-level validation occurs after data is typed into a field, and the user leaves that field, causing the change event to fire. Field-level validation scripts are attached to the following fields in the Membership Application:

- First, middle, and last name fields, which may only contain alphas, spaces, or hyphens.

- A Date of Birth field, which may only contain a proper date.

- An Internet Address field, which must contain a string that matches the pattern of an e-mail address.

- Telephone and FAX fields, which may only contain valid U.S. phone numbers (although you can modify the code to allow for phone numbers in other formats).

Form-level validation takes place at the time of the form's submission, and is initiated by the submit event, which kicks off a script attached to a button.

Not all of the requested data in the Membership Application form is required, so this validation process checks only to see that Mr. or Ms. is selected from the Title menu (shown in Figure 12.1), and that the First Name, Last Name, and Internet Address fields are populated.

Overview of the Membership Application Page

The Membership Application Web page presents a standard Web form to the user, who may then fill it out and submit it in order to join an imaginary club. There are several segments of VBScript included in this page to check the form's input and ensure that the data is reasonably valid, before allowing the actual submission of the form. Here's a pictorial overview of how the page works (see Figures 12.1 through 12.10). You may find it helpful to download the Membership Application page from the companion Web site, and review it in your Internet Explorer browser as you read through the chapter.

> **W W W**   The Membership Application Page is in the Chapter 12 link on the companion Web site, www.wiley.com/compbooks/mara. To use this page on your local system, be sure to download the entire folder, then load memApp.htm into the browser.

Figure 12.1 The Membership Application page contains one selectable menu, seven editable fields, and two buttons.

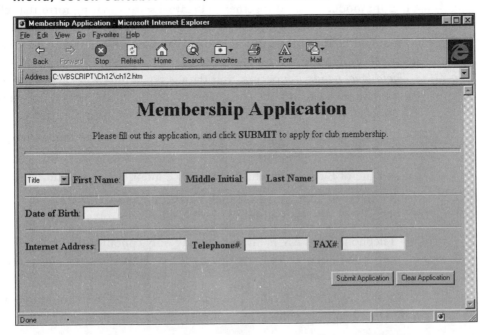

Validation Limits

There are limits to the amount of validation that you can reasonably perform on user input, even with the most sophisticated development environments. And VBScript doesn't rank among the most sophisticated tools for this task.

Furthermore, because this is an intermediate VBScript tutorial, the validation scripts used in this page don't always go as far as you *could* go in detecting errors in the user's input strings (and those gaps are discussed wherever they apply). In some instances, however, total validation of a string simply isn't possible. You cannot determine through VBScript, for instance, whether a user has typed the correct name into the First Name field without knowledge of the user's first name.

Given the limits of technology and personal cognition, when scripting a self-validating form, the emphasis isn't on harvesting completely pure data, but on helping the current user to avoid mistakes and typos. The truth is, if the user isn't serious about giving you the proper information in the first place, then you're just not going to get it. On the other hand, if the user's intentions are good, your validation processes can help that user fill out the fields correctly, and avoid the problems that might arise if the form is submitted with accidentally inaccurate data.

Figure 12.2 The Title menu contains three options: Title (the default selection), Mr., and Ms. The user must select either Mr. or Ms. before the submission of the application is allowed.

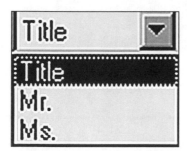

Figure 12.3 When the user inputs data, then tabs or clicks out of either of the three name fields shown in Figure 12.1 (First Name, Middle Initial, and Last Name), the string is validated. If anything other than alphabet characters, spaces, and hyphens appear in the string, this alert is presented.

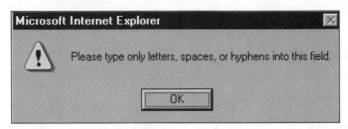

Figure 12.4 The Date of Birth field allows the user to type any string that can be evaluated to a proper date. If the user types the date in European format (shown left in this figure), and the system in use is formatted for U.S. dates, the date string is revised to fit the U.S. format (shown right) as soon as the user leaves the field.

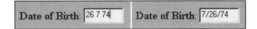

Figure 12.5 If the string typed into the Date of Birth field cannot be evaluated as a proper date, this alert is presented when the user leaves the field.

Figure 12.6 The Internet Address field only accepts a string if it contains the @ and . characters, and if the . character is followed by exactly three chars.

Figure 12.7 If the string in the Email field fails the validation test, this alert is presented.

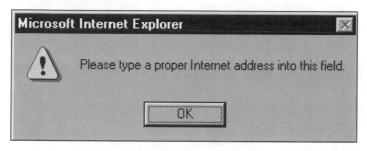

Figure 12.8 The same validation process is used to check the strings typed into the Telephone and FAX fields. If these strings don't meet the U.S. phone format test, this alert is presented. (The example script could be revised to include your country's format, if it varies.)

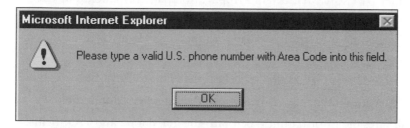

Figure 12.9 When the user clicks the Submit button, the entire application is checked to see if all the required data is present. If not, this alert presents the user with a list of the required data.

Figure 12.10 When the required data test is passed, the form is submitted via e-mail to the mailto: address provided in the answer to the <FORM> tag's ACTION argument. (See Segment 5 in the Individual Scripts section to find out how and why this works this way.)

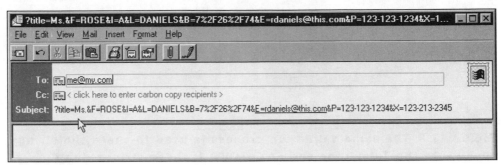

The Membership Application Scripts

Like the Easy Reader page, the Membership Application page is made up of five basic script segments, each of which accomplishes a set of related tasks:

- Segment 1 validates the information typed into the First Name, Middle Initial, and Last Name fields.

- Segment 2 validates the information typed into the Date of Birth field.

- Segment 3 validates the information typed into the Internet Address field.

- Segment 4 validates the information typed into the Telephone and FAX fields.

- Segment 5 checks to see that the application contains all of the required data before allowing the form to be submitted.

Segment 1: Validating the Name Fields

The first script segment checks the input in the First Name, Middle Initial, and Last Name fields to see that only letters, spaces, or hyphens appear in those fields (since some names include spaces or hyphens). This feat is accomplished for all three fields by the same pair of cooperating procedures. This pair consists of a sub called *doAlpha()* and its partner function called *isAlpha()*. Both procedural scripts reside between <SCRIPT> tags in the <HEAD> section of the document.

The doAlpha() sub is called from an onChange script attached to each of the three name fields. When the user tabs or clicks out of any of these fields after making a change to the field, the onChange script executes. Before this script calls doAlpha(), however, it changes the data in the field to uppercase.

TIP Upper and lowercase versions of the same letter are viewed as two different characters in the American Standard Code for Information Interchange (ASCII) character tables. Forcing the input string (the value of the calling field) into uppercase narrows the field of characters that must be tested for by the isAlpha() function, and thereby shortens the necessary script, as noted in the subsequent discussion of isAlpha().

```
<b>First Name</b>:
<INPUT TYPE=text NAME=F SIZE=15

onChange="F.value=uCase(F.value)
doAlpha(F.value)">

<b>Middle Initial</b>:
<INPUT TYPE=text NAME=I SIZE=1

onChange="I.value=uCase(I.value)
doAlpha(I.value)">

<b>Last Name</b>:
<INPUT TYPE=text NAME=L SIZE=15

onChange="L.value=uCase(L.value)
doAlpha(L.value)">
```

As soon as the input string is uppercased, doAlpha() is called by the onChange script. The input string is passed as an answer to doAlpha()'s single required argument, which is the value of the calling field. As you can see in the preceding snippet, the onChange script is virtually the same for each of the three fields. Only the name of the field changes in each instance.

The doAlpha() function is the first block of code placed in the <SCRIPT> tags in the <HEAD> of the Membership Application document. This function receives the input string from the calling field as the answer to its *fldVal* argument, then immediately declares two local variables: *theLen* and *i*. The first variable, theLen, receives the results of the *len()* function, which returns the number of characters in fldVal (which, again, contains the field's input string).

```
DIM theLen,i
theLen = len(fldVal)
```

Next, a *for* repeat loop uses the *i* variable to count its loops (from 1 to the length of the current fldVal string), while it sifts character by character through the string contained in fldVal. The mid() function is executed each time the loop is run, in order to methodically separate each character from the string, and pass that single char to the isAlpha() function.

```
isAlpha(mid(fldVal,i,1))
```

The fldVal (containing the user's original input string) is the answer to the mid() function's string argument, and i contains a number from 1 to the length of that string (depending on which iteration of the for loop is running). The number 1, passed to the mid() function's optional *numberReturned* argument, tells the function to return only the single char (whose string position is indicated by the i variable).

The first time the repeat loop runs, mid() returns the first char in the fldVal string; the second time the repeat loop runs, mid() returns the second char. As the for loop runs its course through the string, each char is passed to the isAlpha() function. If any character is found unacceptable, isAlpha() returns false, and the user receives the alert shown in Figure 12.3.

```
<HTML>
<HEAD>
<TITLE>Membership Application</TITLE>
<SCRIPT LANGUAGE="VBScript">

sub doAlpha(fldVal)

    DIM theLen,i

    theLen = len(fldVal)

    for i = 1 to theLen

        if isAlpha(mid(fldVal,i,1)) = false then

            alert "Please type only letters, spaces, or hyphens into this
field."
            exit for
        end if
    next
end sub
```

The isAlpha() function receives each individual character that is passed to it from doAlpha() as the answer to its *theChar* argument. After declaring *theCharNum* variable, this function employs the built-in VBScript *asc()* function to obtain the ASCII code for the character contained in theChar. If the asc() function returns a 32 (space) or a 45 (hyphen), isAlpha() returns true to doAlpha().

> **WARNING** If isAlpha() returns false at any time, in addition to presenting the alert, the for loop is also exited via the exit for statement. If you didnt exit this statement, it would continue to process the string as soon as the user clicks OK in the alert. If further errors are found in the string, the user will receive an alert for each error. Allowing this alert to needlessly repeat itself is known in development circles as "punishing the user." Professionals would never allow such a harsh treatment of users. It is for this very reason that language elements like exit for exist. The presence of this statement stops the processing of the string as soon as an error is found.

```
if theCharNum = 32 or theCharNum = 45 then
    isAlpha = true
```

If the asc() function does not return 32 or 45, then isAlpha checks to see if theCharNum is less than 65 or greater then 90. The capital letters of the alphabet are ASCII codes 65 through 90. If theCharNum falls outside of this range, the elseif statement is true and isAlpha returns false.

```
elseif theCharNum < 65 or theCharNum > 90 then
    isAlpha = false
```

> **NOTE** If earlier scripts hadn't forced the input string into uppercase, this function would also need to test theChar against the ASCII range of 97 to 122 for lowercase letters—adding yet another branch to the if-then-else conditional. (See Appendix C for an ASCII Chart.)

The final else condition only executes if theCharNum falls between 65–90, making it within the range of uppercase alphabet characters. When this condition is met, isAlpha() returns true to doAlpha().

```
function isAlpha(theChar)

    DIM theCharNum

    theCharNum = asc(theChar)

    if theCharNum = 32 or theCharNum = 45 then

        isAlpha = true

    elseif theCharNum < 65 or theCharNum > 90 then
```

```
        isAlpha = false

    else

        isAlpha = true

    end if

end function
```

Segment 2: Validating the Date Field

The next script segment is also placed between the <SCRIPT> tags in the <HEAD> of the Membership Application document, right below the isAlpha() function. It is a subroutine script, attached to the Date of Birth field (named B) and the onChange event, which executes whenever the user exits field B after changing its contents.

```
sub B_onChange()
```

The *B_onChange()* sub declares a local variable called *theDate*, and initializes it with the contents of the Date of Birth field.

```
DIM theDate
theDate = document.appForm.B.value
```

An if condition uses VBScript's built-in *isDate()* function to see if the string in theDate is a valid date string. If the isDate() function returns true, the built-in *cDate()* function is executed on the string to ensure that it's properly formatted as a date. If the format is already acceptable, nothing happens to the string in the field. If the format is *not* acceptable, however, (for instance, if the user typed 12 13 75), then the string is reformatted. In the example case, the string displays as 12/13/75 if the current system is set for U.S. date format, or 13/12/75 if the system is set for European date format (or other formats may apply if the user has customized the date settings).

If isDate() returns false, the "Please type a proper date..." alert is presented to the user.

```
sub B_onChange()

    DIM theDate

    theDate = document.appForm.B.value
```

```
    if isDate(theDate) then

        document.appForm.B.value = cDate(theDate)

    else

        alert "Please type a proper date into this field."

    end if

end sub
```

TIP   It's possible to make it really tough for the user to submit a "bad" date. Just add statements after the else branch's alert that empty the contents of the date field, and put the user back into the field after the alert is clicked away. To make the script even stricter, you could change the event to onBlur, so that the validation process is initiated whenever the user leaves the field, regardless of whether changes have been made. This script would repeatedly put the user back into the field whenever he or she tries to leave, as long as the input string isn't passing the isDate() test. The only way for the user to stop the process is to type a proper date string into the field or unload the page. You could conceivably script this procedure for every item on the form. Here's how to do it in the current script.

```
sub B_onBlur()

    DIM theDate

    theDate = document.appForm.B.value

    if isDate(theDate) then

        document.appForm.B.value = cDate(theDate)

    else

        alert "Please type a proper date into this field."
        document.appForm.B.value = ""
        document.appForm.B.focus

    end if
end sub
```

Segment 3: Validating the E-mail Address

The third field-level validation script looks for the proper e-mail address pattern in the passed string:

```
username@some.dom
```

Most U.S. Internet addresses begin with an uninterrupted (space-free) string, followed by the @ symbol, followed by the mail server name, followed by a dot, followed by the Internet domain. While there is no way to know ahead of time how long the user and server names will be, there *are* ways to check the string for the @ and dot symbols, and to count the number of chars that follow the dot to make sure there are exactly three, since, at the moment, all domain names have no more and no less than three chars.

The script that accomplishes these feats is called the *doMail()* sub. When the user types into the Internet Address field, and tabs or clicks from the field, the field's onChange script calls doMail(), and passes it the current contents of the field (the field's value).

```
<b>Internet Address</b>:

<INPUT TYPE=text NAME=E SIZE=25

onChange="doMail(E.value)">
```

The doMail() sub declares three local variables, and immediately populates the first two with the @ and dot (.) symbols, respectively. The third variable is left empty for the time being.

```
DIM at,dot,theDomain
at = "@"
dot = "."
```

Next, doMail() uses the built-in *inStr()* function to discover whether the @ symbol appears in the passed string; then uses it again to discover whether the dot symbol appears. If either test returns false, the "Please type a proper Internet address..." alert is presented to the user.

```
if inStr(theStr,at) = false or inStr(theStr,dot) = false then
```

```
    alert "Please type a proper Internet address into this field."
```

If both the @ and the dot symbols appear in the passed string (both inStr() tests return true), then the number of chars in the domain portion of the string can now

> **TIP** Writing effective logical expressions can be tricky at times. In the current situation, you might easily consider that the inStr() tests need to ensure that both the at *and* the dot symbol appear in the string, leading you to erroneously place the *and* operator between the tests. Although it's true that both symbols must be present for the string to represent a proper Internet address, it is also true that the string is invalid if *either* symbol is missing. Therefore, the *or* operator must be used between the two inStr() tests to correctly evaluate the test results. If you ever have trouble getting a script that uses logical operators to perform properly, step yourself v-e-r-y s-l-o-w-l-y through the code to see if your logical operation is taking a wrong turn.

be ascertained. We couldn't test for this until we knew that we had a dot symbol in the string. If this test preceded the test for the dot symbol, then the split() function used to break the string into two pieces would return an error.

Once the presence of a dot in the string is assured, however, theStr can be split into two strings: the first string consisting of all the chars to the left of the dot, and the second consisting of all the chars to the right. By virtue of the split operation, these two strings now populate an array variable called *strArray*. The second string (or second element of the strArray variable) is placed into *theDomain* variable as shown:

```
strArray = split(theStr,".")
theDomain = strArray(1)
```

A second if condition (nested within the first if statement) tests to see if the length of the string contained in theDomain is *not equal* to 3. If it is not, then it cannot be a proper domain name, and the correction alert appears.

```
if len(theDomain) <> 3 then

    alert "Please type a proper Internet address into this field."
```

If theStr passes all of the doMail() tests, the sub statement is exited and no action is taken.

```
sub doMail(theStr)

    DIM at,dot,theDomain

    at = "@"
    dot = "."
```

```
if inStr(theStr,at) = false or inStr(theStr,dot) = false then

    alert "Please type a proper Internet address into this field."

else

    strArray = split(theStr,".")
    theDomain = strArray(1)

    if len(theDomain) <> 3 then

        alert "Please type a proper Internet address into this field."

    else

        exit sub

    end if

end if

end sub
```

Segment 4: Validating the Phone Fields

Like the first segment of scripts in the Membership Application page, the segment that validates the data in the phone fields uses another cooperating pair of user-created procedures: the *doPhone()* sub and the *isPhone()* function. The overall validation process for phone fields is the same as the process used for the name fields.

When the user changes the contents of one of the phone fields, then exits the field, an onChange script is executed that passes the input string to the doPhone() sub. As with the name fields, the same basic onChange script is attached to both phone fields, changing only the field's name.

```
<b>Telephone#</b>:
<INPUT TYPE=text NAME=P SIZE=17

onChange="doPhone(P.value)">

<b>FAX#</b>:
<INPUT TYPE=text NAME=X SIZE=17

onChange="doPhone(X.value)">
```

Filling Gaps in the E-mail Validation Script

There are several gaps in this validation script that you could easily fill if you wanted to flex your VBScript muscles.

First of all, although this script checks for the @ and dot symbols, it doesn't check to see if they appear in the proper order. You could use a variation of the mid() function script in segment 1 to determine where each symbol falls in the string.

Next, there is no test to see if any chars appear before or after the @ symbol. The string @.xxx would test as a valid Internet address. You could modify and combine the mid() function and isAlpha() scripts to see if any chars appear before or after the @ symbol, and whether those chars are valid for the given portion of the address. (At least, you could verify this to some degree; no spaces allowed in either portion, for instance.)

Another thing you could do is check the actual chars contained in theDomain variable against a list of acceptable domain names.

Finally, you may have noted that the current example script is written to verify U.S. Internet addresses only. You could easily expand this script to check for the presence of the two-char country code that appears at the end of international addresses. All you have to do is modify the script to look for a possible second dot using the same split() script procedure. In this new case, however, the result of the split() would be either a two-string array (if there is only one dot in the string) or a three-string array (if there are two dots in the string). From there, you simply write an if condition that checks the number and char types of the third element in the array, if it exists. Any or all of these modifications are excellent exercises to set for yourself in order to expand your working knowledge of VBScript.

The doPhone() sub determines the length of the string, then passes each individual char in the string to a function that determines its datatype. Unlike the name field validation process, however, the length of the input phone string is informative in and of itself. This is because the phone fields are set up to accept only U.S. formatted phone numbers following one of these patterns: 111-111-1111 or (111) 111-1234. The first pattern results in a 12-char string and the second results in a 14-char string.

So, the first thing that doPhone() does (after declaring its necessary local variables) is populate the theLen variable with the length of the passed string, using the len() function. The theLen variable is then used as the single test criterion for a select case statement.

```
DIM theLen,i,theChar
theLen = len(theStr)

select case theLen
```

In the case that theLen is 12 or 14, the string is broken up by the mid() function into single-char pieces, and fed one at a time to the isPhone() function. In addition to sending theChar to isPhone(), the data contained in theLen and i variables are also sent (see isPhone() to find out why). If isPhone() returns false, the valid phone alert is presented to the user, and the for loop is exited. If the isPhone() function reviews the entire string without returning false, then nothing happens.

```
case 12,14

    for i = 1 to theLen

        theChar = mid(theStr,i,1)

        if isPhone(theChar,theLen,i) = false then

            alert "Please type a valid U.S. phone number with Area Code into
this field."

            exit for

        end if

    next
```

In the case where theLen is not 12 or 14, the string is automatically found to be invalid without even calling isPhone(), so the valid phone alert is presented in accordance with the case else condition appearing at the end of the doPhone() sub-routine, show here in its entirety:

```
sub doPhone(theStr)

    DIM theLen,i,theChar

    theLen = len(theStr)

    select case theLen

        case 12,14
```

```
      for i = 1 to theLen

            theChar = mid(theStr,i,1)

            if isPhone(theChar,theLen,i) = false then

                  alert "Please type a valid U.S. phone number with Area
Code into this field."

                  exit for

            end if

      next

   case else

         alert "Please type a valid U.S. phone number with Area Code into
this field."

   end select

end sub
```

Global versus Local Variables

You may have noticed that some of the segments use the same local variables. For instance, doAlpha() and doPhone() both use i and theLen. Why not declare these variables globally if both procedures use them?

It is really only necessary to globalize a variable if data in that variable is needed, as is, by multiple scripts in the page. In the previous Chapter 10's Easy Reader page, the user's name and age information is used by many scripts; so global variables are declared to keep track of this universally accessed data.

In the case of our current example, however, although these variables have the same name, the data that is placed in either is only valid for the local procedure. For instance, in each script, the length of the passed string is placed into theLen. But the length of the string contained in one of the name fields is never of any concern to the doPhone() sub, whose only interest is in the size of the string in its current phone field.

Why use the same names, then, if the variables are actually meant to house different data for different procedures? Once again, the answer is to make the code more readable. Rather than try to come up with several different names for a variable that houses the length of a string, it is completely acceptable to use the same variable name, locally, from script to script. If you adopt the global variable naming convention used in this book, you'll never confuse a similarly named local variable with a g_ prefixed global. And, you'll find it easier to remember what kind of data you're housing in clearly named local variables.

Conversely, if you declare a variable as a global when its actual data isn't needed globally, you may become confused about its use by a local script, or you may even receive script errors if the variable contains leftover data from a previous script. Moreover, whenever the DIM statement executes, a dimension is created in RAM to house that variable and its data.

Also, global variables—whose declarations occur, of necessity, as standalone lines of code that sit outside of any control structure—are dimensioned as soon as the page is loaded. Local variables are dimensioned only if and when their controlling scripts are executed. Thus, if you don't need the data globally, there's no need to allocate memory to the variable until and unless it's needed.

If the phone field's input string meets doPhone's "case 12,14" test, then it's dissected and passed char by char to the isPhone() function. In addition to passing each char, doPhone() also passes the information contained in theLen, which doesn't need to be declared as a variable for isPhone() because it's passed as an answer to an argument (which is a way of sharing data between procedures without declaring a global). The current position of the passed char in the string is also passed to isPhone(). This string position is the same as the current number in the i counter variable used by doPhone's for loop. To clarify, for future reference, what this number means to the isPhone() function, the position data is renamed thePos instead of i (the name of the doPhone() variable that passes it the information).

```
function isPhone(theChar,theLen,thePos)
```

Once again, theLen is used as the acid test for a select case statement containing several other select case statements. The deep-nesting of these statements gives this script a rather complex and foreboding look, but it's actually pretty simple, if you break it down into its component parts. This is true of almost every script, no matter how long and nested its control structures; and of every expression, no matter how many nested operations it contains.

Here is the top select case statement, without the confusing presence of its nested brethren:

```
select case theLen


    case 12


        [statements]


    case 14


        [statements]


    case else


        [statements]


end select
```

As you can see, the first select case statement has three branches. If theLen is 12, then the length of the current string is 12, and the first branch executes. If theLen is 14, the second branch executes. If theLen is neither, the case else branch executes. There are reasons for adding the case else branch, even though doPhone() is already set up to only pass 12- or 14-char strings to isPhone(). The first reason is simply as a fail-safe, just in case some wayward string escapes your first logic trap. Other reasons will become clear with further discussion of the branch scripts.

If theLen is 12, the case 12 branch executes. Here is the case 12 branch, all by itself:

```
case 12


    select case thePos


        case 4,8
```

```
        select case asc(theChar)

            case 32,45

                isPhone = true

            case else

                isPhone = false

            end select

        case else

            isPhone = isNumeric(theChar)

    end select
```

The first action taken by the case 12 branch is to set up another select case statement to test the contents of thePos. This second select case statement has two branches: case 4,8 and case else. If the position of the passed char is number 4 in the string, or number 8 in the string, the first branch executes. If it is neither, then the case else branch executes.

The first case is interested in the 4th and 8th position chars in a string that's already been found to contain 12 chars. These are the characters that fall in the position of the hyphens in the example 12-string: 111-111-1111. If the current char is in either position in the string, then that char is passed to the asc() function whose results are the test for a third select case statement.

```
case 4,8

    select case asc(theChar)

        case 32,45

            isPhone = true

        case else

            isPhone = false

    end select
```

The third select case statement also contains two possible cases. If the first case is met, the isPhone() function returns true to doPhone(). If not, false is returned. The first case is only met if the passed character is either a hyphen or a space. If it is, then it is the expected datatype for its char position. If not, then the entire string is assumed to be an improper phone format.

If thePos select case statement's case else condition is met, this means that the passed character's position in the string is neither 4 nor 8. Since all other chars in the string need to be a number to pass the isPhone() test, theChar is then fed to VBScript's built-in *isNumeric()* function, and the results are assigned to the isPhone() function. If theChar *is* a number, isPhone() is true; if not, isPhone() is false.

```
case else

    isPhone = isNumeric(theChar)
```

Remember the top select case statement that is testing for theLen? Well, the second branch of this statement is executed if the length of the string is 14. Like the case 12 branch, this branch also contains a select case statement that relies on thePos for its test. This time, thePos select case statement has three branches. The first branch executes if the char position is 1 or 5, which would make it the parentheses in a valid 14-char phone string: (111) 111-1111.

The asc() function is again used in a select case statement test, to determine the ASCII value of the current char. If theChar value is 40 or 41 (opening or closing parens), the char is the expected datatype for its position, and isPhone() returns true. If not, isPhone() returns false.

```
case 14

    select case thePos

        case 1,5

            select case asc(theChar)

                case 40,41

                    isPhone = true

                case else

                    isPhone = false

            end select
```

> **TIP** Here's another gap you can fill for yourself with ease if you take a few moments to consider the problem. The case 40,41 test is flawed because it validates the following string as a proper phone number:)111(111-1111. This is because the current script doesn't distinquish between the position of the char in the string, and the type of parenthesis used. Think about it, and if you can't come up with a simple answer, you'll find the answer in the "What's Next" section at the end of this chapter.

The second and third branches of case 14's thePos statement behave exactly the same as the second and third branches of case 12's thePos statement.

If the char position is 6 or 10 in the string (which is either the space or hyphen character in the example string: (111) 111-1111), a select case statement discovers the ASCII value of the char, and returns true if theChar is a space or hyphen, and false if it is anything else.

```
case 6,10

    select case asc(theChar)

        case 32,45

            isPhone = true

        case else

            isPhone = false

    end select
```

If the char occupies any position other than 6 or 10, it must be a number to be a valid phone string, so it is passed to the isNumeric() function for verification. The results of isNumeric() determine whether isPhone() returns true or false.

```
case else

    isPhone = isNumeric(theChar)

end select
```

Here is the entire isPhone() function, with all of its nested select case statements. Surprisingly one of the trickiest things about writing such convoluted logic is making sure that you have an end select statement for each instance of this control structure. You'd be surprised how much a simple omission can trip you up!

```
function isPhone(theChar,theLen,thePos)

    select case theLen

        case 12

            select case thePos

                case 4,8

                    select case asc(theChar)

                        case 32,45

                            isPhone = true

                        case else

                            isPhone = false

                    end select

                case else

                    isPhone = isNumeric(theChar)

            end select

        case 14

            select case thePos

                case 1,5

                    select case asc(theChar)

                        case 40,41

                            isPhone = true

                        case else

                            isPhone = false
```

```
                              end select

                  case 6,10

                      select case asc(theChar)

                          case 32,45

                              isPhone = true

                          case else

                              isPhone = false

                      end select

                  case else

                      isPhone = isNumeric(theChar)

              end select

          case else

              isPhone = false

      end select

end function
```

Segment 5: Checking Required Fields

The last script segment checks to see that all of the required information is (ostensibly) present before allowing submission of the form. As already noted, there's no way to completely ensure the validity of the individual pieces of data, but you can at least check to see that required selections have been made, and required fields have been filled.

The form validation process is implemented by another object/event subroutine. This sub is attached to a button named "submitter" and the onClick event. When the submitter button (which, as you can see, is *not* an official HTML Submit button) is clicked, the sub makes a quick check of all the required items

> **N O T E** Why wait until the form is submitted to alert the user that required information is missing? Because submit is the only form-based event that you have any control over. Although you can check to see if a field is empty when a user leaves it, you cannot force the user to enter the field in the first place. If the user never enters the field, the user will also never leave the field and fire the necessary script-executing event. While you can't force the user to submit a form either, once the user attempts submission you can take control of the process. If the user never submits the form, then the presence or absence of required data is moot anyway.

on the application to determine whether the form is ready for submission. If it is, the *form.submit()* method is executed from within the sub statement.

```
<INPUT TYPE=button NAME=submitter VALUE=" Submit Application ">
```

> **N O T E** This subroutine presents a sneaky way to interfere with the form submission process—and that's not always an easy task for VBScript. JavaScripters may simply call a function from an onClick handler inside a submit button tag, or an onSubmit handler inside the form tag. If the function returns true, the form is submitted; if it returns false, the form is not submitted (and, perhaps, an alert tells the user why). This is not true of VBScript. Even the false results of a called function won't stop the submission of the form once that process has begun. The Microsoft documentation suggests using this syntax: "document.formName.onSubmit = return myFunction" (discussed in the onSubmit section of Chapter 7). However, this procedure either doesn't work with the current version of the browser, or some important point has been left out of the documentation (which seems a frequent occurence). Although this scripting technique may work by the time you read this, this script provides an alternative (and currently working) method for interrupting form submission.

When the Submit Application button is clicked, the *submitter_onClick()* sub declares a variable and then uses the set statement to set that variable to the current form object. It would have been nice to use this object variable in place of the longer name of the form throughout the entire page of scripts, but the current version of the browser was unable to recognize this object as a global. By the time you read this, your version of the browser may have overcome this and other disabilities. Over time, all of the various parts of the VBScript Engine will begin to function better and better. That's the best we can expect from these rapidly realized, and swiftly evolving Web technologies.

```
DIM theForm
SET theForm = document.appForm
```

The submitter sub works hand in glove with a user-created function called *goodApp()*. Using a simple if-then-elseif conditional, the submitter sub simply executes the goodApp() function, and advises the user to provide the required data if goodApp() returns false, or executes the submit method on the object variable, theForm.

```
sub submitter_onClick()

    DIM theForm
    SET theForm = document.appForm

    if goodapp() = false then

        alert "You must select the appropriate Title from the menu, and  fill
in the First Name, Last Name, and Internet fields to submit an application to
this club. Thank you."

    elseif goodApp() = true then

        theForm.submit

    end if

end sub
```

The goodApp() function actually does most of the form-level validation work. To do so, it declares three variables, then sets up a nested if conditional to check for three basic situations. The top if conditional has two branches, if and else. It simply checks to see if the item currently selected in the Title menu is numbered 0 in the options array. If it is, that means that the word "Title" is displayed on the menu. Since the selection of Mr. or Ms. from this menu is required for the Membership Application to be submitted, this condition causes goodApp() to return false to the submitter sub.

```
DIM i,theField,isExempt

if document.appForm.title.options.selectedIndex = 0 then

    goodApp = false
```

> **N O T E** Since this if condition relies on the same test for each branch, couldn't it be written as a select case statement? Absolutely, but it's such a short script—and the if control structure is more English-like than the select case—that sometimes you'll be drawn to its more comprehensible (though more verbose) construction. If you prefer terse code over anything else, however, the select case statement is certainly the better choice for more complex logical progressions (like the one in the Phone Validation Segment). In the current situation, it doesn't save many chars:

```
select case goodapp()

    case false

        alert "You must select the appropriate Title from the menu,
and  fill in the First Name, Last Name, and Internet fields to submit
an application to this club. Thank you."

    case true

        theForm.submit

end select
```

If the array index position of the selected option on the title menu is *not* 0, then the else condition executes. This branch of the top if condition has counting repeat loop and another if condition nested within it:

```
for i = 1 to document.appForm.elements.length-4

    if document.appForm.elements(i).value = "" then
```

The loop counts from 1 to the number of elements in the form, minus 3. This range causes the loop to execute only for the name, date, and e-mail fields on the form. It doesn't execute for the Title menu (which has already been checked), or for the two phone fields (which are not required), or for the two buttons at the end of the form. It can't skip any of the other required fields, because those fields appear between other fields that *are* required.

The if statement checks the value of each field counted by the loop to see if its contents are empty. If not, the else condition is met, and goodApp() returns true. If the field is found empty, however, the if condition is met, and another logical test must be performed to see if the empty field is also a required field. For each empty field tested by the for loop, the name of that field is placed into the previously declared theField variable. This variable is then used as a test for a 2-branch select case statement.

```
for i = 1 to document.appForm.elements.length-5

    if document.appForm.elements(i).value = "" then

        theField = document.appForm.elements(i).name

        select case theField

            case "I","B"

                goodApp = true

            case else

                goodApp = false

                exit for

        end select
```

In the case where the field name is I or B, goodApp() receives true, because the Middle Initial and Date of Birth fields are optional—so it doesn't matter if either is empty. In every case where the if-field-is-empty conditional's else condition is met (i.e., the passed field is not empty), goodApp() receives true. In every other case, where the field is empty and is not named I or B, goodApp() receives false.

All it takes is one false test to stop the form submission and present the "required information" alert. When this happens the for loop is exited, and false is returned to the submitter button. If the entire goodApp() script runs without resulting in a single false test, true is returned to the submitter button, and the form is submitted.

```
function goodApp()

    DIM i,theField,isExempt

    if document.appForm.title.options.selectedIndex = 0 then

        goodApp = false

    else

        for i = 2 to document.appForm.elements.length-3
```

```
      if document.appForm.elements(i).value = "" then

          theField = document.appForm.elements(i).name

          select case theField

              case "I","B","P","X"

                  isExempt = true

              case else

                  goodApp = false
                  exit for

          end select

      else

          goodApp = true

      end if

    next

  end if

end function

</SCRIPT>
</HEAD>
```

Putting the Membership Application Page Together

There's one additional touch needed to complete the setup for this page. As any webmaster knows, the form object requires an answer to its action argument in order for the form to actually be submitted. This can be any forms-processing CGI script, using any viable language, including server-side VBScript or JavaScript. Another option is to submit the form to an e-mail address, and that's the option used in this example. Not because it's a *good* submission method, but just so you can see that the form submission process is, indeed, completed if the form-level validation script is satisfied.

This example page is keyed to the way Internet Explorer responds to the HTML mailto: action string. Unlike Netscape Navigator, Internet Explorer allows you to use any mail client in conjunction with the IE browser. Because of this, IE places all of the resulting form data attached to the mailto: string into the Subject field of the Internet Mail Client (and presumably of any other mail client).

Navigator, on the other hand, can be assured of access to all the fields in an e-mail message since it currently dictates the e-mail client. Because of this, Navigator dissects the string so that—if you passed the following mailto: string—only the word "Test" would appear in the Subject field. The rest of the string, which gets created from the data input into the submitted form, is parsed (divided up nicely) and presented in the message field. All of this takes place "under the covers" when the form is submitted, formatted, and automatically mailed to the given address.

```
<FORM NAME="appForm" ACTION="mailto:me@my.com?Subject=Test">
```

Since Internet Explorer doesn't behave this way yet (though, maybe future versions will assume that the e-mail client is written to ActiveX or other open standard specs, thereby exposing its internal objects to Internet Explorer), the names of all the form elements were shortened to single letters. This results in a form-data string that is short enough (in most cases) to be visible in the Subject field. The word "Test" was removed because it took up extra space.

Again, the purpose of using this action for the form is to provide you with a means of validating the proper behavior of the Membership Application Page. When the form is found to be valid, and is submitted, Internet Explorer doesn't actually attempt to send the resulting e-mail message (because, as previously noted, IE doesn't assume that the e-mail client is Microsoft's Internet Mail). IE merely opens the e-mail client and shows you the string in the Subject field (as shown in Figure 12.11). If your version of IE continues to limit the implementation of the HTML mailto: action, this method of submission is probably impractical for your own forms. Even webmasters who prefer to use Navigator may have to heed this IE limitation, or at least be aware that visitors using Internet Explorer will receive a limited response to mailto: scripts.

The Full Script

```
<HTML>
<HEAD>
<TITLE>Membership Application</TITLE>
<SCRIPT LANGUAGE="VBScript">

sub doAlpha(theStr)
```

Figure 12.11 When an application passes the form-level validation tests, the form is submitted via the mailto: action prescribed within the <FORM> tag. The input from the filled in form is placed into the Subject field in your Internet Mail Client, and displayed for your review.

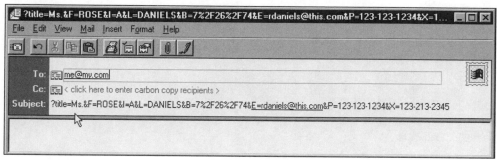

```
    DIM theLen,i

    theLen = len(theStr)

    for i = 1 to theLen

        if isAlpha(mid(theStr,i,1)) = false then

            alert "Please type only letters, spaces, or hyphens into this
field."

            exit for

        end if

    next

end sub

function isAlpha(theChar)

    DIM theCharNum

    theCharNum = asc(theChar)

    if theCharNum = 32 or theCharNum = 45 then
```

```
            isAlpha = true

    elseif theCharNum < 65 or theCharNum > 90 then

        isAlpha = false

    else

        isAlpha = true

    end if

end function

sub B_onChange()

    DIM theDate

    theDate = document.appForm.B.value

    if isDate(theDate) then

        document.appForm.B.value = cDate(theDate)

    else

        alert "Please type a proper date into this field."

    end if

end sub

sub doMail(theStr)

    DIM at,dot,theDomain

    at = "@"
    dot = "."

    if inStr(theStr,at) = false or inStr(theStr,dot) = false then

    alert "Please type a proper Internet address into this field."
```

```
        else

            strArray = split(theStr,".")
            theDomain = strArray(1)

            if len(theDomain) <> 3 then

                alert "Please type a proper Internet address into this field."

            else

                exit sub

            end if

        end if

    end if

end sub

sub doPhone(theStr)

    DIM theLen,i,theChar

    theLen = len(theStr)

    select case theLen

        case 12,14

            for i = 1 to theLen

                theChar = mid(theStr,i,1)

                if isPhone(theChar,theLen,i) = false then

                    alert "Please type a valid U.S. phone number with Area
Code into this field."

                    exit for

                end if
```

```
            next

        case else

            alert "Please type a valid U.S. phone number with Area Code into
this field."

        end select

end sub


function isPhone(theChar,theLen,thePos)

    select case theLen

        case 12

            select case thePos

                case 4,8

                    select case asc(theChar)

                        case 32,45

                            isPhone = true

                        case else

                            isPhone = false

                    end select

                case else

                    isPhone = isNumeric(theChar)

            end select

        case 14
```

```
select case thePos

    case 1,5

        select case asc(theChar)

            case 40,41

                isPhone = true

            case else

                isPhone = false

        end select

    case 6,10

        select case asc(theChar)

            case 32,45

                isPhone = true

            case else

                isPhone = false

        end select

    case else

        isPhone = isNumeric(theChar)

    end select

case else

    isPhone = false

end select
```

```
end function

sub submitter_onClick()

    DIM theForm
    SET theForm = document.appForm

    if goodapp() = false then

        alert "You must select the appropriate Title from the menu, and  fill
in the First Name, Last Name, and Internet fields to submit an application to
this club. Thank you."

    elseif goodApp() = true then

        theForm.submit

    end if

end sub

function goodApp()

    DIM i,theField,isExempt

    if document.appForm.title.options.selectedIndex = 0 then

        goodApp = false

    else

        for i = 1 to document.appForm.elements.length-5

        if document.appForm.elements(i).value = "" then

                theField = document.appForm.elements(i).name

                select case theField

                    case "I","B"
```

```
            isExempt = true

        case else

            goodApp = false
            exit for

      end select

    else

        goodApp = true

    end if

  next

  end if

end function

</SCRIPT>
</HEAD>
<BODY>

<CENTER>
<H1>Membership Application</H1>

<p>Please fill out this application, and click <b>SUBMIT</b> to apply for club
membership.

 </CENTER>
<HR SIZE=6>

<FORM NAME="appForm" ACTION="mailto:me@my.com?Subject=">

<SELECT NAME=title>
<OPTION>Title
<OPTION>Mr.
<OPTION>Ms.
</SELECT>
```

```
<b>First Name</b>:
<INPUT TYPE=text NAME=F SIZE=15

onChange="F.value=uCase(F.value)
doAlpha(F.value)">

<b>Middle Initial</b>:
<INPUT TYPE=text NAME=I SIZE=1

onChange="I.value=uCase(I.value)
doAlpha(I.value)">

<b>Last Name</b>:
<INPUT TYPE=text NAME=L SIZE=15

onChange="L.value=uCase(L.value)
doAlpha(L.value)">

<HR>

<b>Date of Birth</b>:
<INPUT TYPE=text NAME=B SIZE=8>

<HR>

<b>Internet Address</b>:
<INPUT TYPE=text NAME=E SIZE=25

onChange="doMail(E.value)">

<b>Telephone#</b>:
<INPUT TYPE=text NAME=P SIZE=17

onChange="doPhone(P.value)">

<b>FAX#</b>:
<INPUT TYPE=text NAME=X SIZE=17

onChange="doPhone(X.value)">
```

```
<HR>

<TABLE WIDTH=100%>
<TR ALIGN=right>

<INPUT TYPE=button NAME=submitter VALUE=" Submit Application ">

<INPUT TYPE=reset NAME=cancel VALUE=" Clear Application ">

</TR>
</TABLE>
</FORM>
</BODY>
</HTML>
```

What's Next?

A major goal of many Web sites is to gather, as well as provide, information. As a result, the need for data and form validation is high, and—if you check the proper sections in bookstores and script-related Web sites—you'll find an abundance of example VBScripts and JavaScripts that address various methods for performing these feats. Visit the appropriate newsgroups and you'll almost always discover a current thread involving some forms-validation conundrum. The basic methods presented in this chapter for validating string patterns, formatting input, and testing for required conditions should prepare you to enter into and profit from any discussion of this type.

The other purpose of this chapter was to further your education in the scripting of user-created subs and functions, and to show the interactive possibilities of these seemingly self-contained procedures. As the examples in this chapter attest, subs can be extra powerful when partnered with functions that test the sub's passed data and return results that the sub can use to choose among alternate decision paths.

Now that you have some practical knowledge of the inter-behavior of user-written subs and functions to add to your Chapter 11 experience with VBScript's built-in objects, methods, and properties, you're ready for Chapter 13's hands-on exercise in creating and manipulating the equivalent of your own objects and properties through static and dynamic arrays. Before you move on, however, the promised correction to the phone script follows.

Correction to the Phone Script

```
case 14

    select case thePos

        case 1

            select case asc(theChar)

            case 40

                    isPhone = true

                case else

                    isPhone = false

            end select

        case 5

            select case asc(theChar)

                case 41

                    isPhone = true

                case else

                    isPhone = false

            end select
```

The new script separates the case 1,5 branch into two branches. Case 1 tests only char pos 1 in the string to see if it's an open parenthesis, and case 5 tests char pos 5 to see if it's a close parenthesis.

Creating Your
Own Arrays

The lessons of this chapter revolve around the creation and manipulation of *static* and *dynamic* arrays. Unlike JavaScript, VBScript does not (at this time) allow you to create your own objects and object properties (although some ActiveX Controls do allow you to do so within the limits of that control). The reason why object-oriented and object-based languages let users create their own object collections and associated properties in the first place, is so that these uniquely defined collections may be used in a very array-like manner—as user-designed *data-handling structures*. A similar objective is easily achieved with a flexible array-creation system, and may be why Microsoft felt moved to redesignate VBScript's arrays as object collections in the VBS 3.0 documentation.

Here's an example of how you might create a collection of car objects and associated make, model, and year data using the two languages. In JavaScript you'd create 10 instances of a *car* object, then attribute 3 properties to that new object type: make, model, and year. Next, you would assign data to the 3 properties of all 10 instances of your new car object, as a means of programmatically identifying the make, model, and year of the car object in question.

You would accomplish the same feat in VBScript by constructing a two-dimensional array with 3 columns and 10 rows:

```
DIM theCars(2,9)                    ' declares a 3-column, 10-row array

theCars(0,0) = "Ford"
theCars(0,1) = "Fairlane"
theCars(0,2) = "1957"


' populates the make, model, and year columns for the car "object" in the first
row of theCars array

theCars(1,0) = "Chevy"
theCars(1,1) = "Impala"
theCars(1,2) = "1962"


' populates the make, model, and year columns for the car "object" in the sec-
ond row of theCars array
```

These are the basic procedures for creating your own arrays (or object collections) in VBScript. The "Shopping List" Web page example presented in this chapter is calculated to reveal more of the specifics of array creation, as well as some of the subtleties and strategies for making the most of user-created arrays, including the design and implementation of both static and dynamic (resizable) arrays.

Overview of the Shopping List Page

The Shopping List Web page supports two views of the page. The first view is presented when the page is loaded, and the second view is dynamically generated at the user's request, according to choices made by the user in the first page view. To support this design, the first page view presents a table of available products and their prices (shown in Figure 13.1), each prefaced by a checkbox so the user can choose items of interest. Once selections have been made, the user may click one of the two buttons shown in Figure 13.1 to find out more about the chosen items, or to see the items' total cost.

Clicking the Show Items button creates a new table consisting of GIF images of the chosen products. This table is created on-the-fly using a dynamic array to generate the table according to the number of items currently chosen by the user. Each GIF image contains both picture and text descriptions of one of its associated products. A hyperlink allows the user to return to the original view of the page (see Figure 3.2).

If the user clicks the Calculate Order button in the original page, the Shopping List dialog box appears with a list of all the items the user has thus far selected,

Figure 13.1 The top of the Shopping List page displays eight items that may be viewed, placed in the user's Shopping List, or ordered by clicking the associated checkbox.

along with an Order Total. If the user wants to go ahead and order those items, clicking Yes in the dialog scrolls the user to the first field in the Order Form located at the bottom of the first page view.

The following illustrated review of the Shopping List page provides a comprehensive overview of its behavior (see Figures 13.1 through 13.7). For an even better overview, link to the actual page on the companion Web site and try it out in your browser.

> **W W W** The Shopping List page is in the Chapter 13 link on the companion Web site, www.wiley.com/compbooks/mara. To use this page on your local system, be sure to download the entire folder, then load shopList.htm into the browser.

Figure 13.2 The user can view a picture and textual description of any item or group of items by clicking its checkbox, then clicking the Show Items button. A new page view is dynamically generated according to the user's choices. The hyperlink takes the user back to the original Shopping List page.

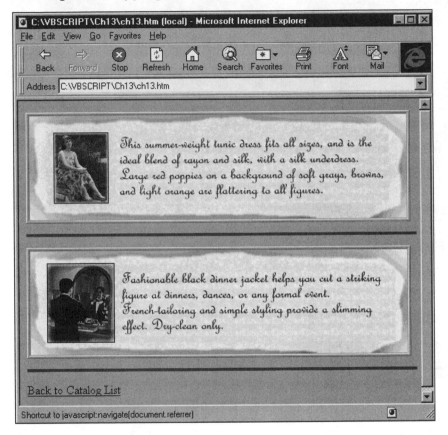

Figure 13.3 If the user clicks either the Show Items or the Calculate Order button without selecting any of the checkbox items, an alert directs the user to select something first.

Figure 13.4 The user can click the Calculate Order button for a Shopping List and Order Total containing any item or group of items whose checkboxes are selected.

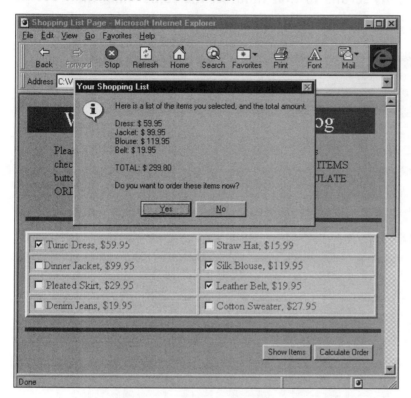

Figure 13.5 If the user clicks the No button in the Shopping List Message Box (shown in Figure 13.4), the selected checkboxes are deselected and the Message Box is closed. If the user click the Yes button in the Message Box, this alert advises the user to fill out the form at the bottom of the page.

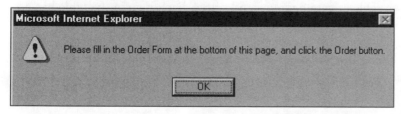

Figure 13.6 When the user clicks OK in the Figure 13.5 alert, focus is sent to the first field in the Order Form section of the page, and the page automatically scrolls to that field. At the same time, the Shopping List information is placed into a hidden field in the Order Application form.

The Shopping List Scripts

The Shopping List page consists of two separate form objects, one named *catalog* and the other named *orderApp*. The first form creates the catalog list portion of the page that displays a table of catalog items and prices. Each item in the table has a checkbox for the user to select, if desired, to view more information on the selected items, to view the items and the calculated total in the Shopping List message box, or to order those items. The Shopping List page accomplishes all of this with the following basic script segments:

- Segment 1 references the first form in the page (the catalog form) to create an array of all the possible items that could become part of the user's Shopping List.

- Segment 2 also references the first form in order to determine the user's chosen items, and to create the user's Shopping List and calculated Order Total.

- Segment 3 also determines the user's chosen items and then displays a tabled list of those items.

- Segment 4 submits the order at the user's request.

Figure 13.7 When the user clicks the Order button, the hidden Shopping List information is appended to the other form data that is sent in a string to the server (or wherever, depending on your form's designated ACTION).

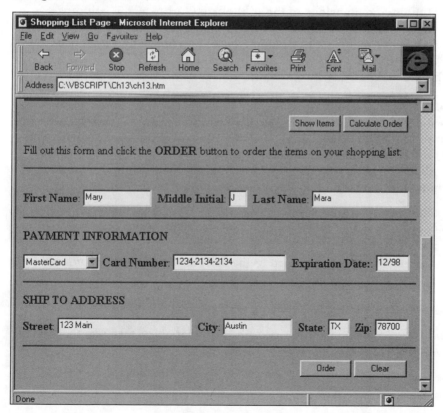

Segment 1: Setting Up the Shopping List Array

As soon as the Shopping List page is loaded into the browser, it declares a global two-dimensional array variable called *g_shopList*. The first dimension of this array variable is initialized for two elements (0 and 1), and its second dimension is initialized for eight elements (0, 1, 2, 3, 4, 5, 6, and 7).

> **N O T E** Like built-in arrays, all created arrays are zero-based, so the number passed to each dimension of the array must be the actual number assigned to its last element, *not* the total number of elements based on a count from 1.
>
> ```
> DIM g_shopList(1,7)
> ```

Working with Two-Dimensional Arrays

Think of the two dimensions of the g_shopList() array as the columns and rows in a table, respectively. The two elements in the first dimension of the array represent two columns. Column 0 is set up to house the NAME information for each checkbox element, and Column 1 is set up to house its VALUE.

The second dimension of the array provides a row for every checkbox element contained in the catalog form. Since this array is created anew each time the page is loaded, you can add or subtract items (i.e., checkboxes) to or from this page by simply adjusting the catalog form's number of <INPUT> tags of TYPE=checkbox, and then adjusting the number of elements in the second dimension of the array accordingly:

```
DIM g_shopList(1,5)  ' changes the number of items to 6
DIM g_shopList(1,9)  ' changes the number of items to 10
```

An *object/event* subroutine (attached to the current window and its *onLoad* event) executes as soon as the window is loaded.

```
sub window_onLoad()
```

The *window/load* sub immediately declares three variables, then sets *theForm* as an object variable containing the catalog form object.

```
DIM theForm,theCol,theRow
SET theForm = document.catalog
```

Now that the needed variables are all in place, a *for* loop is set up to discover the total number of checkbox items contained in the current catalog form (now represented by the object variable theForm). The purpose of the for loop is to read the NAME and VALUE information into the proper slots in the waiting *g_shopList()* array.

```
for theRow = 0 to theForm.elements.length-3


    theCol = 0
    g_shopList(theCol,theRow) = theForm.elements(theRow).name

    theCol = 1
    g_shopList(theCol,theRow) = theForm.elements(theRow).value

next
```

Here's how the for loop works: The loop uses *theCol* and *theRow* variables to designate the first and second dimension positions in the g_shopList() array, in that order. As already explained, we need to place product NAME information into the first column (column 0) of every row in this array, and product VALUE (or price) information into the second column (column 1) of every row. If you page forward and peruse the HTML for the catalog form, you'll notice that every checkbox item in theForm has been given a NAME that reflects a short name for the displayed item, and a VALUE that reflects the item's price.

How g_shopList() Is Populated

Every element in the g_shopList array whose first dimension position is 0 receives the NAME information for the checkbox item (row) specified by the second dimension position:

```
g_shopList(0,0)        ' the name of the first checkbox element
g_shopList(0,1)        ' the name of the second checkbox element
g_shopList(0,2)        ' the name of the third checkbox element
```

Every element in the g_shopList array whose first dimension position is 1 receives the VALUE information for the checkbox item (row) specified by the second dimension position:

```
g_shopList(1,0)        ' the value of the first checkbox element
g_shopList(1,1)        ' the value of the second checkbox element
g_shopList(1,2)        ' the value of the third checkbox element
```

These tasks are accomplished by the following for loop's enclosed statements. The first two statements set theCol variable to 0 (the first column in the array), then place the NAME of the target element into g_shopList at the given position:

```
theCol = 0
g_shopList(theCol,theRow) = theForm.elements(theRow).name
```

The next two statements set theCol variable to 1 (the second column in the array), then place the VALUE of the target element into g_shopList at the given position.

```
theCol = 1
g_shopList(theCol,theRow) = theForm.elements(theRow).value
```

The first time the loop executes, the interpreter reads the script like this, and populates the first row of g_shopList with the name and value of the first checkbox:

```
theCol = 0
g_shopList(0,0) = theForm.elements(0).name

theCol = 1
g_shopList(1,0) = theForm.elements(0).value
```

The second time the loop executes, the interpreter reads the script like this, and populates the first row of g_shopList with the name and value of the second checkbox:

```
theCol = 0
g_shopList(0,1) = theForm.elements(1).name

theCol = 1
g_shopList(1,1) = theForm.elements(1).value
```

The following array index positions represent the name and value of the first checkbox in the catalog form:

```
g_shopList(0,0)      ' the name of the first checkbox
g_shopList(1,0)      ' the value of the first checkbox
```

The following string represents the HTML script that creates the first checkbox in the form, and gives it a name and value:

```
<INPUT TYPE="checkbox" NAME="Dress" VALUE="59.95">
```

When columns 0 and 2 are put together for row 1 of the g_shopList(), the result is the name and value of the first checkbox:

```
g_shopList(0,0) & ", $ " & g_shopList(1,0) = Dress, $ 59.95
```

When the for loop is done executing for all of the elements in the catalog form, except the final buttons, the window/load script is also finished executing. Here's the first segment in its entirety, for a comprehensive review of its operation:

```
<HTML>
<HEAD>

<TITLE>Shopping List Page</TITLE>

<SCRIPT LANGUAGE="VBScript">

DIM g_shopList(1,7)

sub window_onLoad()

    DIM theForm,theCol,theRow
    SET theForm = document.catalog

    for theRow = 0 to theForm.elements.length-3

        theCol = 0
        g_shopList(theCol,theRow) = theForm.elements(theRow).name

        theCol = 1
        g_shopList(theCol,theRow) = theForm.elements(theRow).value

    next

end sub
```

The HTML script for the catalog form that this script references is shown next. As you can see, the first elements in the array are all checkboxes. If you placed new element types (such as text fields) on the form *before* the checkbox elements, the associated scripts will still work as long as the element type takes the NAME and VALUE arguments—as long as you provided an answer to each. The integrity of the page's operations may be upset, however, unless you also redesign necessary segments of the scripts and the presented page to allow for the new element types.

```
<FORM NAME="catalog">

<TABLE WIDTH=100% BORDER=3 CELLSPACING=3 CELLPADDING=3>
<TR>
<TD><INPUT TYPE="checkbox" NAME="Dress" VALUE="59.95">Tunic Dress, $59.95</TD>
```

```
<TD><INPUT TYPE="checkbox" NAME="Hat" VALUE="15.99">Straw Hat, $15.99
</TD>
</TR>
<TR>
<TD><INPUT TYPE="checkbox" NAME="Jacket" VALUE="99.95">Dinner Jacket,
$99.95</TD>
<TD><INPUT TYPE="checkbox" NAME="Blouse" VALUE="119.95">Silk Blouse,
$119.95</TD>
</TR>
<TR>
<TD><INPUT TYPE="checkbox" NAME="Skirt" VALUE="29.95">Pleated Skirt, $29.95</TD>
<TD><INPUT TYPE="checkbox" NAME="Belt" VALUE="19.95">Leather Belt, $19.95</TD>
</TR>
<TR>
<TD><INPUT TYPE="checkbox" NAME="Jeans" VALUE="19.95">Denim Jeans, $19.95</TD>
<TD><INPUT TYPE="checkbox" NAME="Sweater" VALUE="19.95">Cotton Sweater,
$27.95</TD>
</TR>
</TABLE>

<HR SIZE=6>

<TABLE WIDTH=100%>
<TR ALIGN=Right><TD COLSPAN=2>
  <INPUT TYPE="button" NAME="showItems" VALUE=" Show Items ">
<INPUT TYPE="button" NAME="calcOrder" VALUE=" Calculate Order "></TD>
</TR>
</TABLE>

</FORM>
```

Segment 2: Creating the User's Shopping List and Calculating the Order Total

The next segment of script in the Shopping List page is another pair of cooperating procedures: a *sub* attached to the calcOrder button's *click* event, and a *function* that formats the calculated Order Total into a U.S. dollar amount. (The function script can be easily modified if your country's format varies.)

The calcOrder sub executes when the user clicks the Calculate Order button. Its purpose is to determine which (if any) checkboxes are currently selected. If any selected checkboxes are found, it creates a dynamic (zero-dimensioned or unsized) array named *theOrder()*, then redimensions (sizes) it to fit whatever number of checkboxes have been chosen. The newly sized array is then used to list the names and prices of the items represented by these checkboxes in the script-created Message Box, and to calculate the listed prices into an Order Total.

> **TIP**   A dynamic array is created by simply including an empty pair of parentheses at the end of the array variable's name:
>
> ```
> DIM = dynArray()
> ```

To accomplish all of its chores, the calcOrder sub first declares theOrder() as a dynamic array variable, by passing it empty parentheses. At the same time, it declares several other local variables whose purposes are explained as the lesson proceeds. Only *theNum* and *theLen* variables are initialized with data. theNum is set to 0 to establish it both as empty and as a proper data subtype for arithmetic operations; and theLen is set to the length of the catalog form's elements array, less 3 (so that this variable may be used throughout the script, in place of the longer string).

```
DIM theOrder()
DIM
theMsg,theBoxNum,theNum,theChecked,i,theLineItem,orderList,thePrice,orderTotal

theNum = 0
theLen = catalog.elements.length-3
```

The next job of calcOrder() is to determine if any of the checkboxes have been selected, and it uses a simple for counting loop and the previously declared *theBoxNum* and theLen variables to do so.

```
for theBoxNum = 0 to theLen
```

An if statement within the loop looks at the checked property for each separate checkbox. Every time the checked property returns true for the current checkbox, 1 is added to theNum (which originally received a 0 at the beginning of the script), and the actual box number (housed in theBoxNum variable) and a space are concatenated to the current contents of *theChecked*, then reassigned to that variable. (You'll understand why in a moment.)

```
for theBoxNum = 0 to theLen

   if catalog.elements(theBoxNum).checked then
```

```
            theNum = theNum + 1
            theChecked = theChecked & theBoxNum & " "

        end if

    next
```

Next, a *select case* statement is set up to determine if the checked property was found to be true for *any* checkbox. This statement uses the contents of theNum to determine this fact. If theNum is 0, the user is told to select something first, and the calcOrder sub is exited.

```
select case theNum


    case 0

        alert "You must select one or more items before your order can be calcu-
lated."


        exit sub
```

If theNum is not 0, the *case else* branch of the select case statement is executed.

The first order of business for this branch of the select case statement is to redimension the dynamic array variable, theOrder, as a one-dimensional array. At the same time, another new array is created using the split function on the contents of *theChecked*. If you glance back at the initial loop script in the sub, you'll see that theChecked was previously populated with the elements array positions of all the selected checkboxes, delimited by spaces (which is the split function's default delimiter).

```
case else

    REDIM theOrder(theNum-1)
    checkedArray = split(theChecked)
```

The single dimension of theOrder array is set to the number in theNum minus 1, creating an array with the same number of elements as there are selected checkboxes. The single-dimension *checkedArray* has precisely the same number of elements; one element for each selected checkbox. Thus, if the user has selected three checkbox items, both arrays are dynamically sized to contain three elements.

As usual, since all arrays are zero-based, to assign the same number of elements to theOrder() array that is represented by the number in theNum, you must subtract 1 from theNum. If three checkboxes are selected, the number 2 must be assigned to theOrder to create three elements in that array. Since in this instance theNum actually contains the number "3," 1 must be subtracted from that variable's value so that "2" can be assigned to the array.

> **NOTE** Assigning the array variable to the REDIM statement, and passing either a number or an expression that evaluates to a number to each dimension you wish to establish in the array is the standard operating procedure for sizing a previously unsized (thus the name "dynamic") array.

Now that theOrder array has been sized as a single-dimension array with the same number of elements as there are selected checkboxes, a for loop is written to perform the same series of actions on each element in that array. This loop has the dual tasks of (1) populating all of the elements in theOrder array with (2) information from the proper element in the checkedArray.

To do this, the loop must cycle through the elements of both arrays. Luckily, its set range of 0 to theNum-1 is accurate for both theOrder and checkedArray, since these arrays are invariably the same size.

```
for i = 0 to theNum-1
```

The fact that these two arrays are always the same size allows the *i* counter variable to serve both purposes of this loop. With each turn of the loop, the number contained in i reflects the position in theOrder array that is currently up for population, *and* the element in the checkedArray that houses the *catalog.elements* array position of the corresponding checkbox.

Each index position in the array is then assigned a text string containing the NAME and VALUE information for each of the selected checkbox items. This string is created by concatenating column 0 and column 1 data for the row in the *g_shopList* array that corresponds to current value of i, and assigning that string to the element in theOrder array that also corresponds to the current value of i. As you can see in the line of code that follows, i is used in place of the array position number for both theOrder and checkedArray operations:

```
theOrder(i) = g_shopList(0,checkedArray(i)) & ": $ " &
g_shopList(1,checkedArray(i))
```

(If you need clarification of how and why this dual-service strategy works, see the example in "The Double-Purpose Loop at Work" sidebar.)

The Double-Purpose Loop at Work

Here's an example of how the i counter variable in the current loop plays its dual role. Let's say the user selects the checkboxes next to the Dress, Skirt, and Belt items on the Shopping List page. This is the same as selecting rows 0, 4, and 5 in the g_shopList array. By feeding these numbers (0, 4, 5) to theChecked variable, then splitting that variable into a three-element array called checkedArray, we end up with the following information stored in checkedArray:

```
checkedArray(0) = 0
checkedArray(1) = 4
checkedArray(2) = 5
```

Each time a checkbox's elements array position is fed to theChecked, theNum variable is also incremented by 1. This means that if three numbers are fed to theChecked, there will be three elements in the checkedArray and theNum will contain the number 3. When theNum-1 is used to size theOrder array, like the checkedArray, it becomes an array with three elements:

```
theOrder(0)
theOrder(1)
theOrder(2)
```

The for loop's range is set from 0 to theNum-1, which (in this example) is the same as setting the range to 0 to 2. Passing this range to the for statement is going to cause the loop to execute three times. For each iteration of the loop the i variable will sequentially contain the following data:

```
i = 0
i = 1
i = 2
```

As you can see, the sequential numbers appearing in the i variable are an exact match of the index position numbers for theOrder and checkArray variables. Thus, the first time the loop executes, and i contains 0, the 0 element in theOrder array is going to receive the contents of the 0 element in checkedArray. The next execution of the loop is going to populate the 1 element in theOrder with the contents of the 1 element in checkedArray, and the last iteration of the loop is going to populate theOrder(2) with the contents of checkedArray(2).

```
theOrder(0) = g_shopList(0,checkedArray(0)) & ": $ " &
g_shopList(1,checkedArray(0))      ' first iteration

theOrder(1) = g_shopList(0,checkedArray(1)) & ": $ " &
g_shopList(1,checkedArray(1))      ' second iteration
```

```
theOrder(2) = g_shopList(0,checkedArray(2)) & ": $ " &
g_shopList(1,checkedArray(2))      ' third iteration
```

To clarify even further, here is a version of the three sequential statements that shows the contents of checkedArray for each iteration of the loop:

```
theOrder(0) = g_shopList(0,0) & ": $ " & g_shopList(1,0)
' first iteration

theOrder(1) = g_shopList(0,4) & ": $ " & g_shopList(1,4)
' second iteration

theOrder(2) = g_shopList(0,5) & ": $ " & g_shopList(1,5)

' third iteration
```

When the loop is finished executing, theOrder array's elements would contain the following strings:

```
theOrder(0) = Dress: $ 59.95
theOrder(1) = Skirt: $ 29.95
```

After populating the element in theOrder array that corresponds to the current number in i, the string now contained in that element is placed into *theLineItem* variable along with the VBScript constant that creates a carriage return followed by a line feed (vbCrLf). The new contents of theLineItem are then concatenated to the previous contents of the *orderList* variable, then both are placed back into orderList. When the loop is finished executing, orderList contains a hard-return delimited list of all the strings in theOrder array.

```
theLineItem = theOrder(i) & vbCrLf
orderList = orderList & theLineItem
```

The price of the current item must then be added to the Order Total. To do this, the i variable is used again; this time, to discover the price of the element in the checkArray that corresponds to the current value of i:

```
thePrice = abs(g_shopList(1,checkedArray(i))
```

The contents of row 1 in the g_shopList array are returned as a string for the designated element. Before this string can be added to other price data, it must be converted into a subtype that allows arithmetic operations. In this script, the *abs()* function is used to perform this conversion without affecting the absolute value of the number.

> **TIP** Since we're still in a repeat loop, the statement that assigned the current element in theOrder array (the current string) to theLineItem is going to be overwritten every time the loop finds another selected checkbox. How do we keep adding strings to the orderList variable, then, without losing the data that is already in that variable? This is a common problem, and you can see the simple solution in the script just shown. You simply concatenate the current contents of orderList to the new string that is placed into theLineItem each time the loop finds a checked box. The first time the loop is run, orderList is empty, and thus adds nothing to itself but the contents of theLineItem. Each subsequent time that orderList is populated, however, the previous contents of the orderList variable are added to the new contents. This is a time-honored programmer's trick.

Once the price of the current item is discovered and converted, it is added to the previous amount in *orderTotal* using a variation of the previous concatenation trick to continually add the contents of *thePrice* to the existing contents of orderTotal. Instead of creating a list, however, the *addition* operator is used to add each new number in thePrice variable to the previous total in the orderTotal variable.

```
orderTotal = orderTotal + thePrice
```

We now come upon a new problem. If the amount in orderTotal ends up with zeros to the right of the decimal, then the abs() function is going to remove those zeros. To display the Order Total in the proper monetary format, the orderTotal is passed to a function called *doMoney()*, which returns the data in the proper format. (A discussion of this function follows this section.)

```
orderTotal = doMoney(orderTotal)
```

Once the orderList has been compiled, and the orderTotal calculated and properly formatted, the for loop has done its job. The next task for calcOrder is to put all of these pieces together to create the actual list and total amount that appears in the "Your Shopping List" message box. This is done, and the resulting string is placed into *theMsg* variable declared at the top of the sub statement:

```
theMsg = "Here is a list of the items you selected, and the total amount." &
vbCrLf & vbLf & orderList & vbLf & "TOTAL: $ " & orderTotal & vbCrLf & vbLf &
"Do you want to order these items now?"
```

The newly populated theMsg variable is then passed to the *msgBox()* function as the answer to its first argument (which represents the message to be displayed in the resulting dialog box). Two other arguments are also answered for msgBox(). The second answer provides a number that is the sum of three other numbers: the number of the icon to display, the number of the button group to include, and a number representing the modal status of the dialog box. The last answer passed is a literal string that tells the *Interpreter* what to display in the Title bar of the dialog box. (For more information on theMsg() function, see its corresponding section in Chapter 8.)

The Shopping List message box is built from an expression passed as the condition of a *select case* statement:

```
select case msgBox(theMsg,68,"Your Shopping List")
```

Once the msgBox (shown in Figure 13.4) is created and presented to the user, two possible events may occur: the user may click its "Yes" button, or the user may click its "No" button. When the user clicks Yes, the msgBox() function returns a 6, and the first branch (*case 6*) in the current select case statement executes, causing an alert to advise the user to fill out the form at the bottom of the page. At the same time, the all-important orderList information is saved to a hidden field in the *orderApp* form (the second form object created for this page). The first field in that form then receives the document focus, which automatically places the text insertion cursor into that field, and scrolls that field into view for the user (if it's not already visible).

```
case 6

    alert "Please fill in the Order Form at the bottom of this page, and click
the Order button."

    document.orderApp.theHidden.value = orderList
    document.orderApp.First.focus
```

If the user clicks the No button, msgBox() returns 7, and the *case 7* branch is executed. Since clicking "No" means that the user does not wish to order at this time, a for loop methodically unchecks all of the previously selected checkboxes, so the user can select other items for view or to order. The variable previously populated with the length of the catalog form's elements array, minus 3, represents the upper limit of the range passed to the loop:

```
case 7


    for theBoxNum = 0 to theLen
```

```
        catalog.elements(theBoxNum).checked = false

    next
```

Since only these two cases are possible (the user can only click Yes or No), this ends the select case statement. It also ends the *case else* branch of the select case statement that executes if theNum is not 0 (meaning that checkboxes *have* been selected by the user).

Here's the full calcOrder script:

```
sub calcOrder_onClick()

    DIM theOrder()
    DIM
theMsg,theBoxNum,theNum,theLen,theChecked,i,theLineItem,orderList,thePrice,orderT
otal

    theNum = 0
    theLen = catalog.elements.length-3

    for theBoxNum = 0 to theLen

        if catalog.elements(theBoxNum).checked then

            theNum = theNum + 1
            theChecked = theChecked & theBoxNum & " "

        end if

    next

    select case theNum

        case 0

        alert "You must select one or more items before your order can be calcu-
lated."
        exit sub

        case else

            REDIM theOrder(theNum-1)
            checkedArray = split(theChecked)
```

```
        for i = 0 to theNum-1

                theOrder(i) = g_shopList(0,checkedArray(i)) & ": $ " &
g_shopList(1,checkedArray(i))
                theLineItem = theOrder(i) & vbCrLf
                orderList = orderList & theLineItem
                thePrice = abs(g_shopList(1,checkedArray(i)))
                orderTotal = orderTotal + thePrice
                orderTotal = doMoney(orderTotal)

        next

        theMsg = "Here is a list of the items you selected, and the total
amount." & vbCrLf & vbLf & orderList & vbLf & "TOTAL: $ " & orderTotal & vbCrLf
& vbLf & "Do you want to order these items now?"

        select case msgBox(theMsg ,68,"Your Shopping List")

        case 6

                alert "Please fill in the Order Form at the bottom of this
page, and click the Order button."
                document.orderApp.theHidden.value = orderList
                document.orderApp.First.focus

        case 7

                for theBoxNum = 0 to theLen

                    catalog.elements(theBoxNum).checked = false

                next

        end select

    end select

end sub
```

The doMoney() function is a simple script that merely splits *theAmt* (which is passed from doCalc() in the form of the orderTotal variable) into a two-element array to divide the number into dollars and cents.

```
function doMoney(theAmt)

   DIM theDollars,theCents

   theAmtArray = split(theAmt,".")
```

First, doMoney() uses the *uBound()* function to make sure that the upper boundary of the array (the last element) is 1 (as it would be in a two-element array).

```
if uBound(theAmtArray) = 1 then
```

If this condition is true, the first and second elements in the array are placed into the previously declared *theDollars* and *theCents* variables, respectively:

```
theDollars = theAmtArray(0) : theCents = theAmtArray(1)
```

A select case statement then determines whether the length of theCents equals 0 (theCents is empty), 1 (theCents contains one digit), or 2 (theCents contains two digits). If the length of the cents is higher than that, then some error has occurred, and doMoney() returns false. While this is unlikely, it's often good to provide this kind of all-encompassing case else statement *just in case* (so to speak).

```
select case len(theCents)

   case 0

      theCents = theCents & "00"

   case 1

      theCents = theCents & "0"

   case 2

      theCents = theCents

   case else

      doMoney = false

end select
```

If theCents is a zero-length string (empty), then two zeros are placed into theCents. If theCents is a single-char string, then a zero is added to the end of the existing string. If theCents is a double-char string, then theCents is simply repopulated with the current string (because this branch of the select case statement must contains *some* instruction). After theCents has been properly formatted as a two-digit string, theDollars and theCents are strung together with a decimal and fed into orderTotal, then passed back to calcOrder as the new orderTotal:

```
orderTotal = theDollars & "." & theCents
doMoney = orderTotal
```

If doMoney() receives an amount with two zeros to the right of the decimal, uBound() will result in 0, or a one-element array. Even though this is not possible through any calculation of the prices in the current example, the script provides for this eventuality in case you want to use it (or a script like it) with amounts that could calculate to amounts ending in .00.

The following *elseif* statement only executes if *theAmtArray* provides only a dollar amount. In such a case, 00 is forcibly placed into theCents, and theDollars and theCents variables are joined with a decimal and placed into orderTotal, and doMoney() returns the revised orderTotal to calcOrder:

```
elseif uBound(theAmtArray) = 0 then

    theDollars = theAmtArray(0) : theCents = "00"
    orderTotal = theDollars & "." & theCents
    doMoney = orderTotal
```

If uBound() results in anything but 0 or 1 (indicating something other than a one- or two-element array), the else statement executes and doMoney() returns false again (since this means an error occurred which, though unlikely, is not impossible). If false is returned to calcOrder(), the Shopping List dialog displays "false" in place of the Order Total.

Here's the complete doMoney() script:

```
function doMoney(theAmt)

    theAmtArray = split(theAmt,".")

    if uBound(theAmtArray) = 1 then

        theDollars = theAmtArray(0) : theCents = theAmtArray(1)

        select case len(theCents)

            case 0
```

```
                    theCents = theCents & "00"

                case 1

                    theCents = theCents & "0"

            case 2

                theCents = theCents

            case else

                doMoney = false

        end select

    orderTotal = theDollars & "." & theCents

    doMoney = orderTotal

elseif uBound(theAmtArray) = 0 then

    theDollars = theAmtArray(0) : theCents = "00"
    orderTotal = theDollars & "." & theCents
    doMoney = orderTotal

else

    doMoney = false

end if

end function
```

Segment 3: Displaying the Selected Catalog Items

The next script segment is a sub attached to the showItems button in the catalog form, and the click event. This sub performs an operation similar to one of the operations performed by calcOrder(). The *showItems()* sub reviews the checked property of every checkbox in the catalog form, and puts together a list of selected items using a simplified form of the calcOrder for loop.

Note that with each iteration of the loop, *theLineItem* variable receives an HTML string that encloses the referenced GIF image within a table row tag.

```
sub showItems_onClick()

    DIM theBoxNum,theItem,theLineItem,itemList

    for theBoxNum = 0 to catalog.elements.length-3

        if catalog.elements(theBoxNum).checked then

            theItem = g_shopList(0,theBoxNum) & ".gif"
            theLineItem = "<TR><IMG SRC=" & theItem & "></TR>"
            itemList = itemList & theLineItem
            itemList = itemList

        end if

    next
```

If *itemList* is not empty (meaning at least one checkbox item was selected by the user), a new document is open and written to display the GIF file associated with each item in itemList.

Notice that the HTML string passed to the *document.write* method creates a separate table to display each item in the list (which have already been enclosed by table row tags). This string also creates an anchor at the bottom of the new page view (shown in Figure 13.2) that uses the *javascript:* notation to the HREF argument to return the display to the document that referred the user (i.e., the first view of the Shopping List page).

```
if itemList <> "" then

    document.open()

    document.write ("<BODY BGCOLOR='#A0C0A0'>" & itemList & "<A
HREF='javascript:navigate(document.referrer)'>Back to Catalog List</BODY>")

    document.close()
```

> **WARNING** You must *always* follow a *document.open* statement with a *document.close* statement. If you leave the document stream open at the end of your script, the browser may hang.

If the itemList variable is empty, the user is alerted to select one or more items.

```
else

    alert "You must select one or more items."

end if
```

JavaScript Bug in IE4 BETA

The javascript statement passed to the HREF argument is a tried and true technique that not only worked in all versions of IE3, but in Navigator 2 onward. However, it returns an *invalid procedure* error in IE4; an anomalous (buggy) behavior that should surely be fixed in the final release.

Other methods were tried to restore the original page view, but it's difficult to get Internet Explorer to reload a page; and the page *must* be reloaded to restore the display according to the original HTML script. If the HREF argument is answered with the URL of the Shopping List page, it does not reload that page, but simply retrieves the version currently stored in memory. Unfortunately, this version is the list of just-retrieved images. The *history.back* command takes the user back to the page that appeared in the browser window *before* the Shopping List page. Creating a new window might eventually work, but the IE4 BETA also has bugs in its window creation code that makes it difficult to generate dynamic HTML in new windows.

If these bugs aren't fixed in IE4 by the time you find yourself working with the Shopping List page, clicking the Back to Catalog List hyperlink will result in an error. To force a return to the original page, select File > New > Window, and the original page will be displayed in a new window.

Here's the full showItems script:

```
sub showItems_onClick()

    DIM theBoxNum,theItem,theLineItem,itemList

    for theBoxNum = 0 to catalog.elements.length-3

        if catalog.elements(theBoxNum).checked then
```

```
        theItem = g_shopList(0,theBoxNum ) & ".gif"
        theLineItem = "<TABLE BORDER=1><TR><IMG SRC=" & theItem &
"></TR></TABLE><HR SIZE=4 NOSHADE COLOR='teal'>"
        itemList = itemList & theLineItem
        itemList = itemList

    end if

  next

  if itemList <> "" then

    document.open()

    document.write ("<BODY BGCOLOR='#A0C0A0'>" & itemList & "<A
HREF='javascript:navigate(document.referrer)'>Back to Catalog List</BODY>")

    document.close()

  else

    alert "You must select one or more items."

  end if

end sub
```

Segment 4: Submitting the Order Form

This Order Form segment of this page neither contains nor calls on any VBScript. It is a simple HTML form that provides a hidden field that receives the contents of the calcOrder sub's orderList that was accepted by the user. When the form is submitted, the contents of this field are automatically passed to the CGI application (or any other mechanism) that has been set up to harvest the form's data.

```
<FORM NAME="orderApp">

<INPUT TYPE="hidden" NAME="theHidden">

<b>First Name</b>:
<INPUT TYPE=text NAME=First SIZE=15>

<b>Middle Initial</b>:
```

```
<INPUT TYPE=text NAME=Init SIZE=1>

<b>Last Name</b>:
<INPUT TYPE=text NAME=Last SIZE=23>

<HR>

<b>PAYMENT INFORMATION</b>
<P>
<SELECT NAME="Card">
<OPTION>MasterCard
<OPTION>VISA
<OPTION>American Express
</SELECT>

<b>Card Number</b>:
<INPUT TYPE=text NAME="CC#" SIZE=27>
<b>Expiration Date:</b>:
<INPUT TYPE=text NAME="Exp" SIZE=5>

<HR>
<b>SHIP TO ADDRESS</b>
<P>
<b>Street</b>: <INPUT TYPE=text NAME="Street" SIZE=33>
<b>City</b>: <INPUT TYPE=text NAME="Street" SIZE=15>
<b>State</b>: <INPUT TYPE=text NAME="Street" SIZE=2>
<b>Zip</b>: <INPUT TYPE=text NAME="Street" SIZE=5>
<HR>

<TABLE WIDTH=100%>
<TR ALIGN=right>

<INPUT TYPE=submit NAME=submitter VALUE=" Order ">

<INPUT TYPE=reset NAME=cancel VALUE=" Clear ">

</TR>
</TABLE>

</FORM>
</BODY>
</HTML>
```

Putting the Shopping List Page Together

All of the pieces and parts of the Shopping List page described in this chapter go together effortlessly, without any additional scripting and without the need for further explanation or instruction.

The Full Script

```
<HTML>
<HEAD>

<TITLE>Shopping List Page</TITLE>

<SCRIPT LANGUAGE="VBScript">

DIM g_shopList(1,7)

sub window_onLoad()

    DIM theForm,theCol,theRow
    SET theForm = document.catalog

    for theRow = 0 to theForm.elements.length-3

        theCol = 0
        g_shopList(theCol,theRow) = theForm.elements(theRow).name

        theCol = 1
        g_shopList(theCol,theRow) = theForm.elements(theRow).value

    next

end sub

sub calcOrder_onClick()

    DIM theOrder()
    DIM
theMsg,theBoxNum,theNum,theLen,theChecked,i,theLineItem,orderList,thePrice,orderT
otal

    theNum = 0
```

```
theLen = catalog.elements.length-3

for theBoxNum = 0 to theLen

    if catalog.elements(theBoxNum).checked then

        theNum = theNum + 1
        theChecked = theChecked & theBoxNum & " "

    end if

next

select case theNum

    case 0

        alert "You must select one or more items before your order can be cal-
culated."
        exit sub

    case else

        REDIM theOrder(theNum-1)
        checkedArray = split(theChecked)

        for i = 0 to theNum-1

            theOrder(i) = g_shopList(0,checkedArray(i)) & ": $ " &
g_shopList(1,checkedArray(i))
            theLineItem = theOrder(i) & vbCrLf
            orderList = orderList & theLineItem
            thePrice = abs(g_shopList(1,checkedArray(i)))
        orderTotal = orderTotal + thePrice
            orderTotal = doMoney(orderTotal)

        next

        theMsg = "Here is a list of the items you selected, and the total
amount." & vbCrLf & vbLf & orderList & vbLf & "TOTAL: $ " & orderTotal & vbCrLf
& vbLf & "Do you want to order these items now?"
```

```
        select case msgBox(theMsg ,68,"Your Shopping List")

            case 6

                alert "Please fill in the Order Form at the bottom of this
page, and click the Order button."
                document.orderApp.theHidden.value = orderList
                document.orderApp.First.focus

            case 7

                for theBoxNum = 0 to theLen

                    catalog.elements(theBoxNum).checked = false

                next

        end select

    end select

end sub

function doMoney(theAmt)

    theAmtArray = split(theAmt,".")

    if uBound(theAmtArray) = 1 then

        theDollars = theAmtArray(0) : theCents = theAmtArray(1)

        select case len(theCents)

            case 0

                theCents = theCents & "00"

            case 1

                theCents = theCents & "0"

        case 2
```

```
                 theCents = theCents

            case else

                doMoney = false

        end select

        orderTotal = theDollars & "." & theCents

        doMoney = orderTotal

    elseif uBound(theAmtArray) = 0 then

        theDollars = theAmtArray(0) : theCents = "00"

        orderTotal = theDollars & "." & theCents

        doMoney = orderTotal

    else

        doMoney = false

    end if

end function

sub showItems_onClick()

    DIM theBoxNum,theItem,theLineItem,itemList

    for theBoxNum = 0 to catalog.elements.length-3

        if catalog.elements(theBoxNum).checked then

            theItem = g_shopList(0,theBoxNum ) & ".gif"
            theLineItem = "<TABLE BORDER=1><TR><IMG SRC=" & theItem &
"></TR></TABLE><HR SIZE=4 NOSHADE COLOR='teal'>"
            itemList = itemList & theLineItem
            itemList = itemList
```

```
        end if

    next

    if itemList <> "" then

        document.open()

        document.write ("<BODY BGCOLOR='#A0C0A0'>" & itemList & "<A
HREF='javascript:navigate(document.referrer)'>Back to Catalog List</BODY>")

        document.close()

    else

        alert "You must select one or more items."

    end if

end sub

</SCRIPT>

</HEAD>

<BODY BGCOLOR="#A0C0A0">

<TABLE WIDTH=100%>
<TR ALIGN="center" BGCOLOR="teal">
<TD><FONT SIZE="+3" COLOR="white">
Welcome to our Spring Catalog
</FONT>
</TD>
</TR>
</TABLE>

<BLOCKQUOTE>
Please choose the item(s) you wish to order by clicking the item's checkbox.
When you are done selecting items, click the SHOW ITEMS button for more informa-
tion on the selected items, or the CALCULATE ORDER button for a Shopping List
and Order Total:
</BLOCKQUOTE>
```

```
<FORM NAME="catalog">

<HR NOSHADE COLOR="teal" SIZE=6>

<TABLE WIDTH=100% BORDER=3 CELLSPACING=3 CELLPADDING=3 BGCOLOR="#FFD0A0">
<TR>
<TD>
<FONT COLOR="teal">
<INPUT TYPE="checkbox" NAME="Dress" VALUE="59.95">Tunic Dress, $59.95
</FONT>
</TD>
<TD>
<FONT COLOR="teal">
<INPUT TYPE="checkbox" NAME="Hat" VALUE="15.99">Straw Hat, $15.99
</FONT>
</TD>
</TR>
<TR>
<TD>
<FONT COLOR="teal">
<INPUT TYPE="checkbox" NAME="Jacket" VALUE="99.95">Dinner Jacket, $99.95
</FONT>
</TD>
<TD>
<FONT COLOR="teal">
<INPUT TYPE="checkbox" NAME="Blouse" VALUE="119.95">Silk Blouse, $119.95
</FONT>
</TD>
</TR>
<TR>
<TD>
<FONT COLOR="teal">
<INPUT TYPE="checkbox" NAME="Skirt" VALUE="29.95">Pleated Skirt, $29.95
</FONT>
</TD>
<TD>
<FONT COLOR="teal">
<INPUT TYPE="checkbox" NAME="Belt" VALUE="19.95">Leather Belt, $19.95
</FONT>
</TD>
</TR>
```

```
<TR>
<TD>
<FONT COLOR="teal">
<INPUT TYPE="checkbox" NAME="Jeans" VALUE="19.95">Denim Jeans, $19.95
</FONT>
</TD>
<TD>
<FONT COLOR="teal">
<INPUT TYPE="checkbox" NAME="Sweater" VALUE="27.95">Cotton Sweater, $27.95
</FONT>
</TD>
</TR>
</FONT>
</TABLE>

<HR NOSHADE COLOR="teal" SIZE=6>

<TABLE WIDTH=100%>
<TR ALIGN=Right><TD COLSPAN=2>
 <INPUT TYPE="button" NAME="showItems" VALUE=" Show Items ">
<INPUT TYPE="button" NAME="calcOrder" VALUE=" Calculate Order "></TD>
</TR>
</TABLE>

</FORM>
```

Fill out this form and click the <b> ORDER </b> button to order the items on your shopping list:

```
<HR NOSHADE COLOR="teal">

<FORM NAME="orderApp">

<INPUT TYPE="hidden" NAME="theHidden">

<b>First Name</b>:
<INPUT TYPE=text NAME=First SIZE=15>

<b>Middle Initial</b>:
<INPUT TYPE=text NAME=Init SIZE=1>
```

```
<b>Last Name</b>:
<INPUT TYPE=text NAME=Last SIZE=23>

<HR NOSHADE COLOR="teal">

<b>PAYMENT INFORMATION</b>
<P>
<SELECT NAME="Card">
<OPTION>MasterCard
<OPTION>VISA
<OPTION>American Express
</SELECT>

<b>Card Number</b>:
<INPUT TYPE=text NAME="CC#" SIZE=27>
<b>Expiration Date:</b>:
<INPUT TYPE=text NAME="Exp" SIZE=5>

<HR NOSHADE COLOR="teal">

<b>SHIP TO ADDRESS</b>
<P>
<b>Street</b>: <INPUT TYPE=text NAME="Street" SIZE=33>
<b>City</b>: <INPUT TYPE=text NAME="Street" SIZE=15>
<b>State</b>: <INPUT TYPE=text NAME="Street" SIZE=2>
<b>Zip</b>: <INPUT TYPE=text NAME="Street" SIZE=5>

<HR NOSHADE COLOR="teal">

<TABLE WIDTH=100%>
<TR ALIGN=right>

<INPUT TYPE=submit NAME=submitter VALUE=" Order ">

<INPUT TYPE=reset NAME=cancel VALUE=" Clear ">

</TR>
</TABLE>

</FORM>
</BODY>
</HTML>
```

What's Next?

The examples presented in the last three chapters (including this chapter) did not spring into the mind of the author as fully realized, flawlessly functioning pages. Each chapter's scripts resulted from a rather crude basic design that was tediously tested, corrected, retested, recorrected, and tested yet again, until all of its objectives were (more or less) gracefully achieved.

It is par for the average development project to begin with what appears to be a clear initial idea. From that excellent beginning, you'll take the first stab at scripting, fully assured that it's going to be a piece of cake. Reality won't dawn until you begin testing your scripts in the browser (or browsers, if you seek to support more than one). From that point onward you'll be fixing bugs or frantically searching for workarounds to bugs that you cannot fix.

As time goes on and you gain the wisdom that only real experience brings, you'll begin to take the weaknesses of your development environment into account in the initial design stages. You'll hear yourself uttering phrases to your superiors or clients like: "Hmmm . . . you can't really do that very easily in VBScript."

This doesn't mean the VBScript isn't a good Web scripting tool. It is a fact that all environments have their problems. Moreover, the conventional industry wisdom holds that software development is one third design and planning, one third programming, and *one third debugging*. So, regardless of your choice of tools, fixing bugs is obviously no small part of the process. Given its importance to your ultimate success as a VBScripter, the next chapter is dedicated to the fine points and sometimes black art of system debugging.

14

Troubleshooting
Your Scripts

Amidst the chaos of World War II, German atomic physicist Werner Heisenberg brought forth the theory that the mere act of observing a system changes its behavior; thus concluding that you can never observe a system in a completely undisturbed state. In *Instant VBScript,* Alex Homer and Darren Gill use the now-famous Heisenberg principle as a basis for their own Heisen*bug* principle. This new spin on the old theory states that the mere act of fixing a bug in a system introduces new bugs.

Sadly, "bug recycling" (the formal term is *regression*) does indeed occur more often than any software developer would care to admit. Does this mean that you can never completely debug a system? In the volatile atmosphere of Internet software development, veterans of ongoing programming wars (like the one raging between Microsoft and Netscape for net supremacy) would undoubtedly answer with a heart-felt *yes*.

This answer is only true, however, because the software products that these teams are developing *are not standing still*. This means that the platforms you, as a webmaster, are coding *upon* are constantly moving forward and morphing beneath you at breakneck speed. Like any object in an object-based hierarchy, you inherit attributes of the objects that sit above you; in this case, you inherit the problems of the developers of any software that supports your own development efforts.

Browser Support Problems

In Voltaire's best of all possible worlds, there would never have been a World War—let alone a World War *II*—and programmers would have all the time needed to build and debug software, without being driven to add new features and functions before all existing features are smoothly implemented. In our imperfect world, no sooner do you deploy a set of relatively well-behaved scripts on your Web site then new versions of Internet Explorer or Navigator come along to make mincemeat out of once-beautiful pages. So, before you reach the point of debugging your scripts—in fact, before you begin coding or even *designing* your pages—you can save yourself some heartache, additional testing, and eventual debugging by taking the following realities of Web development into account from the very beginning:

- The two most popular browsers (IE and Navigator) are moving in different directions vis-à-vis HTML, DHTML, and the external scripting languages.

- Though many a webmaster has turned a deaf ear to these facts, Internet Explorer and Navigator are *not* the only browsers out there; and PCs are not the only browsing mechanisms. Many PDAs (Personal Digital Assistants) now have built-in browsers—none of which currently support frames, let alone extension scripting languages.

- The scripting engines and debugging tools for extending Web page operations are still fragile and not fully implemented according to their latest specs. This is true (and has been consistently true across versions) for both VBScript and JavaScript.

Given these Web-development realities, many webmasters find it best to design pages and sites as simply as possible, while still taking advantage of the most widely implemented and reasonably dependable offerings of the bleeding-edge technologies.

This approach doesn't preclude the scripting of complex Web sites, as long as you carefully test each script segment as you go along for every browser and version of that browser that you intend to support. If you're providing an alternate page-branch for downlevel or VBScript-unaware browsers, you may find it efficient to design and script the simplest version of your pages first, then use copies of those htm files as a foundation for the more complex (and much cooler) VBScript editions.

Quality Assurance Testing

Before you can debug a system, you must first track down and quantify its anomalous (deviant) behaviors. It is much better, and certainly more professional, to

> **TIP** As new versions of Internet Explorer surface, it is the wise web-master who immediately downloads and tests existing pages against it. If and when Navigator begins to support VBScript, you'll also want to see how your current VBScripted pages fare against this newcomer. As Microsoft finally begins to deliver on its promise to support the Mac and UNIX, you'll need to retest your pages for these platforms as well. Don't be lulled into a false sense of security because these latter browsers are made by Microsoft. True cross-platform compatibility is still more hyperbole than reality, and—despite the supposedly best of intentions—both Internet Explorer and Navigator have been known to behave quite differently across operating systems. The hoardes of nearly disenfranchised Mac users know what I'm talking about.

perform this exercise yourself than to leave it to your unsuspecting users. Although it is difficult—even with third-party testers—to uncover all of the subtle problems in a system, you should certainly be able to track down and root out any *showstoppers* before deploying your pages.

Showstopper is an industry term for misbehavior that brings the functioning of an application (or a page, in this case) to a halt. There's really no excuse for a professional webmaster to deploy pages with problems of this magnitude. If you implement and execute a reasonably good test plan, you'll be able to fine-tune and debug your pages even further—to a degree well beyond the showstopper level—before unleashing those pages on an innocent user community.

When your user community (or any test users, including yourself) actually begin to interact with your pages within a browser, those pages graduate to the status of *software*. You, therefore, need to know how to test and debug software. Thankfully, after all the years spent developing software in this century, the industry has come up with certain recognized standards for testing its efficacy that are not difficult to implement. They simply require you to follow an orderly progression based (perhaps surprisingly) on common sense.

Unit Testing

Unit testing is the first rung on the testing ladder, and it refers to the methodical testing of separate units of code, as those units are written. In VBScript, any sub, function, handler, or other segment of script that you write is considered a unit, and each of these units should be tested as soon as it is written. In fact, you'd be well-advised to test any piece of script, no matter how small, as soon as it is complete enough to be testable (such as a *single repeat loop*, or an *if* or *select case* conditional, or an expression that needs evaluation).

As with HTML, to test a segment of script, all you have to do is load its containing HTML document into the browser (currently, Internet Explorer, or a VBScript-enabled version of Navigator with the *ScriptActive* plug-in), then perform the necessary user actions to execute each statement in the target script.

Since unit testing is performed as the code is written, it is almost always done by the programmer. Testing your own code is fraught with peril, however, because you'll unconsciously avoid "hitting" your application too hard in areas where you know it may be fragile. Nevertheless, in most instances, it is a practical impossibility for anyone else to test the code at this stage of the game.

Sometimes it is only necessary to initiate the proper event and let the script run its course to fully test it. However, if your script contains any conditional statements (such as an if statement or a select case statement), or expressions that are evaluated based on user input (for instance), then you'll need to run the script multiple times to test it in all the different ways that a user might interact with it.

Testing All Conditions

If your script contains a conditional, you'll need to figure out a way to test every branch contained in that conditional. One of the biggest oversights you'll be tempted to make in testing your own code is to assume that if one or some of the branches of a conditional execute properly, then the entire unit of code is working correctly.

This kind of assumption is often made because one or more of the possible conditions is hard to test. However, it is well worth the effort to find some way to produce that condition and thereby test the remaining branch or branches. The costly alternative is to allow your users to discover hidden bugs in these branches themselves; a scenario entirely unacceptable to a conscientious software developer.

Testing All Evaluations

If your script is evaluating expressions based on user input, you'll need to run the script against different data inputs (and maybe even different datatypes) to make sure it evaluates them all correctly—or returns an error if there is something inherently wrong with the user's input. (More on Error Handling later in this chapter.)

If your script is running a repeat loop based on user input, or information passed by variables, or other data that may vary under changing conditions, you should try to test the loop against as many variations of that data as you can create and/or deem necessary and prudent. This is definitely an instance where "less is more" does *not* apply.

Integration Testing

Integration testing occurs after separately coded modules have been linked together to form an application. In Web page scripting circles, this may not seem apropos, but separate pages that are meant to cooperate in a frameset actually fit this scenario quite nicely. *Active Server Pages* (asp) that interact with each other, using both client-side and server-side VBScript, are also coded separately and integrated later (even if just minutes apart).

In any case, if your scripted pages are simple, there is no need *for Integration Testing.* When the page is completed, and each unit tested, you can move right into *System* testing (described next). If pages have been scripted to interact with other pages in a frameset or to interact dynamically between the server and the client, it will be necessary to put these pieces together, and make sure they inter-behave themselves properly.

If you are working on a team, someone other than the original page author may be appointed to pull all the pieces together. If you are the designated integrator, the main thing to check for when joining separate modules is the validity and appropriateness (in terms of content and type) of any data that is passed between the modules.

Passing Variable Data between Modules

Let's say a page in one of the frames in a set includes a script to calculate the total cost of items selected by the user. In unit testing, this script works fine; always calculating the correct amount. A script in a second frame in the set needs to refer to that calculated amount in order to check the amount against the user's set order limit. When the second script is artificially fed an amount during unit testing, it checks it against the user limit just fine. Both units of code are thus found to be performing correctly. When the two pages are put together, however, an error returns. What's the problem?

The problem is that the second frame's script (which refers to the *Total Amount* variable in the first frame) contains a typo in the first frame's name. This is a bug that couldn't be detected in unit testing, where the data was passed artificially, and the statement including the name of the target frame was bypassed.

This example clearly illustrates how underlying integrity problems can percolate to the surface when separate units of code begin to inter-behave. Even when the units in question have been thoroughly tested and found to be executing perfectly on their own, the show isn't over until you've tested all of the dependencies between them.

System Testing

When the scripts have passed *Unit* and *Integration* testing, the time has come to test the system as whole. *System* testing refers to the testing of every feature and function of an application in as many combinations as you can think to test. When applied to Web pages, this means that every way in which you have scripted the page to behave must be tested in as many combinations as possible. Again, the intricacies of this test depend upon the complexity of your page or cooperating pageset.

For complicated pages, it is best to leave the System test to someone other than the author(s) of the scripts. As previously noted, the coder always seems to harbor an unconscious reluctance to test certain parts of his or her own system; especially those parts that presented difficulties in Unit testing. It has also been found through the years that individual testers get into certain habits of testing based on the way that person views the use of the system. It is therefore not only good to get outside testers, but multiple testers as well—since each will "go at" the application in different ways, thereby discovering different problems and weaknesses.

Even if you plan to System test your pages yourself, if the pageset is complex, it's a good idea to prepare a written list of all the responding events and subsequent actions that the page is scripted to support. Certainly if others are doing the testing, some form of testing guide must be prepared so the testers will know what to test.

Rather than wait until you get to the point of System testing, you'll find it efficient to compile the testing guide during Unit and Integration testing. To do a good job in the first two tests, you'll need to make yourself aware of each little operation and every piece of transferred data anyway. Writing this information down during these earlier tests can help at every subsequent stage of testing. When you're done testing and modifying the code to fix bugs and instigate workarounds, you may even want to incorporate some of the gathered test information into comments within the code for future reference.

The tester(s) should treat your test guide only as a basic template for creating the actual System test. Simply going through the system behaviors listed in the guide and testing each operation once or twice isn't thorough enough. The tester must approach the system in the guise of a user, and think in terms of what a user might do; not in terms of what the page is scripted to do. This approach engenders a subtle but all-important change in point of view, and results in a far-better final pageset.

Five Steps to Effective Testing

If the System test is implemented by third-party testers (someone other than yourself), these testers should create a careful, written report (discussed in the "Five Steps" section) for each problem encountered in the system. If you or your third-party testers have never tested software before, the following "Five Steps" will help acclimate you all to the process.

1. **Test slowly and deliberately.**

    Be aware of each action you take, and closely monitor the browser's response. When things go wrong, it's important to remember and carefully document all the actions that lead up to the bad behavior. Knowing the exact sequence may be critical to solving the problem.

2. **Try to replicate the problem.**

   If you can't replicate the problem, then the programmer probably can't fix it either. If Step #1 was followed, however, its resulting step-by-step report of activities leading up to the problem should allow the programmer to replicate it with relative ease. If the programmer can't replicate it, it may be because the problem is relative to the computer system used by the tester. This may require the programmer to debug and retest the code on the original tester's machine, or a similar machine.

3. **Report each problem separately.**

   If third parties are implementing the System test, each instance of anomalous behavior should be reported on a separate piece of paper; written up with as much detail as possible (including, or course, the step-by-step description of how to replicate the behavior).

   If the project requires a close tracking of these *Anomalous Behavior Reports* (ABRs), you may find it helpful to number each report. For large Web site projects, putting each problem in a separate, numbered report makes it easier to keep track of what's been fixed, since each problem is separated from the rest and can be individually identified by number. Whereas, if multiple problems are reported in the same ABR, under a single number, you could fix one or more of the reported problems, yet still have an "outstanding" ABR— causing supervisors or clients to think you're making slow progress.

   Writing up each problem separately has the additional benefit of preventing testers from making assumptions about how problems might be related at the code level. (Ironically, even nonprogramming testers often include instructions in an ABR on how to fix the code.) You, on the other hand, being intimately familiar with that code, can look through the stack of reports and "marry" appropriate problems as you see fit.

4. **Fully test each version.**

   As you fix each reported problem in the system, you should Unit test the affected part of the code again, along with any other part of the code that may be impacted by that fix. If applicable, the module in which the fixed code is contained should be sent through Integration testing again; and, then the whole pageset should be System tested again. Even a few small fixes can introduce new problems (thanks to the Heisenbug principle discussed in the chapter introduction).

5. **Perform random robustness tests and senseless user acts.**

   Once the System has been tested slowly and deliberately (as advised in Step #1), the tester (or, better yet, a newcomer who is completely unfamiliar with the pageset) should test for robustness and the unexpected. It is a practical impossibility to quantify what this means. Suffice it to say that good testing of this type requires a little imagination. The name of the game is to do anything that the objects on the page will allow you to do, without worrying about how these objects are actually scripted to behave.

If you were testing bona fide application software, you'd want your testers to spend a little time executing things in rapid succession: clicking quickly between buttons, typing at high speeds into fields, and so on. It may still be a good idea to do some of this, as long as you realize that many resulting problems will likely be based upon internal misbehaviors of the browser—or even delicacies of the resident computer operating system. These are two areas where you can do nothing to alleviate the problem except, possibly, inform the user of its existence.

Solving Anomalous Behavior Problems

The word "bug" is fired at programmers rather ruthlessly anytime software deviates from its specified behavior. The actual meaning of the term, however, refers exclusively to problems resulting from errors *in the way the code is written*. If all problems were bugs, then all problems could be fixed by rewriting the code. This is not so. In the VBScript environment, some errors result from problems in the browser's interpreter; some result from the user's misunderstanding of the system; some result from errors in the basic design of the system; and some problems occasionally result from frailties in the underlying computer operating system.

The umbrella term "Anomalous Behavior" is used in this chapter instead of bug, because it refers to *any* behavior that deviates from the expected. The first thing to do when a problem is discovered, then, is to identify which part of the system is failing.

Who's Responsible for the Problem?

The steps you need to take to figure out which part of the system is responsible for the problem can be as simple as reading the ABR. Perhaps a user is complaining of an error in an intranet application related to a feature that the user should realize is not fully coded yet. If so, you're dealing with an error in the user's understanding. All you have to do to fix this problem is remind the user (or client) that the feature isn't fully implemented yet. Other problems require fuller investigation; some leading down a dark and winding path from which you may begin to fear there's no return.

When faced with a particularly thorny problem, take some advice from the *Hitchhiker's Guide to the Galaxy* and *don't panic*. Breathe deep and surrender to the process, knowing that all you can do is methodically work through the steps for solving the problem—and no one else could do more. Then, take as many of the following steps as you need to discover the root of the problem.

1. Carefully read the ABR.

2. Replicate the problem.

3. If you can't replicate the problem from the information in the ABR, work directly with the person who wrote the ABR to figure out how to replicate.

4. Once you've replicated the problem, ask yourself the following questions:

    a. Is this a problem with the design of the page?

    b. Does this problem only occur on a particular operating system?

    c. Is this a problem with the interpreter?

    d. Is this a problem with my code?

Design Problems

If the problem is a design issue, you may need to rethink the way in which the page or pageset is architected. It can be downright deflating to have these kinds of problems arise after all the coding and testing is done. Moreover, the correction of such problems can run deep. Fixing them is often time-intensive, sometimes sending you all the way back to the drawing board. The best way to repair severe design problems, however, is to prevent them from occurring in the first place by soliciting user input during the design phase—well before any serious coding commences.

If you're creating a public Web site, an early focus group can help you foresee "application interface" problems that might make it difficult for some users to interact effectively with your pages. If you're creating an intranet site—and maybe even a full-blown custom client-server-type application—you'll save yourself untold agony by running early "prototype" pages by your users prior to starting to code in earnest.

OS Problems

If you are trying to create pages that work across operating systems, or browsers, or both, then you're likely to run into a fair amount of problems that only occur on a particular OS or within a particular browser. At this point, you'll be hitting the delivery gaps in Microsoft's promises of cross-platform/cross-browser support for VBScript. Depending on the problem, you may be able to find a way to modify the script for the errant system. The trouble is, you may end up with multiple implementations of your script; one for each system or browser.

The popular solution to the dilemma of coding for multiple systems and browsers is to code to the lowest common denominator. With this in mind, all testing (starting with Unit testing) should be done for the system or browser that offers the *least* support for VBScript. The assumption inherent in this approach is: "If I can get this page working on the weaker system, it should certainly work in the more muscular environment." While this is not always true, it's true enough to give it the old college try. If you run into exceptions to this assumption, however, you'll need to decide whether to forego the problematical feature entirely—or bow to the necessity of creating separate scripts and multiple page branches on your site.

> **TIP** If you have a supervisor or client who insists on creating a single set of pages for all clients—and those clients may be using multiple browsers and computer systems—at this point in time, the sad truth is, you're better off using JavaScript (or, even safer, no extension scripting language at all). As Microsoft begins to deliver broader support for VBScript across platforms (as it must for VBScript to survive), this situation will surely improve—rapidly, it is hoped.

Interpreter Problems

Both the VBScript and JavaScript interpreters suffer mightily from the pedal-to-the-metal pace of Internet surprise-ware. (Surprise! It freezes up your system—but, what the heck; it has a million features!) The latest engines for both are riddled with bugs and saddled with poor documentation. For VBScript in particular, the documentation problem is acute. Obvious cutting and pasting has left some language elements with identical explanations (which is patently absurd). Other items are so cursorily described that either the documenter didn't understand them, or we're dealing with severe instances of programmer-speak, which assumes ESP on the part of the reader.

As you repeatedly run into these limitations, you'll find yourself falling into the trap of blaming the interpreter for all but the most obvious programming bugs. Sometimes, you'll be right. But beware of taking this route too automatically, or too often. Although this is by far the most aggravating, hair-pulling kind of debugging that exists (is it *me*, or is it *VBScript?*)—careful investigation will oft times point unnervingly at *you*.

If you're going to be doing a lot of VBScripting—or if you're beginning work on a big VBScript project—regularly trolling the VBScript newsgroups is wholeheartedly recommended. You can learn a lot from these targeted discussions about known problems with the interpreter that will help you avoid these weak areas before you commit yourself to code. You can also query the group for help and feedback if you run into a "wall" that you think is founded in the VBScript engine.

> **TIP** Although you can't be expected to beat your head against a risen wall forever, you'd be well advised to make doubly sure that your problem *is* VBScript (and not your own wonderful code) before blaming it on the interpreter in front of supervisors or clients. It could be hazardous to your self-esteem (not to mention your programming career) if a colleague or competitor proved you wrong.

Your Problems

If the problem is in your code, then you're now officially dealing with a "bug." Microsoft has an internal team working on a debugging tool for VBScript and JavaScript called the "Script Debugger." It was available in BETA for earlier versions of Internet Explorer, and had some excellent debugging support features allowing you to automatically check the contents of variables, to "step" through your code to discover the exact place where the code fails (whether the code is VBScript or JavaScript), and other helpful tools.

Unfortunately, the current version of Script Debugger is incompatible with both IE3.02 and IE4. If it is updated and works with your system (and isn't rife with its own bugs), you're strongly encouraged to try it.

> **WWW** Check Microsoft's VBScript site to see if Script Debugger is available yet for IE4:
>
> www.microsoft.com/vbscript/

Like the JavaScript engines for Navigator and Internet Explorer, the VBScript engine provides cursory debugging support that basically tells you the line number (not always right) where the script fails, and a general description (not always accurate) of the error that caused the failure (see Figure 14.1).

This support is better for IE4 than it has ever been. It's a little more thorough, offering both character and line number coordinates for the error; and it appears to be slightly more accurate and clearer in its error descriptions (although the BETA IE still spits out some incorrect data).

Figure 14.1 The VBScript engine returned this error for a script that referred to a field object by the wrong psuedonym. The field's real name is "theFld," but the script used "document.forms(0).thisField" to call it.

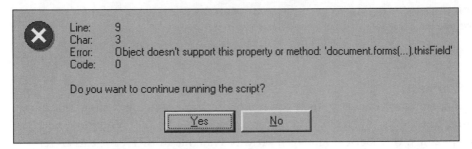

If the Script Debugger isn't ready for prime time, you can still fully debug your scripts without a great deal of difficulty—thanks to the ready availability of the browser to run your scripts, and your debugging tests. You certainly won't be the only developer to ever debug within a fledgling development environment without good tools. Early HyperCard XCMD developers had to write over and over again to something called a "dump" file to test and debug their code. These folks had no runtime equivalent to the browser that lets you easily and quickly revise and execute your code over and over again.

As with everything else concerning software development, standard strategies have coalesced over the years for debugging code. As with testing, there's an orderly, step-by-step process you can follow to track down and fix your bugs. Some may take longer than others to resolve, but the basic rule of thumb is to break the code down into its simplest pieces and test each problem piece separately.

If you've set up a complex conditional or repeat loop (especially nested loops), you may have to start backing out of these conditions and loops, and trying different combinations. You may, for instance, be inadvertently running your larger loop with the wrong condition; perhaps it needs to trade places with a nested loop. You may be making a logical mistake in the expression you're passing to a conditional statement, causing its internal statements to execute in the wrong way for it various branches. As hard as the source of a bug may be to spot, if you just keep breaking the problem down into smaller and smaller increments, you're bound to discover its root.

Whether the problem is simple or complex, exposing it to a standard debugging routine not only provides an orderly means of approaching and solving that current problem, but helps you to refine your debugging techniques and strategies as well.

Where Is the Script Failing?

The first step in fixing any bug is to locate the exact point where your script begins to fail. To do so, walk yourself through a replication of the problem, watching carefully for the very moment when the error occurs.

VBScript Errors

If a script results in a VBScript error during page load, or any other executed user event, then the interpreter's error dialog will provide you with the line and character position where the script failed, along with a short description of the problem and a VBScript error number (as shown in Figure 14.1).

Sometimes, the coordinates given in this error dialog won't be entirely accurate. The line pointed to may, in fact, be empty. The problem is nevertheless close at hand; so, if the designated line seems fine (or is empty), look to the lines directly above or below it for the problem's source.

> **N O T E** VBScript errors are almost always caused by improper syntax or the interpreter's failure to recognize the existence of an object (discussed in the next section, "Figuring Out What Went Wrong").

Execution Errors

If a script results in an incorrect change on the page (like placing the wrong data into a field or selecting the wrong radio button), the VBScript interpreter won't intercept the problem. It isn't sophisticated enough to know exactly what you're trying to do. As long as it finds no syntax or object existence errors, it remains silent.

It's up to you alone to locate the problem causing the incorrect change. The place to start looking is wherever this change is negotiated in your scripted page. You're looking for the actual line of script that places the incorrect data into the field, for instance, or selects the wrong radio button. To find this place in the script, think about the user event and associated object that kicked off the process that ended in the error. If the error occurs when you tab from a field, you need to look at any scripts attached to that field object via the *onBlur* or *onChange* events (both of which are executed by tabbing from the field, assuming the data in the field has changed).

Once you figure out which script is failing (it could even be both), peruse that script for the line that actually implements the environmental change. Once you've located this line, even if it's correctly written, you now have a starting point from which you can work the problem.

Failure to Execute Errors

If the problem is that nothing happens when you execute a scripted event, then you need to determine which script is failing to execute. Again, if you have both an onBlur and an onChange handler associated with a field (to use our prior example), and nothing happens when you tab out of that field after typing new data into it, you need to first isolate the script that contains the problem; then, auger in on the place in the script where the failure occurs.

Since neither event handler's script executed when its event was fired, you'll need to arbitrarily comment out one of the field's handlers (either will do), then place a test alert statement at the top of the remaining handler script:

```
' onChange="[handler script]"
```

```
onBlur="alert 'hello'
[handler script]"
```

Reload the script into the browser, then type and tab from the field again to see if the alert appears. If the alert fails to appear when you execute the necessary event, then the attached script isn't getting called at all. The first thing to consider in this case is whether the attached event is supported by the target object. In the current example, both the blur and change events *are* supported by the <INPUT TYPE="text"> form element, so this kind of error would indicate that the interpreter is somehow failing to recognize and intercept a valid event.

With the helter-skelter addition of DHTML to IE4, this is frankly a problem with the BETA version of the interpreter and some new events. Hopefully the release version will fill all these gaps. If not, you'll need to think of another event or object to use in order to achieve your script's objective.

> **N O T E** Programmers are often forced to take another a coding path to accommodate bugs in the interpreter, compiler, or resident computer operating system that supports their software. This is, in fact, such a frequent necessity that the procedure has earned an unofficial name. It's called a "workaround."

If the alert *does* appear when the event is executed for the field, keep moving the alert statement down in the executing script until it no longer appears. When this happens, you'll find that the error in your script resides in the line *above* the place in the script where the uninvoked alert statement sits.

Since two scripts failed to execute, you should now check the other handler by commenting out the first handler, and performing the same alert test on the second handler.

```
onChange="alert 'hello'
    [handler script]"
```

```
' onBlur="[handler script]"
```

Why Is the Script Failing?

Once you know where the problem resides, you're halfway there. However, although the script may be failing at a particular line, the problem may actually reside elsewhere in the code. In fact, the statements and routines leading up to the failing line of script may even contain multiple errors.

The first thing to do is to read the failing line carefully to be sure you understand exactly what it's supposed to be doing. (This is where previous commenting of the code comes in mighty handy.) Sometimes you'll look at the code and immediately see the problem—though if additional errors are occurring before the line is reached, fixing the line at hand won't solve the entire problem right away. Sometimes, even when there *is* an error in the line, you might not see it right away.

If the line appears to be doing its job correctly (whether it actually is or not), or if you fix the line and the script still fails, you'll need to embark upon a Holmesian investigation to deduce the true cause of the problem. Begin at the place where the script fails and follow the code backwards, looking for the common mistakes chronicled in the next three sections.

Syntax Errors

These errors are usually spotted by the interpreter, which will return an error dialog with a description like "expected end of statement." Look to see that every "if" has an "end if," every "sub" has an "end sub," every "for repeat" has a "next," and so forth; that you aren't missing needed parentheses, or using parentheses when the browser doesn't want them; that you've passed the right arguments to built-in functions or methods; and that all other VBScript language elements are written correctly in your script.

> **TIP** As soon as you type the opening statement of a control structure, type its ending statement at the same time—before you type any of its internal statements. This can help prevent "expected end of statement" errors, especially in a nested control structure that contains lots of loops or conditionals or both. For instance, if you are putting together a sub that begins with a conditional, type your opening and closing statements first. (If you are using the Script Debugger, it'll complete your control structures for you.)

```
sub thisSub()

    if [condition] then

    end if

end sub
```

Although the VBScript error dialog's description of the problem may be incomplete or even incorrect at times, it still provides a clue to the problem. Even when the location coordinates and description of the problem are *both* wrong, taken together, they can usually point you in the right direction.

If the interpreter accuses you of forgetting an end statement in a script that *does* include a proper end statement, perhaps one of the lines above it contains a syntax error that's throwing the interpreter off.

If the interpreter thinks an object doesn't exist, perhaps you've presented it incorrectly; forgetting to precede the name of the object with its parent, or misspelling the object's pseudonym—to name a few possibilities.

> **TIP** Current implementations of the VBScript engine sometimes fail to recognize a properly named object; particularly form elements. If you run into this problem with a form element, here's one of those aforementioned workarounds. Try changing the location of the script that refers to the object to an inline script within the parent form object. Then you can dispense with the formal naming hierarchy (document.formObject), and simply refer to the object by psuedonym or elements array position.

Once you've used the information from the VBScript dialog to determine the exact nature of the problem, you may need to follow it up with a little research to figure out how to correct the problem. If it looks like a particular function or method or property isn't behaving as expected, for instance, you may need to look it up in this book's (or Microsoft's online) reference to review its correct syntax and use.

> **NOTE** Advice to "look up" a misbehaving language element may appear to be a statement of the obvious. Checking a language reference is the first thing you'd do, right? At one time or another, all programmers refuse to believe they've made a mistake in implementing a language element; especially one that they've successfully used in the recent past. If you do any significant amount of VBScripting at all, there'll come a time when you'll wrestle with a bit of script—prehaps for hours—before it even occurs to you that you might be using the crucial language elements incorrectly.

Typos and Spelling Errors

When faced with a failing line of script, immediately check the line for misspelled object, sub, function, method, and property names, in addition to misspelled variable names. In fact, if nothing else seems to be wrong with the code, you might check the spelling of each language element in the failing script against its spelling in Part II of this book, or in any other VBScript language reference.

TIP Typos and misspellings may be the biggest source of bugs in any programming environment. This is especially true in an environment like VBScript that currently requires you to type every line of code by hand (with a little bit of help from the ActiveX Control Pad). You can avoid a large portion of these errors by getting into the habit of using the Copy and Paste functions of your text or HTML editor to copy and paste all previously typed language elements. You can also place an "option explicit" statement at the top of each <SCRIPT> tag to enforce the use of the DIM statement to declare variables. This prevents the browser from treating a mistyped variable name as a completely new variable.

A related error may revolve around the accidental use of a VBScript keyword to name a variable, sub, function, or argument. The interpreter should catch this problem for you, but you might still check a failing line for possible keyword abuses. Adopting a clear naming convention for your self-created elements can help prevent such accidental abuses from ever occurring.

Data Evaluation Errors

Having pinpointed the location of the problem and reviewed the resulting error by running the script in the browser, you should by now have some idea of what's causing the problem. One common source of nonsyntax-related errors is the passage of "bad" data.

Data, as you know, is passed using user-created variables, procedural arguments, or object properties. If you're passing data to the value property of an editable field, then you'll be able to see that data as soon as it is placed into the field. If the wrong data is appearing, you need only to work backward from the line of script that places the data into the field, looking at every mechanism used to collect and pass that data to the field until you discover the place where it goes "bad."

This is also the procedure to follow if a variable, a procedural argument, or any other object property is receiving bad data. But how do you discover if an internal script element, such as a variable, is receiving bad data? If the Script Debugger is available for IE4, you can use it to view information that is being collected and passed in any data container *while the scripting is running*. In lieu of this tool, you can create your own scheme for tracking the values passed using one of the methods discussed in "Tracking Data through an Entire Script" and "Tracking Data through a Repeat Loop."

Once you've found the line of script that's creating bad data, you'll need to figure out why the resulting data is bad:

- Is the data being evaluated from an incorrectly written expression?

- Does the evaluation rely on other variable data containers which could, in turn, contain incorrect data?

- Does every element in the expression conform to the datatype required by the expression's operators?

- Is the data the result of a faulty logical expression (where, perhaps, you used AND when you should have used OR)?

These are the most common reasons for data corruption, but there are almost as many other reasons, and subtle variations on these reasons, as there are programmers. If you've got a good working knowledge of VBScript, put on your thinking cap and study the errant piece of code in earnest. Use your knowledge (or your most handy VBScript reference material) to carefully work through the problem.

What appears to be single failure on the browser side often results from several errors that have accumulated within a long procedure or function, or a many-branched conditional, or a nested repeat loop, or other complex sections of the script. These problems are harder to solve and must be dealt with by working carefully through the code, the logic, each evaluated expression, and so forth, until you've untangled the entire, ugly mess.

If you engage in thorough Unit testing as you build your code, you shouldn't run into severe tangles in the code very often. Proper Unit testing requires you to test and debug each piece of a larger, complex section of script as you piece that section together. Probably the biggest source of "unholy messes" in a carefully designed, tested, and coded project is the unanticipated addition of features or functions after most or all of the project has been coded. Needless to say, such additions should be as carefully analyzed and cautiously incorporated into the existing system as time and resources allow.

Tracking Data through an Entire Script

The simplest technique for tracking data through a script is to use an alert dialog to display the contents of its data container at critical points along the way. To use this technique, place an alert statement just above the line that you suspect is receiving bad data. (You've already determined at least a starting point for this operation by following the "Where Is the Script Failing?" procedures.) Pass the name of the target data container to the alert method. Although you can also pass the alert the name of a procedural argument or an object property, this example tracks the contents of a variable.

```
alert theVariable
```

Debugging Complex Expressions

If you're having trouble getting a complex expression to produce the correct result, try breaking it down into smaller chunks and placing the result of each chunk into its own variable. For instance, if you're unsuccessfully performing a mathematical calculation on data typed into three text fields, try placing the value of each field into its own variable first, then performing the calculation.

To do so, you would take the original expression . . .

```
theTotal = document.forms(0).fld1.value * document.forms(0).fld2.value
/ document.forms(0).fld3.value
```

. . . and break it into these smaller chunks...

```
fld1Val = document.forms(0).fld1.value
fld2Val = document.forms(0).fld2.value
fld3Val = document.forms(0).fld3.value
```

. . . then use the populated variables in a revised version of the expression:

```
theTotal = fld1Val * fld2Val / fld3Val
```

Dividing a complex expression into multiple simple expressions sometimes helps the interpreter to evaluate it properly, but it also helps to pinpoint problems in the way the expression is written. If the expression is broken into smaller chunks and spread out over more lines, when the script fails, it'll point to the particular chunk that is creating the problem.

Perhaps field 3 in the preceding example isn't named "fld3" in its <INPUT> tag. If so, breaking the expression into the sections shown will cause the interpreter to pinpoint the line where this field's value is being assigned to its variable, indicating that the referenced object doesn't exist.

When the script is rerun in the browser with this inserted test statement, the alert dialog box discloses the current contents of the variable passed to it. If the alert discloses the expected value, then something in the line below the alert is corrupting the value of that variable, and that is the line you need to fix. However, you probably reviewed this line when you first identified it as the point of the script's initial failure. If you found no obvious problems at that time, then the alert test is more likely to corroborate the results of the lower line.

If the alert does report the same incorrect value as the line below it, find the previous point in the script where the variable is evaluated (or otherwise manipulated) before it gets to the failing line, and place the alert line below that line of script. When you run the script, the alert will disclose the contents of the variable *right after* the evaluation (or manipulation) has occurred.

If the data is bad at this point, move the alert line above the line that just manipulated it, to see what was in the variable before that line performed its operation on the variable. If running the script discloses a correct version of the data—the line below the alert is the place where the data becomes incorrect—and that's the line that needs fixing.

If the alert reveals the data to be bad before it gets to the line you're testing, keep moving the alert backward in the script's execution sequence; placing it after, then before every point where the data container is manipulated until you find the place where the data is getting corrupted.

> **NOTE** The word script is used loosely here. You shouldn't be limiting your efforts to the current script tag, or event handler, or any other separate script segment. As you know, scripts can call other scripts. You need to trace the data back through the entire calling chain until you find exactly when and where its container receives an incorrect value. You may even discover that it began life with corrupted values (a sad commentary on today's virtual world).

When you finally locate the exact place where the data become corrupted, you've found at least one place in your script that needs reworking. Review the previous discussion and suggestions in this section for insights on how to fix it or fashion a workaround.

> **TIP** An alternative to using the alert method to track the data is to use the *prompt* method. This method can be invoked instead of the alert method as follows. This procedure allows you to artificially inject the correct the data into the target container so the rest of the script can run its course.
>
> ```
> theVariable = prompt theVariable
> ```

Tracking Data through a Repeat Loop

If you just want to verify that a repeat loop is executing correctly, you may only need to let it run once or twice. To do so, temporarily adjust conditions that you are passing to the loop so that it only executes the desired number of test loops. For instance, if you are testing a counting repeat loop, set its high range to the same number as the low range (to run the loop once), or to just 1 or 2 above that range (to run the loop a few times).

In the following example, a counting repeat is supposed to loop as many times as there are elements in *myArray*. To test one iteration of the loop, the expression that represents the high end of the counting loop's range is commented out, and 0 is put in its place. When the script is executed, this loop will only run once, and only perform its internal operation upon the first element in myArray.

```
for i = 0 to 0 ' myArray.length-1
```

If you are passing data through a repeat loop that modifies that data at every turn, you may need to check the contents of the data container at every iteration. If the repeat script is set to run for a large number of loops (say, 10 or more), placing an alert dialog in the loop has its drawbacks—the main one being that the alert dialog box is going to show itself as many times as there are loops. Each time it does, you'll need to make a note of the alert's contents, and click it away. If you need to test the loop repeatedly, you'll quickly tire of the whole exercise. To avoid such tedium, you may prefer to set up a temporary grid of fields on the page to instantly display each evaluation of the data returned during the execution of the entire loop.

To create the grid, go to the bottom of the HTML document that contains the script you want to test. Before the </BODY> tag, create a new <FORM> object, and as many <INPUT TYPE="text"> objects as there are loops in your repeat. If your repeat loop's ending range is based on a variable value, create the highest number of fields that could possibly be needed.

Next, add a line to the repeat loop that places each evaluation of the variable into one of the waiting fields. Here's an example that creates a 15-field at the bottom of the page, then adds a line of script (shown in bold) to a counting repeat loop that will place the value of *theVariable* into a waiting field after each iteration of the loop (see Figures 14.2 and 14.3).

```
<CENTER>
<FORM NAME="thisForm">
<INPUT TYPE="text" size=5>
<INPUT TYPE="text" size=5>
<INPUT TYPE="text" size=5>
<INPUT TYPE="text" size=5>
<INPUT TYPE="text" size=5>
<p>
<INPUT TYPE="text" size=5>
<INPUT TYPE="text" size=5>
<INPUT TYPE="text" size=5>
<INPUT TYPE="text" size=5>
<INPUT TYPE="text" size=5>
```

```
<p>
<INPUT TYPE="text" size=5>
<INPUT TYPE="text" size=5>
<INPUT TYPE="text" size=5>
<INPUT TYPE="text" size=5>
<INPUT TYPE="text" size=5>
<p>
<INPUT TYPE="button"

onClick="for i = 0 to 14
theVariable = theVariable+10
elements(i).value = theVariable
next"

VALUE=" Click Me ">

<CENTER>
</BODY>
</HTML>
```

Figure 14.2 The Variable Watcher Test Grid fields are placed on the page, along with a button that executes the repeat loop script.

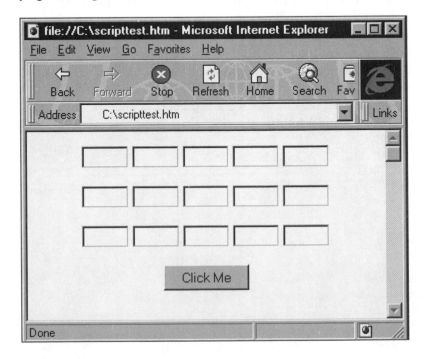

Figure 14.3 When the button is clicked, the results of each iteration of the loop are placed in a successive field, showing the value contained in theVariable at each step in the process.

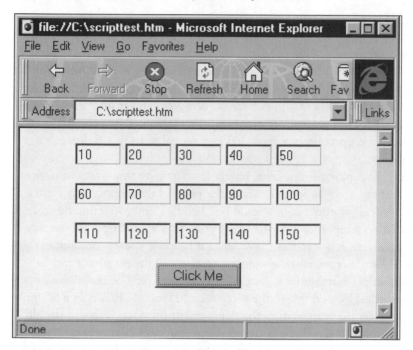

Of course, in a real-life situation, you won't need to create a button to execute the script. You'll execute it in the normal way that it is executed for the particular page. Also, this example supposes that the range passed to the counting loop results in a sequence of numbers that matches the element array positions of the "variable watcher" grid fields.

If this is not the case, you'll need to create enough fields to accommodate all iterations of the loop, even if its beginning number causes it to skip one or more of those fields. The following loop, for instance, would begin populating the fifth field in the elements array. Five more fields must thus be created to accommodate the entire loop.

```
for i = 4 to 18

    theVariable = +10
    document.forms(1).elements(i).value = theVariable

next
```

> **TIP** If you prefer not to look at empty fields, you could create five hidden fields first.

Error Handling

In addition to adopting good coding conventions, user-centered design principles, formal testing procedures, and responsible debugging practices, you can also build a certain amount of error handling directly into your pages. Using a combination of the *on error resume next* statement and the *err* object, you can set up your scripts to anticipate certain VBScript interpreter errors, and code your pages to recover from them—or at least keep your user from having to deal with the interpreter's unfriendly error dialog.

Before discussing the deployment of error-handling scripts, it's important to understand that error handling is not supposed to take the place of debugging. Any errors that result from improperly written code should be "handled" by correcting the code. You can, however, insert temporary error-handling code into your scripts for use as a debugging tool. The *on error...* statement is handy for keeping a script running in the wake of a known VBScript error, and the number property of the *err* object can be used to discover VBScript's number for a particular type of error. The usefulness of this last operation is described by example in the section on "Handling Errors in a Script."

Error-handling scripts that are written for deployment on your Web site should exist only for the purpose of handling errors that you can't fix at the script level, or that would require so much "convoluted" workaround scripting that it isn't worth it, or perhaps isn't possible to code within the crunching timelines of a mission-critical project. This is especially acceptable in cases where the error only occurs in the aftermath of a rare user action or sequence of actions.

Of course, as noted in this chapter's introduction, it is well-nigh impossible to catch every bug in your code, and even the most conscientiously tested software is deployed with undetected bugs. Thus, if you have a page where certain user actions might result in page-debilitating errors (whether due to undetected inadequacies in your own code or in the interpreter's code), it is prudent to provide an error handler within those critical code blocks to tell the user what just occurred.

Bypassing Errors in a Script

The simplest way to implement error handling in your code is to strategically deploy the *on error resume next* statement throughout a page of scripts. By placing this statement at the top of any subroutines, functions, or other blocks of code that instruct the browser to perform multiple actions or call other blocks of code, you can at least be assured that if one action causes an error, it won't halt the execution of remaining actions in the calling chain.

Of course, if one action in a series of actions fails, the consequences may domino, causing subsequent statements to execute improperly as well. The only thing you gain from the *on error...* statement in a situation like this is the shielding of your user from the formidable VBScript error dialog. There are times when this is a worthwhile result all by itself—even if whatever you intended to occur on the page does *not* occur (or occurs improperly)—since there are many instances when such results are not fatal or even particularly important.

An example is a script that performs a mathematical calculation using the current user's age. The age information is obtained when the user types that data into an Age field on the page, and tabs or clicks from the field. The value of the Age field is then used to determine how old the user will be in the year 2000, and the answer is presented to the user in an alert dialog. When the user clicks away the alert, a confirm dialog then asks whether the user wishes to play a game. If the user clicks OK, he or she is taken to the Game Page.

```
sub ageFld_onBlur()


    on error resume next


    DIM theCurYear,theDifYears


    theCurYear = year(date)
    theDifYears = 2000 - theCurYear


    alert "In the year 2000, you will be " & theDifYears +
document.forms(0).ageFld.value & " years old."


    if confirm "Do you want to play a game?" then


        navigate "game.htm"


    end if


end sub
```

The problem with this script is that it might easily run into an error if the user leaves the Age field filled with an alphabetic character, or a number like "2.2.1," or anything other than a whole integer—including, leaving the field empty. In such cases, the line of script that performs the mathematical calculation ends in a VBScript "type mismatch" error.

To avoid this type of error, you could write a routine that checks the data in the field before passing it to the calculating expression. In the current example, however, an *on error resume next* statement has instead been placed on the opening line of the sub. Now, if the user types the wrong type of data into the field (or does anything else in the field that results in a VBScript error), the alert dialog simply fails to appear. In addition, the VBScript error dialog is successfully suppressed, while the subsequent *if* conditional executes just fine.

TIP The trick with this script is to confine any possible error to the line of script that houses the alert statement. After all, the whole idea of this exercise is to surpress the "year 2000" alert if improper age data causes a calculation error. If, instead, you wrote:

```
newAge = document.forms(0).ageFld.value + theDifYears
alert "In the year 2000, you will be " & newAge & " years old."
```

. . . the script would fail at the line that populates the newAge variable, then obey the *on error...* statement's instruction to execute the next line;—the line which invokes the very alert you're seeking to suppress. Because of the previous calculation error, the alert's display message would be written using an empty "newAge" variable. Hardly an efficient way to handle an error that you took such pains to anticipate.

Handling Errors in a Script

While the *on error...* statement does have its solo uses, it is often better employed as a partner in crime to the *err* object. Combining the two gives you more than just a mechanism for suppressing the uninformative VBScript error dialog and resuming the execution of the remaining script. Use of the *err* object provides you with an avenue for informing the user of the error and how it may affect the current operation, as well as an opportunity to tell the user how to recover from the error.

Handling VBScript Errors

A quick and dirty way to add VBScript error-handling to a script would be to include a conditional statement that presents a generic response to the user if *any*

VBScript error occurs. The *err* object's number property can be commandeered for this purpose:

```
if err.number then
```

```
    alert "An error just occurred in the operation you are performing, and the
results will not be accurate. If you wish to begin again, reload this page."
```

```
end if
```

If an error occurs, the err object's number property is populated (and therefore true), and the if condition executes. If no error occurs, this property is empty (and therefore false), and the if condition is not executed.

> **TIP** Since the err object defaults to the number property, you don't actually need to type its name in your script. Simply typing the name of the err object by itself implies the number property.
>
> ```
> if err then
> ```
>
> ```
>     alert "An error just occurred in the operation you are perform-
> ing, and the results will not be accurate. If you wish to begin
> again, reload this page."
> ```
>
> ```
> end if
> ```
>
> Of course, you may wish to explicitly refer to the err object's number property anyway, lest you forget that it's getting called whenever "err" appears alone in a script.

In our previous "year 2000" example, this alert would not be appropriate for the most likely error, which is the type mismatch error. Although this conditional provides for *any* error that might occur, if you know that type mismatches are probable, it would be better to add a branch to your conditional that provides special instructions for this particular error.

The VBScript err object is basically a cut-and-paste of the err object used with any OLE automation object, in any development environment that supports OLE. There's no current documentation for all the error numbers and descriptions specific to VBScript, but you could ferret through Microsoft's OLE documentation for a list of *all* of the errors supported by the err object.

You can also discover the number and official description of any expected error type in VBScript by adding the following conditional to a script, loading the page, and generating the error. In our current example, loading the page with this test script in it, and typing "1.2.2" into the Age field, brings up an alert indicating that the number for this type of error is 13, and its description is "type mismatch."

```
if err then

    alert err.number & "," & err.description

 end if
```

Now that the number of the type mismatch error is known, a branch can be added to the error handling conditional that provides a special response to this particular error. In this example, the conditional control structure is changed from an if statement, to a select case statement (shown below in bold):

```
sub ageFld_onBlur()


    on error resume next


    DIM theCurYear,theDifYears


    theCurYear = year(date)

    theDifYears = 2000 - theCurYear


    alert "In the year 2000, you will be " & theDifYears +
document.forms(0).ageFld.value & " years old."


    select case err.number


        case 13


            alert "Please type a valid age number into this field."
```

```
    case else


        alert "An unrecoverable error has occurred. Please reload the
page."


    end select


    if confirm "Do you want to play a game?" then


        navigate "game.htm"


    end if



end sub
```

Now when the user types the wrong datatype into the field, an alert asks the user to type a valid age number. If any other error occurs, the *case else* clause throws up an alternative alert, advising the user to reload the page (see Figure 14.4).

Figure 14.4 Typing the wrong datatype into the Age field in the "year 2000" page brings up this alert, showing the number and description of the resulting error.

Placing Your Error-Handling Code in Scripts

You'll often find that the best place to put error-handling code in a script block is after the line or lines in the script where the user might encounter errors. If you place the error-handling code at the *top* of the code block (below the *on error...* statement), it will execute on subsequent errors, but not properly.

If you place error-handling code at the *bottom* of the target code block, it will execute after all other operations in the block have executed. If this latter situation is acceptable—and there are times when it may even be preferrable—then, by all means, place your error-handling code at the bottom of the block. But keep in mind that, if your current code block calls other code blocks (subs, functions, etc.) that also open with the *on error resume next* statement, this statement will clear any previous error from the *err* object's memory—a situation that can get you nowhere, fast.

You can fine-tune your error-handling code even further using the err object's *raise* method. You can use this method to create your own errors (discussed momentarily), or to modify the description of existing VBScript errors. The following conditional could be easily added to the previous example select case statement, under its case 13 clause. By passing different text to the raise method's description argument (its third argument), you can then use whatever ends up in the err object's description property to present the appropriate message.

```
select case err.number



    case 13



        if document.forms(0).ageFld.value = "" then



            err.raise 13,,"your age"



        else



            err.raise 13,,"a valid age number"
```

```
end if
```

```
alert "Please type " & err.description & " into this field."
```

Thanks to the addition of this conditional, if and when the user generates a type mismatch error, the error-handling code now further invesigates the error to see if it resulted from the user leaving the field empty, or typing the wrong datatype into the field (see Figures 14.5 and 14.6). The returned alert can now provide more specific information to the user, via the new contents of the description property for error 13.

> **TIP** You cannot skip the second argument of the raise method (which refers to the source of the error), if you intend to answer its third argument. However, as you can see by the structure of the argument string in the bolded raise statements shown in the current example, you *can* pass nothing to this argument if you simply wish to accept its default OLE automation object (which, in this case, is Internet Explorer).

Figure 14.5 If the user leaves the Age field empty, this alert appears.

Figure 14.6 If the user types the wrong datatype into the Age field, this alert appears.

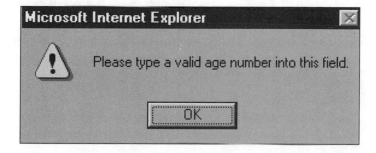

Handling Non-VBScript Errors

Some of the errors generated when users interact with your scripts are not detected by VBScript. Consider, for instance, what happens when an expression in a script is meant to mathematically add together the data input into two fields, and the user fails to type a proper number into one or both fields.

```
theTotal = fld1.value + fld2.value
```

Because of the dual nature of the plus (+) operator, VBScript simply concatenates the values of the fields instead of trying to perform the mathematical calculation. Since no VBScript error is generated by this action, the "bad data" is simply allowed to populate the variable and create whatever havoc it can in your script.

Happily, the err object and its raise method can also be used to handle errors of this type. As with true VBScript errors, you (and your testing team) must anticipate these errors before you can write scripts to handle them. In the current example, the possibility of the user typing something other than a number into either of the target fields is handled as follows:

```
if isNum(theFldVal) = false then

    if theFldVal = ""

        err.raise 1000,,"anything"

    else

        err.raise 2000,,"a number"

    end if

    select case err.number

        case 1000

            alert "You didn't type " & err.description & " into this field."

        case 2000

            alert "You didn't type " & err.description & " into this field."

    end case
```

When the user leaves either calculation field, the value of that field is passed to the *isNum()* function in answer to its theFldVal argument. This function checks the string to determine if it's a valid number. If this function returns false, the raise method creates one of two new errors, depending on whether *theFldVal* is empty, or theFldVal is not a number.

> **WARNING** In the previous example, a valid VBScript error number (13) was passed to the raise method so that its official description property could be modified as desired. In our current example, the idea is to create a unique error (one that isn't already covered by VBScript's existing error codes) to handle problems that wouldn't otherwise generate a VBScript error. For this reason, a unique error *number* must also be passed to the raise method along with an appropriate description. If this number happens to coincide with an existing VBScript error number, you'd be inadvertently revising that error's description for the duration of your script. This only creates a problem if the VBScript error in question occurs during the execution of your script, and you've got code that handles it. Nevertheless, most VBScript programmers takes pains to avoid this possibility by using very high numbers. If you're still worried about conflicts, you can use the err.clear method to erase any changes you may have made to an existing error. Of course, you'll also be erasing your newly created errors.

Centralized Error Handling

If you have several scripts in a page or frameset that are susceptible to errors, you might find it productive to centralize your error-handling code. To do this, you create a subroutine containing one lengthy select case statement that handles all possible errors generated anywhere in the system:

```
sub handleError()
    select case err.number

        case [n]

            [specific error-handling statements]

        case [n]

            [specific error-handling statements]
```

```
        case [n]

            [specific error-handling statements]

        case else

            [generic error-handling statements]

    end select

end sub
```

Insert the following if conditional to check for errors at the appropriate place in each of your vulnerable code blocks. If an error exists, the handleError() sub is duly called to deal with it:

```
if err.number then

    handleError()

end if
```

For more information on the *on error...* statement, see Chapter 9; and for more information on the *err* object and its properties and methods, see Chapters 4, 5, and 6.

What's Next?

Providing for strict testing, debugging, and error-handling in your page-production efforts is the hallmark of excellence in software development. With the close of this chapter, you now have a basic understanding of how these things are done (or *should* be done) in professional development circles. The next step is to put all of this and the previous chapters' knowledge to the test with the advanced scripting projects presented in Part IV.

Part Four
Advanced VBScript

Part IV of the *VBScript Sourcebook* presents fully scripted pages that teach you how to take advantage of DHTML, frames, and external objects (like ActiveX controls) to construct provocative, multimedia-rich Web pages. The emphasis here is the same as it is on today's working Web sites: delivering *dynamic page displays* and *dynamic content* to the breathless browsing public.

The Joys of
Dynamic HTML

Within the context of this book, *dynamic page displays* are displays that rearrange themselves according to the user's actions at run time. An example is this chapter's own advanced scripting tutorial, the *Puzzle Page.*

When the Puzzle Page is initially loaded into the browser, all of the puzzle's pieces are grouped together on the right side of the page (shown in Figure 15.1). As the user clicks and drags one piece of the puzzle into place after another, the display of the page is updated right before the user's eyes (Figure 15.2).

As each piece of the puzzle is moved into place, the user truly appears to be dragging a separate piece of material across the screen. In reality, the browser is working frantically during the entire process, redrawing the screen so quickly and efficiently for each pixel-to-pixel movement that the operation is completely transparent to the naked eye. The beauty of the Dynamic HTML Model is that it allows you to create this impression locally, from a script residing in the displaying page; not from a CGI script posted on a remote server. This local presence of the script is one of the reasons why the update appears so seamless.

In addition to modifying the position, color, and other attributes of already displayed objects on a page, new objects, text, and graphics can be added to that page on-the-fly by a local script. Changing the items that are displayed on the page in reaction to user events is what *dynamic content* is

Figure 15.1 When the Puzzle Page is first displayed in the browser, all of the puzzle pieces appear on the right side of the page.

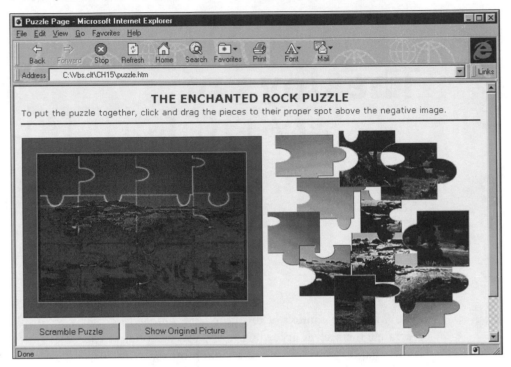

all about. You can decide which images are displayed on a page according to current user choices, or rewrite the titles, link text, paragraph text, and other data on the page as events proceed.

The newly available tools for data-binding bring additional aid to the race for dynamic content, allowing you to attach data in a text file to a specific HTML object on the page (such as a field), so that *records* of data associated with that field can be viewed on-demand by the user, or put into tables that can be resorted at a left-click of the mouse. (See Chapter 16's "Client Address Book" for an in-depth look at how to incorporate data-binding into your own scripts.) Once again, all of this dynamic action takes place without a single return trip to the server.

Chapter Structure

Although Part IV kicks off with a chapter specifically aimed at introducing you to the joys of Dynamic HTML, the truth is that all three chapters in this part of the book rely heavily on the wide-open object model represented by DHTML. Thus,

Figure 15.2 As the user clicks and drags a puzzle piece across the screen, the page display is updated so rapidly that it seems as if the user is moving a real puzzle piece from place to place.

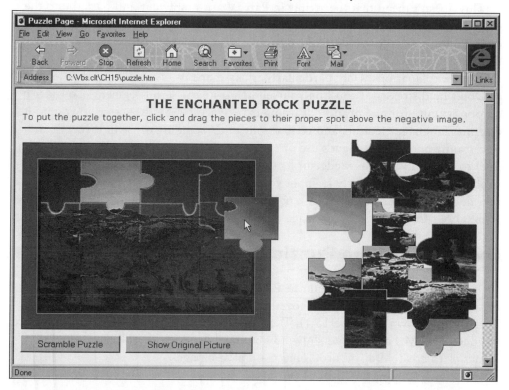

although previous scripts in this book should work well with versions 3.02 *and* 4.0 of Internet Explorer, you *must* install IE4 to view and use the Web page applications described in this part of the book. You'll find it best to load the example page for each chapter into the IE4 browser and review its operation as you read the chapter explanations. Each example is located on the Web site (www.wiley.com/compbooks/mara/).

The chapters in Part IV have been written with the advanced VBScript user in mind. This doesn't mean that the scripts in this part of the book are necessarily more complicated than earlier scripts (many of which were quite complex). It means that the accompanying explanations are shorter, assuming that you understand enough VBScript to figure out what the scripts are doing without a detailed explanation of each and every line.

If you began this book as a new or intermediate VBScript user, and worked your way through all of the previous parts of the book, then you should certainly consider yourself an advanced user. Don't be afraid of tackling the scripts head on; if you take the time to work through the logic, you'll have very little trouble getting the gist of the script, or any other VBScript you care to consume.

This doesn't mean that the scripts in Part IV are simply cut-and-pasted into the chapter text without further ado. As with the Part III Web page examples, each chapter presents an overview of its example page that explains the page's operations; then reviews its script in logical segments—albeit with shorter and less involved explanations. Only particularly tricky maneuvers are discussed at length.

Don't be distressed if you find yourself *at sea* in any script segment. Consider it an opportunity for an advanced learning experience. Break the script down into its essential language elements and review your understanding of each. If there's any uncertainly about an element's use or syntax, look it up in this book's index (or on line) to expand your knowledge of its implementation. If you work through the problem in a steady, orderly fashion, you're bound to find the answer. And when you find the answer through this kind of research, you'll probably end up knowing more about this part of the language than the average VBScripter.

Overview of the Puzzle Page

As explained in the introduction, the Puzzle Page contains a jigsaw puzzle that a browsing user can physically put together by dragging the puzzle pieces onto the Puzzle Bed (shown in Figure 15.1). The tutorial purpose of this page is to introduce the new DHTML model, and show how it may be used with older elements of VBScript to create drag 'n' drop objects on a Web page.

> **W W W** The Puzzle Page is located on the companion Web site. To use this page on your local system, go to www.wiley.com/compbooks/mara with the IE4 browser, link to Chapter 15, and download the entire folder. Then load puzzle.htm into the browser.

The operation of the Puzzle Page is simplicity itself. When the page is loaded into IE4, a Puzzle Bed with a negative view of Enchanted Rock (an ancient power place in the Texas Hill Country) appears on the left, and 12 puzzle pieces appear on the right. Figure 15.1 and 15.2 show the opening view of the page, and how pieces may be clicked and dragged into place on the Puzzle Bed.

Clicking the "Scramble Puzzle" button returns the page to its original condition, emptying the Puzzle Bed and scattering the 12 pieces around on the area to its right (shown in Figure 15.1). If the original picture is in view when the Scramble Puzzle button is clicked, it remains in view in the Puzzle Bed until and unless the user clicks the button to hide it.

The Puzzle Page Scripts

The Puzzle Page is built from the following four script segments:

- Segment 1 handles possible errors

- Segment 2 provides the underlying code dragging and dropping the puzzle pieces.

- Segment 3 rescrambles the puzzle pieces so the user can play again.

- Segment 4 lets the user show or hide a seamless view of the original Enchanted Rock picture (see Figures 15.3 and 15.4).

Figure 15.3 Here's the completed puzzle.

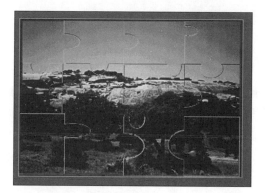

Figure 15.4 Clicking the Show Original Picture button places a seamless view of the Enchanted Rock picture into the Puzzle Bed, and changes the name of the button to "Hide Original Picture." Clicking the button again hides the picture.

Segment 1: Error Handling

In deference to the previous chapter's discussion of error handling—and as a working example of this important programming concept—some error-handling code has been included in this script, centralized in a special subroutine called *handleError()*:

```
sub handleError()

    DIM theMsg,theBtn

    SET theBtn = window.event.srcElement

    theMsg = "The following error has occurred: " & vbCrLf & vbLf & err.description & vbCrLf & vbLf & "If you keep getting this error, reload the page and don't use the " & theBtn.value & " button."

    msgBox theMsg,48,"Error Message"

end sub
```

This handleError() sub is called by the following line of script, at the bottom of the code blocks that execute when the "Scramble Puzzle" or "Show/Hide Original Picture" buttons are clicked:

```
if err.number then handleError()
```

As discussed in Chapter 14, if an error occurs (and the number property of the err object is not empty) then the handleError() routine uses the err object to provide a description of the error in one of the error messages shown in Figures 15.5 and 15.6.

Figure 15.5 This message is presented if an error occurs after clicking the "Scramble Puzzle" button.

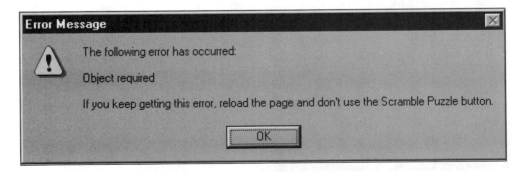

Figure 15.6 This message is presented if an error occurs after clicking the "Show Original Picture" button.

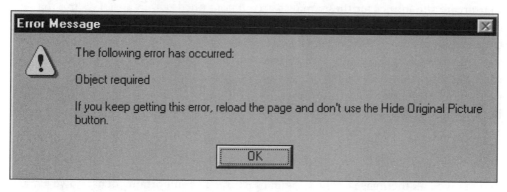

The final bit of error handling is the simple inclusion of the *on error resume next* statement at the top of the script block that contains the drag 'n' drop code. Since it's difficult to anticipate what errors might occur during its execution (none did during testing), no recovery path is provided for this script, and the handleError() sub is not called. However, if an error does occur, the *on error…* statement at least assures that the script will continue to process whatever it can of the user's actions.

> **N O T E** Of particular interest in this script are the lines that set theBtn variable to the object that produced the error.
>
> ```
> DIM theMsg, theBtn
> SET theBtn = window.event.srcElement
> ```
>
> This script uses the new DHTML *event* object and its *srcElement* property to determine which button received the current event (which is a *click*, since this script segment isn't called unless one of the page's two buttons is clicked—*and an error occurs*).

Segment 2: Drag 'n' Drop

The centerpiece of the Puzzle Page is a subroutine that executes for the entire *document* object on the *mouseMove* event. This is another new operation made possible by the dynamic HTML object model, which allows the document object to intercept an event for all of its children. Since the mouseMove sub's job is to animate the current puzzle piece, before discussing its operation, let's review the HTML that provides for the appearance of these individual puzzle pieces.

There are 12 puzzle pieces on this page; each presented as an inline GIF image that has been named pz1.gif, pz2.gif—all the way up to pz12.gif. The <IMG> tags that create the inlines for these images are all contained within a <DIV> tag that defines a region of the page. In this case, that region is as wide as the user makes the current window (100%) but it is always 400 pixels high, regardless of window size. As a result, when you move the pieces around on the page, you'll find that they can't move any further than the page's left and top margins. If you move a piece beyond the right or bottom margins, you won't be stopped but the piece will begin to disappear.

```
<DIV ID="pzDiv" STYLE="POSITION:relative;WIDTH:100%;HEIGHT:400px">
```

The <IMG> tags placed within the <DIV> tag include the image of the Puzzle Bed, as well as the image of the Original Picture. The important focus, however, are the tags that are created for each of the puzzle pieces. These are the only pieces that will move when dragged.

The <IMG> tag for each of the 12 pieces is identical in structure. Each <IMG> is given an ID that numbers it, and reflects its original left (x) and top (y) pixel screen locations. (You'll find out why this is done in the Segment 3 discussion.)

```
    <IMG ID="pz1_190_450"
STYLE="POSITION:absolute;TOP:190pt;LEFT:450pt;WIDTH:89px;HEIGHT:81px;ZINDEX:3;"
SRC="pz1.gif">
```

The GIF file for each image contains its number, and puzzle pieces are numbered starting from the top row of the puzzle and moving right. This is not important; just an orderly means of naming and tracking the images.

> **TIP** The original x,y coordinates for each of <IMG> tags that contain a puzzle piece are set by trial and error. They are set by points in this example, but pixels can also be used. A trial setting was typed for each, the page loaded, and the resulting position of the <IMG> reviewed. If it wasn't in a good spot, the settings were modified, and the page reloaded.

Each puzzle piece is given a *layer* to sit on in the HTML document, defined in its <IMG> tag by the ZINDEX argument.

When this HTML document is loaded into IE4, and the user begins to move the mouse around the page, the mouseMove event's arguments are constantly updated with the latest information on the mouse's activities. It tracks the position of its buttons (if the left mouse button is down, button equals 1), as well as the x,y screen coordinates of its pointer.

> **N O T E** In the case of this particular script, whether the shift key is up or down is irrelevant; the script works the same either way. Nevertheless, proper syntax requires the appearance of this argument in its proper place in the argument string.
>
> ```
> sub document_onMouseMove(button,shift,x,y)
> ```

Three variables are immediately declared: *target* (to hold the document's child object for whom the mouseMove event is to be processed), *newLeft* (to hold the new x coordinate), and *newTop* (to hold the new y coordinate).

```
DIM target,newLeft,newTop
```

If the left mouse button is down, then the mouseMove sub's top if statement executes. (If not, nothing happens, since it has no *else* clause.)

```
if (button = 1) then
```

The first action the script takes *if the left button is down* is to set the "target" variable to the object that fired the event. The event object and its handy *srcElement* property are again used for this purpose, and when this line of script is done executing, "target" becomes an alias to the event-firing object.

```
SET target = window.event.srcElement
```

Next, the script discovers what kind of object fired the event via the *tagname* property (which is valid for any object produced by an HTML tag). If the mouseMove event is fired by an object produced by the <IMG> tag, but the image's ID is "puzzleBed" or ""original," then the *endMove()* sub is called upon to cancel the mouseMove event.

```
if target.tagname = "IMG" then

    if target.id = "puzzleBed" OR target.id = "original" then
```

```
endMove()
```

The endMove() sub actually follows the mouseMove sub in the script, but since it's been called, we'll quickly review it before finishing with the mouseMove script.

```
sub endMove()

    window.event.returnValue = false
    window.event.cancelBubble = true

end sub
```

This simple sub uses the event object's *returnValue* and *cancelBubble* properties to be doubly sure to squash the event. The movement of the mouse is so constant and pervasive in a mouse-driven environment, you want to be sure that nothing happens unless the user is actually clicking and dragging on a puzzle piece.

If the ID of the image is *not puzzleBed* or *original,* then the *else* clause executes a routine that constantly updates the *newLeft* and *newTop* variables with the ongoing information passed to (and processed by) the mouseMove event's x and y arguments. This portion of the script is the heart and soul of the drag 'n' drop routine and here's how it works.

Each time the x information for the currently dragged puzzle piece changes, the *docLeft* property of the enclosing <DIV> tag is subtracted from the new number in x, and half of the width of the puzzle piece is subtracted from the result. If newLeft results in a number less than zero (a coordinate outside the current <DIV> tag region), newLeft is set to 0.

```
newLeft = x - document.all.pzDiv.docLeft - (target.docWidth/2)

if newLeft < 0 then newLeft = 0
```

At the same time, whenever the y information for the currently dragged puzzle piece changes, the *docTop* property of the <DIV> tag is subtracted from the new number in y, and half of the height of the puzzle piece is subtracted from the result. If newTop equals a number less than 0, it is set to 0.

```
newTop = y - document.all.pzDiv.docTop - (target.docHeight/2)

if newTop < 0 then newTop = 0
```

Once the newLeft and newTop variables have been properly populated, the LEFT and TOP arguments of the target puzzle piece's STYLE argument are reset and the onscreen location of the object is changed accordingly.

```
target.style.left = newLeft
target.style.top = newTop
endMove()
```

When all of this is accomplished (and, remember, as the user is moving the object around on the page, this sub is constantly re-executing!), the *endMove()* sub is called upon to perform its double-whammy cancel operation.

Here is the mouseMove sub in its entirety:

```
sub document_onMouseMove(button,shift,x,y)

    on error resume next
    DIM target,newLeft,newTop

    if (button = 1) then

        SET target = window.event.srcElement

        if target.tagname = "IMG" then

            if target.id = "puzzleBed" OR target.id = "original" then

                endMove()

            else
                newLeft = x - document.all.div1.docLeft   (target.docWidth/2)

                if newLeft < 0 then newLeft = 0

                newTo p= y - document.all.div1.docTop - (target.docHeight/2)

                if newTop < 0 then newTop = 0

                target.style.left = newLeft
                target.style.top = newTop

                endMove()

            end if

        end if

    end if

end sub
```

Segment 3: Scramble Operation

The *scramble* operation is a very simple subroutine that executes when the user clicks the Scramble Puzzle button. Its primary code block is a for repeat loop that is executed on every element in the document object's *all* array whose tag name is <IMG>. Within the loop, each image's ID property is reviewed to see if it contains an underscore (_). Only puzzle piece image IDs contain an underscore, so the remaining script only executes for these pieces.

The ID is then split into a three-element array. The first element simply houses its *pz* number, and is not important. Elements 1 and 2, however, end up housing the original x,y coordinates of the puzzle piece. (Now you know why the strange *pz1_190_450* naming convention is used.) The information in elements 1 and 2 of the array are then used to restore the puzzle pieces to their original location to the right of the puzzle bed.

```
sub scramble_onClick()

    on error resume next
    DIM numElements,imgID,thePos
    numElements = document.all.length

    for i = 0 to numElements-1

        if document.all(i).tagname = "IMG" then

            imgID = document.all(i).id

            if inStr(1,imgID,"_") <> 0 then

                thePos = split(document.all(i).id,"_")
                document.all(i).style.top = thePos(1) & "pt"
                document.all(i).style.left = thePos(2) & "pt"

            end if

        end if

        if err.number then handleError()

    next

end sub
```

N O T E   Curiously, when you scramble the puzzle pieces, all of the pieces return to their original locales except the pieces labeled "A" and "B" in Figure 15.7. These two pieces actually end up even further from their original spots than shown here, if their IDs include the original screen coordinates. To adjust their positioning, the IDs for these two images include slightly different coordinates than those given to their enclosing tags' TOP and LEFT arguments. (Check the HTML carefully and you'll see this.) Whether this behavior is related to an error in the interpreter's calculations, or the result of some other problem, it's mentioned here in case you need to provide for this anomaly in your own adaptations of this script.

Segment 4: Viewing Original Picture

The script that powers the "Show Original Picture" button is the simplest of all. When the user first clicks it, a seamless, positive view of the Enchanted Rock picture appears in front of the negative image (or any puzzle pieces) in the Puzzle Bed. At the same time, the display name of the button is changed to "Hide Original Picture."

Figure 15.7 The illustration on the left shows the original position of all the puzzle pieces, and the illustration on the right shows the position of the pieces after clicking the Scramble Puzzle button. The pieces marked "A" and "B" are not returned to their original places.

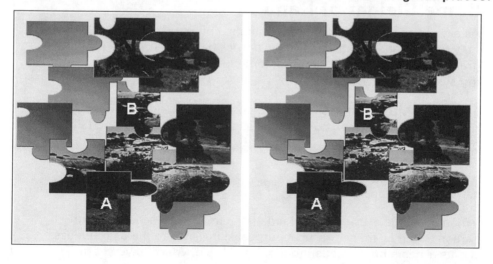

If the user clicks the button while its name contains "Hide," the picture is hidden from view, and the button's name is changed back to "Show Original Picture."

```
sub origBtn_onClick()

    on error resume next

    if document.forms(0).origBtn.value = "Show Original Picture" then

        original.style.top=41
        original.style.left=27
        document.forms(0).origBtn.value = "Hide Original Picture"

    elseif document.forms(0).origBt.value = "Hide Original Picture" then

        original.style.top=3150
        original.style.left=2000
        document.forms(0).origBtn.value = "Show Original Picture"

    end if

        if err.number then handleError()

end sub
```

Some Sleight of Hand

As simple as this script is, it *does* contain a bit of black magic which you may have already spotted. This clever trick has been used by GUI programmers since time immemorial (or at least since the first GUI operating system was invented).

First, the <IMG> tag that creates and positions the "original" image is given impossible screen coordinates as answers to its TOP and LEFT arguments:

```
    <IMG ID="original"
STYLE="POSITION:absolute;TOP:3150pt;LEFT:2000pt;WIDTH:325px;HEIGHT=22
9px; ZINDEX:15;" SRC="seamless.gif">
```

When the page is loaded or reloaded, the image is placed so far off screen that it is, for all practical purposes, invisible to the user (unless the user has a humongous monitor, the likes of which have yet to appear in the mainstream commercial market).

If the user clicks the button to show the picture, its TOP and LEFT arguments are reset to screen coordinates that will place it *exactly* within the Puzzle Bed frame. As before, these coordinates were determined through trial, error, and repeated adjustments.

```
original.style.top=41
original.style.left=27
```

If the user clicks the button to hide the picture again, its TOP and LEFT arguments are set back to the impossible (offscreen) coordinates, and the image is once again hidden from view.

```
original.style.top=3150
original.style.left=2000
```

Putting the Puzzle Page Together

These are the basics of the Puzzle Page. When putting a page like this together, the key is in the coordination of the general HTML with the VBScript portions of the page. All of the moveable elements that are placed on the page via standard HTML must be carefully named and styled to cooperate with the scripting routines that will handle their fired events. Other dynamically updating elements on the page (such as the picture that can be shown and hidden, or the rescrambling of the puzzle pieces) also benefit from careful choreography.

Take a look at the full script, paying particular attention to how the HTML portions have been set up to interact with VBScript.

The Full Script

```
<HTML>
<HEAD>
<TITLE>Puzzle Page</TITLE>
<SCRIPT LANGUAGE="VBScript">

sub handleError()

    DIM theMsg,theBtn
    SET theBtn = window.event.srcElement

    theMsg = "The following error has occurred: " & vbCrLf & vbLf & err.descrip-
tion & vbCrLf & vbLf & "If you keep getting this error, reload the page and
don't use the " & theBtn.value & " button."
```

```
    msgBox theMsg,48,"Error Message"

end sub

sub document_onMouseMove(button,shift,x,y)

    on error resume next
    DIM target,newLeft,newTop

    if (button = 1) then

        SET target = window.event.srcElement

        if target.tagname = "IMG" then    ' if the target tag is <IMG>

            if target.id = "puzzleBed" OR target.id = "original" then

                endMove()

            else

                newLeft = x - document.all.div1.docLeft - (target.docWidth/2)

                if newLeft < 0 then newLeft = 0

                newTop = y - document.all.div1.docTop - (target.docHeight/2)

                if newTop < 0 then newTop = 0

                target.style.left = newLeft
                target.style.top = newTop

                endMove()

            end if

        end if

    end if

end sub
```

```
sub endMove()

   window.event.returnValue = false
   window.event.cancelBubble = true

end sub

sub scramble_onClick()

   on error resume next

   DIM numElements,imgID,thePos
   numElements = document.all.length

   for i = 0 to numElements-1

      if document.all(i).tagname = "IMG" then

         imgID = document.all(i).id

         if inStr(1,imgID,"_") <> 0 then

            thePos = split(document.all(i).id,"_")
            document.all(i).style.top = thePos(1) & "pt"
            document.all(i).style.left = thePos(2) & "pt"

         end if

      end if

      if err.number then handleError()

   next

end sub

sub origBtn_onClick()

   on error resume next

   if document.forms(0).origBtn.value = "Show Original Picture" then
```

```
        original.style.top=41
        original.style.left=27
        document.forms(0).origBtn.value = "Hide Original Picture"

    elseif document.forms(0).origBt.value = "Hide Original Picture" then

        original.style.top=3150
        original.style.left=2000
        document.forms(0).origBtn.value = "Show Original Picture"

    end if

        if err.number then handleError()

end sub

</SCRIPT>
</HEAD>
<BODY TOPMARGIN=10 LEFTMARGIN=10 BGCOLOR="#FFFBEC">
<CENTER>
<FONT COLOR="#800020" FACE="Verdana,Helvetica" SIZE=4>
<B>THE ENCHANTED ROCK PUZZLE</B>
</FONT>
</CENTER>
<FONT COLOR="#800020" FACE="Verdana,Helvetica" SIZE="2">
To put the puzzle together, click and drag the pieces to their proper spot
above the negative image.
</FONT>
<HR SIZE=2 COLOR="#800020" NOSHADE>

<DIV ID="pzDiv" STYLE="POSITION:relative;WIDTH:100%;HEIGHT:400px">

    <IMG ID="puzzleBed" STYLE="POSITION:absolute;TOP:10pt;LEFT:0pt;width: 380px;
height=285px; ZINDEX:2;"  SRC="bed.gif">

    <IMG ID="pz1_190_450"
STYLE="POSITION:absolute;TOP:190pt;LEFT:450pt;WIDTH:89px;HEIGHT:81px;ZINDEX:3;"
SRC="pz1.gif">

    <IMG ID="pz2_10_300"
STYLE="POSITION:absolute;TOP:10pt;LEFT:300pt;WIDTH:112px;HEIGHT:80px;ZINDEX:4;"
SRC="pz2.gif">
```

```
    <IMG ID="pz3_60_325"
STYLE="POSITION:absolute;TOP:60pt;LEFT:325pt;WIDTH:110px;HEIGHT:82px;ZINDEX:5;"
SRC="pz3.gif">


    <IMG ID="pz4_100_290"
STYLE="POSITION:absolute;TOP:100pt;LEFT:290pt;WIDTH:82px;HEIGHT:84px;ZINDEX:6;"
SRC="pz4.gif">


    <IMG ID="pz5_80_400"
STYLE="POSITION:absolute;TOP:100;LEFT:400pt;WIDTH:65px;HEIGHT:102px;ZINDEX:7;"
SRC="pz5.gif">


    <IMG ID="pz6_125_375"
STYLE="POSITION:absolute;TOP:125pt;LEFT:375pt;WIDTH:111px;HEIGHT:78px;ZINDEX:8;"
SRC="pz6.gif">


    <IMG ID="pz7_150_440"

STYLE="POSITION:absolute;TOP:150pt;LEFT:440pt;WIDTH:116px;HEIGHT:95px;ZINDEX:9;"
SRC="pz7.gif">


    <IMG ID="pz8_140_327"
STYLE="POSITION:absolute;TOP:140pt;LEFT:327pt;WIDTH:82px;HEIGHT:80px;ZINDEX:10;"
SRC="pz8.gif">


    <IMG ID="pz9_175_450pt"
STYLE="POSITION:absolute;TOP:175pt;LEFT:368pt;WIDTH:105px;HEIGHT:90px;ZINDEX:11;"
SRC="pz9.gif">


    <IMG ID="pz10_20_425"
STYLE="POSITION:absolute;TOP:20pt;LEFT:425pt;WIDTH:120px;HEIGHT:89px;ZINDEX:12;"
SRC="pz10.gif">


    <IMG ID="pz11_5_375"
STYLE="POSITION:absolute;TOP:5pt;LEFT:375pt;WIDTH:90px;HEIGHT:88px;ZINDEX:13;"
SRC="pz11.gif">


    <IMG ID="pz12_100_450"
STYLE="POSITION:absolute;TOP:100pt;LEFT:450pt;WIDTH:105px;HEIGHT:89px;ZINDEX:14;"
SRC="pz12.gif">
```

```
    <IMG ID="original"
STYLE="POSITION:absolute;TOP:3150pt;LEFT:2000pt;WIDTH:325px; HEIGHT=229px; ZIN-
DEX:15;" SRC="seamless.gif">

<FORM>
<INPUT TYPE="button" VALUE="Scramble Puzzle" NAME="scramble"
STYLE="POSITION:absolute;TOP:230pt;LEFT:0pt">
<INPUT TYPE="button" VALUE="Show Original Picture" NAME="origBtn" STYLE="POSI-
TION:absolute;TOP:230pt;LEFT:120pt">
</FORM>

</DIV>
</BODY>
</HTML>
```

What's Next?

The script you've just studied contains highly adaptable code for creating drag-gable/droppable objects on a Web page—and what could be more useful and friendly in a GUI environment (or more *dynamic*) than objects that can be moved around at the user's will? Just replace the images (reducing or adding the number of <IMG> tags as needed), and change the attached scripts and underlying HTML accordingly, to incorporate this state-of-the-art user interface feature into pages of your own.

In addition to the essentials of creating moveable objects, perhaps this chapter's tutorial has also shown you the twin benefits of the wide-open dynamic HTML object model. This object model not only bestows greater power upon you to perform complicated tasks (benefit #1), but it also makes these tasks *easier* to accomplish. Thanks to DHTML, you've probably noticed in this chapter's example that *you can do more with less VBScript.*

Chapter 16 continues to explore the added power and ease that DHTML brings to the VBScript table with a "Client Address Book" page that takes you through the fine points of local data binding—and also shows you how to use VBScript across interactive frames.

Working with Bound
Data Across Frames

The Web application that comprises this chapter's tutorial provides two valuable lessons. It shows you how to use the essential tools provided by DHTML to incorporate *data-binding* into Web pages; and it also teaches you how to deploy VBScript across frames. Before digging into the Web page example, here's a quick look at the basic procedures for performing both feats.

Data-Binding

One of DHTML's most exciting new offerings to Web page scripters is the ability to bind data from external text files to specific HTML objects. For instance, if you had a form with a Name field and a Phone field, you could create a text file of *records* that could be used to sequentially populate those fields with the *next* record in the file upon each subsequent click of a button specially scripted for the purpose.

The text file can be created in any text editor, such as Notepad, as long as it is constructed in the following way:

1. The first line of the file is used as a *header* by the HTML tag that supports it (discussed in a moment) and must contain a comma-delimited list of the target objects (in this case, the two form fields).

2. The lines of text following the header are used to populate the fields. These lines should follow the exact same construction as the header—except, instead of a comma-delimited list of the names of the target data display objects (fields in this example), each *data* line must be a comma-delimited list of the actual data to be placed into the *bound* fields.

    Each new line begins a new record, and a hard return placed at the end of that line marks its end. Only the last line can be left without a hard return, although the presence of a hard return won't cause an error.

```
NAME,PHONE
John Smith,222-2202
Mary Jones,123-2345
Tom Terrific,233-9999
```

Once this text file is properly created, it should be named and saved as a "txt" file, and placed into the same folder as the HTML document that generates the Name and Phone fields.

The next step is to insert an <OBJECT> tag into the Web page's HTML document. This tag is used to bind the text file to the page and give it object status. Once it receives this status, it can be referred to in a script that drives, say, a button that browses through the text file's three records—showing each one in the order that they appear in the file, one after the other as the user clicks the button. (More details are included in the subsequent tutorial.)

```
<OBJECT ID="phoneList" CLASSID="clsid:333C7BC4-460F-11D0-BC04-0080C7055A83"
BORDER="0" WIDTH="0" HEIGHT="0">

    <PARAM NAME="DataURL" VALUE="phoneList.txt">
    <PARAM NAME="UseHeader" VALUE="True">

</OBJECT>
```

> **NOTE** You may be surprised to see the <OBJECT> tag used in this example to call something that isn't an ActiveX control (Chapter 17 covers that particular use of the tag). It is used here to instantiate the previously created text file as an external object. Your attention is also drawn to the fact that, any time you need to refer to a text file in an <OBJECT> tag, the answer to its CLASSID argument is always:
>
> ```
> clsid:333C7BC4-460F-11D0-BC04-0080C7055A83
> ```

Scripting Across Frames

Your VBScripts can communicate with any other VBScript that is currently running in the browser. This means that all of the pages that are currently populating the frames in a <FRAMESET> can be scripted to interact with each other.

To do this, the only thing that you need to take into account is the location of each object or code block that the current script is manipulating or calling. If the object or code block (such as a user-created sub or function) resides in another page in the <FRAMESET>, then you must include a reference to both the parent <FRAMESET> and the frame where the target element's supporting page sits. For this reason, if you're setting up a series of interactive scripts within a <FRAME-SET>, it's a good idea to name each <FRAME> in the set for later reference.

```
<FRAMESET ROWS="75%,25%"

        <FRAME SRC="frame1.htm" NAME="frame1">

        <FRAME SRC="frame2.htm" NAME="frame2">

</FRAMESET>
```

Any item that you need to call from across frames can now make use of that frame's name in its *calling* statement. Thus, if you created a global variable called g_thisVar in the frame1.htm document used in our current <FRAMESET> example, and you needed to retrieve its housed data from a script in the frame2.htm document, you'd use one of the following lines of script (or something similar) to accomplish the deed:

```
g_thisVar2 = parent.frame1.g_thisVar
```

-OR-

```
g_thisVar2 = top.frame1.g_thisVar
```

By the same token, if you needed to invoke a sub called *myProc()* in the frame2.htm from a script residing in the frame1.htm document, you'd call it like this:

```
parent.frame2.myProc()
```

Working with VBScript elements between frames is as simple as this. As the chapter progresses you'll see variations of this calling procedure used throughout.

Overview of the Client Address Book

Now that you've got a bead on how data-binding and scripting across frames are accomplished, let's take a quick look at how the Client Address Book page behaves before delving into the details of its supporting scripts (see Figures 16.1 through 16.5).

> **W W W**   The Client Address Book page is in the Chapter 16 link on the companion Web site (www.wiley.com/compbooks/mara). To use this page on your local system, be sure to copy the entire folder, then load addressFr.htm into the browser.

Figure 16.1 The top frame in the Address Book page contains a row of Alphabet buttons, a Table View button, and Previous and Next buttons for browsing through the stored addresses. The bottom frame provides all the fields needed to display the data for each record.

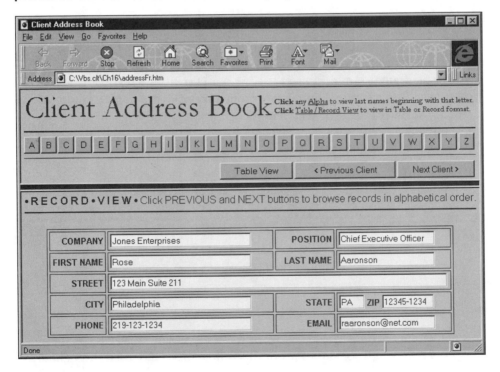

Figure 16.2 The user can browse the "database" in a record-by-record fashion using the Previous or Next buttons; or the user can click any Alpha button to go right to the first record stored in that letter's record set.

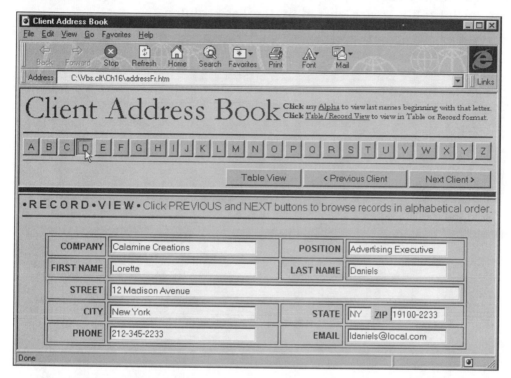

If the user clicks any Alpha button while in Table View, then the table is revised to display that letter's record set. If, on the other hand, the user clicks either the Previous or Next button while in Table View, nothing happens. The user can resume viewing and browser the data as separate, more detailed records by clicking the "Record View" button. This resets the page in the bottom frame to the record view page, and resets the name of the button to "Table View."

The Client Address Book Scripts

In addition to having its share of script segments, the Client Address Book page is also scattered across frames. Its parent <FRAMESET> creates three frames, although the middle frame is only an empty page with a maroon background

**Figure 16.3 If the user clicks the "Table View" button, the current
letter's record set is reorganized into a table containing only the
Company, First, Last, and Phone data for each record. Since the
record set is already alphabetized (within its text file) by Last Name,
the initial table is also sorted by the Last column.**

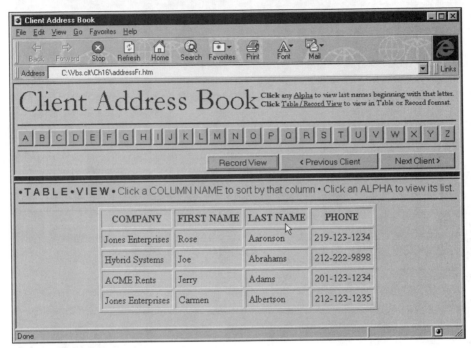

(shown as black in this book and in color if you've loaded the <FRAMESET> from the browser—with a color monitor). Its purpose is only to create the dark band that separates the top and bottom frames (see Figures 16.6 and 16.7). Although it *could* house additional scripts, if needed, the middle frame contains no scripts in this example.

Here's the script that generates the Client Address Book <FRAMESET>:

```
<HTML>
<HEAD>
<TITLE>Client Address Book</TITLE>
</HEAD>

<FRAMESET FRAMEBORDER="1" BORDER=NO FRAMESPACING="0" ROWS="150,10,*">

        <FRAME MARGINWIDTH="0" MARGINHEIGHT="0" SRC="controls.htm"
NAME="controls" NORESIZE SCROLLING="no">
```

```
        <FRAME MARGINWIDTH="0" MARGINHEIGHT="0" SRC="bar.htm" NORESIZE
SCROLLING="no">

        <FRAME MARGINWIDTH="0" MARGINHEIGHT="0" SRC="addresses.htm"
NAME="viewer" SCROLLING="auto">

</FRAMESET>
</HTML>
```

All of the Address application's scripts are contained in the pages that populate the top and bottom frames. As long as the Client Address Book page is on display in the browser, its top frame always contains the document named *controls.htm*. The <FRAME> tag that sources this file is also called "controls," because all of the buttons that control the Address Book application are presented by this page (although the scripts that drive the Previous and Next buttons are actually contained in the addresses.htm, discussed next).

The bottom frame is named *viewer* in its <FRAME> tag, because it is the frame that presents views of the data. The viewer <FRAME> sources a file called

Figure 16.4 If the user clicks the name of another column (such as Company), the table is resorted by the items in that column.

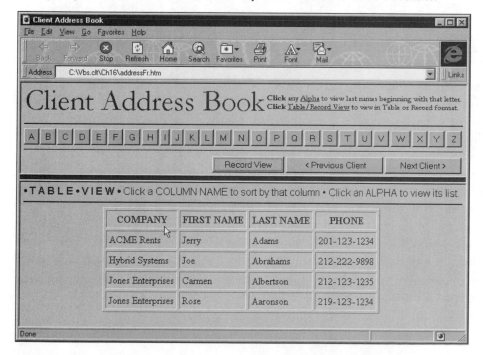

Figure 16.5 If the items in the sort-by column are alphas, they are alphabetized (as shown in Figures 16.3 and 16.4). If they are numbers, they are sorted in numeric order, low to high, as shown in the Phone column in this illustration.

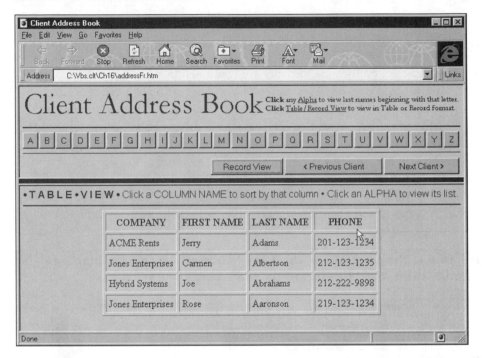

addresses.htm, which displays the Record View of the address data. If the user clicks the Table View button, the Record View page is replaced by the Table View page. The HTML document that supports the Table View page is called *tables.htm*.

This means that—while there are only two "working" frames that display pages with VBScript—at various times during the operation of this Web application, a total of three pages may be used to populate those frames: controls.htm, addresses.htm, and tables.htm.

In addition to the HTML files that interact to produce the Client Address Book application, 26 separate text files were also created and bound to those pages. Each file houses all of the records in the Client Address "database" where the Last Name field begins with that file's alphabet letter. Thus, the text file named *addresses1.htm* (shown in Figure 16.8) contains all of the records where the Last Name begins with A; addresses2.htm contains records where Last Name begins with B; and so on, all the way through to the Zs.

Figure 16.6 The highlighted file in this folder is the HTML file that contains the <FRAMESET> script. The same folder houses the separate HTML files that are used to populate the frames. The bar.htm file is the empty page that creates the dark bar between the top and bottom frames.

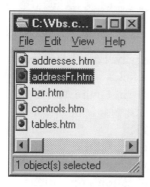

Figure 16.7 The three frame areas created by the addressFr.htm document are labeled in this illustration. The top frame is the *controls* frame; the middle frame is unnamed because it doesn't participate in the scripting; and the bottom frame is the viewer frame.

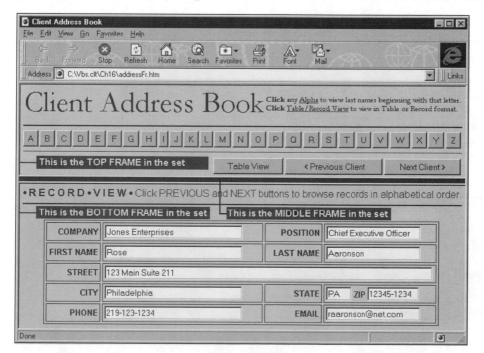

> **WARNING** As this chapter progresses, you'll learn how to set-up the text files that provide the data for the Address Book. At the same time, you'll discover how to add data to your own copy of the Address Book application by working directly with these text files. Be advised, however, that the Address Book application *does not* support data entry via the pages themselves. You can only add data to the Address Book by opening the supporting text files using a standard text editor.

All 26 of the data files are constructed in exactly the same way. Each begins with the same header, which is a comma-delimited list of all of the fields presented by the addresses.htm (or Record View) page (shown most recently in Figure 16.7). This header is followed by a line for each record where the Last Name begins with the data file's associated letter (see Figures 16.9 through 16.11).

As you can see, numerous documents cooperate to produce the Client Address Book application. In addition, several script segments have been set up to interact between the three VBScripted pages to perform all of the application's operations.

The controls.htm script in the Controls frame contains the following two segments:

- Segment 1 controls the operation of the Alpha buttons.

- Segment 2 controls the operations of the Table/Record View button.

Figure 16.8 The folder that contains the HTML files that drive the Client Address Book application also contains the 26 text files that comprise the Client Address database.

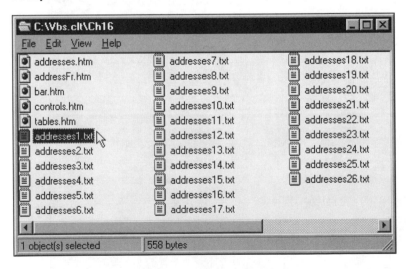

Figure 16.9 The highlighted header line lists all of the fields presented by the Record View page. Each line below contains a comma-separated list of data that will be used to populate each field when that line's record is selected for display.

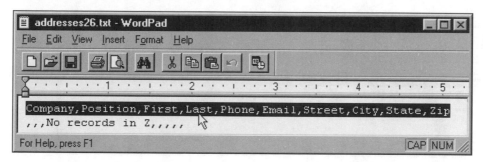

The addresses.htm script in the Viewer frame contains the following two segments:

- Segment 1 tracks and binds the appropriate text file to the page's fields.
- Segment 2 controls the browsing of records (called by scripts in controls.htm where the browse buttons actually reside)

The tables.htm script in the Viewer frame contains the following two segments:

- Segment 1 tracks and binds the appropriate text file to the page's table cells.
- Segment 2 controls column sorting

Figure 16.10 When there are no names stored for a given letter of the alphabet, a single data line is created below the header that leaves every field empty except the Last Name field. This field is set to display a notice that there are "No records in [*letter*]."

COMPANY		POSITION	
FIRST NAME		LAST NAME	No records in Z
STREET			
CITY		STATE	ZIP
PHONE		EMAIL	

Figure 16.11 When the user browses to the Zs, the "no records" record is displayed. Since this is an example application, most of the files contain the "no records" notice. Only A through D actually contain records to display.

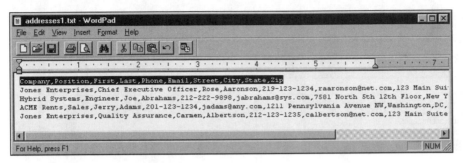

Segment 1 of controls.htm: Alpha Buttons

The first script in the Controls page declares two important global variables that will be used throughout the <FRAMESET>:

```
DIM alphaSet,txtFile
alphaSet = "1"
txtFile = "addresses1.txt"
```

The script that choreographs the clicking of the A–Z buttons is attached to those buttons by its <FORM> object, which is named "alphas." Before viewing the script, here's the HTML that creates the <FORM> and the <INPUT> elements that interact with the controlling script:

```
<FORM NAME="alphas">
        <TD ALIGN="left"><INPUT TYPE="button" ID="x1" VALUE=" A "></TD>
        <TD ALIGN="left"><INPUT TYPE="button" ID="x2" VALUE=" B "></TD>
        <TD ALIGN="left"><INPUT TYPE="button" ID="x3" VALUE=" C "></TD>
        <TD ALIGN="left"><INPUT TYPE="button" ID="x4" VALUE=" D "></TD>
        <TD ALIGN="left"><INPUT TYPE="button" ID="x5" VALUE=" E "></TD>
        <TD ALIGN="left"><INPUT TYPE="button" ID="x6" VALUE=" F "></TD>
        <TD ALIGN="left"><INPUT TYPE="button" ID="x7" VALUE=" G "></TD>
        <TD ALIGN="left"><INPUT TYPE="button" ID="x8" VALUE=" H "></TD>
        <TD ALIGN="left"><INPUT TYPE="button" ID="x9" VALUE=" I "></TD>
        <TD ALIGN="left"><INPUT TYPE="button" ID="x10" VALUE=" J "></TD>
        <TD ALIGN="left"><INPUT TYPE="button" ID="x11" VALUE=" K "></TD>
        <TD ALIGN="left"><INPUT TYPE="button" ID="x11" VALUE=" L "></TD>
        <TD ALIGN="left"><INPUT TYPE="button" ID="x13" VALUE=" M "></TD>
        <TD ALIGN="left"><INPUT TYPE="button" ID="x14" VALUE=" N "></TD>
```

```
        <TD ALIGN="left"><INPUT TYPE="button" ID="x15" VALUE=" O "></TD>
        <TD ALIGN="left"><INPUT TYPE="button" ID="x16" VALUE=" P "></TD>
        <TD ALIGN="left"><INPUT TYPE="button" ID="x17" VALUE=" Q "></TD>
        <TD ALIGN="left"><INPUT TYPE="button" ID="x18" VALUE=" R "></TD>
        <TD ALIGN="left"><INPUT TYPE="button" ID="x19" VALUE=" S "></TD>
        <TD ALIGN="left"><INPUT TYPE="button" ID="x20" VALUE=" T "></TD>
        <TD ALIGN="left"><INPUT TYPE="button" ID="x21" VALUE=" U "></TD>
        <TD ALIGN="left"><INPUT TYPE="button" ID="x22" VALUE=" V "></TD>
        <TD ALIGN="left"><INPUT TYPE="button" ID="x23" VALUE=" W "></TD>
        <TD ALIGN="left"><INPUT TYPE="button" ID="x24" VALUE=" X "></TD>
        <TD ALIGN="left"><INPUT TYPE="button" ID="x25" VALUE=" Y "></TD>
        <TD ALIGN="left"><INPUT TYPE="button" ID="x26" VALUE=" Z "></TD>
</FORM>
```

A subroutine attaches the click event to every button contained in the *alphas* form object:

```
sub alphas_onClick()
```

After an opening *on error…* statement, the *alphaSet* variable receives the ID of the button within the form that was actually clicked. Since you can't begin an object's name with a number in VBScript, an "x" is used as the first character in each button's ID. This x is replaced with the empty literal. The alphaSet variable is then used in a concatenated string that creates the name of the text file associated with the clicked button, and places this filename into the txtFile variable. (Thus, if button D is clicked, txtFile becomes address4.txt.) Next, the dataURL used by the page in the *viewer* frame is changed to the contents of txtFile.

```
alphaSet = window.event.srcElement.id
alphaSet = replace(alphaSet,"x","")
txtFile = "addresses" & alphaSet & ".txt"
parent.viewer.addresses.dataURL = txtFile
```

Finally, the database object that was created from an <OBJECT> tag named "addresses" (discussed later) is forced to update itself via the reset() method.

```
parent.viewer.addresses.reset()
```

Here's the complete segment:

```
DIM alphaSet,txtFile
alphaSet = "1"
txtFile = "addresses1.txt"

sub alphas_onClick()
```

```
on error resume next

alphaSet = window.event.srcElement.id
alphaSet = replace(alphaSet,"x","")
txtFile = "addresses" & alphaSet & ".txt"


parent.viewer.addresses.dataURL = txtFile
parent.viewer.addresses.reset()
```

end sub

Segment 2 of controls.htm: Table/Record View

The button that toggles between Table View and Record View is generated by a second <FORM> object on the controls.htm page, along with the Previous and Next buttons.

<FORM>

```
      <TD ALIGN="top"><INPUT TYPE="button" ID="view" VALUE=" Table View
"></TD>
      <TD ALIGN="top"><INPUT TYPE="button" ID="backward"

      onClick="if view.value = ' Table View ' then

   parent.viewer.moveBack()

end if" VALUE=" < Previous Client "></TD>

      <TD ALIGN="top"><INPUT TYPE="button" ID="forward"

      onClick="if view.value = ' Table View ' then

       parent.viewer.moveForward()

end if" VALUE=" Next Client > "></TD>

   </FORM>
```

When the "view" button is clicked, its attached subroutine immediately declares a new variable to house the current value, or displayed name, of the button (whether it is "Table View" or "Record View").

> **NOTE** The view and browse button <INPUT> elements were segregated inside their own <FORM> tag to make it easier to attach the alphas sub to the click event for the Alpha buttons only. If there had been <INPUT> elements within the *alphas* form that were not Alpha buttons, it would have required additional scripting to ensure that the statements in the alphas sub only executed for the Alpha buttons.

```
sub view_onClick()

    DIM theView
    theView = document.forms(1).view.value
```

The txtFile variable is then updated with the current contents of the dataURL property of the Viewer frame's addresses object. This is the property that houses the name of the currently bound text file (whether it is addresses1.txt, addresses2.txt, etc.). If the user has been browsing the records by clicking the Previous or Next buttons, the currently bound file could easily be different from the file last tracked by, say, the alphas sub.

```
txtFile = parent.viewer.addresses.dataURL
```

> **NOTE** Although the information in txtFile isn't used by this script, it is important to update the data in this global variable every chance you get so that other scripts will know which text file is currently bound to the addresses object. With so many scripts working across frames, this data could easily become confused.

As you review this code segment, remember that this script is running because the user just clicked the "view" button. If theView variable isn't "Record View," then the button is reset to display "Record View" as its name, and the page in the Viewer frame is replaced with the tables.htm, which redisplays the data in table format. If theView isn't "Table View," the button is reset to "Table View," and the Viewer frame reloads addresses.htm, which redisplays the data in record format.

```
if theView <> "Record View" then

    document.forms(1).view.value = "Record View"
    parent.viewer.location.replace("tables.htm")

elseif theView <> "Table View" then
```

```
document.forms(1).view.value = "Table View"
parent.viewer.location.replace("addresses.htm")
```

end if

Here's the complete script segment:

```
sub view_onClick()

    DIM theView
    theView = document.forms(1).view.value
    txtFile = parent.viewer.addresses.dataURL

    if theView <> "Record View" then

        document.forms(1).view.value = "Record View"
        parent.viewer.location.replace("tables.htm")

    elseif theView <> "Table View" then

        document.forms(1).view.value = "Table View"
        parent.viewer.location.replace("addresses.htm")

    end if

end sub
```

Segment 1 of addresses.htm: Data-Binding

The addresses.htm document contains the <OBJECT> tag that binds the data in the 26 text files to the fields on the page generated by addresses.htm. To do this, two global variables are declared at the top of the page. These variables are copies of the information housed in the alphaSet and txtFile variables declared by the controls.htm script, and they are set to the current contents of those variables:

```
DIM alphaSet2,txtFile2
alphaSet2 = parent.controls.alphaSet
txtFile2 = parent.controls.txtFile
```

The <OBJECT> tag is inserted into the <BODY> of the document, using the standard CLASSID for text files—and giving it no physical space within the page by setting its BORDER, WIDTH, and HEIGHT arguments to zero. The VALUE argument is initially answered with the first text file, addresses1.txt (the A's). The new object is given the name (or ID) "addresses." The page now has an "addresses" object that refers to the currently bound text file.

```
<OBJECT ID="addresses" CLASSID="clsid:333C7BC4-460F-11D0-BC04-0080C7055A83"
BORDER="0" WIDTH="0" HEIGHT="0">

        <PARAM NAME="dataURL" VALUE="addresses1.txt">
        <PARAM NAME="useHeader" VALUE="True">

</OBJECT>
```

After instantiating the text file, it is necessary to update its dataURL property to the current value in txtFile2 as soon as the page is loaded. (You'll remember that the contents of txtFile2 received the current contents of parent.controls.txtFile when the page was loaded.) A sub that attached the load event to the current window object (the viewer frame) is placed immediately after the <OBJECT> tag in the <BODY> of the addresses.htm document. This sub rebinds the addresses object to the file whose name is contained in txtFile2, then resets the object.

```
<SCRIPT LANGUAGE="VBScript">

sub window_onLoad()

    addresses.dataURL = txtFile2
    addresses.reset()

end sub

</SCRIPT>
```

The fields generated by the addresses.htm document are bound to the fields described in the header of each of the 26 text files (all of the files contain the exact same header) by including DATASRC and DATAFLD arguments in each field's <INPUT> tag. These arguments are answered with the name of the <OBJECT> tag preceded by #, and the name of the field as it appears in the header:

```
<INPUT TYPE="text" SIZE=30 ID="company" DATASRC="#addresses"
DATAFLD="Company"></TD>
```

Segment 2 of addresses.htm: Browsing

The Previous and Next buttons are actually generated by the controls.htm page, as <INPUT> elements in its second <FORM> tag:

```
<FORM>

        <TD ALIGN="top"><INPUT TYPE="button" ID="view" VALUE=" Table View "></TD>
        <TD ALIGN="top"><INPUT TYPE="button" ID="backward"

        onClick="if view.value = ' Table View ' then

          parent.viewer.moveBack()

end if" VALUE=" < Previous Client "></TD>

        <TD ALIGN="top"><INPUT TYPE="button" ID="forward"

        onClick="if view.value = ' Table View ' then

    parent.viewer.moveForward()

end if" VALUE=" Next Client > "></TD>

</FORM>
```

As you can see by the bolded text in the preceding script, each button contains
an onClick handler that checks the current value of the view button (also generated
as <INPUT> elements in the same parent form). If that button's displayed name is
"Table View," this means that the Viewer frame is currently displaying data in
record format.

The browsing buttons are only set up to browse the data if the data *is* on display
in record format. Thus, if the button's name is *not* "Table View," nothing happens
when the user clicks either the Previous or Next button. If it *is* "Table View," then
the appropriate sub in the Viewer frame is called upon to execute.

These two subs—*moveForward()* and *moveBack()*—reside in the addresses.htm,
so this HTML document must be the currently displayed page in the Viewer frame
for these subs to execute. This is no problem. Since these subs are only called if the
data is on display in record format, the addresses.htm file (which provides the
record format) *must be* the current display document.

If the "Previous" button is clicked, the moveBack() sub is called. As its first act,
it populates thePos (a global declared along with alphaSet2 and txtFile2) with the
number of the currently displayed record. This is provided by the *absolutePosition*
property of the addresses object's *recordset*.

```
sub moveBack()
```

```
    thePos = addresses.recordset.absolutePosition
```

If necessary, the alphaSet2 and txtFile2 variable are updated to the current contents of the parent.controls frame object's version of these variables.

```
if alphaSet2 <> parent.controls.alphaSet then
```

```
    alphaSet2 = parent.controls.alphaSet
    txtFile2 = parent.controls.txtFile
```

```
end if
```

Depending on which record in the current recordset is on display, various actions occur.

```
select case thePos
```

If the first record in a set is on display (and the user is moving backwards in the data), then the user is sent to the last record in the previous alphaSet. Thus, if the user clicked the Previous button from the first record in addresses4.htm (D), the last record in addresses3.htm (C) is then displayed. This is accomplished by subtracting 1 from the contents of alphaSet2 (which contains the number portion of the text file's name), and by invoking the recordset objects moveLast method.

If subtracting 1 from the current contents of alphaSet results in 0, the user is shown the last record in addresses26.htm (Z).

```
case 1
```

```
            alphaSet2 = alphaSet2 - 1
```

```
        if alphaSet2 = 0 then
```

```
            alphaSet2 = 26
```

```
        end if
```

```
        txtFile2 = "addresses" & alphaSet2 & ".txt"
        addresses.dataURL = txtFile2
        addresses.reset()
        addresses.recordset.moveLast()
```

```
        parent.controls.alphaSet = alphaSet2
        parent.controls.txtFile = txtFile2
```

If the current record is *not* the first record in the set, the user is simply taken to the previous record in that same set, via the movePrevious method.

```
    case else


        addresses.recordset.movePrevious()


    end select


end sub
```

The *moveForward()* sub follows the same logic from the angle of moving *forward*. Thus, if the current record is the last in the set, the script is written to move the user to the first record in the next set (from A to B, for instance). The script determines whether thePos (current record number) is the last record by using recordset's *recordCount* property, which returns the total number of records in the set. Since, when a new text file is bound to the addresses object, its first record is automatically displayed, no special method is needed to move to the first record in this set.

If the user is anywhere else in a record set (other than the last record), the user is moved to the next record in the set via the *moveNext* method.

```
sub moveForward()

    thePos = addresses.recordset.absolutePosition

    if alphaSet2 <> parent.controls.alphaSet then

        alphaSet2 = parent.controls.alphaSet
        txtFile2 = parent.controls.txtFile

    end if

    select case thePos

        case addresses.recordset.recordCount

            alphaSet2 = alphaSet2 + 1
```

```
        if alphaSet2 = 27 then

            alphaSet2 = 1

        end if

        txtFile2 = "addresses" & alphaSet2 & ".txt"
        addresses.dataURL = txtFile2
        addresses.reset()

        parent.controls.alphaSet = alphaSet2
        parent.controls.txtFile = txtFile2

    case else

        addresses.recordset.moveNext()

    end select

end sub
```

Segment 1 of tables.htm: Data Binding

The same variables and <OBJECT> tag instantiation are performed in tables.htm as
was previously described for the addresses.htm document. And the same
window_onLoad() sub is used to update the path of the bound file:

```
DIM alphaSet2,txtFile2
alphaSet2 = parent.controls.alphaSet
txtFile2 = parent.controls.txtFile

<OBJECT ID="addresses" CLASSID="clsid:333C7BC4-460F-11D0-BC04-0080C7055A83"
BORDER="0" WIDTH="0" HEIGHT="0">

        <PARAM NAME="dataURL" VALUE="addresses1.txt">
        <PARAM NAME="useHeader" VALUE="True">

</OBJECT>

<SCRIPT LANGUAGE="VBScript">

sub window_onLoad()
```

```
        addresses.dataURL = txtFile2
        addresses.reset()

end sub

</SCRIPT>
```

The tables.htm, however, is going to present the data differently in two ways. First of all, it is only going to include Company, First, Last, and Phone information for each record. Secondly, it is going to present this data in table cells.

To accomplish the first objective, tables.htm merely needs to ignore all of the fields in the header of the text files that it wishes to disclude from the display. To accomplish the second objective, the data is bound to the cells by creating a <THEAD> element that includes the list of fields that *are* to be displayed. A <DIV> object is then created for each column head, and given an ID that matches the field in the text file header whose contents that column will display.

```
<THEAD>
<TR>
        <TD ALIGN="center"><FONT COLOR="#800020">
        <B><DIV ID="company">COMPANY</DIV></B></FONT></TD>

        <TD ALIGN=CENTER><font color="#800020">
        <B><DIV ID=first>FIRST NAME</DIV></B></FONT></TD>

        <TD ALIGN=CENTER><font color="#800020">
        <B><DIV ID=last>LAST NAME</DIV></B></FONT></TD>

        <TD ALIGN=CENTER><font color="#800020">
        <B><DIV ID=phone>PHONE</DIV></B></FONT></TD>

</TR>
</THEAD>
```

Next, a <TBODY> element is created to enclose a single row of four <TD> elements; one for each of the four column (or fields) whose data these cells shall house. Each table data element encloses a <DIV> tag with a DATAFLD argument that is answered with the name of the field whose data it is meant to display. When the script runs, the number of rows needed to display the recordset of each of the 26 text files are generated on-the-fly.

```
<TBODY>
<TR>
```

```
<TD><DIV DATAFLD="company"></DIV></TD>
<TD><DIV DATAFLD="first"></DIV></TD>
<TD><DIV DATAFLD="last"></DIV></TD>
<TD><DIV DATAFLD="phone"></DIV></TD>
```

```
</TR>
</TBODY>
```

> **N O T E** When the Table View button is clicked, and the tables.htm
> page is loaded, the data in the addresses1.htm file is displayed first
> because this is the filename that is initially passed to the addresses
> object's dataURL argument. The display then rapidly updates to a view of
> data in the current text file whose name is contained in txtFile2. Various
> methods of passing this information to the <OBJECT> tag's dataURL
> argument using the txtFile2 variable were tried, but none worked in the
> version of IE4 tested.

Segment 2 of tables.htm: Column Sorting

You'll be pleasantly shocked at how easy it is to script the table in this page to sort by the column head that the user clicks. To do so, each column created by the four <TD> elements in the <THEAD> portion of this page is attached to its own short subroutine. Each sub consists of two simple statements. The first statement passes the name of the just-clicked column head to the addresses object's sortColumn method, which duly sorts the data. The second statement updates the addresses object so the user can see the results of sortColumn.

Here are the four little scripts that accomplish this wonderful feat:

```
<SCRIPT LANGUAGE="VBScript">

sub company_onClick()

    addresses.sortColumn = "Company"
    addresses.reset()

end sub

sub first_onClick()

    addresses.sortColumn = "First"
    addresses.reset()
```

```
end sub

sub last_onClick()

    addresses.sortColumn = "Last"
    addresses.reset()

end sub

sub phone_onClick()

    addresses.sortColumn = "Phone"
    addresses.reset()

end sub

</SCRIPT>
```

Putting the "Addresses" Frameset Together

Putting this application together is a little more complicated than it would be for a single-page application. Like the Puzzle Page before it, it also requires very careful choreography between its HTML elements and the VBScripts that drive them. This close coordination of the two languages are a critical aspect of DHTML.

Here are the full scripts for each page that is used to orchestrate the Client Address Book application. Look this <FRAMESET) over in its entirety and see if you can appreciate the intense interplay between the HTML and VBScript in its pages.

The FRAMESET Script

```
<HTML>
<HEAD>
<TITLE>Client Address Book</TITLE>
</HEAD>

<FRAMESET FRAMEBORDER="1" BORDER=NO FRAMESPACING="0" ROWS="150,10,*">

        <FRAME MARGINWIDTH="0" MARGINHEIGHT="0" SRC="controls.htm"
NAME="controls" NORESIZE SCROLLING="no">
```

```
        <FRAME MARGINWIDTH="0" MARGINHEIGHT="0" SRC="bar.htm" NORESIZE
SCROLLING="no">

        <FRAME MARGINWIDTH="0" MARGINHEIGHT="0" SRC="addresses.htm"
NAME="viewer" SCROLLING="auto">

</FRAMESET>
</HTML>
```

The CONTROLS FRAME Script

```
<HTML>
<HEAD>

<TITLE>Alpha Tabs</TITLE>

<SCRIPT LANGUAGE="VBScript">

DIM alphaSet,txtFile
alphaSet = "1"
txtFile = "addresses1.txt"

sub alphas_onClick()

    on error resume next

    alphaSet = window.event.srcElement.id
    alphaSet = replace(alphaSet,"x","")
    txtFile = "addresses" & alphaSet & ".txt"

    parent.viewer.addresses.dataURL = txtFile
    parent.viewer.addresses.reset()

end sub

sub view_onClick()

    DIM theView
    theView = document.forms(1).view.value
    txtFile = parent.viewer.addresses.dataURL

    if theView <> "Record View" then
```

```
            document.forms(1).view.value = "Record View"
            parent.viewer.location.replace("tables.htm")

    elseif theView <> "Table View" then

            document.forms(1).view.value = "Table View"
            parent.viewer.location.replace("addresses.htm")

    end if

end sub

</SCRIPT>
</HEAD>
<BODY TOPMARGIN=0 LEFTMARGIN=5 RIGHTMARGIN=5 BGCOLOR="pink" TEXT="#000000">


<TABLE WIDTH=100% CELLPADDING=1 CELLSPACING=1>
<TD NOWRAP>
<FONT FACE="garamond,arial,helvetica" SIZE=7 COLOR="#800020">
Client Address Book</FONT></TD>
<TD><FONT FACE="garamond,arial,helvetica" SIZE=2 COLOR="#800020">
<B>Click</B> any <U>Alpha</U> to view last names beginning with that letter.
<BR>
<B>Click</B> <U>Table/Record View</U> to view in Table or Record format.
</FONT>
</TD>
</TABLE>


<HR SIZE=2 COLOR="#800020" NOSHADE>
<TABLE WIDTH=100% CELLSPACING=0 CELLPADDING=0>
<TR>
<FORM NAME="alphas">
        <TD ALIGN="left"><INPUT TYPE="button" ID="x1" VALUE=" A "></TD>
        <TD ALIGN="left"><INPUT TYPE="button" ID="x2" VALUE=" B "></TD>
        <TD ALIGN="left"><INPUT TYPE="button" ID="x3" VALUE=" C "></TD>
        <TD ALIGN="left"><INPUT TYPE="button" ID="x4" VALUE=" D "></TD>
        <TD ALIGN="left"><INPUT TYPE="button" ID="x5" VALUE=" E "></TD>
        <TD ALIGN="left"><INPUT TYPE="button" ID="x6" VALUE=" F "></TD>
        <TD ALIGN="left"><INPUT TYPE="button" ID="x7" VALUE=" G "></TD>
        <TD ALIGN="left"><INPUT TYPE="button" ID="x8" VALUE=" H "></TD>
        <TD ALIGN="left"><INPUT TYPE="button" ID="x9" VALUE=" I "></TD>
        <TD ALIGN="left"><INPUT TYPE="button" ID="x10" VALUE=" J "></TD>
        <TD ALIGN="left"><INPUT TYPE="button" ID="x11" VALUE=" K "></TD>
```

```
        <TD ALIGN="left"><INPUT TYPE="button" ID="x11" VALUE=" L "></TD>
        <TD ALIGN="left"><INPUT TYPE="button" ID="x13" VALUE=" M "></TD>
        <TD ALIGN="left"><INPUT TYPE="button" ID="x14" VALUE=" N "></TD>
        <TD ALIGN="left"><INPUT TYPE="button" ID="x15" VALUE=" O "></TD>
        <TD ALIGN="left"><INPUT TYPE="button" ID="x16" VALUE=" P "></TD>
        <TD ALIGN="left"><INPUT TYPE="button" ID="x17" VALUE=" Q "></TD>
        <TD ALIGN="left"><INPUT TYPE="button" ID="x18" VALUE=" R "></TD>
        <TD ALIGN="left"><INPUT TYPE="button" ID="x19" VALUE=" S "></TD>
        <TD ALIGN="left"><INPUT TYPE="button" ID="x20" VALUE=" T "></TD>
        <TD ALIGN="left"><INPUT TYPE="button" ID="x21" VALUE=" U "></TD>
        <TD ALIGN="left"><INPUT TYPE="button" ID="x22" VALUE=" V "></TD>
        <TD ALIGN="left"><INPUT TYPE="button" ID="x23" VALUE=" W "></TD>
        <TD ALIGN="left"><INPUT TYPE="button" ID="x24" VALUE=" X "></TD>
        <TD ALIGN="left"><INPUT TYPE="button" ID="x25" VALUE=" Y "></TD>
        <TD ALIGN="left"><INPUT TYPE="button" ID="x26" VALUE=" Z "></TD>
</FORM>
</TR>
</TABLE>

<HR WIDTH=100% SIZE=1 COLOR="#800020" NOSHADE>
<TABLE CELLSPACING=1 CELLPADDING=1 ALIGN="right">
<FORM>
<TR>
        <TD ALIGN="top"><INPUT TYPE="button" ID="view" VALUE=" Table View
"></TD>
        <TD ALIGN="top"><INPUT TYPE="button" ID="backward"

        onClick="if view.value = ' Table View ' then

         parent.viewer.moveBack()

end if" VALUE=" < Previous Client "></TD>

        <TD ALIGN="top"><INPUT TYPE="button" ID="forward"

        onClick="if view.value = ' Table View ' then

         parent.viewer.moveForward()

end if" VALUE=" Next Client > "></TD>

</FORM>
</TR>
```

```
</TABLE>
</BODY>
</HTML>
```

The MIDDLE Frame Script

```
<HTML>
<HEAD>
</HEAD>

<BODY BGCOLOR="#800020">

</BODY>
</HTML>
```

The VIEWER Frame Scripts

The addresses.htm Script

```
<HTML>
<HEAD>
<SCRIPT LANGUAGE=VBSCRIPT>

DIM alphaSet2,txtFile2,thePos
alphaSet2 = parent.controls.alphaSet
txtFile2 = parent.controls.txtFile

sub moveBack()

    thePos = addresses.recordset.AbsolutePosition

    if alphaSet2 <> parent.controls.alphaSet then

        alphaSet2 = parent.controls.alphaSet
        txtFile2 = parent.controls.txtFile

    end if

    select case thePos

        case 1

            alphaSet2 = alphaSet2 - 1
```

```
        if alphaSet2 = 0 then

            alphaSet2 = 26

        end if

        txtFile2 = "addresses" & alphaSet2 & ".txt"
        addresses.dataURL = txtFile2
        addresses.reset()
        addresses.recordset.moveLast()

        parent.controls.alphaSet = alphaSet2
        parent.controls.txtFile = txtFile2

    case else

        addresses.recordset.movePrevious()

    end select

end sub

sub moveForward()

    thePos = addresses.recordset.absolutePosition

    if alphaSet2 <> parent.controls.alphaSet then

        alphaSet2 = parent.controls.alphaSet
        txtFile2 = parent.controls.txtFile

    end if

    select case thePos

        case addresses.recordset.recordCount

            alphaSet2 = alphaSet2 + 1

            if alphaSet2 = 27 then

                alphaSet2 = 1
```

```
            end if

            txtFile2 = "addresses" & alphaSet2 & ".txt"
            addresses.dataURL = txtFile2
            addresses.reset()

            parent.controls.alphaSet = alphaSet2
            parent.controls.txtFile = txtFile2

        case else

            addresses.recordset.moveNext()

    end select

end sub

</SCRIPT>

<TITLE>Client Addresses</TITLE>
</HEAD>

<BODY TOPMARGIN=5 LEFTMARGIN=5 RIGHTMARGIN=5 BGCOLOR="#CDCDCD">

<OBJECT ID="addresses" CLASSID="clsid:333C7BC4-460F-11D0-BC04-0080C7055A83"
BORDER="0" WIDTH="0" HEIGHT="0">

        <PARAM NAME="dataURL" VALUE="addresses1.txt">
        <PARAM NAME="useHeader" VALUE="True">

</OBJECT>

<SCRIPT LANGUAGE="VBScript">

sub window_onLoad()

    addresses.dataURL = txtFile2
    addresses.reset()

end sub
</SCRIPT>

<FONT SIZE=3 COLOR="#800020" FACE="helvetica,arial">
```

```
<B>• R E C O R D • V I E W • </B>Click PREVIOUS and NEXT buttons to browse
records in alphabetical order.
</FONT>
<HR SIZE=2 COLOR="#800020" NOSHADE>
<P>
<TABLE WIDTH=90% ALIGN=CENTER CELLSPACING=3 CELLPADDING=3 BGCOLOR="pink" BORDER-
COLOR="#800020" BORDER=1>
<TR>
<TD ALIGN="right" VALIGN="middle">
<FONT SIZE=2 COLOR="#800020" FACE="helvetica,arial">
<B>COMPANY</B></FONT></TD>
<TD ALIGN="left" VALIGN="middle">
<INPUT TYPE="text" SIZE=30 ID="company" DATASRC="#addresses"
DATAFLD="Company"></TD>

<TD ALIGN="right" VALIGN="middle">
<FONT SIZE=2 COLOR="#800020" FACE="helvetica,arial">
<B>POSITION</B></FONT></TD>
<TD ALIGN="left" VALIGN="middle">
<INPUT TYPE="text" ID="position" DATASRC="#addresses" DATAFLD="Position"></TD>
</TR>

<TR>
<TD ALIGN="right" VALIGN="middle" NOWRAP>
<FONT SIZE=2 COLOR="#800020" FACE="helvetica,arial">
<B>FIRST NAME</B></FONT></TD>
<TD ALIGN="left" VALIGN="middle">
<INPUT TYPE="text" SIZE=30 ID="first" DATASRC="#addresses" DATAFLD="First"></TD>

<TD ALIGN="right" VALIGN="middle" NOWRAP>
<FONT SIZE=2 COLOR="#800020" FACE="helvetica,arial">
<B>LAST NAME</B></FONT></TD>
<TD ALIGN="left" VALIGN="middle">
<INPUT TYPE="text" ID="last" DATASRC="#addresses" DATAFLD="Last"></TD>
</TR>

<TR>
<TD ALIGN="right" VALIGN="middle">
<FONT SIZE=2 COLOR="#800020" FACE="helvetica,arial">
<B>STREET</B></FONT></TD>
<TD ALIGN="left" VALIGN="middle" COLSPAN=3>
<INPUT TYPE="text" ID="street" SIZE=74 DATASRC="#addresses"
DATAFLD="Street"></TD>
```

```
</TR>

<TR>
<TD ALIGN="right" VALIGN="middle">
<FONT SIZE=2 COLOR="#800020" FACE="helvetica,arial">
<B>CITY</B></FONT></TD>
<TD ALIGN="left" VALIGN="middle">
<INPUT TYPE="text" ID="city" SIZE=30 DATASRC="#addresses" DATAFLD="City"></TD>

<TD ALIGN="right" VALIGN="middle">
<FONT SIZE=2 COLOR="#800020" FACE="helvetica,arial">
<B>STATE</B></FONT></TD>
<TD ALIGN="left" VALIGN="middle">
<INPUT TYPE="text" ID="state" SIZE=4 DATASRC="#addresses" DATAFLD="State">
<FONT SIZE=2 COLOR="#800020" FACE="helvetica,arial">
<B> ZIP <INPUT TYPE="text" ID="zip" SIZE=10 DATASRC="#addresses" DATAFLD="Zip">
</B></FONT></TD></TR>

<TR>
<TD ALIGN="right" VALIGN="middle">
<FONT SIZE=2 COLOR="#800020" FACE="helvetica,arial">
<B>PHONE</B></FONT></TD>
<TD ALIGN="left" VALIGN="middle">
<INPUT TYPE="text" SIZE=30 ID="phone" DATASRC="#addresses" DATAFLD="Phone"></TD>

<TD ALIGN="right" VALIGN="middle">
<FONT SIZE=2 COLOR="#800020" FACE="helvetica,arial">
<B>EMAIL</B></FONT></TD>
<TD ALIGN="left" VALIGN="middle">
<INPUT TYPE="text" ID="email" DATASRC="#addresses" DATAFLD="Email"></TD>
</TR>
</TABLE>
</body>
</html>
```

The tables.htm Script

```
<HTML>
<HEAD>
<SCRIPT LANGUAGE="VBScript">

DIM alphaSet2,txtFile2
```

```
alphaSet2 = parent.controls.alphaSet
txtFile2 = parent.controls.txtFile

sub company_onClick()

    addresses.sortColumn = "Company"
    addresses.reset()

end sub

sub first_onClick()

    addresses.sortColumn = "First"
    addresses.reset()

end sub

sub last_onClick()

    addresses.sortColumn = "Last"
    addresses.reset()

end sub

sub phone_onClick()

    addresses.sortColumn = "Phone"
    addresses.reset()

end sub

</SCRIPT>

<TITLE>Address Tables</TITLE>
</HEAD>

<BODY TOPMARGIN=5 LEFTMARGIN=5 RIGHTMARGIN=5 BGCOLOR="#CDCDCD">

<OBJECT ID="addresses" CLASSID="clsid:333C7BC4-460F-11D0-BC04-0080C7055A83"
BORDER="0" WIDTH="0" HEIGHT="0">

        <PARAM NAME="dataURL" value="addresses1.txt">
```

```
        <PARAM NAME="useHeader" value="True">

</OBJECT>

<SCRIPT LANGUAGE="VBScript">

sub window_onLoad()

    addresses.dataURL = txtFile2
    addresses.reset()

end sub

</SCRIPT>

<FONT SIZE=3 COLOR="#800020" FACE="helvetica,arial">
<B>• T A B L E • V I E W • </B>Click a COLUMN NAME to sort by that column •
Click an ALPHA to view its list.
</FONT>
<HR SIZE=2 COLOR="#800020" NOSHADE>

<TABLE ALIGN="center" BGCOLOR="pink" BORDER=1 CELLSPACING=4 CELLPADDING=4
DATASRC="#addresses">

<THEAD>
<TR>
        <TD ALIGN="center"><FONT COLOR="#800020">
        <B><DIV ID="company">COMPANY</DIV></B></FONT></TD>

        <TD ALIGN=CENTER><font color="#800020">
        <B><DIV ID=first>FIRST NAME</DIV></B></FONT></TD>

        <TD ALIGN=CENTER><font color="#800020">
        <B><DIV ID=last>LAST NAME</DIV></B></FONT></TD>

        <TD ALIGN=CENTER><font color="#800020">
        <B><DIV ID=phone>PHONE</DIV></B></FONT></TD>

</TR>
</THEAD>

<TBODY>
```

```
<TR>

        <TD><DIV DATAFLD="company"></DIV></TD>
        <TD><DIV DATAFLD="first"></DIV></TD>
        <TD><DIV DATAFLD="last"></DIV></TD>
        <TD><DIV DATAFLD="phone"></DIV></TD>

</TR>
</TBODY>

</TABLE>
</BODY>
</HTML>
```

What's Next?

If the nonstop excitement of VBScript, DHTML, data-binding, and working across frames isn't enough for you, you'll be pleased to know that the next chapter presents the ins and outs of working with ActiveX controls. A basic understanding of how to embed and run these separately coded, self-contained external objects in your Web pages will open up a whole new bag of operational and multimedia tricks to draw upon as you script your Web site into the 21st century.

Chapter

17

Working with
External Objects

This book's final exercise uses VBScript to orchestrate the behavior of external objects that have been embedded into a Web page using the <OBJECT> tag. The strategy for embedding objects into a page is actually more appropriately termed *dynamic* HTML than the strategy for allowing extension languages to interact with HTML. This is because the <OBJECT>, <APPLET>, and <PLUGIN> tags allow webmasters to extend the functionality, interactivity, and multimedia nature of their pages with *nothing but* HTML.

As a seasoned webmaster, you've probably already used embedded objects and are, thus, quite aware of the immediate shot in the arm that these external components can give to your pages. It's not much more than a hop, skip, and jump to add the might of VBScript to this equation. The <OBJECT> and <APPLET> tags already allow you to determine an embedded object's presentation height, width, and other cosmetic attributes (as appropriate to the object). Both tags also allow you to include parameter information, further defining the appearance and behavior of the object on your page, by enclosing <PARAM> tags within the parent tag:

```
<OBJECT CLASSID=[registered id that uniquely identifies the object to the
browser] HEIGHT=[n] WIDTH=[n]>
```

```
        <PARAM NAME=[property or method name as defined by the author of the exter-
        nal object] VALUE=[string defined by you]>


        <PARAM NAME=[property or method name] VALUE=[string]>


</OBJECT>
```

The problem with using the <OBJECT> tag alone to set the stage for an external component is that you only get to set its appearance and behavior when the page is loaded into the browser. With VBScript, you can continue to modify an object's attributes as other events are fired through user actions.

This chapter's lesson provides example scripts that refine the behavior and appearance of the Marquee ActiveX Control, which is used in three different places on the example page. The tutorial focus is the simplicity with which VBScript "speaks" to the control. You already know how to write scripts that manipulate the properties, invoke the methods, and run on the events allowed by VBScript's own objects. It is really only necessary to apply this knowledge to the properties, methods, and events that are allowed by the control's (or applet's) author in order to further script that object's behavior.

The catch-22 when working with outside objects is a combination of the quality of the object's external code, and the availability of information about its properties, methods, and events. Microsoft publishes brief descriptions of each of its free controls on its Web site, including the Marquee.ocx.

> **W W W**   The latest documentation on the Marquee ActiveX Control, as well as other freely available Microsoft controls can be found at:
>
> www.microsoft.com/activex/gallery/default.htm

Because of the brevity of documentation on freely distributed controls and applets, when the object doesn't respond to a request for information about a known property; or a method appears to behave badly; or the object fails to respond to a supposedly attached event; it is difficult (if not impossible) to determine whether the problem is in the code or the published information.

Overview of the Recipe Page

The Web application that provides the backdrop for this lesson in working with external objects is called the "Recipe Page." Although it's comprised of several pages, the result is a simple though provocative presentation of a "daily" recipe.

> **TIP** If you run into trouble working with a free control or applet, travel to other sites where that object is (or you suspect it may be) in use, and look at the source code driving it. Also, try the newsgroups for discussion on its use (or to ask direct questions about it). Example scripts traditionally shed more light on the use of external objects (as well as, VBScript's own objects) than the scanty documentation developers understandably provide with free software. Of course, if you paid for the external component, you should receive ample documentation and technical support from its publisher.

Three separate instances of the *marquee* object are used to display the current recipe's title, its ingredients, and its preparation instructions. The first marquee object (in the top frame) scrolls the title of the recipe horizontally across the page. The second and third marquees sit in two column frames below the top frame. The left frame houses a marquee that vertically scrolls the recipe's ingredients, and the right frame's marquee vertically scrolls its instructions (see Figures 17.1 through 17.3).

Each marquee object is set to display its own separate HTML document, so changing the recipe every day merely requires the site master to replace the source file for each marquee object. The name of the three files can remain the same; only the contents need to change.

> **WWW** The Recipe Page is on companion Web site (www.wiley.com/ compbooks/mara). To use this page on your local system, be sure to copy the entire folder, then load marqueeFr.htm into the browser. If you don't already have the Marquee control, copy the Marquee.ocx file from the Chapter 17 folder to your Windows/System directory.

> **NOTE** Sometimes, when the marqueeFr.htm was loaded into the BETA version of IE4 (used for this portion of the book), some of the buttons didn't appear. If this happens, collapse the IE4 window to the Start bar and open it again (or click another window in front and then behind the browser window) to coerce a screen update. The BETA IE4 also had trouble resizing this window on-the-fly, and presented buttons and marquees out of alignment. Resize it again to fix it.

The Recipe Page Scripts

Like the Client Address Book page in the previous chapter, the Recipe Page is built with a <FRAMESET> that generates three frames:

```
<HTML>
<HEAD>
<TITLE>Recipe Page</TITLE>
</HEAD>
<FRAMESET BORDER=0 ROWS="200,*">

        <FRAME NAME="banner" SRC="banner.htm" SCROLLING="auto" NORESIZE>

        <FRAMESET BORDER=0 COLS="50%,50%">

                <FRAME NAME="viewerx" SRC="marqueex.htm" SCROLLING="auto" NORE-
        SIZE>
                <FRAME NAME="viewery" SRC="marqueey.htm" SCROLLING="auto" NORE-
        SIZE>

        </FRAMESET>
</FRAMESET>
</HTML>
```

Figure 17.1 The Recipe Page uses three frames, and three instances of the ActiveX Marquee control. A marquee in the top frame moves the recipe's title across the page, and a marquee in each bottom frame scrolls the Ingredients and Instructions.

Figure 17.2 Clicking the Zoom button below the scrolling Ingredients or Instructions list causes the view to toggle between 75% and 100% views of the scrolling text. Clicking a Pause or Resume button stops or starts the scroll action in the related marquee.

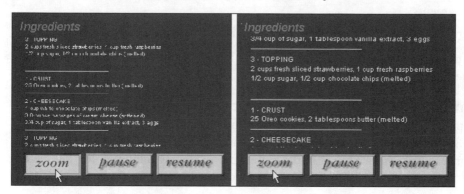

As long as this <FRAMESET> is on display in the browser, its frames always contain the source documents shown in the preceding script. However, in addition to the pages that populate these frames, there *are* three other HTML documents necessary to the pageset. These three documents are displayed by the three instances of the Marquee ActiveX control (and are shown in the "Putting the Recipe Frameset Together" section at the end of the chapter). The only documents that contain VBScript, however, are the pages displayed in the frames: banner.htm, marqueex.htm, and marqueey.htm.

The banner.htm script in the banner frame contains the following three segments:

- Segment 1 instantiates the Horizontal Title Marquee.

- Segment 2 intercepts the *mouseDown* event, and sets the "depress" state for the appropriate button.

- Segment 3 intercepts the *mouseUp* event, and processes button behaviors.

Figure 17.3 Clicking the Slow or Fast button slows down or speeds up the scrolling title text.

The viewerx.htm and viewery.htm scripts are exactly the same. The only differences are the name (and contents) of the source file fed to the Marquee control, and the internal names used for the Zoom, Pause, and Resume buttons (so the banner .htm scripts can differentiate between them). Each page contains the following two script segments:

- Segment 1 instantiates the Vertical Ingredients or Instructions marquee.

- Segment 2 identifies the currently clicked button to the button processing routines in the banner frame

Segment 1 of banner.htm: Horizontal Marquee

An instance of the marquee object is created by placing the following tag into the banner.htm document at the point where the marquee is to appear. Height, width, and border information are set in the main <OBJECT> tag, along with a unique ID (which is necessary to allow VBScript to talk to this instance of the object).

```
<OBJECT ID="marquee1" CLASSID="CLSID:1A4DA620-6217-11CF-BE62-0080C72EDD2D"
TYPE="application/x-oleobject" WIDTH=99% BORDER=0 HEIGHT=40>

        <PARAM NAME="szURL" VALUE="recipeTitle.htm">
        <PARAM NAME="scrollStyleX" VALUE="circular">
        <PARAM NAME="LoopsX" VALUE="-1">
        <PARAM NAME="ScrollPixelsX" VALUE="-60">

</OBJECT>
```

The marquee's *szURL* property determines its display file. In this example, any HTML document titled recipeTitle.htm residing in the current directory or folder is presented in the resulting marquee.

The *scrollStyleX* property is set to *circular* so that the text scrolls along the horizontal (x) plane of the page in a steady flow. Setting this property to *bounce* would cause the text to bounce back and forth between the left and right margins. Setting the *LoopsX* value to –1 causes it to scroll infinitely.

If a positive number is passed to the *ScrollPixelsX* property the text scrolls from left to right. To scroll the text from right to left, a negative number is passed to this property. The relatively high number passed results in a rather rapid scrolling of the text, modifiable by the user via the Slow button.

Segment 2 of banner.htm: Mouse Down

The banner.htm (which sits in the top frame produced by the marqueeFr.htm file) processes all mouse down events for the entire Recipe <FRAMESET>. This page contains two buttons of its own: Slow and Fast. In addition, a set of Zoom, Pause,

Figure 17.4 To use the ActiveX Control Pad to insert an <OBJECT> tag into your page, select Insert ActiveX Control from the Edit menu.

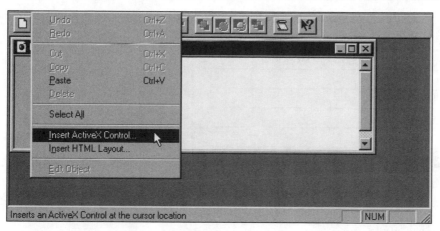

> **T I P** You can automate the production of the <OBJECT> tag by using the ActiveX Control Pad. The Control Pad not only creates a template of the tag for you, but it presents you with a list of all of your installed controls and their parameters; plus it grabs the pesky, long-winded (but required) CLASSID for the object (see Figures 17.4 through 17.7).

> **W W W** Download the ActiveX Control Pad from the Microsoft site at
>
> www.microsoft.com/

Figure 17.5 Choose the target control from the Control Pad browser.

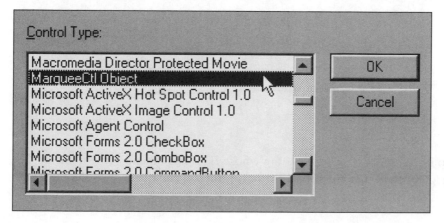

Figure 17.6 Choose the arguments and parameters you wish to use, and edit them accordingly.

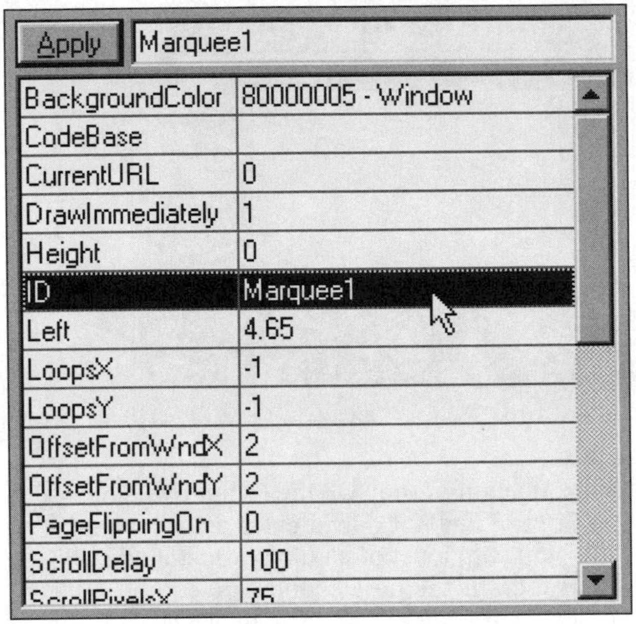

and Resume buttons resides on each page in the bottom two frames. All eight of these "buttons" are actually <IMG> objects, which (thanks to DHTML) now process a number of events, including *mouseDown* and *mouseUp*.

When any of the eight <IMG> buttons receives a mouseDown event (meaning the user is holding down the left mouse button while the pointer is above that button), *theBtn* global variable uses the *window.event.srcElement* property to assign that object to itself.

```
DIM theBtn

sub document_onMouseDown(x,y,shift,button)

    SET theBtn = window.event.srcElement
    doDown()

end sub
```

If the source element is an <IMG> tag whose ID is *not* "menu" (the name of the banner image presented at the top of the page), then it must be one of the buttons.

Figure 17.7 If you prefer to use your favorite HTML text editor (instead of the Control Pad), select the finished tag, and copy it into your waiting HTML document.

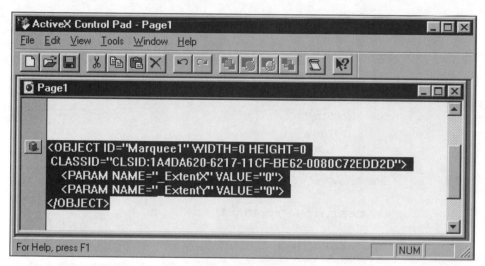

The ID of that button is used to determine the name of the GIF file that contains a picture of that button in a depressed state; and that GIF is then displayed in the button's place.

```
sub doDown()

    if theBtn.tagname = "IMG" then

        if theBtn.id <> "menu" then

            select case theBtn.id

                case "pauseBtnx"

                    theBtn.src = "pauseDN.gif"

                case "resumeBtnx"

                    theBtn.src = "resumeDN.gif"

                case "zoomBtnx"
```

```
                        theBtn.src = "zoomDN.gif"

                case "pauseBtny"

                        theBtn.src = "pauseDN.gif"

                case "resumeBtny"

                        theBtn.src = "resumeDN.gif"

                case "zoomBtny"

                        theBtn.src = "zoomDN.gif"

                case "slowBtn"

                        theBtn.src = "slowDN.gif"

                case "fastBtn"

                        theBtn.src = "fastDN.gif"

            end select

        end if

    end if

end sub
```

Segment 3 of banner.htm: Mouse Up

When the user releases the mouse button when the point is above the button, the
same basic scripting procedures are used to discover whether the source element
that fired the event is a button, and to redisplay its original GIF file (which shows it
as undepressed).

```
sub document_onMouseUp(x,y,shift,button)

    SET theBtn = window.event.srcElement
    doUp()

end sub
```

In addition to revising the button's display, various properties are set—or methods invoked—depending on which button was "clicked." If a Zoom, Pause, or Resume button was clicked, the marquee.ocx zoom, pause, or resume method is invoked (respectively) for the associated marquee. If the Slow or Fast button was clicked, the number 20 is added to or subtracted from the *ScrollPixelsX* property of the Horizontal Title marquee. Adding to the original negative number of this property slows it down; subtracting from it speeds it up.

```
sub doUp()

    DIM theSpeed
    theSpeed = document.marquee1.scrollPixelsX

    if theBtn.tagname = "IMG" then

        if theBtn.id <> "menu" then

            select case theBtn.id

                case "pauseBtnx"

                    theBtn.src = "pauseUP.gif"
                    parent.viewerx.document.forms(0).marquee2.pause

                case "resumeBtnx"

                    theBtn.src = "resumeUP.gif"
                    parent.viewerx.document.forms(0).marquee2.resume

                case "zoomBtnx"

                    theBtn.src = "zoomUP.gif"

                    if parent.viewerx.document.forms(0).marquee2.zoom = "100"
then

                        parent.viewerx.document.forms(0).marquee2.zoom = "75"

                    else

                        parent.viewerx.document.forms(0).marquee2.zoom = "100"
```

```
                    end if

          case "pauseBtny"

                    theBtn.src = "pauseUP.gif"
                    parent.viewery.document.forms(0).marquee2.pause

          case "resumeBtny"

                    theBtn.src = "resumeUP.gif"
                    parent.viewery.document.forms(0).marquee2.resume

          case "zoomBtny"

                    theBtn.src = "zoomUP.gif"

                    if parent.viewery.document.forms(0).marquee2.zoom = "100"
then

                          parent.vicwery.document.forms(0).marquee2.zoom = "75"

                    else

                          parent.viewery.document.forms(0).marquee2.zoom = "100"

                    end if

          case "slowBtn"

                    theBtn.src = "slowUP.gif"

                    if theSpeed <> "0" then

                          document.marquee1.scrollPixelsX = theSpeed+20

                    else

                          alert "This demo doesn't go any slower."

                    end if

          case "fastBtn"
```

```
                    theBtn.src = "fastUP.gif"

                    if theSpeed <> "-60" then

                            document.marquee1.scrollPixelsX = theSpeed-20

                    else

                            alert "This demo doesn't go any faster."

                    end if

            end select

        end if

    end if

end sub
```

Segment 1 of viewerx.htm: Vertical Marquee

The instantiation of the Ingredients Marquee in the left column frame (viewerx) and the Instructions Marquee in the right column frame (viewery) are almost identical. Even the IDs are the same, since any reference to either marquee across frames must include the parent name (like using a child's last name), which makes the object IDs unique within the <FRAMESET>:

```
parent.viewerx.marquee2
parent.viewery.marquee2
```

The only difference between the <OBJECT> tag used to create the Ingredients Marquee, and the <OBJECT> tag used to create the Instructions Marquee is the name of the sourced file. The Ingredients source file is recipex.htm, and the Instructions source file is recipey.htm.

```
<OBJECT ID="marquee2" CLASSID="CLSID:1A4DA620-6217-11CF-BE62-0080C72EDD2D"
TYPE="application/x-oleobject" BORDER=1 WIDTH=95% HEIGHT=150 ALIGN=right>

        <PARAM NAME="szURL" VALUE="recipex.htm">
        <PARAM NAME="ScrollPixelsX" VALUE="0">
        <PARAM NAME="ScrollPixelsY" VALUE="-2">
```

```
          <PARAM NAME="ScrollDelay" VALUE="300">
          <PARAM NAME="Whitespace" VALUE="0">
          <PARAM NAME="zoom" VALUE="75">

</OBJECT>
```

Both marquees are implicitly set to a circular scrolling style (which happens by default if you don't include a *ScrollStyle* property. The *ScrollPixelsX* property is set to 0, *ScrollPixelsY* (vertical plane) is set to –2, and the *ScrollDelay* is set to 300 milliseconds (the default is 100) to describe a slow, vertical scroll. *WhiteSpace* is set to 0 (the default) to show you this property, which lets you define the size of an empty white space between "scroll frames," if you desire it.

Segment 2 of viewerx.htm: The Button

The only VBScript that appears in the viewerx.htm or viewery.htm file are two subroutines that process the mouseUp and mouseDown events for each document. Like similar subs already described in the banner.htm section, these two subs identify the source elements that fired the given mouse event, and then call banner.htm's *doDown()* or *doUp()* sub, accordingly. The only difference between these scripts in the viewerx and viewery HTML files, and the scripts in the banner.htm file, is the use of the parent object (bolded in the following script) to call the user-created subroutines across frames:

```
sub document_onMouseDown(x,y,shift,button)

    SET parent.banner.theBtn = window.event.srcElement
    parent.banner.doDown()

end sub

sub document_onMouseUp(x,y,shift,button)

    SET parent.banner.theBtn = window.event.srcElement
    parent.banner.doUp()

end sub
```

Putting the "Recipe" Frameset Together

Although several documents must be created to achieve the full effect of this page, the individual pieces go together quite easily. Here are the scripts for each page displayed by the Recipe <FRAMESET>, along with the three HTML files used by the three marquee objects to display the different parts of the "Tuxedo Cheesecake" recipe (which, by the way, is *unbelievable*).

The FRAMESET Script

```
<HTML>
<HEAD>
<TITLE>Recipe Page</TITLE>
</HEAD>
<FRAMESET BORDER=0 ROWS="200,*">

        <FRAME NAME="banner" SRC="banner.htm" SCROLLING="auto" NORESIZE>

        <FRAMESET BORDER=0 COLS="50%,50%">

                <FRAME NAME="viewerx" SRC="marqueex.htm" SCROLLING="auto" NORE-
        SIZE>
                <FRAME NAME="viewery" SRC="marqueey.htm" SCROLLING="auto" NORE-
        SIZE>

        </FRAMESET>
</FRAMESET>
</HTML>
```

The BANNER Frame Script

```
<HTML>
<HEAD>
<TITLE>Banner</TITLE>
<SCRIPT LANGUAGE="VBScript">

DIM theBtn

sub document_onMouseDown(x,y,shift,button)
    SET theBtn = window.event.srcElement
    doDown()

end sub

sub doDown()

    if theBtn.tagname = "IMG" then

        if theBtn.id <> "menu" then
```

```
    select case theBtn.id

        case "pauseBtnx"

            theBtn.src = "pauseDN.gif"

    case "resumeBtnx"
                        theBtn.src = "resumeDN.gif"

        case "zoomBtnx"

            theBtn.src = "zoomDN.gif"

        case "pauseBtny"

            theBtn.src = "pauseDN.gif"

        case "resumeBtny"

            theBtn.src = "resumeDN.gif"

        case "zoomBtny"

            theBtn.src = "zoomDN.gif"

        case "slowBtn"

            theBtn.src = "slowDN.gif"

        case "fastBtn"

            theBtn.src = "fastDN.gif"

        end select

    end if

    end if

end sub
```

```
sub document_onMouseUp(x,y,shift,button)

    SET theBtn = window.event.srcElement
    doUp()

end sub

sub doUp()

    DIM theSpeed
    theSpeed = document.marquee1.scrollPixelsX

    if theBtn.tagname = "IMG" then

        if theBtn.id <> "menu" then

        select case theBtn.id

            case "pauseBtnx"

                theBtn.src = "pauseUP.gif"
                parent.viewerx.document.forms(0).marquee2.pause

            case "resumeBtnx"

                theBtn.src = "resumeUP.gif"
                parent.viewerx.document.forms(0).marquee2.resume

            case "zoomBtnx"

                theBtn.src = "zoomUP.gif"

                if parent.viewerx.document.forms(0).marquee2.zoom = "100" then

                        parent.viewerx.document.forms(0).marquee2.zoom = "75"

                    else

                        parent.viewerx.document.forms(0).marquee2.zoom = "100"

                    end if
```

```
                    case "pauseBtny"

                          theBtn.src = "pauseUP.gif"
                          parent.viewery.document.forms(0).marquee2.pause

              case "resumeBtny"

                          theBtn.src = "resumeUP.gif"
                          parent.viewery.document.forms(0).marquee2.resume

              case "zoomBtny"

                          theBtn.src = "zoomUP.gif"

                          if parent.viewery.document.forms(0).marquee2.zoom = "100"
      then

                                parent.viewery.document.forms(0).marquee2.zoom = "75"

                          else

                                parent.viewery.document.forms(0).marquee2.zoom = "100"

                          end if

              case "slowBtn"

                          theBtn.src = "slowUP.gif"

                          if theSpeed <> "0" then

                                document.marquee1.scrollPixelsX = theSpeed+20

                          else

                                alert "This demo doesn't go any slower."

                          end if

              case "fastBtn"

                          theBtn.src = "fastUP.gif"
```

```
            if theSpeed <> "-60" then

                document.marquee1.scrollPixelsX = theSpeed-20

            else

                alert "This demo doesn't go any faster."

            end if

        end select

      end if

  end if

end sub

</SCRIPT>

</HEAD>
<BODY TOPMARGIN=10 BACKGROUND="copper.gif">
<CENTER>
<TABLE WIDTH=90%>
<TR NOWRAP><TD ROWSPAN=2 VALIGN=middle>
<IMG BORDER=0 ID="slowBtn" WIDTH=84 HEIGHT=33 SRC="slowUP.gif">
<p><IMG BORDER=0 ID="fastBtn" WIDTH=84 HEIGHT=33 SRC="fastUP.gif">
</TD><TD>
<IMG ALIGN=right SRC="menu.gif" ID="menu" WIDTH=544 HEIGHT=150></TD>
</TR></TD></TABLE></CENTER>

<CENTER>
<OBJECT ID="marquee1" CLASSID="CLSID:1A4DA620-6217-11CF-BE62-0080C72EDD2D"
TYPE="application/x-oleobject" WIDTH=99% BORDER=0 HEIGHT=40>

        <PARAM NAME="szURL" VALUE="recipeTitle.htm">
        <PARAM NAME="scrollStyleX" VALUE="circular">
        <PARAM NAME="LoopsX" VALUE="-1">
        <PARAM NAME="ScrollPixelsX" VALUE="-60">

</OBJECT>
</CENTER>
```

```
</BODY>
</HTML>
```

The VIEWERX Frame Script

```
<HTML>
<HEAD>
<TITLE>Marquee</TITLE>
<SCRIPT LANGUAGE="VBScript">

sub document_onMouseDown(x,y,shift,button)

    SET parent.banner.theBtn = window.event.srcElement
    parent.banner.doDown()

end sub

sub document_onMouseUp(x,y,shift,button)

    SET parent.banner.theBtn = window.event.srcElement
    parent.banner.doUp()

end sub

</SCRIPT>
</HEAD>
<BODY TOPMARGIN=5 BACKGROUND="copper.gif">
<FORM><TABLE WIDTH=100% CELLPADDING=2><TR><TD ALIGN=left>
<FONT SIZE=3 FACE="helvetica,arial"
COLOR="#E47843"><b><i>Ingredients</b></i></FONT>
</TD></TR></TABLE>

<CENTER>
<OBJECT ID="marquee2" CLASSID="CLSID:1A4DA620-6217-11CF-BE62-0080C72EDD2D"
TYPE="application/x-oleobject" BORDER=1 WIDTH=95% HEIGHT=150 ALIGN=center>

        <PARAM NAME="szURL" VALUE="recipex.htm">
        <PARAM NAME="ScrollPixelsX" VALUE="0">
        <PARAM NAME="ScrollPixelsY" VALUE="-2">
        <PARAM NAME="ScrollDelay" VALUE="300">
        <PARAM NAME="Whitespace" VALUE="0">
        <PARAM NAME="zoom" VALUE="75">

</OBJECT>
```

```
</CENTER>

<TABLE WIDTH=100% CELLPADDING=6>
<TR><TD ALIGN=left>
        <IMG BORDER=0 ID="zoomBtnx" WIDTH=84 HEIGHT=33 SRC="zoomUP.gif">
        <IMG BORDER=0 ID="pauseBtnx" WIDTH=95 HEIGHT=33 SRC="pauseUP.gif">
        <IMG BORDER=0 ID="resumeBtnx" WIDTH=95 HEIGHT=33 SRC="resumeUP.gif">
</TD></TR>
</TABLE>

</FORM>
</BODY>
</HTML>
```

The VIEWERY Frame Script

```
<HTML>
<HEAD>
<TITLE>Marquee</TITLE>
<SCRIPT LANGUAGE="VBScript">

sub document_onMouseDown(x,y,shift,button)

    SET parent.banner.theBtn = window.event.srcElement
    parent.banner.doDown()

end sub

sub document_onMouseUp(x,y,shift,button)

    SET parent.banner.theBtn = window.event.srcElement
    parent.banner.doUp()

end sub

</SCRIPT>
</HEAD>
<BODY TOPMARGIN=5 BACKGROUND="copper.gif">
<FORM><TABLE WIDTH=100% CELLPADDING=2><TR><TD ALIGN=left>
<FONT SIZE=3 FACE="helvetica,arial" COLOR="#E47843"><b><i>
Instructions</b></i></FONT></TD></TR></TABLE>

<CENTER>
<OBJECT ID="marquee2" CLASSID="CLSID:1A4DA620-6217-11CF-BE62-0080C72EDD2D"
```

```
TYPE="application/x-oleobject" BORDER=1 WIDTH=95% HEIGHT=150 ALIGN=right>

        <PARAM NAME="szURL" VALUE="recipey.htm">
        <PARAM NAME="ScrollPixelsX" VALUE="0">
        <PARAM NAME="ScrollPixelsY" VALUE="-2">
        <PARAM NAME="ScrollDelay" VALUE="300">
        <PARAM NAME="Whitespace" VALUE="0">
        <PARAM NAME="zoom" VALUE="75">

</OBJECT>
</CENTER>


<TABLE WIDTH=100% CELLPADDING=6>
<TR><TD ALIGN=left>
        <IMG BORDER=0 ID="zoomBtny" WIDTH=84 HEIGHT=33 SRC="zoomUP.gif">
        <IMG BORDER=0 ID="pauseBtny" WIDTH=95 HEIGHT=33 SRC="pauseUP.gif">
        <IMG BORDER=0 ID="resumeBtny" WIDTH=95 HEIGHT=33 SRC="resumeUP.gif">
</TD></TR>
</TABLE>
</FORM>
</BODY>
</HTML>
```

The TITLE Marquee Script

```
<HTML>
<HEAD>
<TITLE>Title</TITLE>
</HEAD>
<BODY BACKGROUND="copper.gif" TOPMARGIN=2 LEFTMARGIN=10>
<FONT FACE="helvetica,arial" SIZE=5 COLOR="turquoise">
<b>
Tuxedo
</b></FONT>
<FONT FACE="helvetica,arial" SIZE=5 COLOR="gold">
<b>
Cheesecake
</b></FONT>
<FONT FACE="helvetica,arial" SIZE=5 COLOR="violet">
<b>
with
</b></FONT>
<FONT FACE="helvetica,arial" SIZE=5 COLOR="limegreen">
```

```
<b>
Summer
</b></FONT>
<FONT FACE="helvetica,arial" SIZE=5 COLOR="salmon">
<b>
Berries
</b></FONT>

</BODY>
</HTML>
```

The INGREDIENTS Marquee Script

```
<HTML>
<HEAD>
</HEAD>
<BODY BACKGROUND="copper.gif" TEXT="white" LEFTMARGIN="6" TOPMARGIN="0">
<FONT SIZE=1 FACE="helvetica,arial">
<HR ALIGN=left WIDTH=25%>

<B>1 - CRUST</B>
<BR>25 Oreo cookies, 2 tablespoons butter (melted)

<HR ALIGN=left WIDTH=25%>

<B>2 - CHEESECAKE</B>
<BR>1 cup white chocolate chips (melted)
<BR>3 8-ounce packages of cream cheese (softened)
<BR>3/4 cup of sugar, 1 tablespoon vanilla extract, 3 eggs

<HR ALIGN=left WIDTH=25%>

<B>3 - TOPPING</B>
<BR>2 cups fresh sliced strawberries, 1 cup fresh raspberries
<BR>1/2 cup sugar, 1/2 cup chocolate chips (melted)
</font>

</BODY>
</HTML>
```

The INSTRUCTIONS Marquee Script

```
<HTML>
<HEAD>
```

```
</HEAD>
<BODY BACKGROUND="copper.gif" TEXT="white" LEFTMARGIN="6" TOPMARGIN="0">
<FONT SIZE=1 FACE="helvetica,arial">
<HR ALIGN=left WIDTH=25%>

<B>1 - CRUST</B>
<BR>Pulverize cookies and butter in food processor or blender
<BR>Press into 10-in. springform pan; bake at 350° for 10 mins.

<HR ALIGN=left WIDTH=25%>

<B>2 - CHEESECAKE</B>
<BR>Beat cheese, sugar, vanilla, eggs, and melted white chips
<BR>Pour into crust; bake at 350° 'til edges set (45 mins.)

<HR ALIGN=left WIDTH=25%>

<B>3 - TOPPING</B>
<BR>Mix berries and sugar in bowl; spoon over chilled cheesecake
<BR>Drizzle melted chocolate chips over berries

</FONT>
</BODY>
</HTML>
```

More to Come

The promise of the Web is just beginning to be fulfilled, and the trajectory of its technologies describe a steep ascent; high, fast, and almost out of sight. The only saving grace is that we're all traveling in the same shaky rocket ship, hurtling along the same uncharted course, at the same mind-numbing speed. Updates to the *VBScript Sourcebook* will be posted on the companion Web site as needed. Go to www.wiley.com/compbooks/mara.

As the trip progresses, it is hoped that companies like Netscape and Microsoft and Sun who propose to be our standard-bearers will keep in mind our most pressing need. The development tools and languages that drive the expansion of the Web must subscribe to common and cohesive patterns, so that our knowledge of any one technology can be woven into the next with the least amount of learning curve. If so, we'll be standing on the shoulders of true giants who saw to it that the technical knowledge gained from works like the *VBScript Sourcebook* would be embryonic to our understanding of the technologies yet to come.

What's on the
Web site?

The Companion Web site contains scripts and ancillary files for viewing all of the Web applications discussed in Parts III and IV of this book. Each set of files appears within the folder that corresponds to its chapter. For instance, all of the files for running the "Puzzle Page" application are found in the Chapter 15 folder.

Details on how to copy the files to your hard drive, and which file to open within IE4 so you can begin viewing and using the application (or Web pages), are provided at the beginning of each chapter, following the "Web site" heading.

> **NOTE** This book was written in "Internet time," which means that versions can change quickly. For up-to-the-minute updates, please visit the companion Web site at www.wiley.com/compbooks/mara

Color
Chart

Popular Hexadecimal Equivalents

Basic Colors

Color	Code	Color	Code
Black	#000000	Magenta	#FF00FF
Blue	#0000FF	Red	#FF0000
Cyan	#00FFFF	White	#FFFFFF
Green	#00FF00	Yellow	#FFFF00

Other Colors

Color	Code	Color	Code
Aquamarine	#70DB93	Bright Yellow	#EC9800
Baker's Chocolate	#5C3317	Brown	#A62A2A
Blue Violet	#9F5F9F	Bronze	#8C7853
Brass	#B5A642	Bronze II	#A67D3D
Bright Gold	#D9D919	Burgundy	#C50067
Burnt Sienna	#DC6000	Goldenrod	#DBDB70
Cadet Blue	#5F9F9F	Grass Green	#4DA619
Cool Copper	#D98719	Grey	#C0C0C0
Copper	#B87333	Green Copper	#527F76
Coral	#FF7F00	Green Yellow	#93DB70
Corn Flower Blue	#42426F	Hunter Green	#215E21
Dark Brown	#5C4033	Indian Red	#4E2F2F
Dark Green	#2F4F2F	Khaki	#9F9F5F

Color	Code	Color	Code
Dark Green Copper	#4A766E	Light Blue	#C0D9D9
Dark Olive Green	#4F4F2F	Light Grey	#E6E6E6
Dark Orchid	#9932CD	Light Grass Green	#92C000
Dark Purple	#53005D	Light Steel Blue	#8F8FBD
Dark Navy Blue	#003D84	Light Wood	#E9C2A6
Dark Slate	#1A1A1A	Lime Green	#32CD32
Dark Slate Blue	#1C0B5A	Mandarin Orange	#E47833
Dark Slate Grey	#2F4F4F	Maroon	#8E236B
Dark Tan	#97694F	Maroon Purple	#7C005F
Dark Teal	#008F93	Medium Aquamarine	#32CD99
Dark Turquoise	#7093DB	Medium Blue	#3232CD
Dark Wood	#855E42	Medium Dark Grey	#666666
Darkest Grey	#0D0D0D	Medium Forest Green	#008740
Dim Grey	#545454	Medium Goldenrod	#EAEAAE
Dusty Rose	#856363	Medium Orchid	#9370DB
Feldspar	#D19275	Medium Sea Green	#426F42
Firebrick	#8E2323	Medium Sky Blue	#00A0DD
Forest Green	#238E23	Medium Slate	#4D4D4D
Gold	#CD7F32	Medium Slate Blue	#7F00FF
Medium Spring Green	#7FFF00	Scarlet	#8C1717
Medium Turquoise	#70DBDB	Sea Green	#238E68
Medium Violet Red	#DB7093	Semi-Sweet Chocolate	#6B4226
Medium Wood	#A68064	Sienna	#8E6B23
Midnight Blue	#2F2F4F	Silver	#E6E8FA
Mulberry	#C40026	Sky Blue	#3299CC
Navy Blue	#23238E	Slate Blue	#007FFF
Neon Blue	#4D4DFF	Spicy Pink	#FF1CAE
Neon Pink	#FF6EC7	Spring Green	#00FF7F
New Midnight Blue	#00009C	Steel Blue	#236B8E
New Tan	#EBC79E	Summer Sky	#38B0DE
Old Gold	#CFB53B	Tan	#DB9370
Orange	#FF7F00	Thistle	#D8BFD8
Orange Red	#FF2400	Turquoise	#ADEAEA
Orchid	#DB70DB	Very Dark Brown	#5C4033
Pale Green	#8FBC8F	Very Light Grey	#CDCDCD
Pink	#BC8F8F	Violet	#4F2F4F
Plum	#EAADEA	Violet Red	#CC3299
Quartz	#D9D9F3	Wheat	#D8D8BF
Rich Blue	#5959AB	Yellow Green	#99CC32
Salmon	#6F4242	Yellow Gold	#FFEB00

Appendix

C

Most Commonly
Used ASCII Codes

0 through 127Char	Code	0 through 127Char	Code
NUL	0	S0	14
SOH	1	SI	15
STX	2	DLE	16
ETX	3	DC1	17
EOT	4	DC2	18
ENQ	5	DC3	19
ACK	6	D4	20
BEL	7	NAK	21
BS	8	SYN	22
HT	9	ETB	23
LF	10	CAN	24
VT	11	EM	25
FF	12	SUB	26
CR	13	ESC	27
FS	28	7	55
GS	29	8	56
RS	30	9	57
US	31	:	58
SP	32	;	59
!	33	<	60
"	34	=	61
#	35	>	62
$	36	?	63

0 through 127Char	Code	0 through 127Char	Code
%	37	@	64
&	38	A	65
'	39	B	66
(	40	C	67
)	41	D	68
*	42	E	69
+	43	F	70
,	44	G	71
-	45	H	72
.	46	I	73
/	47	J	74
0	48	K	75
1	49	L	76
2	50	M	77
3	51	N	78
4	52	0	79
5	53	P	80
6	54	Q	81
R	82	i	105
S	83	j	106
T	84	k	107
U	85	l	108
V	86	m	109
W	87	n	110
X	88	o	111
Y	89	p	112
Z	90	q	113
[	91	r	114
\	92	s	115
]	93	t	116
^	94	u	117
	95	v	118
`	96	w	119
a	97	x	120
b	98	y	121
c	99	z	122
d	100	{	123
e	101	|	124
f	102	}	125
g	103	~	126
h	104	DEL	127

Index

A

ABRs. *See* Anomalous Behavior Reports
Abs function, 251
ACTION argument, 5, 25, 149, 161, 211
Action property, 149
Actions, PreProgrammed sets, 38
Active Server Pages, 20, 459
ActiveX, 3–4, 406
ActiveX Control. *See* Marquee ActiveX Control
ActiveX Control Pad, 14, 60
ActiveX controls, 117, 545
ActiveX Scripting Engine languages, 23
ActiveX scripting engines, 4–5
ActiveX SDK, 21
Add method, 173
Addition operator, 320, 334
Address. *See* E-mail address
Address book. *See* Client address book
Addresses frameset, assembly, 534–545
addresses.htm, 526–531
addresses.htm script, 538–542
Advanced HTML, 489–570
Agent Control, 7
Alert dialog box, 53
Alert method, 173–174
ALinkColor property, 149–150
All array, 87
All object, 31
Alpha buttons, 522–524
Anchor object, 87–88
<ANCHOR> tag, 24, 87, 111, 113, 142, 157, 166
Anchors, 30
Anchors array, 87, 94
And operator, 334–335

Animal sounds game, 362–364
Anomalous behavior problems
responsibility, 462–466
solving, 462–478
Anomalous Behavior Reports (ABRs), 461–463
AppCodeName property, 150–151
<APPLET> tag, 30, 32, 88, 547
Applets, 30
Applets array, 88
Application interface problems, 463
Application page. *See* Membership application page
Applications, VBScript usage restrictions, 22–23
AppName property, 151
AppVersion property, 151–152
Argument labels, 40
Arguments,
creation, process/timing, 68
inclusion, timing, 42–43
omitting, timing, 42–43
Arithmetic operations, 347, 433
Arithmetic Operator, 334, 336, 342, 343
Array function, 251–252
Array index position, 403
Array length property, 318
Array objects, 43. *See also* Built-in array objects
Array position, 67, 102, 123. *See also* Forms array position
information, 47
Array variables, 252. *See also* Global two-dimensional array variable
creation, 51
Array-creation system, 417

Arrays, 56
creating, 417–453
understanding, 43–47
usage, 43–47
Asc function, 252
ASCII code, 384, 385
number, 255
ASCII value, 252, 397
Assignment operator, 48
Assignment statement, 62, 172
Atn function, 252–253

B

Back method, 174–175
BANNER Frame script, 561–566
banner.htm, 552–559
Behavior problems. *See* Anomalous behavior problems
bgColor property, 367
Binary comparison, 296
Bit-wise comparison operator, 335
Blur event, 227, 228
Blur method, 175–176
Body object, 31, 88–89
<BODY> section, 359, 360
<BODY> tag, 10, 24, 29, 41, 144, 156, 214, 239, 247, 475
Boolean expression, 339, 347
Boolean value, 227, 343
Boolean variable, 57
Bound data across frames, working, 511–545

 tag, 360
Branch scripts, 395
Branches, 323, 396, 458. *See also* Case else branch
Browser application. *See* Web-enabled browser application
Browser support problems, 456

Browsing, 527–531
Built-in array objects, 160
Built-in arrays, 45
Built-in behavior, 360
Built-in browsers, 456
Built-in element, 56
Built-in Event Handlers, 131
Built-in functions, 43
Built-in methods, 88. *See also*
    VBScript objects
Built-in object methods, 38
Built-in objects behavior,
    scripting, 353–375
Built-in properties. *See*
    VBScript objects
Built-in statements, 60, 65–67
Built-in VBScript objects, 375
Button game, 368–370
Buttons, 36, 560
Byte subtype, 253

C

C++, 48. *See also* Object-
    oriented C++
Call statement, 72, 304–305
Calling button script, 329
Calling object, 183
Calling script, 69
Case else branch, 430
Case else keywords, 76
Case else statement, 438
Case insensitivity, 61
Case sensitivity. *See* VBScript
Case statements, 75–76, 363
Catalog items. *See* Selected
    catalog items
CBool function, 253
CByte function, 253–254
CCur function, 254
CDate function, 254–255
CDbl function, 255
Ceiling constant, 305
Centralized error handling,
    487–488
CGI. *See* Common Gateway
    Interface
Change event, 230
Character comparison, 296
Checkbox elements, 427
Checkbox object, 91–93

Checkboxes, 36, 73, 91, 92,
    102, 418, 426,
    428–431, 440
Checked property, 152
Chr function, 255–256
CInt function, 256–257
CLASSID, 526, 552
    argument, 512
Clear method, 176–179
ClearTimeout method,
    179–181
Click event, 232, 233, 428
Click method, 182
Clicked-and-held link, 149
Client address book, 492
    overview, 514–515
Client address book scripts,
    515–534
    segments, 522–534
Client-server-type
    application, 463
CLng function, 257–258
Close method, 182–183
Code, commenting, 65–66
Code problems, 465–466
Collapse method, 183
Collapsed format, 63
Color constants, 250, 258
Color game, 364–367
Color literals, 169
Column sorting, 533–534
Comma-delimited list, 40,
    511, 512
Comma-delimited
    numbers, 266
Common Gateway Interface
    (CGI), 152
    application, 443
    script, 491. *See also* Forms-
        processing CGI script
CommonParentElement
    method, 184
compareType, 266
Comparison operations, 347
Comparison Operator, 337,
    340, 341, 342
Concatenation operations, 347
Concatenation operator,
    320, 335
Conditional control
    structure, 63

Conditional expression, 368
Conditions, testing, 458
Confirm method, 184–185
confirm() method, 184, 185
Const statement, 305–307
Constants, 249–301. *See also*
    Color constants;
    VBScript constants
Constant/value, usage
    choice, 307
Contains method, 185–186
Control structures, 51, 239,
    395. *See also*
    Conditional control
    structure; Decision
    control structures; For
    loop control structure; If-
    then-else control
    structure; If-then-elseif
    control structure; Repeat
    loop control structure
    combining, 81–82
    exiting, 81–82
    looping, 77–81
    usage, 72–82
CONTROLS FRAME script,
    535–538
controls.htm, 522–526
Cookie array, 94
Cookie controversy, 155
Cookie object, 21
Cookie property, 152–155
Cookie text file, 249
Cookies, definition, 21
Cos function, 259
Counting variable, 77
CreateElement method, 186
CreateRange method,
    186–187
CreateTextRange method, 187
Cross-platform/cross-browser
    support, 463
CSng function, 259
CStr function, 259–260

D

Data. *See* Modules
    passing, 47–57
Data binding, 227, 531–533
Data container, 474

Data evaluation, 47–57
Data evaluation errors,
    471–478
Data across frames. *See*
    Bound data across
    frames
Data subtype, 337
    constants, 300
Data tracking. *See* Repeat
    loops; Scripts
Data-binding, 492, 511–512,
    514, 526–527, 545
Data-driven script, 37
Data-handling structures, 417
Datatype, 397, 483, 485
Datatype conversion function,
    256, 257, 259
Datatype handling. *See*
    VBScript
dataURL, 523
Date field, validation,
    386–387
Date functions, 250, 260–265
dateDiff() function, 262
Datestring, 262
Decimal delimiter, 39
Decimal separators, 254, 258
Decision control statement,
    323, 326
Decision control structures,
    73–77
Default delimiter, 43, 294
DefaultChecked property, 155
DefaultValue property, 156
Delimited substrings, 294
Delimiter, 42, 43. *See also*
    Decimal delimiter;
    Default delimiter; Group
    delimited; Semicolon
    delimiter
Design problems, 463
DHTML. *See* Dynamic
    HTML
dim statement, 48
Dim statement, 307–310
<DIV> tag, 500, 532
Division operators, 336. *See*
    also Floating Point
    Division operator;
    Integer Division operator
Do loops, 79–81
Do until, 80–81

Do Until statement, 310–311
Do while, 79–80
Do while statement, 79
Do While statement, 311–312
doAlpha(), 382–384, 393
Document, 18, 24. *See also*
    Hypertext markup
    language document
HTML writing reasons,
    214–215
Document method, 183, 198
Document object, 29, 30, 36,
    93–97, 128
model. *See* Hypertext
    markup language
    document object model
Document Object Model
    (DOM), 4, 22
Documentary sources, 85–86
Does Not Equal operator,
    336–337
DOM. *See* Document Object
    Model
Domain variable, 391
Double purpose loop,
    432–433
Drag 'n' drop, 494, 497–501
Duplicate method, 187
Dynamic array, 51, 309, 312,
    325, 346, 417, 418, 428
    variable, 429
Dynamic HTML (DHTML),
    6, 9, 23, 25, 26, 29, 100,
    147, 223, 224, 456, 468,
    491–510, 534, 545, 547
documentation page, 170
extensions, 24
model, 491, 497
object model, 171
properties, 148
Dynamic page displays, 491
Dynamic page generation,
    359–361

E

Easy Reader page, 393
    assembly, 370–374
    full script, 371–374
    overview, 353–356
Easy Reader scripts, 356–370
    segments, 356–370

Easy Reader Web page, 353
ElementFromPoint
    method, 187
Elements array, 46, 91,
    97–100, 108, 124,
    127, 162
Else clause, 323
else statement, 439
elseif statement, 439
E-mail address, 405
    validation, 388–390
E-mail validation script, gap
    filling, 391
<EMBED> tag, 30, 32, 100
Embedded control, 117
Embedded objects, 32, 547
Embeds, 30
Embeds array, 100–101
Empty field, 403
Empty keyword, 337
Empty method, 187–188
Encoding property, 156
ENCTYPE argument, 156
End function statement, 69
Equals operator, 337–338
Equivalence operator, 338
Erase statement, 312–313
Err object, 101–102
Error handling, 324, 458,
    478–488, 496–497. *See*
    also Centralized error
    handling; Scripts
code, placement. *See* Scripts
    conditional, 482
Error-handling code, 484, 496
Error-handling scripts, 478
Errors. *See* Data evaluation
    errors; Execution errors;
    Failure to execute errors;
    Non-VBScript errors;
    Spelling errors; Syntax
    errors; Typographical
    errors; VBScript errors
bypassing. *See* Scripts
Euler's constant, 265
Evaluations, testing, 458
EVENT=, 8
EVENT argument, 90, 93,
    130, 133, 136, 139, 144,
    224
Event bubbling, 6, 225

Event handlers, 10, 88, 223–248, 328
Event handling, 88–91, 93, 97, 100, 101, 104–105, 107, 109–111, 113, 116–119, 121, 124–126, 130–131, 133, 136, 139–141, 144–145
Event object, 29, 101
Event-driven languages, 24–27 first steps, 25–27
Event-driven scripting language, 4, 24
Event-firing actions, 47
Events, 4, 24. *See also* Blur event; Change event; Click event; Focus event; Hypertext markup languages events; onBlur event; onFocus event processing, 224–225 working, 26–27
Event-triggered script, 47
Exclusion Or operator, 345–346
ExecuteCommand method, 188
Execution errors, 467
Exit Do statement, 313
Exit For statement, 314
Exit Function statement, 314–315
Exit statement, 82
Exit Sub statement, 315
Exp function, 265
Expand method, 188
Expanded format, 64
Exponent operator, 339
Exponentiation operator, 265
Expressions
  construction process, 54–56
  evaluation process, 54–56
  values, supplying, 55–56
Extension scripting languages, comparison. *See* Hypertext markup language
External objects, working, 547–570

F

Failure to execute errors, 467–468
False keyword, 339
fgColor property, 367
FgColor property, 156–157
Field. *See* Date field; Empty field; Multiple-line fields; Name fields; Phone fields; Text field checking, 400–405 value, 68
Field-level validation, 377
Filter function, 265–266
Fix function, 267
Floating Point Division operator, 336
Floating point number, 336
Focus event, 235
Focus method, 188–190
FOR=, 8
FOR argument, 90, 93, 130, 133, 136, 144, 224
For each loop, 314
For each statement, 319
For loop, 314, 425
For loop control structure, 81
For statement, 77, 139, 316–318
For Each statement, 318–319
Form, script, 103
Form elements, 24, 97
Form object, 91, 102–105, 128
<FORM> object, 475, 524
<FORM> tag, 5, 25, 29–32, 45, 46, 70, 102, 104, 117, 126, 149, 156, 161, 166, 211, 363, 368, 522, 527
Format. *See* Collapsed format; Expanded format
FormatCurrency function, 267
FormatDateTime function, 268
FormatNumber function, 268–269
FormatPercent function, 269–270
Form-data string, 406

Form-level validation, 377
Forms array, 94
Forms array position, 138
Forms object, 31
Forms-processing CGI script, 405
Forward method, 190
Fourth-tier objects, 91, 97, 107, 137
Fourth-tier select object, 118
Frame object, 105–107
Frame script. *See* BANNER Frame script; MIDDLE Frame script; VIEWER Frame script; VIEWERX Frame script; VIEWERY Frame script
FRAME script. *See* CONTROLS FRAME script
<FRAME> tag, 44, 45, 105, 142, 513, 517
Frames, scripting, 513
Frames array, 44
Frames object, 31
Frameset, 73, 141, 307, 321. *See also* Addresses frameset; Recipe frameset
FRAMESET script, 534–535, 561
<FRAMESET> tag, 44, 107, 144, 513, 515, 516, 534, 549, 551, 559, 560
Frequently asked questions. *See* VBScript
Function statement, 319–321. *See also* End function statement set, 69
Functions, 41–43, 56, 62, 63, 69–70, 249–301, 304, 305 parentheses usage, 250–251

G

Game. *See* Animal sounds game; Button game; Color game
Genie, 7

GET, 104, 161
GetMember method, 190
GIF file, 555, 556
GIF image, 110, 418, 498
Global two-dimensional array
    variable, 424
Global variables, 308, 310,
    357, 358, 369, 522
    local variables, comparison,
    393–394
    scope, 51–52
Go method, 190
Greater Than operator,
    339–340
Greenwich Mean Time
    date, 153
Group delimiter, 269
GUI applications, 38
GUI elements, 353

H

Hard-coded value, 44
Hardware requirements. *See*
    VBScript
Hash property, 157
<HEAD> section, 357, 359,
    360, 382, 386
<HEAD> tag, 9, 29, 41,
    70, 383
Heisenberg, Werner, 455
Heisenberg principle, 455
Heisenbug principle, 455, 461
Hex function, 270
Hidden object, 107–109
History object, 29, 109–110
Home page, 116
Horizontal marquee, 552
Horizontal Title
    marquee, 557
Host property, 157–158
Hostname property, 158
<HR> tag, 9, 360
HREF argument, 87, 111,
    233, 441, 442
Href property, 158
HTML. *See* Hypertext
    markup language
HTMLcode, 172
HTMLSelectionNone, 188
HyperCard XCMD, 466
Hyperlink, 418

Hypertext link, 165, 226
Hypertext markup language
    (HTML), 176, 213, 325.
    See also Advanced
    HTML; Dynamic HTML
arguments, 39, 85
convention, 122
dialog, 144
document, 45, 114, 126,
    210, 370, 458, 475,
    498, 518, 549, 551, 552
document object model,
    23–58
documentation. *See* Internet
    Explorer
editor, 13, 60
elements, 534
events, 24–25
extension scripting
    languages comparison,
    5–7
file, 114, 518, 560
form, 443
items, 215, 220
mailto:, 406
Object Model, 224
objects, 24, 190, 204,
    205, 511
page, 13, 103, 142
script, 95, 97, 139, 359, 427
string, 198, 218, 220,
    365, 441
tags, 30, 39, 72, 87, 148,
    186, 190, 204, 213,
    218, 219, 224, 370, 499
VBScript usage, 9–12
writing reasons. *See*
    Document

I

IE. *See* Internet Explorer
If conditional, 313, 402, 457
If conditions, 358
If statement, 321–324
if-field-is-empty conditional,
    404
If-then-else conditionals, 303
If-then-else conditions, 66,
    73–75
If-then-else control
    structure, 66

If-then-else script, 243
If-then-elseif control
    structure, 358
IIS. *See* Internet Information
    Server
Image object, 110–111, 226
<IMG> buttons, 554
<IMG> objects, 554
<IMG> tag, 24, 110, 498,
    499, 502, 510, 554
Implication operator,
    340–341
Inclusion Or operator, 345
Index position, 44–47
INGREDIENTS
    Marquee, 559
INGREDIENTS Marquee
    script, 569
Inline scripts, 10
Input string, 383
<INPUT> elements, 528
<INPUT> tag, 24, 41, 89,
    90–93, 108, 119–125,
    130, 132–136, 368, 370,
    522, 527
InputBox function, 271–272
InRange method, 191
InStr function, 272–274
InStrRev function, 274–276
INSTRUCTIONS
    Marquee, 559
INSTRUCTIONS Marquee
    script, 569–570
Int function, 270–271
Integer Division operator, 336
Integer subtypes, 257
Integration testing, 458–459
Internet addresses. *See* U.S.
    Internet addresses
Internet Explorer (IE), 13, 63,
    74, 116, 126, 129–130,
    148, 151, 152, 167, 172,
    182, 194, 195, 207, 209,
    251, 310, 378, 406, 456,
    465, 493
    download pages, 13, 14
    HTML documentation, 148
    IE4, 465, 468, 493, 494
    IE4 Beta, JavaScript
        bug, 442
Internet Explorer 3.0, 12

Internet Explorer 4.0, 12, 224
Internet Information Server
  (IIS) 3.0, 20, 21
Interpreter, 435. *See also*
  JavaScript; VBScript
  problems, 464–465
I/O commands, 21
Is operator, 341
isAlpha(), 382, 384–386
IsArray function, 276
IsDate function, 276–277
IsEmpty function, 277
IsEqual method, 191
IsNull function, 277–278
IsNumeric function, 278
IsObject function, 279
Item method, 191
IViewTransition, 210, 211
IViewTransitionSite, 210, 211

J

Java, 48
  VBScript relationship, 19
Java Virtual Machine, 19
JavaScript, 3, 5, 10, 18, 20,
  25, 33, 41, 44, 48, 49,
  55, 56, 60, 63, 66, 67,
  86, 94, 100, 150, 151,
  209. *See also* Server-side
  JavaScript
  bug. *See* Internet Explorer
  interpreters, 464
  usage, 7–9
Join function, 279–281
JScript, 5

K

keyDown event, 237
keyPress event, 238
Keywords, 333–349. *See also*
  Empty keyword; False
  keyword; Nothing
  keyword; Null keyword;
  Preserve keyword; True
  keyword; VBScript
  keywords

L

Labels. *See* Argument labels
LANGUAGE argument,
  7, 364

Languages. *See* Event-driven
  languages; Extension
  scripting languages;
  Hypertext markup
  language; Object-based
  languages; VBScript
  language
LastModified property,
  158–159
LBound function, 281
LCase function, 281–282
Left function, 282
Len function, 282
Length property, 44, 159–160
Less Than operator, 341–342
Lines, 63–65
Line-space-tab blindness, 64
Link object, 111–113
LinkColor property, 160
Links, 24, 30. *See also*
  Clicked-and-held link
Links array, 94
Literal string, 258
Local variables
  comparison. *See* Global
    variables
  scope, 52–54
Location object, 29, 114–116
Log function, 282–283
Logical Conjunction
  Operator, 334
Logical Disjunction
  Operator, 345
Logical Equivalence
  Operator, 338
Logical Implication
  Operator, 340
Logical Negation
  Operator, 343
Looping. *See* Control
  structures
Loops. *See* Do loops; Double
  purpose loop; Repeat
  loops
LTrim function, 283, 291

M

Marquee. *See* Horizontal
  marquee; Vertical
  marquee
  object, 549

script. *See* INGREDIENTS
  Marquee script;
  INSTRUCTIONS
  Marquee script; TITLE
  Marquee script
Marquee ActiveX Control,
  548, 551
Membership application page
  assembly, 405–415
  full script, 406–415
  overview, 378–382
Membership application
  scripts, 382–405
  segments, 382–405
Message string, 42
<META> tag, 9
METHOD argument, 25, 161
Method property, 160–162
Methods, 18, 38–41, 62, 63,
  88–90, 92–93, 97,
  100–102, 104, 106,
  109–111, 113, 116–119,
  121, 124, 125, 130, 131,
  133, 136, 139–141, 144
  parentheses usage, 172
Methods without objects. *See*
  Objectless methods
Methods/arguments, 39–41
Microsoft Office suite, 20
Microsoft Script
  Debugger, 14
Mid function, 287
MIDDLE Frame script, 538
MIME type, 104, 156
Modules, variable data
  passage, 459
Modulus operator, 342
Mouse Down, 552–556
Mouse Up, 556–559
mouseDown, 554
mouseDown event, 240
mouseMove event, 241,
  497, 500
mouseMove sub, 501
mouseOut event, 241
mouseOver event, 241
mouseUp, 554
mouseUp event, 243
Move method, 191–193
MoveEnd method, 192
MoveStart method, 192
Mozilla, 151

MsgBox function, 283–287
Multidimensional array, 281, 299
Multiple-line fields, 137
Multiplication operator, 54, 342–343

N

NAME argument, 30, 87, 88, 90, 92, 98, 105, 108, 111, 118, 120, 125, 130, 133, 136, 138, 157, 162, 427
Name fields, validation, 382–386
NAME information, 425, 431
Name position, 102
Name property, 162
Named array, 279
Naming. *See* Variables
Navigate method, 193
Navigator. *See* Netscape Navigator
Navigator object, 29, 116–117
NCSA Mosaic code, 151
Negation operator, 343
Nesting statements, 64
Netscape Navigator, 4, 74, 150–152, 167, 195, 455, 570
  supporting, 14–15
  top object, 31
Next statement, 77
<NOBR> tag, 9
<NOFRAMES> tag, 9
Non-VBScript errors, handling, 486–488
Not operator, 343–344
Nothing keyword, 344
Null keyword, 344

O

1-dimensional arrays, 281
Object collections, 43
Object hierarchy, 6, 29. *See also* VBScript object hierarchy
Object methods, 32–43, 171–221

Object model. *See* Hypertext markup language document object model
Object pathname, 96
Object properties, 32–43, 147–170
  reading, 35–36
  writing, 35–36
<OBJECT> tag, 30, 32, 98, 100, 102, 117–118, 512, 523, 526, 527, 531, 547, 548, 552, 559
Object variables, 344
Object-based languages, 24–27
  first steps, 25–27
Object-based scripting languages, 4
Object-centric coding environments, 27
Object/event focus, 24
Object/event subroutine, 424
Objectless methods, 41–43
Object-oriented C++, 19
Object-oriented languages, 4
Object-oriented programming (OOP), 4, 19
Objects, 56
Oct function, 287
OLE automation object, 481
On Error Resume Next statement, 324
onAbort handler, 226
onAfterUpdate handler, 226–227
onBeforeUpdate handler, 227
onBlur event, 175, 467
onBlur handler, 227–229
onBounce event handler, 229
onBounce handler, 229–230
onChange event, 467
onChange event handler, 230
onChange handler, 230–231, 468
onChange script, 362, 364, 390
onClick argument, 368
onClick handler, 231–233, 528
onClick script, 182, 369
onDblClick handler, 233–235
onError handler, 235
onEventHandler scripts, 72

onFinish handler, 235
onFocus event, 188
onFocus handler, 235–236
onFocus script, 189
onHelp handler, 236–237
onKeyDown handler, 237
onKeyPress handler, 238
onKeyUp handler, 238
onLoad event, 72
onLoad handler, 214, 238–239
onMouseDown handler, 239–240
onMouseMove handler, 240–241
onMouseOut handler, 241
onMouseOver handler, 241–243
onMouseUp handler, 243–244
onReadyStateChange handler, 244
onReset handler, 244
onSelect handler, 244
onStart handler, 244–245
onSubmit event handler, 104
onSubmit handler, 105, 245
onUnload handler, 245–248
OOP. *See* Object-oriented programming
Open method, 193–198
Opener property, 163
Opening prompts, 357–358
Operation. *See* Scramble operation
Operator precedence, 347–348
  importance, 54–55
Operators, 333–349
<OPTION> tag, 9, 32, 362
Options array, 118–119, 165
  position, 366
<OPTIONS>, 118
Or operators, 345–346. *See also* Exclusion Or operator; Inclusion Or operator
Order form, submitting, 443–444
Order Total, 419, 423
Order total, calculation, 428–440

Original picture, viewing, 503–505
OS problems, 463–464

P

Page. *See* Membership application page; Puzzle page; Recipe page; Shopping list page; VBScripted pages
Page generation. *See* Dynamic page generation
<PARAM> tag, 9
Parent property, 163
ParentElement method, 198
Parentheses, usage, 61–63. *See also* Functions; Methods
Parse time, 215
Passed condition, 311
Passed string, 297, 370
Passed variable, 297
Password object, 119–121
PasteHTML method, 198
Pathname property, 163–164
PDAs. *See* Personal Digital Assistants
Personal Digital Assistants, 456
Phone fields, validation, 390–400
Picture. *See* Original picture
<PLUGIN> tag, 121, 547
Plugins, 30
Plugins array, 121
Port property, 164
Position. *See* Array position; Index position; Name position
POST, 104, 161
<PRE> tags, 219
Precedence. *See* Operator precedence
PreProgrammed sets. *See* Actions
Preserve keyword, 346
Private functions, 321
Problems. *See* Anomalous behavior problems; Code problems; Design

problems; Interpreter problems; OS problems replication, 461
Procedure-based functions, 251
Procedure-level variables, 52
Procedures
calling, 70–72
writing, 67–72, 377–416
Program flow, control, 303–330
Prompt method, 199–202, 357
Prompts. *See* Opening prompts
Properties, 88–90, 92, 96–97, 100–102, 104, 106, 108–113, 115, 117–121, 123–125, 127, 130, 131, 133, 136, 138, 139, 141–143
information sources, 32–38
Property-setting statement, 369
Protocol property, 164
Pure object, 37
Puzzle page, 491
assembly, 505–510
full script, 505–510
overview, 494
Puzzle page scripts, 495–505
segments, 495–505

Q

Quality assurance testing, 456–462
QueryCommandEnabled method, 202
QueryCommandIndeterm method, 202–203
QueryCommandState method, 203
QueryCommandSupported method, 203
QueryCommandText method, 203
Quotes, 63–65

R

Radio object, 121–124
Radios, 36

Radio-specific scripts, 122
Random value, 290
Randomize statement, 324
RangeFromElement method, 203
Reader page. *See* Easy Reader page
Read-only, 148, 162
Read-only value, 35
Read-write, 148
Read-write properties, 35
Real world, VBScript, 351–488
Recipe frameset, assembly, 560–570
Recipe page, overview, 548–549
Recipe page scripts, 549–560
segments, 552–560
Record view. *See* Table/Record view
redim statement, 51
Redim statement, 324–325
Referrer property, 164–165
Regression, 455
Related script, 70
Reload method, 204
Rem statement, 325–326
REM statement, 65
Remove method, 204
RemoveMember method, 204
Repeat loop control structure, 63, 316, 319
Repeat loops, 44, 80, 303, 369, 466, 471, 472, 474. *See also* Single repeat loop
counting, 77–78
data tracking, 474–478
Replace function, 288–289
Replace method, 204
Reset button, 125
Reset event, 244
Reset method, 204
Reset object, 124–126
RGB color, 161
Right function, 289
Right-most char, 289
Rnd function, 289–290, 324
Rnd() function, eccentricities, 291

Round function, 290–291
Routines. *See* Subroutines
RTrim function, 283, 291

S

Safe subset, 21
Scientific notation, 290
Scramble operation, 502–503
Screen coordinates, 187
Script Debugger, 465, 466.
    See also Microsoft Script
    Debugger
Script failure
  location, 467–468
  reason, 468–478
Script module, 365
Script object, 126–127
Script segment, 363
<SCRIPT> tag, 7–9, 31, 41,
    51, 71, 72, 90, 93, 116,
    130, 136, 139, 207, 224,
    239, 308, 357, 359, 360,
    364, 382, 383, 386
ScriptActive, 14, 15
  plug-in, 458
ScriptEngine function, 292
ScriptEngineBuildVersion
    function, 292
ScriptEngineMajorlMinorVers
    ion function, 292
Scripting, 445. *See also* Built-
    in objects; Frames
  devices, 249
  operations, 328
  power, 5–12
  starting, 12–19
Scripting engines, 456. *See*
    also ActiveX scripting
    engines
Scripting languages. *See*
    Event-driven scripting
    languages; Hypertext
    markup language;
    Object-based scripting
    languages
Scripting Object Model, 4
Script-level constant, 307
Script-level variables, 51
Script-related Web sites, 415

Scripts. *See* addresses.htm
    script; BANNER Frame
    script; Calling button
    script; Calling script;
    CONTROLS FRAME
    script; Data-driven script;
    Easy Reader page; Easy
    Reader scripts; Event-
    triggered script; Form;
    FRAMESET script;
    Hypertext markup
    language script; If-then-
    else script;
    INGREDIENTS
    Marquee script; Inline
    scripts; INSTRUCTIONS
    Marquee script;
    Membership application
    page; Membership
    application scripts;
    MIDDLE Frame script;
    onChange script; onClick
    script; onEventHandler
    scripts; onFocus script;
    Puzzle page; Puzzle page
    scripts; Radio-specific
    scripts; Recipe page
    scripts; Related script;
    setTimcout() script;
    Shopping list scripts;
    Shopping list page;
    tables.htm script; Tag-
    level scripts; TITLE
    Marquee script;
    VIEWER Frame script;
    VIEWERX Frame script;
    VIEWERY Frame script
  data tracking, 472–474
  error handling code,
    placement, 484
  errors, bypassing, 476–480
  errors, handling, 480–488
  object, 31
  troubleshooting, 455–488
Scroll method, 205
ScrollIntoView method, 205
Search property, 165
Second-tier objects, 94, 101,
    105, 114, 116, 140, 141
Select case conditional, 457

Select case statement, 75,
    362, 365, 396–398, 430,
    435, 436, 439
Select event, 244
Select method, 205–206
Select object, 127–131
Select statement, 326–327
<SELECT> tag, 31, 32, 118,
    127, 128, 130, 362, 365
Select-case statements, 66
Selected catalog items,
    displaying, 440–443
SelectedIndex property, 165
Selection object, 31, 131
Self property, 166
Semicolon delimiter, 154
Server-side JavaScript, 405
Server-side VBScript, 405
Set statement, 327, 341
SetMember method, 206–207
SetTimeout() anomalies,
    209–210
SetTimeout method, 179,
    207–210
setTimeout() script, 179
Sgn function, 292–293
Shared methods, 38–39
Shared properties, 36–38
shopList(), population
    process, 425–426
Shopping list. *See* User
    shopping list
Shopping list array, setting
    up, 424–428
Shopping list page
  assembly, 445–452
  full script, 445–452
  overview, 418–422
Shopping list scripts,
    422–444
  segments, 424–444
ShowModalDialog
    method, 210
Showstoppers, 457
Simple-to-complex
    expressions, 333
Simple-to-complex series, 38
Sin function, 293
Single repeat loop, 457
Single-dimension array, 431

Single-dimension
   checkedArray, 430
Site/server side, VBScript
   usage, 20–21
Soft coding, 44
Software requirements. *See*
   VBScript
Sorting. *See* Column sorting
Space function, 293–294
Spaces, 63–65
Spelling errors, 470–471
Spin-off language, 29
Split function, 294–295
Sqr function, 295
SRC=, 8
Start event, 245
Start method, 210
Start-onClick() sub
   statement, 181
StartPainting method, 210
Statements, 303–331
Static array, 309, 312, 417
Status property, 166
Stop method, 211
StopPainting method, 211
strArray, 389, 390
StrComp function, 296
String function, 296
String literal, 315
String position, 394
String subtype, 259
String variable, 48
strReverse function, 296–297
Structures. *See* Control
   structures
STYLE argument, 500
Sub statement, 18, 68, 225.
   See also Start-onClick()
   sub statement
Sub Statement, 315,
   328–330. *See also* Exit
   Sub statement
Sub-arguments, 41, 194
Subindex argument, 191
Subs, 56, 62, 304, 305, 315
Submit Application
   button, 401
Submit button, 7, 99, 132,
   245, 400
Submit event, 245

Submit method, 211–212
Submit object, 131–133
Submitter button, 400, 404
Subroutines, 11, 67–68. *See
   also* VBScript
Sun Microsystems, 4
Support problems. *See*
   Browser support
   problems
Switch-case statements, 66
Syntax, VBScript rules, 59–67
Syntax errors, 469–470
System testing, 459–460

T

3DField, 94
Table/Record view, 524–526
tables.htm, 531–534
tables.htm script, 542–545
Tabs, 63–65
Tag-level scripts, 9
Tags method, 212–213
Tan function, 297
Target argument, 195, 196
TARGET argument, 142, 166
Target array variable, 298
Target object, 341
Target property, 166–167
<TBODY> element, 532
<TD> element, 532, 533
Term listing, 250
Testing. *See* Conditions;
   Evaluations; Integration
   testing; Quality
   assurance testing; System
   testing; Unit testing
   steps, 460–462
TEXT argument, 156
Text field, 35, 40, 427, 511
Text file, 530
Text object, 36, 134–136
Text stream, 39
Text string, 40, 49, 65, 111,
   173, 337
Textarea object, 136–139
<TEXTAREA> tag, 32, 138
textRange object, 183,
   192, 203
TextRange object, 139–140

<THEAD> element, 532
<THEAD> portion, 533
Third-party code, 118
Third-tier object, 88, 102,
   126, 131
Three-element array, 295, 502
Time functions, 250,
   260–265
timeSerial() function, 263
<TITLE> information, 109
TITLE Marquee script,
   568–569
<TITLE> tags, 167
Title property, 167
Top property, 167
True keyword, 347
True-only condition, 338
Two dimensional arrays, 424
Two-element array, 437, 438
TypeName function, 297–298
Typographical errors (typos),
   470–471
Typos. *See* Typographical
   errors

U

UBound function, 298–299
UCase function, 299
UI display, 188
Unit testing, 457–460
UNIX, 256
Upper-lowercase sequence, 60
URL, 8, 40, 104, 109, 114,
   115, 143, 149, 157, 158,
   161, 163–166, 193, 194,
   204, 217, 233, 249. *See
   also* dataURL
   argument, 193, 195, 196
U.S. Internet addresses, 388
User inputs, 78
User shopping list, creation,
   428–440
userAgent property, 167–168
User-created arrays, 418
User-created features, 359
User-created functions, 69,
   71, 402, 513
User-created procedures, 390
User-created sub, 513

User-defined functions, 249
User-generated event, 220

V

Validation. *See* Date field; E-mail address; Field-level validation; Form-level validation; Name fields; Phone fields
limits, 379
script. *See* E-mail validation script
Value, choice. *See* Constant/value
VALUE argument, 33, 37, 90, 92, 108, 120, 123, 125, 133, 136, 168, 370, 427, 526
VALUE information, 425, 431
Value property, 168–169
Values, supplying. *See* Expressions
var statement, 48
Variable container, 278
Variable data, passage. *See* Modules
Variable watcher grid fields, 477
Variables. *See* Array variables; Boolean variable; Counting variable; Domain variable; Global variables; Local variables; Object variables; Procedure-level variables; Script-level variables
naming, 56–57
restrictions, 57
scoping, 51–54
working, 48–51
Variant, 50
VarType function, 300
VBA. *See* Visual Basic for Applications
VBScript, 25. *See also* Real world; Server-side VBScript

basics, 59–82
case sensitivity, 60–61
datatype handling, 50–51
first script, 15–19
frequently asked questions (FAQs), 19–22
hardware requirements, 15–17
home page, 13
information, 86
interpreter, 33, 172, 464, 467, 478
introduction, 1–82
relationship. *See* Java; Visual Basic
rules. *See* Syntax
secureness, 21
software requirements, 15–17
subroutine, 16
usage, 7–9. *See also* Hypertext markup language tags; Site/server side
usage restrictions. *See* Applications
VBScript arguments, 85
VBScript comparison constants, 273, 275, 288, 295
VBScript constants, 250–300, 433
VBScript container, 276, 279
VBScript developers, 43
VBScript documentation, 61, 63, 86
VBScript Engine, 401, 464
VBScript environment, 462
VBScript error dialog, 101, 324, 469, 479
VBScript errors, 467, 480, 484, 485. *See also* Non-VBScript errors
handling, 480–485
VBScript event handlers, 225–248
VBScript functions, 250–300
VBScript keywords, 333–348, 471

VBScript language, 83–349, 469
reference, 43
VBScript modules, 353
VBScript object hierarchy, 27–32, 86, 97, 100–102, 107, 110, 119, 121, 126, 127, 131, 134, 137, 139, 140
VBScript objects, 85–145. *See also* Built-in VBScript objects
built-in methods, 171–221
built-in properties, 147–170
VBScript operators, 333–348
VBScript prompt dialog box, 199
VBScript properties, 85, 147
VBScript table, 248
VBScript user, 493
VBScript value, 277
VBScript-aware browser window, 238, 246
VBScripted pages, 307, 310, 321, 330, 457, 520
VBScripter, 453, 494
VBScript-unaware browsers, 456
Vertical marquee, 559–560
VIEWER Frame script, 538–545
VIEWERX Frame script, 566–567
VIEWERY Frame script, 567–568
viewerx.htm, 559–560
Visual Basic, 3, 19
Development Environment, 20
VBScript relationship, 20
Visual Basic for Applications (VBA), 20
Visual object, 29, 140–141
VLinkColor property, 169–170

W

Web browser, 38
Web development, 456

Web page operations, 456
Web pages, 25, 29, 207, 333, 371, 378, 418, 459, 510, 512, 545, 547. *See also* Easy Reader Web page
Web scripting language, 24
Web sites, 463, 478, 545, 548. *See also* Script-related Web sites
Web-based educational playscape, 353
Web-enabled browser application, 24

Web-enabling technologies, 23
Window method, 183, 193–197
Window object, 36, 141–145, 202
Window Object, 30
Window/load script, 427
Window/load sub, 424
Window.open() method, undocumented features, 196
write, 19
    writeLn comparison, 361

Windows API, 21
Windows NT 4.0, 20
World War II, 455, 456
Write method, 213–218, 220
writeLn, comparison. *See* write
WriteLn method, 218–220

Z

Zero-based array, 299, 430
Zero-length string, 335, 438
ZINDEX argument, 498
ZOrder method, 220–221